Presented to:

_____

From:

_____

Date:

_____

Becoming
A Leader of
Worth

Becoming
A Leader of
Worth

— Ilka V. Chavez —

A 365-day Leadership Devotional
Reflections that will guide you to becoming the purposeful,
faithful, and successful leader God has ordained you to be in
your family, career, ministry and in life.

Becoming a Leader of Worth
Copyright © 2021 by Ilka V. Chavez

ISBN 978-1-63760-876-0

Printed in the USA

Dedication

I dedicate this devotional to my Mom and Dad (deceased),
Alfonso and Herrieth Wilson, and My Grandmother (deceased),
Lyneth Sutherland Vallee, for being true leaders of worth.

Forward

My friend, my soul sister Ilka, has done it again. She has been obedient, and she continues to show us all what it means to be obedient while leading by example. Ilka's devotional book Becoming a Leader of Worth – A 365-Day Devotional is about relationship with our Heavenly Father. It completely aligns with her book titled What Leaders Say and Do. Ilka tells us we are all leaders, whether we are leading a country, a business, a school, a government, a home, or ourselves. Ilka's obedient leadership is developing and fostering leadership qualities in all of us, she is being used by our Heavenly Father to share His words and make us better leaders. This book required listening and paying attention to God's voice. Every one of the devotions was a result of a conversation, Ilka would say reflection, I call it revelation. However, all of them are everyday occurrences that if we are walking in God's will, we would see how much God is saying to us. Time and time again, Ilka reveals to us what is means to be doers of the word. What it means to trust in the Lord and not to lean upon our own understanding. What it looks like to see God do exceedingly and abundantly more than we could ask or imagine. What it means to be a leader.

This devotional allows us to improve on our leadership skills by allowing us to step away from the daily routine and focus on our relationship with God. This devotional gives us food for thought, prayers, and practical steps. When you are ready to submit, surrender, obey, and become a better leader and person, this 365- Devotional book will give you a first- hand view of what that looks like. It will invite you to personally experience what it feels like to fully trust God. Learn to lead like Jesus, spend time with God so that at the end you will hear, "well done good and faithful servant."

Elisa Bracero
Financial Steward

Aknowledgements

"God has been a constant Helper, a faithful Friend, a victorious Defender, a wise Leader, and a great Redeemer to me, and He can be all of this to you too."
-Charles F. Stanley

Leading without God's help, your leadership will perish. You will stray from your values and may even rely and trust yourself more than you trust God. When, not if, your leadership falters (of self, family, vocation, relationships, time, and money freedom) you will notice that you fell away from your creator. I affectionately refer to this as losing your compass. I pray this devotional serves as a daily compass to leaders of all walks, levels, and anchors them on the importance of their leadership. I wrote this devotional for leaders because of the lessons I learned and realized nothing can sustain or succeed without starting your day in prayer, meditation, or in conversation with God. He guides and is the compass that will transform you into a leader of worth.

I thank God for planting the seed to create this devotional and guiding me to share as I wrote. It takes faith, trust, and courage to do so. To my Parents (Alfonso and Herrieth Wilson) and Grandmother (Lyneth Sutherland Vallee), my gratitude is infinite for instilling strong faith in me and guiding me to the truth and wisdom to press through every storm that will come my way. To my children, R.J. and Gabrielle who inspire me daily to become a leader of worth, one who stands in truth, in life, and in faith. I remain a work in progress (WIP.) Their prayers and faith keep me anchored. My siblings, Luanna, Ronna, and Arturo, their spouses and all my nieces and nephews. They are my biggest cheerleaders and raise me up when I want to quit. To my prayer warriors (aka soul sisters Angela, Amy, Elisa, Charmaine, Fanny, LaKeshia), my butterfly tribe (Celina, Dalys, Delicia, Jaenine, Xiomara), my Powerful and Blessed Tribe (Kisha and Ronnell), my God is good tribe (Valina, Patricia and Liza) and last but not least my bold moves tribe (BMT) (Aleks, Samira, and Yolanda), I can't thank each of you enough for praying daily for me as I navigate the hurdles that life brings. Leaders, we have many tribes that sustain us and hold us accountable as we become leaders of worth. Cherish them all. They are your "Board of Directors." I encourage you to find and define your micro tribes, the purpose each serve in your life and growth as a leader of worth and most importantly in designing your legacy blueprint.

To my marketing team in Panama who remain faithful and stay the course towards the vision we set almost four years ago. Thank you for designing this beautiful book cover. "We will continue to rise by lifting each other." To Elisa Bracero, you continue to keep your promise to stand by me during every storm, celebration, or sorrow that life brings. Thank you for writing the foreword for this book. Your continued prayers, accountability, guidance, and mentorship helps me lead in excellence. You truly are a leader of worth. To Royal Writer Company, thank you for your hard work in perfecting this book and preparing it with excellence that can only come from our Father Almighty. God bless you. Your patience with me in stopping and starting this project when I was so close, is commendable. I highly recommend your services. And finally, to all those who took the time to read my devotionals and provided feedback, comments, testimonial, support, registered or follows my devotional blog, thank you. Your encourage-ment not to give up served as a midwife to birth this book. I humbly bring this devotional/journal to life.

I express my deep gratitude to Heather Goble, Tiffany Turley and Greg Turley at Evolution Printing for rescuing me yet again and providing me with a quality product that reflects who I am. "Remain Coura-geous" and I look forward to working with you again on many more projects.

I leave you with this verse:
> *"Call to Me and I will answer you, and I will tell you*
> *great and mighty things, which you do not know."*
> *Jeremiah 33:3*

Testimonials

"This devotional allows us to improve on our leadership skills by allowing us to step away from the daily routine and focus on our relationship with God. This devotional gives us food for thought, prayers, and practical steps. When you are ready to submit, surrender, obey, and become a better leader and person, this 365- Devotional book will give you a first- hand view of what that looks like. It will invite you to personally experience what it feels like to fully trust God. Learn to lead like Jesus, spend time with God so that at the end you will hear, "well done good and faithful servant."

-Elisa Bracero

"I found it to be simply beautiful. As I read each devotion, I felt them blossoming in me points of discovery in the scripture, God, and myself - all at the same time. The devotional seamlessly moved the reader from the anchor, through the insightful quote, and opens up into revelation, which invokes communication - a prayer. Finally, you challenge the reader to do something - with practical steps for living and leading. Simply, beautiful. What a wonderful tool and a blessing for those on this long journey home. Thank you for your obedience to the voice of God and your diligence to do an excellent job.

-Rev. Sharahn Harris Morgan

What an awesome and amazing job you have done of really providing great content with practical steps, scriptures, and stories to guide the reader and allow them to journal their thoughts. I cannot wait to purchase my copy of this masterpiece.

- Charmaine Dunn

This book will help guide true believers in a deeper relationship with God. His salvation (Grace) His mercies, Our pilgrimage (sanctification and the promises of God. I love the emphasis on a strong prayer life and humility. Thanks for opportunity. May Christ grow us in truth and love.

-Arusha Morgan

This was a delightfully informative and inspirational work. I liked that you took examples and situations from your experiences to make the Bible quotes relevant to a modern audience. It is also great that you took quotes from other people that are not always centered around the Bible as I think that is a great way to draw in those who may not adhere to scripture as closely as others. Even for the non-religious, this workbook contains some great advice and guidelines in general; from practicing patience to uplifting others, focusing on what one has instead of what other people are doing. The numerous applications for each day are not impossible tasks but small, easy things that anyone can do if they take some time out of their schedule, such as praying for thirty minutes each day or taking the time to appreciate what you have. And there are more substantial applications in the workbook that require more thought such as realizing one's fears and anxieties and working to lessen them. This workbook is a great guide on loving not only God but yourself and others around you. It is an eye-opening experience that, if nothing else, will leave people with a new perspective on their life and how they affect the people they are surrounded by.

- Jazmin Gousse

Working on the layout of this devotional has been so inspirational on tough days-- each day reminds us of something we already know deep down, but the reminders help us make each day beautiful and to accept that in a positive way. I have worked with Ilka many times in the past, I find her to be one of the most upbeat, inspirational, understanding individuals I've ever had the pleasure of knowing and I truly feel that this devotional will help guide me to something close to that same inner peace and positivity.

-Heather Goble

Introduction
A bit about my journey into devotionals

Hi! My name is Ilka V. Chavez. In 2014, I was diagnosed with a very rare form of cancer known as a Gastrointestinal Stromal Tumor (GIST.) At the same time, my marriage, as I knew it, was dissolving after 27 years. This all seemed too much for one person during a very delicate time in my life. Then to add to two already weighty trials, I began to question my purpose, which included my career and all I was currently doing for my family, community, and friends. To say the least I was totally lost.

As I woman of faith, after the initial shock that lasted over one year and through many tears, I began to anchor on what I knew best to do, pray, and ask God for guidance. The first was what to do about my health, then what to do about my marriage, and last what to do about anchoring my children and myself during this very tough and uncertain season. As usual, God was faithful and guided me through turbulent waters.

One area of major concern for me were our two beautiful children, whose lives were torn apart after we worked so hard to build a strong foundation for them. I asked God what I could do to show our children that this is part of life and to ensure this experience did not ruin their future. I heard "show them my word, show them the truth." Of course, I wondered was it one specific thing. It was not. I started sharing my daily devotional reads and prayers with them. Slowly I started sharing with my brother as he was having a difficult time with my separation and pending divorce. Slowly I began sharing this devotional with a larger community nationally and internationally. Next came the nudge to elevate and I did not see it coming.

Through the journey since 2014, God made it possible for me to become a best-selling author and international speaker. On June 5th, 2017, the day before the devolution of my marriage of 32 years, while in prayer and reflection, I heard why do you continue to forward other people's devotional? I made you a best-seller author, write your own devotional and share that. By the way, share it as you write and do not let the perfect be the enemy of the good. Write a one-year devotional and publish that. What do you do when you hear clear and specific instructions; you simply obey and do it in all your imperfections. I continue to write occasionally but not daily or frequently throughout the week as I was used to doing. I thought, may be the quarantine was the pause I need to complete and publish this devotional of the daily downloads our Father has guided me to share. I pray it helps each of you as you continue to lead yourself, your family, your business and ultimately your purpose. To God be the glory.

My slogan is Learn it. Live it. Lead it.

I believe the messages here are for leaders of countries, companies, churches, communities and families. So, meditate on them with all your heart and let God minister to you. I love you.

Ilka V.

January

LOVE

ANCHOR SCRIPTURE: 1 CORINTHIANS 13:1-3

"If I speak in the tongues of men or of angels, but do not have love, I am only a resounding gong or a clanging cymbal. If I have the gift of prophecy and can fathom all mysteries and all knowledge, and if I have a faith that can move mountains, but do not have love, I am nothing. If I give all I possess to the poor and give over my body to hardship that I may boast, but do not have love, I gain nothing."

L-O-V-E is the missing link in Leadership.
Live Our Values Everyday (LOVE)
-Ilka V. Chavez

One important ingredient missing from leadership today is LOVE. How can you lead someone or something you do not love? How can you hurt and take advantage of someone you say you love? It seems hypocritical, don't you think?

If you do not love yourself, how can you lead yourself? If you do not love others, how can you lead them? We are not created to hate, envy, chastise, or be jealous of each other. We are created to LOVE.

The word reminds us, "If I have the gift of prophecy and can fathom all mysteries and all knowledge, and if I have a faith that can move mountains, but do not have love, I am nothing." That means no amount of power, influence, or gift we wield can surpass love. That is why Jesus set the example of leadership for us by describing it as a life of service and not control, a good leader loves and serves his people.

1

Ponder on this: leaders must be patient, kind, not envious, not boastful, not proud (be humble), must not dishonor others, must not be self-seeking (never about you or your desires), not easily angered, keeps no record of wrong doing (forgiving), does not delight in evil, always protects, always trusts (this is one of the biggest areas that threaten leaders), hopes always, and always persevere.

Do you exhibit these traits as a leader? Do you need to improve on any of these key LOVE principles needed to successfully lead your tribe? I once saw an acronym that defined the word love:

LOVE = Living Our Values Everyday

I leave you with this reminder

- Love is patient: leaders must be patient and understanding.
- Love is kind: leaders must not use their positions to wield authority with blustery, cutting words.
- It does not envy: leaders must elevate people. They should not be threatened by the success of others.
- It does not boast: leaders should boast of the successes of their people rather than their own success.
- It is not proud: leaders remain humble.
- It does not dishonor others: leaders must honor and respect all people. Always.
- It is not self-seeking: leaders must serve others, not themselves nor their own agendas.
- It is not easily angered: leaders must have control of their emotions (to have self-control). They should not be quick to anger.
- It keeps no record of wrongs: leaders must help others when they fall, not berate them, or keep a tally of people's failures. Yes, great leaders forgive easily.
- Love does not delight in evil but rejoices with the truth: leaders do not partake in evil or permit it on their teams. They speak and operate from truth.
- It always protects: leaders must protect their people the way parents protect their children.

- Always trusts: leaders must believe the best of their people and trust them. Begin all relationships from a place of trust.
- Always hopes: leaders must be positive about their people and their mission. Leaders are hopeful.
- Always perseveres: leaders must not give up on their tribe even when the going gets tough.

PRAYER FOR THE DAY:

Dear Father,
Thank you for the reminder that to lead, we must love. I pray for the grace to remember to love as I lead. That the words in 1 Corinthians 13:1-3 become life to me, and most importantly that you are Love and I love like you. I ask this in Jesus' name. Amen!

Maintaining Momentum

ANCHOR SCRIPTURE: PHILIPPIANS 3:12-14 (NIV)

"Not that I have already obtained all this, or have already arrived at my goal, but I press on to take hold of that for which Christ Jesus took hold of me. Brothers and sisters, I do not consider myself yet to have taken hold of it. But one thing I do: Forgetting what is behind and straining toward what is ahead, I press on toward the goal to win the prize for which God has called me heavenward in Christ Jesus."

Belief in oneself is incredibly infectious. It generates momentum, the collective force of which far outweighs any kernel of self-doubt that may creep in.
-Aimee Mullins

Swings are sometimes hazardous. However, there are several benefits to swings, for instance they promote physical, social and cognitive development, and it can be therapeutic as well. It is interesting to realize the freedom that getting on a swing and pumping your way to great heights brings. The more you pump your feet, the more momentum you get to go higher. I want you to capture this exhilarating experience in your mind as you swing pleasantly through the air. However, note that if you stop pumping, or someone or something stops pushing, you will eventually stop.

Like the lessons learned in swinging, you must continue to pump your leg to maintain momentum. Just small strokes to keep you moving. What small steps and actions do you take to maintain your momentum in life and in your leadership? Even when you are tired, what is the one thing you do that can change things for you in just a few areas of your life and leadership? Maintaining momentum primarily

4

depends on you, your mindset, and your willingness to pump your leg just one more time, to shift your mindset and belief to maintain your momentum. Colin Powell is quoted as saying; "Perpetual optimism is a force multiplier."

Today's scripture is a reminder, "Not that I have already obtained all this, or have already arrived at my goal, but I press on to take hold of that for which Christ Jesus took hold of me. Brothers and sisters, I do not consider myself yet to have taken hold of it. But one thing I do: Forgetting what is behind and straining toward what is ahead, I press on toward the goal to win the prize for which God has called me heavenward in Christ Jesus. I encourage you to read Philippians 3 in its entirety and ensure that as you go through today, you maintain your momentum.

──────────────── **PRAYER FOR THE DAY:** ────────────────

Dear Father,
Thank you for the reminder to maintain my momentum. Not that I have already obtained all this, or have already arrived at my goal, but I press on to take hold of that for which Christ Jesus took hold of me. I pray that the Holy Spirit gives me grace to forget what is behind and strive towards what is ahead. That I yield to your word in Philippians 3 and maintain my momentum. I ask this in your son Jesus' name. Amen!

What you say and do

ANCHOR SCRIPTURE: PROVERBS 16:3

"Commit to the Lord whatever you do, and he will establish your plans."

We must let go of the life we have planned, so as to accept the one that is waiting for us."
-Joseph Campbell

Entering new endeavors, starting a new relationship, starting a new home or work project, or doing something you have never done before, is sometimes scary. You are entering the unknown, which I sometimes refer to as an "uncomfortable zone." As I reflect on the number of times I entered the 'unknown' without overthinking, I am realized that these experiences have been critical to my growth. These events and moments were pivotal in defining who I am today.

Today's verse reminds us to commit to the Lord whatever we do, and he will establish our plans. I recall hearing from a mentor, "Commit whatever you say, do, and think to the Lord first and your path will remain straight." Sounds easy right? I can attest that it is not. Fear, doubt, unease, "control factors" show up frequently when we commit it all to the Lord.

I encourage you today to look at ways you are not committing what you say, do and think to the Lord. If you find that it is hard, consider today's verse. Which plan do you think will succeed? Be encouraged, it is okay to let go and let God have His way.

Dear God,
Thank you for the reminder to commit, not some things, but all that I do to you, and for the promise that you will establish my plans. You are the master planner and your way; your plans are perfect. I pray that this reminder will quicken me to commit all to you. That I do not allow fear of the unknown to get in the way of what I say, do and think. I ask this in your son Jesus's name. Amen!

JANUARY 4

Seeking Purpose

ANCHOR SCRIPTURE: HEBREWS 13:21

" *Equip you with everything good for doing his will, and may he work in us what is pleasing to him, through Jesus Christ, to whom be glory for ever and ever.* "

"The meaning of life is to find your gift.
The purpose of life is to give it away."
- Pablo Picasso

Finding and living your purpose is a desire many people seek. It takes longer for some than others. I realize that finding quiet time in meditation, truly remaining present, and trusting God to equip you with everything you need at exactly the time you need it, is key.

7

Today's verse provides guidance and hope. Hope that the Good Lord will equip you with everything good for doing His will, and may He work in us what is pleasing to him, through Jesus Christ, to whom be glory for ever and ever.

If we allow God to equip us with the tools necessary to fulfill our purpose; if we are still, listen and obey as we search for our own purpose, we will find the purpose for which we are here on earth.

I encourage you today to seek your true purpose and how you are to serve others. Confidently ask God to guide and lead you to that purpose that is pleasing to him. Never compare your purpose with someone else's. We are all here to serve our unique purpose.

 **PRAYER FOR THE DAY:**

Dear God,
Thank you for the encouragement and hope that you are mighty and will equip me with everything good for doing your will. I give you all the praise, honor, and glory. I pray that as I seek my purpose in you today, you will reveal it to me and show me the way to go. I trust you to equip me with all I need to fulfill my purpose in alignment with your will. I ask this in your son Jesus's name. Amen!

Greener grass syndrome

ANCHOR SCRIPTURE: PSALM 1:3

"That person is like a tree planted by streams of water, which yields its fruit in season and whose leaf does not wither-whatever they do prospers."

"The grass isn't always greener on the other side!"
- *Ricky Gervais*

I recently listened to a sermon that discussed how many of us constantly fall prey to what I refer to as "the greener grass syndrome." We long to have what someone else has. We believe that "the grass is greener on the other side." We begin to focus on the wrong goals and false outcomes. We focus on someone else's yard instead of our own. However, the supposed glitter and sheen of the grass on the other side may not be so once we chose the greener grass.

We fail to realize that if our grass is not green, it relates directly to us. Our lens and our thoughts may be out of focus yet still we hope for a great outcome. This sermon truly led me to think, to have great outcomes, do I continue to focus on the wrong things or focus on things of God? Today's verse reminds us to focus on God and His plans for our own lives. "That person is like a tree planted by streams of water, which yields its fruit in season and whose leaf does not wither-whatever they do prospers." (Read Psalm 1)

The sermon continued to discuss "If we focus on God and His outcome for our lives, we will not be fooled by the green grass in someone else yard because we are focusing on our own and being happy with what God is doing in our lives. If we focus on what God has blessed us with and work hard to maintain it, our lives will be different, especially as it pertains to the different relationships we have with people in our lives." This emphasizes the importance of us focusing on God and allowing Him to water our grass. The grass is always greener where God is, and He is the living water that will make your grass green.

────────────────── **PRAYER FOR THE DAY:** ──────────────────

Dear God,

Thank you for the reminder to always focus on You and the outcomes you have for my life. That my grass is as green as I make it. I am grateful. I pray that I remember to always focus on you so I too can be like a tree planted by streams of water, which yields its fruit in season and whose leaf does not wither, and whatever I do prospers. I ask this in your son Jesus' name. Amen!

Obey, Love, and Serve

ANCHOR SCRIPTURE: DEUTERONOMY 11:13-15

*"So if you faithfully obey the commands I am giving you
today—to love the LORD your God and to serve him with
all your heart and with all your soul, then I will send rain on
your land in its season, both autumn and spring rains,
so that you may gather in your grain, new wine and olive oil.
I will provide grass in the fields for your cattle,
and you will eat and be satisfied."*

"The purpose of human life is to serve, and
to show compassion and the will to help others."
-Albert Schweitzer

Many people today live in what we refer to as the "sandwich generations." They are raising their own children and taking care of their parents all at the same time. For many, this is no easy feat especially when you add all other responsibilities like work, home, and general family responsibilities. However, we are called to serve and take care of those who no longer can either be alone or take care of themselves. We must learn to love and serve.

Today's verse is a reminder of a very important command to love the Lord your God and to serve him with all your heart and with all your soul. When we love God, we love all people, we obey his commands and we joyfully serve the lord and his children. Being a part of the sandwich generation may not be easy, but when you see the blessing of serving the Lord and his people, the burden is light. You can serve with ease, joy, and love.

I encourage you today to live by this important command. Obey, Love and Serve the lord with all your heart and soul. As Matthew 11:30 reminds us- "His yoke is easy and His burden is light."

Dear God,
Thank you for the reminder that the key to walking on your
straight path entails loving, obeying, and serving you with all
our heart and soul. I pray that you help me put you first in my
life. That I love, obey, and serve you above all. I ask this all in
Jesus name. Amen!

●

JANUARY 7

Justice

ANCHOR SCRIPTURE: ISAIAH 56:1

"This is what the Lord says: "Maintain justice and
do what is right, for my salvation is close at hand and
my righteousness will soon be revealed."

"I have always found that mercy bears richer fruits than strict justice"
- Abraham Lincoln

Have you ever found yourself in a situation where you want to seek justice? Where you take matters into your own hands. You try to get back at someone who hurt you, or who has done wrong to your loved one.

Today's verse guides us to maintain justice and do the right thing. There is no need to do wrong to someone in return for the wrong they did to you. It serves no one any good. The Word states that you should do the right thing because the Lord's salvation is close at hand and his righteousness will soon be revealed. This message to me is one of hope.

Next time you have the urge to repay someone with the same or worse wrong than they have done to you or your loved one, remember, this is not necessary. The Lord's righteousness will be revealed. Live according to God's law. He will handle the rest.

─────────────── PRAYER FOR THE DAY: ───────────────

Dear God,
Thank you for the reminder that doing the right thing and living by your law is the way to go. I pray that I maintain justice and do the right thing every day. That I do not repay evil for evil, and I remember your righteousness will be revealed. I ask this in your son Jesus' name. Amen!

JANUARY 8

Power

ANCHOR SCRIPTURE: ACTS 19:20

"In this way the word of the Lord spread widely and grew in power"

─────────────

"The past cannot be changed. The future is yet in your power."
- Unknown

─────────────

I often think about fashion trends and how they become popular. Someone designs the product; someone famous or the primary target group endorses that product; before you know it, there is a high demand for the product. Then the product gains power enough to influence the lifestyle and fashion choices of people.

I wonder if the Lord's word could spread the same way. If it was treated like high fashion, the word would spread widely and grow in power. Today's verse reminds us that the word of the Lord has power to spread widely. (Read Acts 19.) The Lord's word has power to break strongholds. It is key to setting many free.

I encourage you today to believe in the power of the Lord's word and the power you inherited. But do not just believe and use that word for your life and success, go into the world and share that power with the people you interact with on a daily basis to as to cause the Word to become of great influence in the lives of people like high fashion.

─────────────── **PRAYER FOR THE DAY:** ───────────────

Dear God,
Today's reminder that spreading your word widely grows in power. I thank you for the power that your word brings me. I pray that all your children continue to widely spread your word, the truth so it grows in power. I ask this in your son Jesus' name. Amen!

●

JANUARY 9

Created in his image

ANCHOR SCRIPTURE: GENESIS 1:27

"So, God created mankind in his own image, in the image of God he created them; male and female he created them."

"Life isn't about finding yourself. Life is about creating yourself."
- George Bernard Shaw

14

I recently attended a networking meeting and met a very interesting woman who caught my attention. After the meeting, we engaged in conversation and she indicated that she loved to write - that writing brought out her creativity. She also shared that her ten-year-old daughter just became an author. She created a story about two sisters in Africa and was inspired to publish this story into a book.

As I left the meeting, I thought, "Wow, we are all truly created to create." The greatest creator created us in His likeness, in his image to do the same. I thought, a ten-year-old figured that out early. From our birth, we were all created with the innate ability to create. However, somewhere along our journey called life, we lose our way and forget this truth, "We've been made in the image and likeness of God."

I wonder what stops us from fully tapping into our creativity. Is it that we don't believe we have the ability? Is it that, as we grow older, we are exposed to sin and feel unworthy? Today, I encourage each of you to tap into your God-given creativity, your gift. No matter your age, if you have been thinking about creating something, create it now. If you have been thinking about starting something, start working on it today. We are God's good work; made in God's image, part of God's family. What will you create today?

PRAYER FOR THE DAY:

Dear God,
Thank you for creating me in your own image, for giving me the greatest gift of spirit within to help me be creative. To help me remember that, even if I sin, I should not allow that to block my creativity. Your son already paid the price. I pray that all your children remember that they were created to create and are members of your family. I ask this in your son Jesus' name. Amen!

Made Free

ANCHOR SCRIPTURE: JOHN 8:31-32

"To the Jews who had believed him, Jesus said, "If you hold to my teaching, you are really my disciples. Then you will know the truth, and the truth will set you free."

"Knowing is not enough; we must apply.
Willing is not enough; we must do."
- *Johann Wolfgang von Goethe*

Have you ever heard anyone say, "I have been living a lie?" Someone once said this to me, and I wondered why. Apparently, this person had come in contact with a piece of information from someone she trusted, that she lived her entire life on, even though it was contrary to the norm and was not easy to live with. Only to find out later, that the information was not as true as she believed, and this made her hurt and disappointment. But despite the disappointment, once she discovered the truth, she was able to come to terms with it and began to experience freedom in her heart.

We cannot give or share what we don't have. Knowing the truth and practicing the truth is the key to freedom. Everyone values truth and freedom. Yet, we have many people who do not really know the truth, live their lives based on lie, and do not enjoy freedom. Sometimes, they are simply enslaved by their fear of guilt, condemnation, or their sinful desires.

Whether we admit it or not, the truth is freely available to every one of us. If we don't know the truth and exercise it, it is useless. "The Bible is full of truths, but you must be careful that the 'truth' you follow is an original and Biblical truth and not an interpretation from man, especially a man with an agenda. Once you know what the Bible says, then you can apply that truth to your life." James 1:25 says: "But whoever looks intently into the perfect law that gives freedom, and continues in it—not forgetting what they have heard, but doing it—they will be blessed in what they do." I encourage you to continue to seek the truth. Set yourself free.

——————————— **PRAYER FOR THE DAY:**———————————

Dear God,
Thank you for setting me free with your truth. I pray that all your children seek your truth and their freedom. I ask this in your son Jesus' name. Amen!

JANUARY 11

Patience is a Virtue

ANCHOR SCRIPTURE: ROMANS 12:12

"Let your hope keep you joyful, be patient in your troubles, and pray at all times."

"Patience is a bitter plant that produces sweet fruit."
- Charles Swindoll

Society today seems to have lost patience. Everyone wants everything done now or done their way. When they don't have whatever they desire, they complain, take matters into their own hands, retaliate or pout. One definition of patience is "the capacity to accept or tolerate delay, trouble, or suffering without getting angry or upset." Patience is also a fruit of the Spirit.

17

Can you imagine activating patience in the most uncomfortable situation? Going through any uncomfortable situation without whining or complaining? We all have the power to activate patience and self-control (another fruit of the Spirit) to persevere during tough times, during the wait and during uncomfortable situations. One point to note: complaining during the wait is different than speaking out about something that is totally wrong based on the truth.

As your patience is tested today or another day, I encourage you to remember the saying, "Patience is a virtue." Before you react to a situation, take the time (be patient) to collect all the facts. Today's verse serves as a reminder to be patient in your troubles, let your hope keep you joyful, and always pray. Patience, trust, hope, faith, and love are all tied to the spirit and good character.

PRAYER FOR THE DAY:

Dear God,
Thank you for the reminder that during tough times I can activate patience, a fruit of the Spirit. It reminds me that You remain in control. I pray that help me activate the gift of patience you have given us today, and every day of my life. That I am reminded that you are in control and that I allow you to drive. I ask this in your son Jesus' name. Amen.

Seeking Happiness

ANCHOR SCRIPTURE: PSALM 37:4

*"Take delight in the Lord, and he will give you
the desires of your heart".*

Your heart is where your treasure is, and you must find your treasure
in order to make sense of everything."
- Paulo Coelho

Going through life, I have met a lot of people who are simply not happy
with life. They are not happy with their jobs, they are not happy with
their weight, they are not happy with their spouses, they are not
happy with their relatives, they are not happy with themselves and
the list goes on. No matter what it is, they are never happy.

Some people spend their entire lives seeking or chasing after happiness.
I compare it to a treasure hunt. If only they knew that the secret to
finding their treasure - their happiness - is to seek God. Happiness is
within. They don't need to go looking for happiness through someone
else; they can't find it through a job, or some miraculous occurrence
such as winning the lottery, and meeting prince or princess charming
still won't guarantee happiness.

Today, I encourage you and hope you encourage others to delight in
the Lord. Serve the Lord, continue to strengthen your relationship
with God and he will give you the desires of your heart. He will lead
you to genuine happiness and peace. Our quest for happiness is born
out of a dislocation from the realm of God in our hearts.

Our heart was created to host God, and the more of God we carry, the
more happiness we have, irrespective of the current situation around
us. This is because happiness is the atmosphere of God, and we are
sure, that once we are close to God, whatever current situation we are
in will find solution.

This is why the secret to through happiness is not seeking physical or mundane things that can be here today and gone tomorrow, but seeking the eternal God, who can furnish happiness on our hearts unconditionally.

Dear God,
Thank you for leading me to happiness, my true treasure. To know that you live in me and by my taking delight in you, you will give me the desires of my heart. I pray that from now on, my gaze and delight is in you, Lord, so I can find true happiness through you. I ask this in your son Jesus' name. Amen.

JANUARY 13

Comfort

ANCHOR SCRIPTURE: 2 CORINTHIANS 1:3-4

"Praise be to God and Father of our Lord Jesus Christ, the Father of compassion and the God of all comfort, who comforts us in all our troubles, so that we can comfort those in any trouble with the comfort we ourselves receive from God."

"Cultivating compassion for ourselves and others can bring balance and harmony to our lives in a way we never dreamed of."
- Thubten Chodron

I wonder why it takes a disaster for people to come together, to work for, rather than against each another. We need to learn to make it a habit, rather than a reaction, to pray together as a nation. To comfort one another the same way God comforts us. Wouldn't it be beautiful, if we simply did that as part of our daily lives, disaster or not?

Should it take situations that place our backs against the wall to show our goodness, compassion, to comfort one another and share love for one another as children of God? The reality is we get busy in our daily lives and sometimes forget who we are and what we should do. We forget to pray for each other and even forget to pray for ourselves.

We are all good people. It just takes extra effort and a deeper dive to tap into the goodness within. Today's verse reminds us to praise God the Father of compassion and the God of all comfort. He comforts us in our troubles so we can share that same comforts with others especially in their times of trouble. I encourage you today to remain in the present, pray together often and seek opportunities to comfort others in times of trouble. I leave you with 1 Thessalonians 3:12(NIV) - May the Lord make your love increase and overflow for each other and for everyone else, just as ours does for you.

--------------------- **PRAYER FOR THE DAY:** ---------------------

Dear God,
Thank you for your compassion and constant comfort in times of trouble. For teaching me that the same comfort I receive from you, I should share with others in their times of trouble. I pray that I remember to praise you for the compassion and the comfort you give to me in hard times. That I remember to share this same compassion and comfort with others. I ask this in your son Jesus' name. Amen!

Leading in Excellence

ANCHOR SCRIPTURE: EPHESIANS 6:4

"Fathers, do not exasperate your children; instead, bring them up in the training and instruction of the Lord."

"We are what we repeatedly do. Excellence, then,
is not an act, but a habit."

- Aristotle

Fathers play a critical role in each of our lives. They provide for us, instruct us, and are there for us through the good and the bad. Being a father is a tough job. Can you imagine the whole world relying on you day in and day out? Can you imagine, "lights, camera, action" on you every minute of the day? Living up to so many expectations while leading a family?

Today's scripture reminds fathers not to exasperate their children; instead, to bring them up in the training and instruction of the Lord. Whether you are a father, father-to-be, or serve as a father figure to someone, be encouraged that God has provided you with all the tools and instructions to lead your children and family in excellence and in truth. Seek Him daily to help you in your walk and in turn help your children walk a life of excellence.

Note, excellence is not perfection. Perfection is focused on "doing the thing right," according to others' perception. Excellence is about "doing the right thing," regardless of your audience. Deuteronomy 6:6-9 guides each of us to leave a legacy of God's law by committing ourselves to His commandments then teaching them to our children and their children, etc.

Dads, I encourage you to continue to do the right thing. Be you a Father at Home or a Father of employees at work, any scope of leadership is Fatherhood.

My hats off to all dads, fathers and fathers-to-be. "Learn it. Live it. Lead it." Lead your legacy! Set an example of excellence that you want your children or followers to be and guide them through the path into that height of excellence, then you will have left a lasting legacy.

--------------------- **PRAYER FOR THE DAY:** ---------------------

Dear God,
Thank you for all fathers, including those who are in heaven. I thank you for all my brothers who read this today and most importantly thank you for all men preparing to be fathers. Continue to be the force that brings them up in the training and instructions of the Lord so they can do the same for their children and their families. I pray that you strengthen all families and lead them to your will and your way. That all your children follow your law so they may live in truth and in excellence. I asked this in your son Jesus' name. Amen!

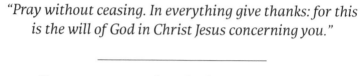

JANUARY 15

Reactive or Proactive Prayer

ANCHOR SCRIPTURE: 1 THESSALONIANS 5:17-18

"Pray without ceasing. In everything give thanks: for this is the will of God in Christ Jesus concerning you."

"Is prayer your steering wheel or your spare tire?"
- Corrie ten Boom

Today, I prayed for increase in my prayer life, and that others increase theirs. I thought about whether our prayer lives have become more reactive than proactive. Have we stopped praying in the good times and only pray in the bad? If we prayed as hard as we do in good times as we do in the bad, how powerful would that be? What joy would that bring to our Father above- each of us constantly talking to him and strengthening our relationship with him?

The word cease is defined as; "cause to come to an end especially gradually: no longer continue." Today's verse reminds us to pray without ceasing. This is a clear instruction to never stop praying. Additionally, verse 18 reminds us that as we pray continuously, we must give thanks for everything: for this is the will of God in Christ Jesus concerning you. To me, this means no matter what the situation, good or bad, pray continuously and give thanks for everything. God has a plan. We must never stop praying.

Next time someone asks you to pray for something on his or her behalf, will you be able to say, "It's already done?" Whenever I forget how to pray, I usually go back to Mathew 6:5-15, which includes the Lord's Prayer and gives specific instructions on how to pray. I also visit Psalm 86; A prayer of David, which reminds me on how to pray to God fully and openly. I encourage you today, to pray without ceasing, in the good times and in the bad.

Dear God,
Thank you for your clear instructions to never cease my prayers,
to be thankful for all I have and endure as I know you remain
in control. I pray that I obey your instructions to pray without
ceasing. To be thankful for all things and to trust that you are in
control and your will is best for us all. I ask this in your son Jesus'
name. Amen!

JANUARY 16

Wisdom and Wealth

ANCHOR SCRIPTURE: PSALM 49:20

"People who have wealth but lack understanding
are like the beast that perish."

"The real measure of your wealth is how much you'd be worth
if you lost all your money."
- Unknown

I once read an article and it said, "Life is about righteousness, not riches." Many people focus on getting rich. Everyone wants to be rich and famous. In pursuing this dream, some focus simply on getting rich. Many never pause to think that nothing they possess right now goes to eternity with them.

I recently met an actress who shared her story of having wealth for some time. Somewhere along the way, she lost her gigs, became depressed and lost all her wealth. She admits that she lacked wisdom and the foundation to manage her wealth. I am sure you have heard many stories of recording artists, actors, and millionaires who went from rags to riches and back to rags.

Did they lack wisdom and the tools to manage their wealth or did they simply lose sight of the bigger picture? Today's verse warns that people who have wealth but lack understanding are like the beasts that perish. Understanding the facts of life, God's word, and his truth, seeking righteousness, seeking wisdom, and understanding provides the greatest wealth for our internal life. Today I encourage you to read Psalm 49 and seek wisdom as you aim for wealth and fame.

─────────────── **PRAYER FOR THE DAY:** ───────────────

Dear God,
Thank you for your guidance on what is needed for my life in your
kingdom. I pray that I learn to have wealth with understanding.
That I remember "It's not the riches, it's the riches with the foun-
dation and understanding that comes from earning those riches"
that truly matters. I ask this in your son Jesus' name. Amen!

───────────────●───────────────
JANUARY 17

Adhesive

ANCHOR SCRIPTURE: COLOSSIANS 1:17

"He is before all things, and in him all things hold together."

───────────────

Man is born broken. He lives by mending. The grace of God is glue.
- Eugene

───────────────

An adhesive is sometimes defined as a substance that causes some-thing to adhere, as glue or rubber cement. In physics, it relates to

26

the molecular force that exists in the area of contact between unlike bodies and that acts to unite them. If you look around your current surroundings, you will see many items held together by different types of adhesives.

Have you ever thought about what holds you together? Is it your family, your career, your community, your faith/prayer life? How do you make it through life without falling apart? When you fall apart who puts you together again, what "adhesive" or anchor keeps you from totally falling apart? Or are you like the egg of the English nursery rhyme Humpy Dumpty?

Today's verse reminds us that in Christ, all things hold together. He did not only create the universe, but He is the power behind the gravity that holds things together! (Read Colossians 1) This is why Christ is before all things, because in him all things hold together. He is the adhesive!

─────────── **PRAYER FOR THE DAY:** ───────────

Dear God,
Thank you for the reminder that you are before all things. That in you, ALL THINGS hold together. As I go through the day, help me to remember you are before all things and that you are the adhesive that holds all things together. I ask this in your son Jesus' name. Amen!

Tests and Trials Strengthen Character

ANCHOR SCRIPTURE: JOB 23:10

*"But he knows the way that I take; when he has tested me,
I will come forth as gold."*

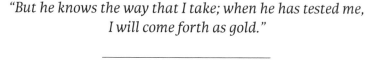

"Beautiful souls are shaped by ugly experiences"
-Matshona Dhliwayo

Testing your faith through trials is hard. Plain and simple. And some trials are tougher than others. The Bible mentions in several places the process of refining gold; there are several detailed stages involved in purifying gold, and a large part of that process involves heat. The gold ore is placed under fire to separate pure gold from other less precious metals. This process is referred to as removing impurities.

Life trials to me are like the process of refining gold. Impurities are removed so our worth shines, and our character is strengthened. We go through the fire and some even feel like they will not make it when the heat is turned on high. They wonder if God is with them or question why He is making them go through such trying times? See the story of Shadrach, Meschach, and Abednego from the Bible book of Daniel 3.

Today's verse reminds us that God knows what you are going through, He is with you and knows the path you are walking in. He is testing you, your faith in Him, and separating your impurities from pure gold. 1 Peter 1:6-7 says – "In all this, you greatly rejoice, though now for a little while you may have had to suffer grief in all kinds of trials. These have come so that the proven genuineness of your faith—of greater worth than gold, which perishes even though refined by fire—may result in praise, glory, and honor when Jesus Christ is revealed."

Dear God,
Thank you for removing my impurities by bringing me through the heat. For the reminder that it all strengthens my character and my faith. I pray I trust you through all my trials and believe that with obedience I will come out with my character strengthened and shining like gold. I ask this in your son Jesus' name. Amen!

JANUARY 19

Confidently Connected

ANCHOR SCRIPTURE: 1 JOHN 3:22

"And receive from him anything we ask, because we keep his commands and do what pleases him."

"It is not hard to obey when we love the one whom we obey."
- Saint Ignatius

As a young child, do you recall wanting that latest toy you saw on the television? Were you excited because it was coming to a store near you very soon? Whether it was the latest Barbie or Ken doll, you did all that was required to have that toy in your possession on the day it was available for purchase. Most of the time getting this toy was tied with getting all your chores done, doing your homework, obeying your parents, teachers or those who raised you. You obeyed the rules and did what pleased your parents to get what you wanted.

29

Today's verse is a reminder that the same with the requirements of your parent, God requires us to obey and follow his commandments. Keeping his commands and doing what pleases him assures us that we will receive all that we ask according to his will. We all disobey God's command at one point or the other and then forget this when we ask for something. However, we serve a faithful and merciful God. He works with us and helps us be obedient to his commands and guide us to do the things that pleases him. He wants to give us everything we ask of Him.

1 John 3:1 reminds us, "See what great love the Father has lavished on us, that we should be called children of God. And that is what we are! The reason the world does not know us is that it did not know him." (Read 1 John 3). Yes, you are God's child and he wants to give you everything you ask. I encourage you to seek to please God and keep his commands. Be confidently connected to God and his word and he will guide you to keeping his commands and be abundantly rewarded according to his will.

PRAYER FOR THE DAY:

Dear God,
Thank you for the reminder that keeping your commands and doing what pleases you is important. There is a reward for doing so, whether it is received right away or later. I pray that I confidently connect with you, keep your commands, and do what pleases you. I ask this all in Jesus' name. Amen!

Peace I Give You

ANCHOR SCRIPTURE: JOHN 14:27

"Peace I leave with you; my peace I give you. I do not give to you as the world gives. Do not let your hearts be troubled and do not be afraid."

"Peace is not something you wish for; it's something you make, something you do, something you are, and something you give away.
– *John Lennon*

It is interesting how so many leaders and others in the limelight say they seek peace, asking for world peace or sometimes even peace that surpasses all understanding. I sometimes wonder if they themselves are taking the necessary steps to live and breathe that peace. I ask, am I living and walking in that peace that Jesus gave to me or am I walking in the peace that the world gives to me?

Sometimes it takes a simple reminder to awaken us to our inheritance. To the promises made to each of us here on earth. Today's verse serves as a reminder that we have the power and have been given a gift. Yes, that gift is peace...Jesus said in John 14:26, "But the Advocate, the Holy Spirit, whom the Father will send in my name, will teach you all things and will remind you of everything I have said to you."

There is so much devastation occurring in this world. Yes, it is easy to despair and focus on what is happening in the world. I encourage you to continue to pray and hang on to the promise that will never be broken... "Peace I leave with you; my peace I give you. I do not give to you as the world gives. Do not let your hearts be troubled and do not be afraid." I encourage you today to anchor on the peace given to you by the almighty.

Dear God,
Thank you for the reminder to not let my heart be troubled or
afraid. You left me with peace and I will believe this no matter
what may be happening in this world. I pray that I learn to seek
the peace that you freely left for me and that I remember you
do not give as the world gives. I ask this in your son Jesus' name.
Amen

●

JANUARY 21

Influence

ANCHOR SCRIPTURE: GALATIANS 5:7-9

"You were running the race so well. Who has held you back from
following the truth? It certainly isn't God, for he is the one who
called you to freedom. This false teaching is like a little yeast
that spreads through the whole batch of dough!"

"The key to successful leadership today is influence, not authority."
- Ken Blanchard

Influence is sometimes defined as the capacity to have an effect on
the character, development, or behavior of someone or something, or
the effect itself. I thought today, what are somethings or people that
influence you? Are these positive or negative influencers? Do I even
pause to think about how I am being influenced or how I influence
others?

To have influence is a powerful trait. Think about it, some people don't have to say a word and their presence influences your actions, thoughts, and behavior. I wonder how great this world will be if all of us allowed God and his words to be the sole influencer of our thoughts, actions and words. However, this is not the case.

Today's verse serves as a reminder to pause and think... you were running the race so well. Who has held you back from following the truth? It certainly isn't God, for he is the one who called you to freedom. This false teaching is like a little yeast that spreads through the whole batch of dough! I encourage you to reflect today on this verse and write down the things that are influencing you today. Are these taking you in the right or wrong direction? You decide and don't forget to check-in with God's word. The truth!

―――――――――― **PRAYER FOR THE DAY:** ――――――――――

Dear God,
Thank you for the reminder that there is so much surrounding me to influence what I say, do, and think. That unless I learn and memorize your truth, I can be swayed to follow wrong teachings. I pray that I seek you to influence my thoughts, words, and actions. I ask this in your son Jesus' name. Amen!

Wait and Grow

ANCHOR SCRIPTURE: PSALM 27:14

*"Wait for the Lord; be strong and take heart
and wait for the Lord."*

When things do not go your way, remember that
every challenge — every adversity — contains within it
the seeds of opportunity and growth.
- Roy T. Bennett

These days, everyone expects things to happen in an instant. We now have shortcuts to prepare quick meals. We have trains that can take you from one location to the other in half the time it took before. We also now have drive-thru restaurants to get your food in a hurry. It seems that we have become a "microwave" society. Where everything must happen now, we set a plan and expect it to happen overnight. When it doesn't happen right away, we are disappointed; we simply give up during the process.

Waiting is mentioned a lot in the Bible. I remember my Grandmother saying that when you see something mentioned often in the Bible, pay attention. This is a clue. Waiting is part of our journey to maturing spiritually, mentally, and emotionally. However, our flesh is very impatient, the stillness drives us crazy and we stop waiting. We think being still and waiting for guidance from God is wasting precious time or it is something we must do to get what we want.

Waiting is part of the growth process. Consider when you plant a seed. It is essential that you wait for it to grow. Waiting may be the most opportune time to mature, to grow in hope, patience, faith, and gratitude. Today's verse is a reminder that no matter how long the wait, be strong, take heart and wait for the Lord. Use the time to strengthen a few spiritual muscles. Wait and grow!

Dear God,
Thank you for the reminder to be strong, take heart and wait
for you. To use the time of waiting to grow, and strengthen my
spiritual muscles. I pray that I learn to remain strong, take heart,
and wait on you. That I take the wait time to strengthen my
spiritual muscles. I ask this in your son Jesus' name. Amen!

JANUARY 23

Rejoice Always

ANCHOR SCRIPTURE: 1 THESSALONIANS 5:16–18

"Rejoice always, pray continually, give thanks in all
circumstances; for this is God's will for you in Christ Jesus."

"Rejoicing is grounded in gratitude, with a keen appreciation for
yourself, others, your abundance, and the beauty around you."
- Susan C. Young

I once saw an article in an Oprah magazine, where Danielle Brooks
describes one of her best childhood memories: At age 12, she won a
raffle for $10 after her bible study. She described that win as the first
time she had won anything, and it felt as though she won tickets to
Willy Wonka's chocolate factory.

As I reflect on the difference of winning ten dollars vs. one million
dollars, I thought, bottom line, it is all a win. You may, however, have
difficulty appreciating the win because you could not appreciate the
value or the blessing of winning no matter the amount. You may even
say thanks but, I wish it was ten million dollars. You simply could not

feel the joy either because you are comparing, or you are not satisfied with what you have or what you won.

Imagine if you would rejoice over finding a penny in the street as though you won one million dollars. It shouldn't matter, money is money, right? Are you able to embrace and rejoice in that moment? Are you able to remove the urge to compare the amount and rejoice in having more even if it is one penny more? Today's verse is a reminder to rejoice always, pray continually, give thanks in all circumstances; for this is God's will for you in Christ Jesus. I encourage you today and every day to resist the urge to compare and rejoice always!

──────────── **PRAYER FOR THE DAY:** ────────────

Dear God,
Thank you for the reminder to rejoice always, pray continually and give thanks in all circumstances. That wherever I am, that whatever I have, is your will for me. I pray that I will yield to the guidance you provided in today's verse, rejoice always, pray continually, and give thanks in all circumstances. That I appreciate this is your will for me. I ask this in your son Jesus' name. Amen!

Two Wrongs Don't Make a Right

ANCHOR SCRIPTURE: MATTHEW 5:39

"But I tell you, do not resist an evil person. If anyone slaps you on the right cheek, turn to them the other cheek also."

"If thy brother wrongs thee, remember not so much his wrong-doing, but more than that he is thy brother."
— *Epictetus*

There is something fascinating about maturing. It seems as you mature, your spirit is calm, your mind is renewed, and the power to understand and discern situations increases. The things of old that would unnerve you, you can now tolerate. You no longer want to get back at someone when they do you or a loved one wrong. Revenge is no longer part of your strategy. Understanding peace and love becomes your center.

Seeking revenge no longer satisfies your heart. As you mature, you see that getting back at someone for doing you or someone you love wrong can lead to a hardened heart, plenty of bitterness, and plain old anger in your heart. That does the heart no good. As we mature, we learn to guard our hearts by making choices based on wisdom and life experiences more than feelings and reactive actions. Simply speaking, we learn "two wrong don't make a right." We learn to lead with God's truth.

Today's scripture reminds us of Jesus' words, "But I tell you, do not resist an evil person. If anyone slaps you on the right cheek, turn to them the other cheek also." This is very hard for most of us to do. Our natural reaction is to fight back. One thing I learned, is that God is always testing our character. He gives us instructions on how to live in his likeness. When we obey and seek his guidance on how to handle the many situations we face, our character and patience are strengthened. No need to seek vengeance, God says in Romans 12:19, Vengeance is Mine, I will repay. Maturity involves seeing things from the other person's perspective and knowing they are doing wrong because they do not know any other way of doing thing. So, in maturing, we learn to always trust God's and forgive people like Jesus did on the cross when He was being crucified, rather than seeking revenge by ourselves. We let God be the judge of all things and learn to forgive in everything.

--- **PRAYER FOR THE DAY:** ---

Dear God,
Thank you for the reminder to not resist an evil person. I pray that you help me seek your help to deal with those that me wrong. That I see it is far better to forgive than to seek revenge. I ask this in your son Jesus' name. Amen!

JANUARY 25

Managing Fear

ANCHOR SCRIPTURE: JAMES 4:7

"Submit yourselves, then, to God. Resist the devil,
and he will flee from you."

"Don't let your fear of what could happen, make nothing happen."
- Doe Zantamata

Many of us have fears -we fear snakes, spiders, the dark, other people, heights, fear of confrontation, just to name a few. Have you ever thought why or how this fear developed? Have you tried to overcome this fear? Is your fear warranted or not? Has fear stolen your joy?

Some fear is reasonable and warranted, it is a gift from God built into us to serve as a warning factor. I read an article about overcoming fear by Bill Bouknight that helps define and classify the degrees of fear we have, "The most common fears relate to matters we cannot control. Abnormal or excessive fear is a monster which can paralyze and destroy. Panic is fear out of control." The article continued to state, "Excessive fear is caused when our source of security is not strong enough to sustain us." This statement came as a form of revelation that gave me more insight into what fear really is.

Think about this, who or what do you fear? Who are what are you trusting to be the source of your security and strength? Can this source sustain you through all your fears? Reminder, the enemy is there to insight fear. Who will you believe? The Bible tells many stories where fear rather than trusting Jesus caused many to panic when it seems it was the end. Today's verse reminds us to submit yourselves, then, to God. Resist the devil, and he will flee from you. I encourage you to have a fearless day.

———————————— PRAYER FOR THE DAY: ————————————

Dear God,
Thank you for the reminder that with you sustaining me, I shall fear not. I pray for grace to submit to you and fear not. That I am able to resist the devil and watch fear and evil flee from my life. I ask this in Jesus name. Amen!

Victorious Living

ANCHOR SCRIPTURE: 1 CORINTHIANS 16:13-14

"Be on your guard; stand firm in the faith; be courageous; be strong. Do everything in love."

"Victorious living does not mean freedom from temptation, nor does it mean freedom from mistakes."
- E. Stanley Jones

As I continue to mature spiritual, I am always seeking instructions on how to stand strong in order to make it through the many battles and temptations we all face. Sometimes, these instructions show up as a remembrance of something my grandmother, father or mother taught me. Other times, it comes as a reminder of a lesson I or someone learned through life. However, as I mature spiritually, I seek God's instructions and guidance from the Bible. I realize that as I seek these instructions in the Bible, all the steps are written for us. These instructions were always readily available to us. That is one of the many truths I was taught.

As one of God's children, I know God will always have the victory. Many of you may have been told while you were going through a particular battle or storm in life to "be strong." I know when I heard this, "be strong", I said how? Today's verse, which some compare it to a military command or instruction before war, provides us with five steps to win our battles. Some who have served in the military may relate to these instructions;

1 —*Be on guard which means be vigilant and stay awake.*

2 — *Stand firm in your faith. Anchor on God's word and promises.*

3 — Be courageous, do not be shaken by danger or pain, know that God is with you.

4 — Be Strong, don't seek your strength, instead rely on God's strength.

5 — Do everything in love. If you forget how to do this, read 1 Corinthians 13:1-7.

Today I encourage you to read 1 Corinthians 13 and 16. Victory is yours. Happy Victorious living!

──────────── **PRAYER FOR THE DAY:** ────────────

Dear God,
Thank you for your instructions on how to live a victorious life. You never instruct me in the wrong way to go. I pray that all heed your clear instructions so they can win every battle I face. Simply, so I can live victoriously. I ask this in your son Jesus name. Amen!

JANUARY 27

Contentment

ANCHOR SCRIPTURE: PHILIPPIANS 4:11

"Am not saying this because I am in need, for I have learned to be content whatever the circumstances."

"Many people lose the small joys in the hope for the big happiness."
- Pearl S. Buck

41

The word contentment is sometimes defined as a state of pure satisfaction. You are joyous with all you have, where you are and who you are. I was awakened to the fact that being content is a learned behavior. Contentment isn't denying your feelings about wanting and desiring what you can't have, but it frees you from being controlled by your feelings. It is a learned behavior not to have your emotions and feelings control you.

Jesus tells us to be content with what we have in Matthews 6:25 "Therefore I tell you, do not worry about your life, what you will eat or drink; or about your body, what you will wear. Is not life more important than food, and the body more important than clothes?" This to me means to remain in the present, live one day at a time. Let go of the past and worrying about the future. Be content with having one slice of the pie, you don't need the entire pie. God provides exactly what you need, not more, not less. Be content with knowing who you are, and whose you are, a child of God perfectly and wonderfully made. And never forget the sacrifice that Jesus made for you.

Today's verse is a reminder to learn to be content whatever the circumstances. I encourage you today to practice and learn contentment. It is not easy, but I know with God's help, you can do it. Be content!

——————————— PRAYER FOR THE DAY: ———————————

Dear God,
Thank you for the reminder to learn to be content no matter my circumstances. That I have all I need. I pray that you help me find the strength to learn contentment, control my feelings and emotions and find peace no matter my circumstances. That I remember I lack nothing. I ask this in your son Jesus' name. Amen!

Forgotten Dreams

ANCHOR SCRIPTURE: EPHESIANS 3:20 (NLT)

"There is no fear in love. But perfect love drives out fear because fear has to do with punishment. The one who fears is not made perfect in love."

This morning do something different: When you wake up in the morning, wake your forgotten and forsaken dreams up as well, wake them up like an insisting rooster!
-*Mehmet Murat Ildan*

As a child, do you remember dreaming about something that at the time seemed unattainable? Or maybe an idea landed in your spirit and because what it entailed to get there was too arduous, required patience and persistence, or plainly seemed impossible, you laid it to rest.

What if you took a few minutes and brought that forgotten dream back to life? Mary Morrissey says, "If you think you can or you think you can't, you are right". Why not always think you can and do the work to live that dream? It may not be easy and may even seem utterly impossible. Why not believe the words in Luke 1:37, "For nothing will be impossible with God?"

Today's verse is a reminder, "Now all glory to God, who is able, through his mighty power at work within us, to accomplish infinitely more than we might ask or think". Mark Twain once said, "Twenty years from now you will be more disappointed by the things that you didn't do than by the ones you did do. So, throw off the bowlines. Sail away from the safe harbor. Catch the trade winds in your sails. Explore. Dream. Discover." Go ahead, do something different today, wake up your forgotten dream!

Dear Father,
Thank you for the reminder to not put my dreams to rest. That nothing will be impossible with you. That through your mighty power at work within us, we can accomplish infinitely more than we might ask or think. I receive grace to wake up my forgotten dream. That I remember that through your mighty power at work within me, I can accomplish infinitely more than I might ask or think. For nothing will be impossible with You. I ask this in your son Jesus' name. Amen

JANUARY 29

Stand United

ANCHOR SCRIPTURE: ECCLESIASTES 4:9-10

"Two are better than one, because they have a good return for their labor: if either of them falls down, one can help the other up. But pity anyone who falls and has no one to help them up."

"Two heads are better than one, not because either is infallible, but because they are unlikely to go wrong in the same direction."
- C.S. Lewis

Have you ever considered that isolating yourself from others is a form of vanity? Even trying to do things yourself is a sign of conceit and self-righteousness. We all need each other. Proverbs 18:1 says: "Whoever isolates himself seeks his own desire; he breaks out against all sound judgment."

Even some of us that know God's word forget that God is always there helping us. When the lights shine on us and we are elevated to another level or achieve a goal or fame, we take all the credit. I am not saying that we have not put in the work, but we can't forget that God is our constant helper. He is showing us to work together. No one stands alone. I have always appreciated teamwork as many have helped me along this journey called life. Doing things together makes the victory even sweeter.

Today's Reflection is a reminder that two are better than one, because they have a good return for their labor: if either of them falls, one can help the other up. I encourage you today to read Ecclesiastes 4 and work together with others. You are stronger together than apart. Stand United!

PRAYER FOR THE DAY:

Dear God,
Thank you for the reminder that two are better than one. So, if one falls, the other can help the other up. This way we have a good return for our labor. I pray I take this reminder to heart, that two are better than one and to stand united. I ask this in your son Jesus' name. Amen!

Words and Works

ANCHOR SCRIPTURE: JAMES 2:18

"But someone will say, "You have faith; I have deeds." Show me your faith without deeds, and I will show you my faith by my deeds."

"Good works is giving to the poor and the helpless, but divine works is showing them their worth to the one who matters."
- Criss Jami

I recently had a conversation with an acquaintance about my thoughts on words and works. Of course, this question came because of a book I recently wrote about what leaders say and do. The gist of my response was, as I continue to mature, I pay closer attention to whether my words and my works are aligned. I also pay attention to whether others are doing the same. Where I fail or fall short, I work hard to make immediate corrections. To influence others, I realize it is important to align our words, works, and actions.

The beauty is, most of the time you don't need to say anything. You just show by your works and your deeds. For example, you don't need to say you have faith, you simply show. Yep, many may call you crazy when they see your faith in action. Words could never explain some of the things I have done by faith. Can you recall the last time you acted by faith? No words necessary.

As I seek more wisdom through the Bible, I realize that Jesus' words and works were always aligned. This is something I thought important enough to learn and practice. As humans, it is a continuous improvement process. Today's verse is a reminder to show your faith by your deeds. Let your works speak louder than your words.

Dear God,
Thank you for sending your son Jesus to teach me about words
and works. That my words and works must align. I pray that
all your children continue to work on aligning their words with
their works. That they show their faith more by their deeds and
their works. I ask this in your son Jesus' name. Amen!

JANUARY 31

Knowledge and Wisdom

ANCHOR SCRIPTURE: 1 KINGS 3:9

"So, give your servant a discerning heart to govern your people
and to distinguish between right and wrong. For who is able
to govern this great people of yours?"

"Knowledge without application is simply knowledge. Applying the
knowledge to one's life is wisdom — and that is the ultimate virtue."
- Kasi Kaye Iliopoulos

Part of growth and maturity is understanding how to best use your
knowledge. Many powerful people have great knowledge but lack the
wisdom on the right use of this knowledge. This is either because wisdom
is the missing link or their wisdom is compromised, they tend to
guide others solely with knowledge. Knowledge alone is not sufficient
to lead others. Something that is compromised is unable to function
optimally. I akin this to a ship lost in the ocean without a compass.

King Solomon was on the right path (See 1 Kings 3-4). He realized that
having knowledge without the right application could harm his lead-

ership. So instead of asking God for riches and other things, he asked God for wisdom. God granted Solomon wisdom and much more. Imagine asking God simply for wisdom. Ensuring that your wisdom is not compromised. As humans, many situations will present to lead us to solely rely on knowledge.

Today's verse is a reminder of Solomon's ask to God for wisdom, "So give your servant a discerning heart to govern your people and to distinguish between right and wrong. For who is able to govern this great people of yours?" Today I encourage you to read 1 Kings 3-4. Ask God for wisdom and watch him over deliver.

--------- **PRAYER FOR THE DAY:** ---------

Dear God,
Thank you for the reminder that sometimes all we need to request from you is wisdom. You will show me how to best apply the knowledge with which you have equipped me. I pray that all your children seek a discerning heart to distinguish between right and wrong. That they understand that knowledge with the proper application is wisdom. I ask this in your son Jesus' name. Amen!

FEBRUARY 1

God is Still Working

ANCHOR SCRIPTURE: HABAKKUK 1:5

*"Look at the nations and watch and be utterly amazed.
For I am going to do something in your days that you
would not believe, even if you were told."*

"You are where God wants you to be at this very moment. Every
experience is part of His divine plan."

When we look at our world and our life, we are faced with disappointment, dissolution, and even desperation when things that are happening simply don't make sense. When we don't understand what is happening, we worry, we get angry, and we give up.

Habakkuk witness so much and was desperate, he was simply puzzled. He didn't understand what God was doing by allowing him to look at injustice. Why God tolerated wrongdoing? Why he allowed destruction, violence, strife, and conflict to happen. Habakkuk accused God of simply not caring and of inaction. In Habakkuk 1:2 he cried out saying, how long, Lord, must I call for help, but you do not listen? Or cry out to you, "Violence!" but you do not save?

In today's verse, God assured Habakkuk that he was going to do something in his days that he would not believe, even if he were told. To me, this is the assurance of things to hope for but not yet seen. God is still working and despite what things may look like, destruction, violence, strife, and conflict, he is working it all out for our good. Have you ever felt like Habakkuk? When you do, what actions do you take? Be encouraged, God is still working!

49

Dear God,
Thank you for the assurance that no matter what I may face today, that you are still working it all out for my good. I pray that all your children stand strong in this assurance that you are working hard in their favor, no matter what they face today. You are working it out for their good. I ask this in Jesus' name. Amen!

FEBRUARY 2

The Power of God's Grace

ANCHOR SCRIPTURE: PHILIPPIANS 2:13

"For it is God who works in you to will and to act in order to fulfill his good purpose."

"God answers the mess of life with one word: "grace."
- Max Lucado

It is amazing to see how we take advantage of God's powerful grace. I wonder if it is sometimes misunderstood when shown outside of sin? I recently had a conversation with a friend who long to receive a promotion. This person felt undervalued, overlooked and abused. Diving deeper into the conversation we were able to uncover that his thoughts were misplaced. He was unable to see God's grace and favor in serving from his current position. He truly was straying towards his own desires than God's plans.

I thought, ahh, the "saving grace" of God. God's grace is there to greet us each morning. I sometimes wonder how many pay attention to this. God's grace comes from the love he has for each of us. It is a gift that we cannot buy, earn, or deserve. Without God's grace, there can be no salvation since grace is fundamental to salvation. (Eph. 2:4-9). "God will never ask you to do anything he doesn't give you the ability and the power to do. That power and ability is called grace." To me, this was the lesson learned from the above conversation. Today's verse is a reminder for it is God who works in you to will and to act to fulfill his good purpose. Today I encourage you to pay attention to God's powerful grace in your life and write down the many ways his grace has saved you.

──────────────── **PRAYER FOR THE DAY:** ────────────────

Dear God,
Thank you for the reminder that it is you who work in me to act to fulfill your good purpose. I pray that all your children remain aware of the power of your grace in their life and that they become more obedient to your good purpose for them. I ask this in your son Jesus' name. Amen!

Equipped for Victory

ANCHOR SCRIPTURE: PSALM 119:98

"Your commands are always with me and make me wiser than my enemies."

"God has equipped you to handle difficult things. In fact, He has already planted the seeds of discipline and self-control inside you. You just have to water those seeds with His Word to make them grow!"

- Joyce Meyer

Have you ever had a situation where someone tried to outsmart or deceive you? Whether it is trying to sell you a counterfeit item, have you done something that is against your values, or take you to a place that does not align with your core beliefs? Do you recall how you handle this situation once you realized what transpired?

We are warned many times to beware of many things in life. We are told not to do certain things or frequent certain areas because of danger. We are taught commands and equipped with the truth from very young. However, we tend to flirt with the very things that we receive clear instructions to keep clear of. I recalled recently being in such a situation. Once I realized that the situation was not aligned with God's commands, I was able to walk away free and clear. I was grateful to have God's commands with me that awakened me to the enemy's deception.

I realized that by studying and learning God's word and his commands, the truth equips you with the tools for victory. Today's verse is a reminder that keeping God's commands with you always, makes you wiser than your enemies. No matter how the enemy may try to outsmart you, God's word equips you for victory!

Dear God,
Thank you for the reminder to always keep your commands with
me as it makes me wiser than my enemies. That the truth always
sets me free. I pray that all your children keep your commands so
that they too can be wiser than their enemies. I ask this in your
son Jesus' name. Amen!

●

FEBRUARY 4

Self-Care

ANCHOR SCRIPTURE: MATTHEW 22:39

Jesus said, "You shall love your neighbor as yourself."

"Love yourself first and everything else falls into line.
You really have to love yourself to get anything done in this world."
- Lucille Ball

It is interesting how many times we hear these instructions on plane rides or as advice from someone else, "put the mask on yourself before placing it on others." We, however, seem to not know how to yield to these instructions.

As someone who thought it was selfish to put yourself first or to place your needs and desires above everyone', I was relieved when I finally learned that taking care of self-first was not a selfish act. That there is no way you can take care of others before yourself. Think about it for a minute. You are running around ensuring the children are okay, your Mom and Dad are okay, your family is okay and never stop to check on whether you are okay. At some point, if you don't check-in on you, you will run out of steam.

Today's verse reminds us that the same love we give to others, we should give to ourselves. So many of us love others more than ourselves. Jesus said it, love yourself the same as you love your neighbor. Note the part of "love yourself." I encourage you to reflect on loving you and if you don't already love you, start today. You are wonderfully and perfectly made. Love who you are!

──────────────── **PRAYER FOR THE DAY:** ────────────────

Dear God,
Thank you for the reminder that I must love myself the same as my neighbor. That there is no reason to feel that this is a self-ish act. I pray that all your children love themselves the same as their neighbor and that this reminder set them free. I ask this in your son Jesus' name. Amen!

───────────────────── ● ─────────────────────

FEBRUARY 5

Strength in numbers

ANCHOR SCRIPTURE: HEBREWS 10:24-25

"And let us consider how we may spur one another on toward love and good deeds, not giving up meeting together, as some are in the habit of doing, but encouraging one another—and all the more as you see the Day approaching..."

There is strength in numbers. Once we show the world that we're together, they can't stop us."
- *Cory Hardrict*

I have a few friends who have expressed to me reasons why they choose not to congregate to worship God and strengthen their faith. Some feel they are worshipping with hypocrites; others rather be alone; some just don't know why but they simply chose not to worship. I reflected on the joy of gathering with family during holidays, special occasions and just because moments. The strength that is replenished by being "in community", in fellowship with others cannot be described. The best description that comes to mind is "iron sharpens iron" when you gather with family, with all your brothers and sisters.

God knew that trying to live life solo would not be easy. That we would continually fall and stray from his purpose for our lives. He knew that for the plans he has for us to succeed, we will have to have the support and encouragement of our brothers and sisters. He instills this when he created the earth and created Eve to be with Adam. He knew this when he created animals to travel in a pack. However, it seems some of us forget the basics.

Today's verse is a reminder that there is strength in numbers... And let us consider how we may spur one another on toward love and good deeds, not giving up meeting together, as some are in the habit of doing, but encouraging one another—and all the more as you see the Day approaching... I encourage you today to not give up gathering, no special occasion needed. There is strength in numbers.

———————————— PRAYER FOR THE DAY: ————————————

Dear God,
Thank you for the reminder that there is strength in numbers. To not give up on gathering and to spur one another on toward love and good deeds. I pray that all your children do not give up on gathering and that they encourage each other toward love and good deeds. I ask this in your son Jesus' name. Amen!

FEBRUARY 6

Favor

ANCHOR SCRIPTURE: PROVERBS 8.35

*"For those who find me, find life and receive favor
from the LORD."*

Humility is the gateway into the grace and the favor of God."
- *Harold Warner*

Have you ever heard the statement "I am blessed and highly favored"
I hear that from so many people but when you look up the meaning,
those who make this statement are not walking in the favor they claim
to have. Favor is defined as gaining approval, acceptance, or special
benefits or blessings.

I recalled hearing a story of a teacher who taught her students to
claim God's favor daily. One day, one of her students came to class
disappointed saying that God's favor was not with her last evening
because she had to park her car on the other side of the school cam-
pus instead of in front of her dorm room. The student later found out
that due to a storm that same evening all the cars near her dorm room
were damaged from debris from the storm. Her car was untouched.

This gave the student a fresh prospective on God's favor. That what
she thought was meant for harm was favor. Today's verse is a reminder that for those who find the Lord, find life, and receive favor from
the LORD. V32-36 gives us instructions on how to maintain this favor,
listen and keep God's ways and do not disregard, seek God and his
goodness and do not fail to find him as you will cause harm to yourself. Today I encourage you to read Proverbs 8 and do not forget that
you are blessed and highly favored.

Dear God,
Thank you for the reminder of your favor and the instructions
on how to remain in this favor. I pray that all your children will
learn that they are favored. That they must listen, obey, and keep
your ways, seek you and your goodness for those who find you,
find life and receive favor from you. I ask this in your son Jesus'
name. Amen!

FEBRUARY 7

Are you ready to listen?

ANCHOR SCRIPTURE: PROVERBS 16:20

"Those who listen to instruction will prosper;
those who trust the LORD will be joyful."

"One of the most sincere forms of respect is actually
listening to what another has to say."
-Bryant H. McGill

I remember as a child, jumping on the bed was prohibited. Our parents had many reasons why this was not allowed including damaging the furniture and the risk of injury. However, when we could get away with it, we still chose to disobey. I recently saw a child jumping on her bed and I asked, are you allowed to do that? She said no and stopped. I said thank you and asked, are you ready to listen now? She hung her head and said yes.

Sometimes, doing what we feel like doing feels good at the time even when we know it is wrong. We even convince ourselves that what we are doing is okay and sometimes go as far as saying I heard a message from the Lord. I heard this statement recently, "God communicates in many forms but most often through your mind." I wondered, if our minds are filled, how can we hear from God? He communicates through our thoughts so we should pay attention to our thoughts.

Today's verse is a reminder that those who listen to instructions will prosper, and those who trust the Lord will be joyful. If we are not sure what we are hearing, keep in mind that God will never send you a message that contradicts his truth or his principles. (His reference manual is available to all, including a little child.) We live in a world filled with noise so our listening to God's guidance must be intentional. I wonder if this is why my Mom prays at 3:00 -5:00 am most times... When most of the world is still asleep and she can have the quiet to listen to God's instructions for her day.

_____ **PRAYER FOR THE DAY:** _____

Dear God,
Thank you for the reminder that those who listen to your instructions will prosper. That submitting, obeying, and surrendering to your will, your instructions, brings joy. I pray that all your children continue to draw closer to you to listen to your instructions so they can prosper and have joy. I ask this in your son Jesus' name. Amen!

Greater is coming

ANCHOR SCRIPTURE: PSALM 139:16

*"You saw me before I was born. Every day of my life
was recorded in your book. Every moment was laid out
before a single day had passed."*

Do not give up when dark times come. The more storms you face in
life, the stronger you'll be. Hold on. Your greater is coming.

- Germany Kent

Can you imagine being 37 or 50 years of age and saying that your life
is over? You have done so many horrible things in life that you believe
God will never bless you. Or another thought, you have been working
for 39 years to reach your goal or find your purpose and you decide,
it will never happen, so you give up. What if you believe greater is
coming and you keep moving forward?

Think of the stories in the Bible, Job had to wait for God to heal and
deliver him; Abraham waited 25 years for God's promise to give him
a son, Joseph had 13 years of tribulation, Moses spent 40 years in the
wilderness, David waited 15 years to be King. Let us not forget that
Sarah, Leah, Hannah, the Woman with the issue of blood, and Martha
also had to wait. It seems God's strategy is to bring you through a
process and part of that process is waiting, trusting, believing and
keep things moving.

Sometimes we allow the enemy to convince us that it is over, that we
should just give up, that we will never make it or that you will never
be a good person. Today's verse is a reminder that God saw you before
you were born. Every day of your life was recorded in his book. Every
moment was laid out before a single day had passed. Yes, God knows
the plans he has for you and those plans are for greater. Don't give-up!

Remember no matter how long your wait, you are in good company. Greater is coming! Today, I encourage you to read Psalm 139.

Dear God,
Thank you for the reminder that you saw me before I was born. That every day of my life is recorded in your book. That every moment was laid out before a single day had passed. I pray that all your children are reminded that you saw them before they were born. That every day of their life was recorded in your book. That every moment was laid out before a single day had passed. That although the wait may be long, they must endure and believe. Greater is coming! I ask this in your son Jesus' name. Amen!

Let there be peace

ANCHOR SCRIPTURE: ROMANS 12:18

*"If it is possible, as far as it depends on you,
live at peace with everyone."*

Peace is the result of retraining your mind to process life as it is,
rather than as you think it should be."
- Wayne Dyer

There's a song that says, "Let there be peace on earth...and let it begin with me." This song reminds us in its lyrics that peace was meant to be. That with God as our father, we are all brothers and sisters and we should walk in harmony with each other. The song ends by reminding us to take each moment, and live each moment in peace eternally, let there be peace on earth and let it begin with me.

It is easy to forget that one person can be the catalyst for peace. That one person can be you. Sometimes because we don't have inner peace, we walk around with guilt, or we have insecurities, we are not able to tap into the peace that is ours to have. Instead, we stew about everything that is said or done to or around us. I find that letting go of un-beneficial thoughts is one way to find peace. I saw a quote recently that said, "Letting go is hard but holding on is harder." Which will you choose today?

Today's verse is a reminder that, as much as possible, whenever it is within your power, live at peace with everyone. I encourage you today to search for peace and work to maintain it every day of your life. Let there be peace on earth and let it begin with you. May peace be with you.

Dear God,
Thank you for the reminder that as far as it depends on me, live at peace with everyone. I pray that all your children remember that peace begins with each of them. That they can be the single catalyst to bring peace. I ask this in your son Jesus' name. Amen!

───────────●───────────

FEBRUARY 10

Do Not Be Afraid

ANCHOR SCRIPTURE: LUKE 2:10

"But the angel said to them, "Do not be afraid. I bring you good news that will cause great joy for all the people."

"Why settle for a lesser vision? When you are
destined for greatness!"
- Laila Gifty Akita

Jesus came to liberate us from all sin, the lies of the enemy and to save us all. It is sometimes perplexing that we know these truths but persist to believe the lies of the enemy, the lies we tell ourselves and pursue the flesh desires rather than that of the spirit. We are destined for greatness but pursue lesser because of fear.

Despite our disobedience, our refusal to praise, honor and give God thanks for all he does for us each day, he still willingly showers us with his Amazing Grace. His grace to help each of us achieve the greatness he intended. This is love. Like the song Amazing Grace by John Newton says, that saved us when we were lost, when we were blind, through many dangers, toils and snares his grace has brought us safe thus far, and grace will lead us home. Another portion of the song reminds us that the Lord has promised good to us, his word secures our hope, he will be our shield and portion be if life endures.

Today's verse is a reminder of the Angel's message when the glory of the Lord shone around the terrified shepherds; do not be afraid. I bring you good news that will cause great joy for all the people. Jesus' birth was great news and came to bring us great joy. Since we should have great joy, we are destined for greatness, why do we continue to let fear keep us in bondage, rule our hearts and our minds? I encourage you today to read Luke 2.

———————————— **PRAYER FOR THE DAY:** ————————————

Dear God,
Thank you for the reminder of the good news that Jesus' birth came to cause me great joy. That there is no need to fear. I pray that all your children have great joy, fear no longer and embrace the freedom that Jesus came to give us all. That they embrace God's Amazing Grace and the greatness to which they are destined. I ask this in your son Jesus' name. Amen!

Year-Round Joy

ANCHOR SCRIPTURE: PHILIPPIANS 1:27

*"Whatever happens, conduct yourselves in a manner worthy
of the gospel of Christ. Then, whether I come and see you
or only hear about you in my absence, I will know that you
stand firm in the one Spirit, striving together as one for
the faith of the gospel."*

"Year-round joy begins with gratitude for what you have."
- *Ilka V. Chavez*

Wouldn't it be amazing to keep the Christmas spirit alive year-round? That joy-filled feeling day after day. It may be hard for some to embrace this idea. How can I have enough money to shower my friends, family and the needy with gifts and blessings all year long? How can I remain joyful every single day? How can I be intentional to reach out to my Grandma or Mom throughout the year and not just at Christmas time?

Some may have given up hope with the first question. You may say this is impossible. There is no way a human being can maintain this hope, peace, joy and love we feel at Christmas year-round. Life happens, problems surface and pursue you, loved ones die, someone dear to you is diagnosed with cancer, you get the picture. You say, how is it possible to keep this joy of Christmas year-round?

What if I said it is possible and may not be so difficult? Here are a few ways: 1- Be grateful for all and annotate those things daily; 2-Do something for someone else. Sharing a smile or a hug counts; 3- Be intentional about gathering often with loved ones and spending quality time; 4-Increase your prayer and meditation time; 5-Make love the center of your life. Today's verse is a reminder that whatever happens, conduct yourselves in a manner worthy of the gospel of Christ. Then you stand firm in the one Spirit, striving together as one for the faith of the gospel. I encourage you today to strive to conduct yourself in the same manner you do for Christmas throughout the year.

────────────── PRAYER FOR THE DAY: ──────────────

Dear God,

Thank you for the reminder to conduct myself in a manner worthy of the gospel and to stand firm in one Spirit. I pray that all your children conduct themselves in a manner worthy of the gospel. That the hope, peace, love, and joy they experience during the holidays, remain in their hearts throughout the year. I ask this in your son Jesus' name. Amen!

The Sky is Not the Limit!

ANCHOR SCRIPTURE: PSALM 78:41-42

"Again, and again they put God to the test; they vexed the Holy One of Israel. They did not remember his power— the day he redeemed them from the oppressor..."

"The sky is not the limit. Your mind is."
- Marilyn Monroe

As a child, I always wondered if the sky was really the limit. As I continue to mature and strengthen my relationship with God, I realize that if I believe that the sky is as far as I could go, then I am putting limits on God. Being part of God's family, we are not allowed to limit what God can do. Trust Him and watch how there is no limit or boundaries with God. In fact, with God the sky is not the limit.

Job 11:8-9 says the sky is no limit for God, but it lies beyond your reach. God knows the world of the dead, but you do not know it. God's greatness is broader than the earth, wider than the sea. I said, here is the answer to the question I wondered about as a child...the sky is no limit for God. His greatness is broader than the earth. He is the Almighty.

Today's verse is a reminder that again and again they put God to the test; they vexed the Holy One of Israel. They did not remember his power— the day he redeemed them from the oppressor. I hope and pray that you don't limit God. He passed every test of achieving the impossible. Don't forget his power. I encourage you today to read Psalm 78 and Job 11.

Dear God,
Thank you for the reminder that the sky is no limit for you.
That you have passed every test when I tried to put limits on your
power. I pray that all your children do not vex you by putting
limits on what you can do. That they remember your mighty
power. I ask this in your son Jesus' name. Amen!

FEBRUARY 13

He Knows Your Order

ANCHOR SCRIPTURE: MATTHEW 6:8

"Do not be like them, for your Father knows
what you need before you ask him."

"Let God's promises shine on your problems."
- Corrie ten Boom

Do you have a favorite restaurant or coffee shop you visit often?
When you walk in these locations, they know your name and what
you will order. Sometimes they even see you coming down the block
and by the time you enter the door, your order is ready. Your request
is known, and it brings you joy to feel special.

I thought about prayer. We pray and ask God for things he already
knows about. He already knew what we would ask for because he
knows our every need. Your request can be simple. No need for fancy

prayers or like is described in Matthew 6:7, when you pray, do not keep on babbling like pagans, for they think they will be heard because of their many words. Pray and speak to God from your heart because he already knows your request, he already knows what you will order.

Matthew 6 also says when you pray, go into your room, close the door, and pray to your Father, who is unseen. Then your Father, who sees what is done in secret, will reward you. I remind you that your story was written before you were born. Today's verse is a reminder that God knows what you need before you ask him. Ask, then spend a bit more time listening for the answer. It may not be the answer you want to hear, but his answer is best. He already knows what you will order and knows what you need. He created the plan for your life.

──────────────── **PRAYER FOR THE DAY:** ────────────────

Dear God,
Thank you for the reminder that you already know everything that I will pray for. That I should ask and spend more time listening for your answer. That you already know what I need. I pray that all your children trust that you know what they will ask for and what they need before they ask. That they spend time listening for your answer and understand that you know best. I ask this in your son Jesus' name. Amen!

Purpose and Priorities

ANCHOR SCRIPTURE: EPHESIANS 1:11

"In him we have obtained an inheritance, having b een predestined according to the purpose of him who works all things according to the counsel of his will."

"Put First Things First"
- *Stephen Covey*

So many of us ask the question, what is my purpose? Pursuing and prioritizing your purpose is no simple task. It takes some decades to find their purpose, while others find it very early in life. There are so many competing factors that distract us from finding and walking in our purpose. The book, The Purpose-Driven Life by Pastor Rick Warren discusses that we are not here for our own our purpose. We are here to serve God's purpose and his needs. So, thinking of yourself when seeking your purpose may land you in a maze with no exit.

Every person possesses gifts, talents, and abilities. I wise woman I met briefly in a casual conversation said to me that many fail at this thing called life because they are out of alignment with their purpose and fail to set the right priorities. We waste our abilities, talents, and gifts by not keeping our priorities straight and remaining laser focused on finding our purpose and then walking in it. This made sense to me. Of course, I will lose my way if I am focusing on what is in it for me instead of what God wants me to do for him and his Kingdom.

We spend a lot of time seeking fulfillment through achievements, success, and a materialism mindset when God has already pre-planned our purpose. Ephesians 1:11 says, in him we have obtained an inheritance, having been predestined according to the purpose of him who works all things according to the counsel of his will. It seems that strengthening our relationship with God may be a good place to start searching for our purpose. Then remember your purpose is not about you, it is for a much larger purpose. Don't think small, start thinking big and think eternity.

PRAYER FOR THE DAY:

Dear God,
Thank you for the reminder that you predestined my purpose.
That my purpose is to serve you and your Kingdom. To decrease
me and increase you. I pray that all your children seek you as
they pursue their purpose and priorities. That they are remind-
ed that you are the author of their purpose. I ask this in your son
Jesus' name. Amen!

●

FEBRUARY 15

Don't Fret the Old or the New Year

ANCHOR SCRIPTURE: PSALM 90:14

"Satisfy us in the morning with your unfailing love,
that we may sing for joy and be glad all our days."

"Treat every day as a New Year"

As another year comes to an end, some may spend today reflecting on the bad things that happen this year, some may focus on the great things that happen this year, and some may just focus on celebrating the passing of another year. I wonder, why do we fret and fuss about the passing of another year? Shouldn't this just be another day to rejoice in God's grace? Should the focus be to reflect on living our days in a such a way that they count regardless of the passing of a year or not, regardless of whether we met our goals or not? Should the focus be on whether we meet God's goals for us rather than the ones we set for ourselves?

My girlfriend and sister shared this with me, "Start with God, Stay with God, and End with God." Is this where our focus should be daily. The passing of the time here on earth is irrelevant if we are not doing these three things, start with God, Stay with God, End with God. If we are not strengthening our relationship with God, if we are not thanking him for his daily grace does the change of the calendar year really matter? Amid the good, bad, and the ugly there is always God's grace.

Today's verse is a reminder that God satisfies us in the morning with his unfailing love, that we may sing for joy and be glad all our days. Therefore, I encourage you to not fret about the passing year or the one to come. God's unfailing love, his faithfulness and grace greet us each morning. Focus on living your days in such a way that they count for God's glory, for his kingdom, and for eternity.

--------- PRAYER FOR THE DAY: ---------

Dear God,
Thank you for the reminder that your unfailing love satisfies me each morning regardless of the change in days or calendar year. That I shall sing for joy and be glad all my days. I pray that all your children remember that your unfailing love satisfies them each morning. That they focus on living each day in an easy manner that counts for your glory, your kingdom and for eternity. I ask this in your son Jesus' name. Amen!

New Beginnings

ANCHOR SCRIPTURE: 2 CORINTHIANS 5:17

"Therefore, if anyone is in Christ, the new creation has come: The old has gone, the new is here!"

"Every page you have the courage to turn is a chance for a new beginning. Don't let fear keep you from turning the page"

Today is one day we all give ourselves permission to start a new chapter, to renew our minds, heart, and soul, to start fresh. What does a new beginning look like to you? Is it a time of hope, expectation and believing that all things are possible? Is it a time that you decide to throw out all your hurt, pain, sorrow, and anger and forgive no matter what? Is it a time you decide to move forward with joy, peace, in harmony and one step at a time? Is a new beginning a time you chose to believe without seeing?

Walking by faith is not easy. This is what each of us do when we resolve to make a change or several changes in the New Year. We have faith and believe that we will achieve the things we set out to do. Sometimes, we have no idea of the steps we will take to achieve our goals, but we believe we will reach them. I wonder what the anchors are some use to remain focus on reaching their goals and remain committed to self. Are they truly committed to self or just want to have what they see others have?

To me, when you focus on you, your plans, your goals, and the truth aka God's word, you have a better chance of success. You focus on God's plans for your life not someone else's, you let go and let God lead the change and transformation you seek. My experience is that he usually exceeds my expectations. Today's verse is a reminder that if anyone is in Christ, the new creation has come: The old has gone, the new is here! I encourage you to read 2 Corinthians 5. Let God lead your New Year resolutions, obey the steps he orders you to take at all cost and watch him exceed your expectations.

———————————— **PRAYER FOR THE DAY:** ————————————

Dear God,
Thank you for the reminder that you must be a critical part of the changes I seek. Without you, it means nothing. That in you, the new creation has come: The old has gone and the new is here. I pray that all your children include you, and better yet, let you lead the changes, the visions, and the goals they seek. That they realize that without you, it is nothing. I ask this in your son Jesus' name. Amen!

Beauty

ANCHOR SCRIPTURE: 1 PETER 3:3-4

"Your beauty should not come from outward adornment,
such as elaborate hairstyles and the wearing of gold jewelry
or fine clothes. Rather, it should be that of your inner self,
the unfading beauty of a gentle and quiet spirit, which is
of great worth in God's sight."

"Everything has beauty, but not everyone sees it."
- *Confucius*

Many of you may have heard this saying "Beauty is in the eye of the beholder." I thought about how God uses nature to whisper to us, to teach us and to feed us. He uses it to show us the many colors life has to offer, to teach us that life has seasons, and he uses it to grow the crop we eat.

What abundance God has provided through nature. What beauty! When you have a hard time seeing the beauty God has provided through you and around you remember all that he allows to unfold right in your midst. It costs you nothing to experience this beauty. What if I told you that the same beauty you see through nature, God sees in you?

Today's verse is a reminder that your beauty should not come from outward adornment, such as elaborate hairstyles and the wearing of gold jewelry or fine clothes. Rather, it should be that of your inner self, the unfading beauty of a gentle and quiet spirit, which is of great worth in God's sight. I encourage you to read 1 Peter 3.

Dear God,
Thank you for the reminder that my beauty should not come
from outward adornment. It should be of my inner self. Same
as my happiness which comes from my inner self. I pray that all
your children see that beauty comes from their inner self and not
from outward adornments. I ask this in your son Jesus' name.
Amen!

FEBRUARY 18

Courage

ANCHOR SCRIPTURE: 1 CORINTHIANS 16:13

"Be on your guard; stand firm in the faith;
be courageous; be strong."

"Courage is resistance to fear, mastery of fear, not absence of fear."
- Mark Twain

I recently watched an old movie entitled Courageous. It is about four police officers who struggle with their faith, roles as husbands and fathers after tragedy strikes close to home. Together they made a decision that changed their lives. It is not easy living up to so many expectations as parents, children and as a family. It takes courage to take a stand, lean on faith and do the right thing against all odds.

This made me think of courage. Courage is sometimes defined as bravery. It also has been defined as "fear that has said its prayers." I loved this when I saw it written by Pastor Greg Laurie some time ago. "Courage doesn't mean you don't get afraid; it means you don't let fear stop you." We all have fears and have exercised courage at one point in our lives.

Courage is required for so many aspects of our life. Courage is needed to do the right thing every single time; it is needed to change; it is needed to always tell the truth; it is needed to handle death and life; it is needed to live a life in integrity; it is needed to grow; it is needed to trust God during the good and the bad; it is needed to wait on God; and it is needed to obey God. It seems courage is necessary to make it through life. Today's verse is a reminder to be on your guard; stand firm in the faith; be courageous; be strong. I encourage you to read 1 Corinthians 16. Be courageous!

─────────────── **PRAYER FOR THE DAY:** ───────────────

Dear God,
Thank you for the reminder that to make it through life, I must be on my guard, stand firm in my faith, be courageous and strong. I pray that all your children be on guard, stand firm and strong in their faith and are courageous. That no matter how fear may try to get in the way, that they overcome their fears with courage. I ask this in your son Jesus' name. Amen!

FEBRUARY 19

Detachment

ANCHOR SCRIPTURE: LUKE 18:22

*"When Jesus heard this, he said to him, "You still lack one thing.
Sell everything you have and give to the poor, and you will
have treasure in heaven. Then come, follow me."*

"Your heart must become a sea of love. Your mind must
become a river of detachment."
- Sri Chinmoy

Detaching from "things" is a process. During the end and the start of
the year we focus on getting rid of the old and bringing in the new. We
focus on decluttering and removing the things that no longer serve
us. I say, it is a process to make room for more blessings. But there are
always those things to which we are attached whether for sentimental
or other reasons that we have held onto for decades.

Neal Donald Walsh wrote this, "You must be willing to lose it all before
you can have it all. It means that until you can let go of everything,
you will find it hard to hold onto anything. Detachment is the key.
If you are so attached to something that you are deeply unhappy
without it, then you are not simply attached, you are addicted." This
statement made me say hmm or as my Pastor says made me say "ouch."
But it made sense after reading several times. Nothing belongs to us,
it all belongs to God including our treasures, talents, and our time.

Detaching from so many things including our treasures, is still
difficult for most. One key to God's teaching in my eyes is detachment.
We should not attach ourselves to anything of this world as it is all
temporary and does not belong to us. Would you be willing to sell
everything you have, be left with nothing, let go of your treasures,

your ego to follow God? That is the challenge. We have all experienced loss. As we grow spiritually, we understand that nothing lasts forever. That change is constant. Would you rather anchor on something that is permanent or something that is temporary? Today's verse is a reminder of the answer God gave to a rich ruler when he asked "Good teacher, what must I do to inherit eternal life? I encourage you to read Luke 18.

PRAYER FOR THE DAY:

Dear God,
Thank you for the reminder that detachment not attachment is key. That anchoring on worldly attachments yields very little. That detaching from fear of losing all and focusing on your kingdom is the way to true joy, peace, and happiness. I pray that all your children grow to learn this important lesson of detachment and understand that eternity is all that matters. I ask this in your son Jesus' name. Amen!

Thanks for Your Gifts

ANCHOR SCRIPTURE: PHILIPPIANS 4:11-13

"I am not saying this because I am in need, for I have learned to be content whatever the circumstances."

"If what's ahead scares you and what's behind hurts you,
then just look above. God never fails to help you. Trust Him."
– Unknown

Do you know someone no matter what, they are always crying and complaining? They are never satisfied with their situation. They could win one million dollars and still find a reason to complain. I wonder if this has anything to do with learning to be content no matter your situation. I am not saying it is easy.

Philippians 4:12-13 says I know what it is to be in need, and I know what it is to have plenty. I have learned the secret of being content in any and every situation, whether well fed or hungry, whether living in plenty or in want. I can do all this through him who gives me strength. This last sentence is key.

If we all truly believe this, no matter our age, the barriers we face, our past or negative thoughts that surface, we would quickly overcome complaining and be content no matter what may be going on in our lives. Look at the situation as a gift, be content, and know that you can do all things through Christ who gives you strength. I encourage you to read Philippians 4:10-20.

Dear God,
Thank you for the reminder that I can do all things through you.
To look to you to supply the strength I need to be content and
persevere through all situations. I pray that all your children
remember that through you, who give them strength, they can
do all things. I ask this in your son Jesus' name. Amen!

●

FEBRUARY 21

Infinity

ANCHOR SCRIPTURE: EPHESIANS 3:20

"Now all glory to God, who is able, through his mighty power
at work within us, to accomplish infinitely more
than we might ask or think."

"Your greatest awakening comes, when you are aware
about your infinite nature"
- Amit Ray

Merriam Webster defines infinity as unlimited extent of time, space, or quantity. Have you ever thought about infinity, without limits, not even been limited by the sky? Some of you may recall the Pixar animated film Toy Story where one of the featured characters Buzz Lightyear used the catchphrase "to infinity and beyond. I decided to look up the meaning of this catchphrase.

Scientist, philosophers, and bloggers try to put their own spin on the meaning of this catchphrase. I, however, found this discussion in a blog written by Vincenzo Dimonte in 2014 that caught my attention. It references Buzz Lightyear and it talked about being trapped in our human limits, without escape but in the end, it is just an illusion. Although this is an animated film, Buzz is helping us recognize the illusion, challenging us to change our perspective, break free and go! Leaving all our chains behind and going where it was previously unthinkable and unimaginable.

I have a dear friend that wrote a book entitled Unveiling the Illusion and this is generally the same thing she challenges us to do through her book, recognize the illusion, break the chains, and unveil. All through God's truth. Stop limiting what God can do in your life. Yes, he can take you from homeless to being a billionaire, he can take you from death diagnosis to abundant life, he can fix your broken-ness in a flash, and he can change your unbelief to belief. I am sure many or all of you could serve as a witness to this truth. I know I can. Today's verse is a reminder that our God who is able, through his mighty power at work within us, to accomplish infinitely more than we might ask or think. Glory be to God!

——————————— **PRAYER FOR THE DAY:** ———————————

Dear God,
Thank you for the reminder that I should never put limits on what you can do in my life. That you can do exceedingly and abundantly much more through your mighty power at work within me, to accomplish infinitely more than I might ask, think, or imagine. I pray that all your children free themselves from human limits and are reminded that through your mighty power at work within them, you can accomplish infinitely more than they might ask, think or imagine. I ask this in your son Jesus' name. Amen!

Sin Makes Us Stupid

ANCHOR SCRIPTURE: HEBREWS 12:1

"Let us lay aside every weight, and the sin which so easily ensnares us."

The price of sin is very high, though now it may seem low;
and if we let it go unchecked, its crippling power will grow."
— *Fitzhugh*

As I continue to release what no longer serves me, I scanned through a few documents and I found a copy of the Daily Bread dated September 28, 2006. I recalled, saving this to be reminded that "Sin makes us stupid." No matter how wise, or smart you may be, you can be tempted and remain vulnerable to the foolishness of the mind. I was grateful for this reminder and thought to share with you. Don't let sin break you from your power source. Thank you, Daily Bread, for the reminder to remain connected. Hope it encourages you as it did me.

Daily Bread - Sin makes us stupid by Bill Crowder
"I was having lunch with a pastor-friend when the discussion sadly turned to a mutual friend in ministry who had failed morally. As we grieved together over this fallen comrade, now out of ministry, I wondered aloud, "I know anyone can be tempted and anyone can stumble, but he's a smart guy. How could he think he could get away with it?" Without blinking, my friend responded, "Sin makes us stupid." It was an abrupt statement intended to get my attention, and it worked.

I have often thought of that statement in the ensuing years, and I continue to affirm the wisdom of those words. How else can you explain the actions of King David, the man after God's own heart turned adulterer and murderer? Or the reckless choices of Samson? Or the public denials of Christ by Peter, the most public of Jesus' disciples? We are flawed people who are vulnerable to temptation and to the foolishness of mind that can rationalize and justify almost any course of action if we try hard enough.

If we are to have a measure of victory over the power of sin, it will come only as we lean on the strength and wisdom of Christ (Rom. 7:24-25). As His grace strengthens our hearts and minds, we can overcome our own worst inclination to make foolish choices. God's Spirit is your power source, don't let sin break the connection."

Today's verse is a reminder to lay aside every weight, and the sin which so easily ensnares us. I encourage you today to never lose connection to your power source. "Fully Rely On God" (FROG)!

———————————— **PRAYER FOR THE DAY:** ————————————

Dear God,
Thank you for the reminder that sin makes us stupid. That you are our power source, not sin. I pray that all your children lean on your strength and grace to strengthen their hearts and minds and turn from making foolish choices. I ask this in your son Jesus' name. Amen!

Eliminating Distractions

ANCHOR SCRIPTURE: LUKE 8:7

*"Other seed fell in the weeds; the weeds grew with it
and strangled it."*

"Starve your distractions, feed your focus."
— Unknown

It seems that the theme of the month for many of us is eliminating distractions. Eliminating distractions requires discipline. There are so many things that show up in life as distractions such as social media, watching television, "handy-dandy cell phones", unexpected events, "the problem of the day", clutter in your physical space, clutter in your mental space (your thoughts) just to mention a few.

Sometimes the things that show up as distractions include making a living (yes, work can be at times a distraction if it consumes all the hours you are awake), living "your life" (partying and pursuing flesh desires instead of spiritual desires can keep you from your destiny), or being concerned about someone else's life (yes minding someone else's business and not your own can be a distraction.)

We are all guilty of falling prey to distractions. Distraction is the very thing that keeps us from finishing the race God set out for us. It keeps us from moving forward, it keeps us from hearing what God has to say to us, it keeps us from walking and living on purpose. Shutting down distractions is important to live a full life, a life that is purposeful and meets God's goals for your life. Today's verse serves as a reminder that distractions are like seeds that fall in the weeds. Don't let distractions strangle or stifle your purpose. Extinguish it!

Dear God,
Thank you for the reminder that eliminating distractions is key to hearing from you and meeting the goals you set for my life. I pray that all your children focus on eliminating distractions that may be keeping them off the path you set out for them. That they eliminate distractions to hear from you. I ask this in your son Jesus' name. Amen!

FEBRUARY 24

Obey

ANCHOR SCRIPTURE: JOHN 14:15

"If you love me, you will obey what I command."

"When obedience ceases to be an irritant and becomes our quest, in that moment God will endow us with power."
- Ezra Taft Benson

The word obey seems to at one point turned from a good thing to a bad thing. Some feel if they obey, they are giving in to something against their will. Some feel obeying is a sign of weakness. Think about the peer pressure children undergo daily. They are teased because they are obedient to their teacher, parent, or someone of authority. They were taught to be obedient.

Sometimes we ourselves create the confusion about why we should obey and who we should obey. Listen to this advice but don't listen to someone else. I wonder if we just trained our ears to listen to God, seek him, trust what he tells us to do and just do what he asks. If we listen for his soft voice and yield to his request, how much different our lives would be.

I am the first to admit that obedience is not easy, and it is complicated by all the noise in our life. It makes it hard to hear from God. However, when you see the rewards of your obedience time and time again, obedience becomes easier. (See also Exodus 3:11... Moses' experience.) God loves us and he would never ask us to do something that would not benefit us at the end or that will not benefit the Kingdom. Think about it, he said he works all things out for those who love him. Today's verse is a reminder that if you love the Lord, you will obey what he commands. No matter how impossible it may seem or whether it made sense or not. If you love him, you obey, you trust, and you act on his command.

--------- PRAYER FOR THE DAY: ---------

Dear God,
Thank you for the reminder that if I love you, I will obey your command. I love you, so I obey your every command. No matter what the flesh may think. I pray that all your children remember that to love you is to obey what you command. That to love you is to trust you and to act on what you ask. I ask this in your son Jesus' name.

Equality

ANCHOR SCRIPTURE: ROMANS 2:11

"For God does not show favoritism"

"We hold these truths to be self-evident:
that all men are created equal."
- *Martin Luther King Jr.*

Today, I reflect on a statement made in the "I Have a Dream speech delivered by American civil rights activist Martin Luther King Jr. during the March on Washington for Jobs and Freedom on August 28, 1963, in which he calls for an end to racism in the United States and called for civil and economic rights." The statement is "We hold these truths to be self-evident: that all men are created equal."

I reflect on this statement and the word equality. What does it mean to be equal or have equality? Equality is sometimes defined as the state of being equal, especially in status, rights, and opportunities. If all men are created equal and if we are created in God's image and likeness, why is this world so hard pressed to embrace humanity? Seeing each other in God's likeness no matter who you are, where you came from, what you look like, we are all God's children. One family.

Deuteronomy 10:17 says For the LORD your God is God of gods and Lord of lords, the great God, mighty and awesome, who shows no partiality and accepts no bribes. Can you imagine treating everyone equally, no partiality, simply as humans and sharing unconditional love no matter what? Jesus did that for us. Why can't we do that with others? Today's verse is a reminder that God does not show favoritism. We are all equal in his eyes and treated with equality.

Dear God,
Thank you for the reminder that you do not show favoritism.
That you treat all your children the same way and pour the same
love into each of us. I pray that all your children are reminded
that you do not play favorites. That if they show favoritism and
not equality, they have sinned and are convicted by the law as
lawbreakers. That they remember your commandment to Love
your neighbor as yourself." I ask this in your son Jesus' name.
Amen!

FEBRUARY 26

Think Like a Winner

ANCHOR SCRIPTURE: 2 CORINTHIANS 4:8-9

"We are hard pressed on every side, but not crushed;
perplexed, but not in despair; persecuted, but not abandoned;
struck down, but not destroyed."

"If losing is mostly all you know, then it's obvious
you haven't been thinking, acting, working, persisting,
persevering, and walking like winners do."
- Edmond Mbiaka

A few years ago, I attended a class entitled "Think like a Winner"
taught by my friend Rabbi Baars. Although the concepts taught in this
class seemed obvious, without the reminders and the tools he taught

in the class it is easy to forget how to think like a winner. Reflecting on the value I gained from this class reminded me that more believers need to always "think like winners."

No matter what battle or challenge shows up in your life, believe that you have already won the battle. That God is fighting alongside, for and with you. That no matter what, he wins and as a member of God's family, if he wins, you win. As you go through difficulties in life how wonderful would it be to simply ride the waves, keep your head above water because you know who wins at the end. You train your mind to "Think like a winner." Things are never what it seems.

Today's verse is a reminder that you are set-up to win. To never seize to "Think like a winner." Refresh your thoughts with God's words and promises daily. If we believe God's promises and refuse to quit, we cannot lose. That we may be hard pressed on every side, but not crushed; perplexed, but not in despair; persecuted, but not abandoned; struck down, but not destroyed. Get back-up because you are part of God's family... A family that thinks and are winners!

--------- PRAYER FOR THE DAY: ---------

Dear God,
Thank you for the reminder that as a member of your family, I must think like a winner. That claiming defeat is surrendering to the enemy. I pray that all your children think like winners. That they remember they are part of your family and have already won through their relationship with you. That they remember they may be hard pressed on every side, but not crushed; perplexed, but not in despair; persecuted, but not abandoned; struck down, but not destroyed. I ask this in your son Jesus' name. Amen!

Have Your Cake and Eat It Too

ANCHOR SCRIPTURE: MATTHEW 6:24

"No one can serve two masters. Either you will hate the one and love the other, or you will be devoted to the one and despise the other. You cannot serve both God and money."

"You can't have it both ways. You can't have both free will and a benevolent higher power who protects you from yourself."
— *Arthur C. Clarke*

It would be nice to have all the things I want in this world. Many people including children often daydream about having everything they desire. However, I wonder how many take it one step further to ask what will it cost me to have it all? What will I have to give up? Of course, no one wants to give up anything, they want it all. They want to consume their cake and still expect it to be there a few days later. Think about it, is this possible?

This brought me to think about so many of us desiring all the riches of this world and the riches of God's Kingdom. Can we have it both ways? Can you really have the things that break God's laws, that brings you temporary pleasure and yet seek those things for God's Kingdom? Can you stray from your values for a temporary satisfaction and yet still honor your values? The reality is that many of us try to do this all the time. We want to serve God and man at the same time. We want worldly things that drives us to disobey God's laws, sell our souls, and yet still want salvation and a seat in God's Kingdom.

We are all human and will be tempted and fall into temptation. However, when reminded which will you choose? You can't have it both ways. Today's verse is a reminder that no one can serve two masters.

Either you will hate the one and love the other, or you will be devoted to the one and despise the other. You cannot serve both God and money. You cannot have your cake and eat it too.

—————————— PRAYER FOR THE DAY: ——————————

Dear God,
Thank you for the reminder that I cannot serve two masters.
That I must choose. I pray that all your children are reminded
that they cannot serve two masters. Either they will hate the one
and love the other, or they will be devoted to the one and despise
the other. That they cannot serve both God and money. I ask this
in your son Jesus' name. Amen!

FEBRUARY 28

One Day at a Time

ANCHOR SCRIPTURE: PSALM 68:19

"Praise be to the Lord, to God our Savior,
who daily bears our burdens."

Realize that the now is all we have. The past is just a story
and the future is a complete mystery. This is it. Now.
- Eckhart Tolle

Have you ever thought how difficult it is to adhere to the advice given by the wise and in many parts of the Bible to "Take one day at a time"? You probably ask, how am I supposed to do this when I know that there are things like bills, an exam, an unpleasant appointment, or something major pending for tomorrow? When I know what today looks like and my lack of hope propels me to think that there is no way tomorrow can be better than today? When you look ahead, and you are not able to see light.

Remaining in the present, controlling your thoughts to solely remain in the present is certainly a challenge. A wise person once told me this "Realize that the now is all we have. The past is just a story and the future is a complete mystery. This is it. Now." Predicting, assuming, replaying, or guessing does us no good. It is better to focus on what you have, the things you can see now what is in front of you.

Training your thoughts and actions to remain in the present and to take one day at a time, requires, gratitude to experience the present day, trust to know that God is in control, self-control not to take your thoughts to the past or to the future, and faith to know that all you need for today is already provided. Today's verse is a reminder that Praise be to the Lord, to God our Savior, who daily bears our burdens. He has us in the palm of his hands, he provides everything we need for today, and he gives us the strength to take life one day at a time, one step at a time.

──────────────── **PRAYER FOR THE DAY:** ────────────────

Dear God,
Thank you for the reminder to take life one day at a time. That replaying the past or trying to forecast the future does no good. I pray that all your children know that you replenish them daily with what they need. You bear their burdens daily. That they learn to trust you one day at a time. I ask this in your son Jesus' name. Amen!

March

MARCH 1

Vitality

ANCHOR SCRIPTURE: ISAIAH 40:31

"But those who hope in the Lord will renew their strength. They will soar on wings like eagles, they will run and not grow weary, they will walk and not be faint."

"Vitality shows in not only the ability to persist but the ability to start over."
- *F. Scott Fitzgerald*

Merriam Webster defines vitality as the power of enduring; the peculiarity distinguishing the living from the nonliving; capacity to live and develop; physical or mental vigor especially when highly developed. I recently read an article by Yohan Perera on how to wait on the Lord. It was fascinating to read about the Eagle's journey and the purpose for using an Eagle to explain the act of waiting.

The article explained that Legend says that an Eagle at the age of 30-50, flies to a high place and there it endures a harsh trial of endurance and change. It can't fly because its feathers are overgrown. Therefore, it plucks all the feathers from its body. It plucks its talons from its feet because the talons have grown curled and useless. Its beak has grown too long and curled. It breaks its beak against a rock. Defenseless, it cries out and waits for the time of renewal. Other Eagles hear its cry and come to aid. They fly overhead, scaring off predators, and they bring food to their incapacitated friend.

Today's verse is a reminder that at the end of the test, the Lord will renew your strength, you will soar on wings like eagles, you will run and not grow weary, and you will walk and not be faint. The renewing of our strength requires that we wait upon the Lord even during great trials. Our faith and trust must be tested to gain strength like the eagle.

PRAYER FOR THE DAY:

Dear God,
Thank you for the reminder to wait on you! That you will renew my strength and I will soar on wings like eagles. I pray that all your children learn to wait on you! That they trust that you will renew their strength and they will soar on wings like eagles. That they will be rewarded with increased vitality. I ask this in your son Jesus' name. Amen!

Provision

ANCHOR SCRIPTURE: PHILIPPIANS 4:19

"And my God will supply every need of yours according to his riches in glory in Christ Jesus."

"...You say to God, "I have never seen you provide for me."
God says to you, "You have never trusted Me."
- Corallie Buchanan

As I reflect on life, I sometimes wonder, "How did I make it from point A to point B?" Sometimes it looks like you have exhausted all your options to make ends meet, sometimes you feel that you have done all in your power to fix a health or personal situation, sometimes your tank is on empty and you have no idea how to fill it. Then suddenly, a blessing shows up to allow you to make it from point B to point C. This may be in the form of lost treasure found in unlikely places, you begin to feel better after a long illness, or you are blessed by a stranger. You then realize, you have just what you need, not more, not less.

Believing and having unshakable faith is critical to make it in this world. When the going gets tough, sometimes all you have left is your belief that God will provide for you, to never lose hope, to never doubt God's promises, to not worry and smile through the "going gets tough." Anchor on the fact that you know that God has got you. He will provide everything you need. He is your provider. Look back at your life, do you have a story to share when the going got tough and God provided just what you need through someone else or by finding a loss treasure?

Today's verse is a reminder that no matter your current situation, do not worry, God will supply every need you have according to his riches in glory in Christ Jesus. He is your provider, not man. Put your faith in God not man and watch him provide just what you need.

Dear God,
Thank you for the reminder that you are my provider. That you will supply every need of mine according to your riches in glory in Christ Jesus. I pray that all your children remember that you are the provider, not man. That you will supply every need they have according to your riches. I ask this in Jesus' name. Amen!

●

MARCH 3

Fear and Trust

ANCHOR SCRIPTURE: PSALM 56:3

"When I am afraid, I put my trust in you."

"Fear arises when we imagine that everything depends on us."
~ Elisabeth Elliot

Can we fear and trust at the same time? I always wondered how the two match-up. Does this have anything to do with control or lack thereof? Imagine sky diving. I do not know many people who would want to try this. I ask a friend if she would skydive and she said no, I love my life too much. I thought is the "fear thing" connected with lack of control? You have no idea what will happen, but your mind says "be afraid" if you lack control.

I thought if we trust the Lord, why do we fear? Is fear a natural reaction and trust not an automatic reaction? Is it just a fact that as human beings we want to be in control of everything? I read an article by Rachel Cohen and she described fear as "Fear is what happens when our desire to be in control is confronted with our complete inability to control anything." When fear shows up, you realize that you are powerless. Your first instinct on the sight of fear may be to go into panic mode, try to fix the situation or run from the thing that causes you fear.

If we know and trust God, we know he is our almighty Father. 2 Timothy 1:7 says for God has not given us a spirit of fear, but of power and of love and of a sound mind. So why do we still fear and not trust God? Why don't we run to God when we mess up, find that fear has taken over our being, instead of running away from God. He loves us. Today's verse is a reminder that when I am afraid, I put my trust in God. Maybe the answer to overcoming fear is to put your trust in God? He is the fixer of all things not you.

——————————— PRAYER FOR THE DAY: ———————————

Dear God,
Thank you for the reminder that when I am afraid, I must put my trust in you. That you know best. I pray that all your children run to you when they are afraid. That they wholeheartedly put their trust in you. I ask this in your son Jesus' name. Amen!

The Role Is Not the Reward

ANCHOR SCRIPTURE: JOHN 3:30

"He must become greater; I must become less."

"God cannot approve of a system of servitude, in which
the master is guilty of assuming absolute power - of assuming
God's place and relation towards his fellow-men."
- Gerrit Smith

Do you remember the time you received your first promotion, I bet it
was a time of extreme pride? If you are an actress or actor imagine the
first leading role you were assigned, you probably felt on top of the
world. When we are assigned key roles, we sometimes forget that "the
role is not our reward."

I was reading an article by John Bloom on Desiring God. "He stated
in this article that we must remember that our role is not our reward.
Jesus is our reward. Roles will begin and they will end. And the only
way for us to end well is if in our heart Jesus has increased and we
have decreased." Can you imagine this, being named the President
of a multi-million dollar company or you are called to lead a nation,
would you be able to trust God and give him his rightful place, to
decrease you and increase him? To know that despite holding this
powerful position, there is no reward in the role, the reward is in Jesus.

I believe when we truly adopt an attitude of humility and servitude,
we learn to completely rely on God and know that we are his humble
servants. No matter our title, position, or role, we understand we
are here to serve God and his kingdom. Once we understand this, it
may be easier to accept that God must become greater and we must
become less. Nothing is about us; it is all about him. The struggle to
remove self is real. I encourage you to read John 3:25–36.

Dear God,
Thank you for the reminder that in all things you must become
greater; I must become less. That nothing is about me, it is all
about you, your kingdom and eternity. I pray that all your chil-
dren remember that no matter their position, title, or role it is
all temporary. That they must remain focused that it is all about
you, your kingdom, and eternity, and not about them. That you
become greater; and they must become less. I ask this in your son
Jesus' name. Amen!

MARCH 5

Live Bold

ANCHOR SCRIPTURE: LUKE 12:32

"Do not be afraid, little flock, for your Father has
been pleased to give you the kingdom."

Virtue is bold, and goodness never fearful.
William Shakespeare

The word boldly sometimes refers to not hesitating or fearful in the
face of actual or possible danger or be courageous and daring. Someone asks me what does living bold means to me. It means knowing
who you are, whose you are and living and walking in this truth. It is
walking your talk, speaking truth, knowing your purpose, and using it
for the greater good and for God's kingdom. It is living freely, fearless
and filled with joy. What is living bold to you?

After providing this response, I reflected on why for so long I lived in fear and questioned my courage. Why dims my light? I realized that knowing whose you are was key. Jesus served as a great example of living boldly. He was so bold and loved us so much he gave his life for us. If we know the truth (who we are, and whose we are), if we learn his word and speak his truth honestly and authentically, and we know the authority he has given us, why not live bold? Acts 4:29 says and now, Lord, look upon their threats and grant to your servants to continue to speak your word with all boldness.

Today's verse is a reminder to not be afraid, your Father has been pleased to give you the kingdom. Does this mean not to fear, trust God, he will provide for you, his intent all along was to give you the Kingdom? If this is true, why not live bold. I encourage you to live bold and in truth. I encourage you to read Luke 12.

──────────────── PRAYER FOR THE DAY: ────────────────

Dear God,
Thank you for the reminder that there is no need to fear that you are pleased to give me the kingdom. That knowing and speaking your truth gives me the courage to live bold. I pray that all your children find courage and do not fear. That they speak your word with all boldness. That they remember you are pleased to give them the kingdom. They must live bold. I ask this in your son Jesus' name Amen!

Sticking to Your New Years' Resolution?

ANCHOR SCRIPTURE: LUKE 18:22 (NIV)

When Jesus heard this, he said to him, "You still lack one thing. Sell everything you have and give to the poor, and you will have treasure in heaven. Then come, follow me."

"Your heart must become a sea of love.
Your mind must become a river of detachment."
- *Sri Chinmoy*

Keeping your New Years' resolutions beyond the first month of the year is not easy. When you are called to lead others, it is especially difficult because all the demands of the group under your supervision or influence consume the 1440 minutes of your day. In attempting to forge forward with any goals, let alone my resolutions for the New Year, I have discovered the importance of the following factors: self-confidence, consistency, prioritization, discipline, and desiring change over stagnancy.

As you continue to pursue your 2018 resolutions past the first month of the year ask yourself these five questions:

1— *How badly do I want to experience this change?*

2— *Am I prepared to hold myself to a higher standard of accountability?*

3— *Am I prepared to lead myself before leading others (this includes your family, your tribe, and your projects)?*

4— *Am I equipped with the tools to succeed?*

5— *Am I using the same strategies to get different results?*

Once you answer these questions, I encourage you to do the following:

- Keep first things first.

- Take it one day at a time.

- Find an accountability partner

- Try new strategies to meet your new goals. (You know what Einstein said about doing the same thing and expecting different results.)

- Remain in the present.

- Do your best.

- Get the help you need to succeed.

- Never give up on you. Don't ever let yourself off the hook! You will inspire your tribe, and don't be surprised if you even inspire yourself.

- Remain focused.

- Do your best! (Yes, this second reminder is intentional) Here is to overwhelming success in achieving your resolutions and goals. You can do it! Remember it is mind over matter.

PRAYER FOR THE DAY:

Dear God,
Thank you for the reminder that detachment not attachment is key. That anchoring on worldly attachments yields very little. That detaching from fear of losing all and focusing on your kingdom is the way to true joy, peace, and happiness. I pray that all your children grow to learn this important lesson of detachment and understand that eternity is all that matters. I ask this in your son Jesus' name. Amen!

Anchor Your Soul

ANCHOR SCRIPTURE: HEBREWS 6:19

"This hope we have as an anchor of the soul, a hope both sure and steadfast and one which enters within the veil..."

"We should not moor a ship with one anchor,
or our life with one hope."
- *Epictetus*

I have worked for over three decades. I recall two different occasions when two different supervisors (one male and one female) mentioned to me that I am a hopeful person. I say why do you say that? They both said that I use the word "hope" often. They highlighted that my use of this word hopes also helped them believe that the assignment they gave to me would be accomplished. Weird, right? I never gave much thought to this conversation until recently.

The word hope is defined in the Merriam Webster dictionary as to desire with expectation of obtainment or fulfillment. It seems in my subconscious; I always hope and believe in others. It seems that this hope anchored my soul. That no matter if a storm came and shifted my anchor, I faced a difficult situation or assignment, my soul (heart, mind, and body) would eventually anchor on hope. Hope keeps you steady. I now realize that hope is part of my faith, my belief system.

Hope to me is a gift from God. It is the assurance that God will do what he said he will do. No matter how long it takes. Hebrews 6:11 says, "And we desire that each one of you show the same diligence to the full assurance of hope until the end." I ask, what do you hope for? Are you anchored on hope? Today's verse reminds us that hope is the anchor to our soul, it is sure and steadfast, and it enters within the veil. I encourage you to read Hebrews 6 today. Hope it anchors your soul.

Dear God,
Thank you for the reminder that Hope steadies our soul. I pray
that all your children remember that hope is the anchor to their
soul. It is sure, steadfast and enters within the veil. I ask this in
your son Jesus' name. Amen!

MARCH 8

Emotional Maturity

ANCHOR SCRIPTURE: 1 JOHN 4:7

"Dear friends, let us love one another, for love comes from God.
Everyone who loves has been born of God and knows God."

"Fear is the glue that keeps you stuck.
Faith is the solvent that sets you free."
- Shannon L. Alder

The word love is a word that makes life so complicated. Some believe that love only relates to romance and sexual attraction. Others believe you can only love someone if they are in your tribe, is someone to whom you are affectionate, or it is someone you like or know. If none of these apply, then there is no reason to love that person.

Love defined is not solely related to affection, sentiment, or romance, it is part of our fabric, how we came to exist and key to who we are. Love flows from God. We are created in God's image and God is love. As our relationship with our Father grows and strengthens, so does our love for every being on this earth. No matter their make, model, or sin, we learn to love all that belongs to God.

Today's verse is a reminder to let us love one another, for love comes from God. Everyone who loves has been born of God and knows God. To me, as you mature spiritually, you mature emotionally. They go hand in hand. I encourage you today to love one another no matter what someone says, does or the past that transpired. Exercise your spiritual and emotional maturity today and every day. Find it in your heart to love like Jesus.

────────────── PRAYER FOR THE DAY: ──────────────

Dear God,
Thank you for the reminder that I am created in your likeness.
That we must love one another as love comes from you. Everyone
who loves knows you. I pray that all your children will continue
to strengthen their relationship with you, to live and love in your
likeness. I ask this in your son Jesus' name. Amen!

Heart Trouble

ANCHOR SCRIPTURE: JOHN 14:1

"Do not let your hearts be troubled.
You believe in God; believe also in me."

"The heart of the human problem is the problem
of the human heart."
- *Adrian Rogers*

Are you caring for your heart? It is no secret that heart disease and complications are leading cause of death. There are many ways to care for your heart, you can exercise, eat healthy, have a physical, and minimize stress just to mention a few. It is important to keep a healthy and pure heart. I wondered... are we trusting our heart and mind more than God?

I recently read a devotion by Joyce Meyer where she said "taking time to keep your heart pure is like cleaning out your basement or attic. Once you turn on the lights and start looking around in there, don't be surprised to find some things you didn't expect." Keeping your heart in good condition, guarding it, and asking God for help when it is not well is important.

We all have our hearts broken at some point in our journey. If we don't take the time to deal with the hurt, with the ailment and brokenness of our heart, we develop a heart condition. Some never deal with the many hurts and eventually their heart become troubled beyond repair. I encourage you to seek help from God if you have never taken time to work on your troubled heart. Don't turn your heart into your basement or attic. Constantly work on keeping your heart right. Connect with God often. He will help you. Today's verse is a reminder, do not let your hearts be troubled.

Dear God,
Thank you for the reminder not to let my heart be troubled. To
believe and trust you instead. I pray that all your children do not
let their hearts be troubled. That they keep their heart in good
condition, they guard it and ask you for help when their heart is
not well. I ask this in your son Jesus' name. Amen!

———————————————●———————————————

MARCH 10

Obey, Serve, and Love

ANCHOR SCRIPTURE: DEUTERONOMY 11:13-15

"So if you faithfully obey the commands I am giving you today—to
love the LORD your God and to serve him with all your heart and
with all your soul, then I will send rain on your land in its season,
both autumn and spring rains, so that you may gather in your
grain, new wine and olive oil. I will provide grass in the fields for
your cattle, and you will eat and be satisfied."

"The purpose of human life is to serve, to show compassion
and the will to help others."
- *Albert Schweitzer*

Many people today live in what we refer to as the "sandwich generation." They are raising their children and taking care of their parents
all at the same time. For many, this is no easy feat especially when
you add all other responsibilities like work, home, and other general
family responsibilities. However, we are called to serve and take care
of those who no longer can either be alone or take care of themselves.
We must love and serve.

Today's verse is a reminder of a very important command to love the Lord your God and to serve him with all your heart and with all your soul. When we love God, we love all people, we obey his commands and we joyfully serve the lord and his children. Being a part of a sandwich generation may not be easy, but when you see the blessing of serving the Lord and his people, the burden is light. You serve with ease, with joy and filled with love.

I encourage you today to live by this important command. Obey, Love and Serve the lord with all your heart and soul. As Matthew 11:30 reminds us- "For my yoke is easy and my burden light."

PRAYER FOR THE DAY:

Dear God,
Thank you for the reminder that the key to walking on your straight path is to obey, serve and love with all my heart and soul. I pray that all your children put you first in their lives. That they obey, love, and serve you and your family with all their heart and soul. I ask this in your son Jesus' name. Amen!

First Things First

ANCHOR SCRIPTURE: PSALM 119:2-3

"Blessed are those who keep his statutes and seek him with all their heart—they do no wrong but follow his ways."

"Most of us spend too much time on what is urgent and not enough time on what is important."
- Stephen R. Covey

With the influx of social media, we are all inundated with requests to follow and like many people, pages, and things. It is so overwhelming at times even deciding if you want to or should follow this person, product, or place. We are often distracted by all the "noise" and forget what should go first. Trying to prioritize who or what will be most beneficial for you can be daunting. I wonder, are we prioritizing urgency or importance? Which should be first?

Sometimes the things we seek and pray for are delayed because we are prioritizing and following the wrong direction or guidance? With so many things, people and responsibilities clamoring for our attention prioritizing is not easy. Today's verse seems to provide the formula for receiving blessings. This seems simple enough, keep God's statutes, seek him with all your heart, do no wrong and follow his ways. Keep God first.

To me this means connect with God first daily, being obedient to his word and submitting and surrendering to his will for me. Does this sound easy? NO! Because we all know some of the things we are asked to do seem impossible. However, today's verse assures us that we are blessed when we keep God's statutes, seek him with all our hearts, do no wrong and follow his ways. Keep first things first. I encourage you today to reflect on psalm 119:2-3. What does this mean to you?

Dear God,
Thank you for the reminder that seeking you, following you, and doing no wrong is the key to blessings. To keep you first and as the priority in my life. I pray that all your children remember that your laws and decrees provide them with the perfect path to you, eternal joy, and many blessings. I ask this in Jesus name. Amen!

MARCH 12

Pollution of Anger

ANCHOR SCRIPTURE: COLOSSIANS 3:8

"But now you must also rid yourselves of all such things as these: anger, rage, malice, slander, and filthy language from your lips."

"If you're going to pursue revenge, you'd better dig two graves"
- Chinese proverb

The word anger is sometimes defined as a strong feeling of displeasure and usually of opposition toward someone or something. Do you know anyone who has never experienced anger? Even the nicest people have been pushed to a place of anger at least once in their lifetime. There are so many reasons why we get angry including loss of power, disappointment, our ego, not getting our way, and sometimes just because we lost control of something. Resisting the feeling and emotion of anger is not easy. However, one fruit of the spirit is self-control. If we can activate self-control, could we avoid the continued pollution that anger causes?

Have you thought about how anger pollutes us and the world in which we live? Exercising more self-control would lead us to choose to respond to offensive words and actions with kindness. Many of us rather be right than kind. Today's verse is a reminder that we must also rid ourselves of all such things as these: anger, rage, malice, slander, and filthy language from our lips. Which will you choose, kindness or anger? I encourage you to read Colossians 3.

──────────── **PRAYER FOR THE DAY:** ────────────

Dear God,
Thank you for the reminder that I must rid myself of all such things as anger, rage, malice, slander, and filthy language from my lips. I pray that all your children remember that anger is a pollutant. That they must rid themselves of anger, rage, malice, slander, and filthy language. I ask this in your son Jesus' name. Amen!

Idols in the Heart

ANCHOR SCRIPTURE: EZEKIEL 14:3

*"Son of man, these leaders have set up idols in their hearts.
They have embraced things that will make them fall into sin.
Why should I listen to their requests?"*

"Idolatry is really not good for anyone. Not even the idols."
- John Bach

As a former workaholic, I never thought about how working around the clock a form of idolatry could be. I truly thought it was the right thing to do and to show my loyalty to my organization. I even recalled putting work in front of my prayer time and my family. I made the choice to have work consume most of the hours in my day that there was only time for the required hour of Sunday church service and the five to ten minutes daily for devotion.

For me one of the idols in my heart was work. There are so many idols that we allow or crave in our hearts; money, power, materialism, pleasure, sex to name a few. Some of these idols are birth and defined by worldly desires. We allow these idols to take over our hearts and become more important than our relationship with God. If we continue to embrace things that are not of God, if we continue to invite "idols" in our hearts, how can we develop a strong relationship with God?

Today's verse is a reminder of Ezekiel's revelation when "leaders came insincerely seeking God's counsel, their facade was revealed, and they were indicted for determining to pursue their evil way and defy God's will. They had set up their idols in their hearts." A reminder that "you shall have no other gods before me." (Exodus 20:3) What idols are you storing in your heart that is preventing you from developing a rich and intimate relationship with God? I encourage you to read Ezekiel 14.

Dear God,
Thank you for the reminder that I have set-up idols in my heart.
That I must repent and turn away from my idols. I pray that all
your children recognize the idols they have stored in their hearts,
and that they repent and turn away from all idols. That they
place their relationship with you as their priority. I ask this in
your son Jesus' name. Amen!

MARCH 14

Temptation vs. Inspiration

ANCHOR SCRIPTURE: 1 CORINTHIANS 10:13

"No temptation has overtaken you except what is common to
mankind. And God is faithful; he will not let you be tempted
beyond what you can bear. But when you are tempted, he will
also provide a way out so that you can endure it."

"Every time I say 'no' to a small temptation, I strengthen
my will to say 'no' to a greater one."
- Mother Angelica

As I continue to grow spiritually, I constantly seek guidance from the
almighty and seek his word, his truth. I say the Lord's Prayer daily, and
today I thought about temptation. What causes us to be weak and fall
prey to the enemy's temptation? We find all sorts of excuses for why
we give in and why saying no to temptation was so difficult.

I recently heard a sermon by Pastor Rick Warren. In this sermon Pastor Rick discusses that by saying that you were helpless, you were weak or simply had no choice but to give in implies that you are calling God a liar. He promised he will always offer you a way out when faced with temptation. Your thoughts are where the battle begins. The sermon also discussed that when God gives us an idea, that is inspiration, and when the enemy plants an idea, that is temptation. "Every moment of resistance to temptation is a victory."

We must be aware of our thoughts and make careful choices daily. We each can activate God's power daily by knowing his word, his truth, and his promises. God fulfills all His promises. Which will you choose today, temptation or inspiration? I encourage you to read 1 Corinthians 10. Hope it inspires you to resist temptation.

———————————— **PRAYER FOR THE DAY:** ————————————

Dear God,
Thank you for the reminder that you are always near when I face temptation. That I have the option to yield to your power to resist temptation. I pray that all your children remember that you are always near when they face temptation. That they have the option to yield to your power to resist temptation. If they fall into temptation, you always provide a way out. I ask this in your son Jesus' name. Amen!

Agape Love

ANCHOR SCRIPTURE: 1 JOHN 4:9

"This is how God showed his love among us: He sent his one and only Son into the world that we might live through him."

The only way love can last a lifetime is if it is unconditional. The truth is this: love is not determined by the one being loved but rather by the one choosing to love.
- Stephen Kendrick

Love shows up in so many ways. We love certain things, people, and places. I wonder how deep is that love? Are you willing to sacrifice all for the things, people, and places you love deeply? There are four types of love, love as it relates to romance, love as it relates to your brother or to one another, love of your family and then there is Agape love. Agape Love is unconditional, selfless, and sacrificial love.

Can you imagine walking a life where love is your compass, your guide, and the center of your being? That no matter what anyone does or says to you, you are still able to just love everyone just the way they are? That you automatically forgive every sin committed. I know many of you may be struggling with this thought....But God, he killed someone, but God she left me when I needed her the most, but God, they hurt me, but God it still hurts. Can you imagine if God said all of this about you and refuses to love or forgive you? We however know that God will never withhold his love from us.

Today's verse is a reminder that this is how God showed his love among us: He sent his one and only Son into the world that we might live through him. Wow, simply said, Agape Love. Are you able to gain the strength and courage to follow God's example and walk in this way of love (Ephesians 5:1-2)? I encourage you today to read 1 John 4 and meditate on that sacrificial love.

Dear God,
Thank you for the reminder that you sent your only son into
the world so that we may live through him. To show me what
unconditional, selfless, and sacrificial love looks like. I pray that
all your children find it in their hearts to walk in this way of love.
Agape love, unconditional, selfless, and sacrificial love. I ask this
in your son Jesus' name. Amen!

●

MARCH 16

Channeling Peace

ANCHOR SCRIPTURE: PHILIPPIANS 4:7

"And the peace of God, which transcends all understanding,
will guard your hearts and your minds in Christ Jesus."

"Peace is the result of retraining your mind to process life as it is,
rather than as you think it should be.

Have you ever said or heard someone said I need peace? Some think
of peace as being in a quiet isolated place. What if I said you could be
in the middle of a noisy and crowded fish market and still have peace?
When the noise of life takes over your mind and heart, when you are
filled with worry, anxiety, doubt and are not able to be at peace what
do you do?

Do you ever ask God for his peace and to share his peace? The peace that transcends all understanding. If God is in me, then I already have the peace that he gives. I can also channel that peace to others. 2 Thessalonians 3:16 says now may always the Lord of peace himself give you peace and in every way. The Lord be with all of you.

I recalled learning the prayer of St. Francis at a tender age. It was a hymn sang at church. In this prayer, I asked to be a channel of the Lord's peace. Where there is hatred let me bring love. Where there is injury, pardon. Where there is doubt bring faith. Where there is despair let me bring hope. Where there is darkness let me bring only light and where there is sadness let me bring joy. Decades later this prayer makes much more sense than ever.

Today's verse is a reminder that the peace of God, which transcends all understanding, will guard your hearts and your minds in Christ Jesus. I encourage you to read Philippians 4 and revisit the prayer of St. Francis. Become a channel of peace.

———————————— **PRAYER FOR THE DAY:** ————————————

Dear God,
Thank you for the reminder that I am a vessel to channel your peace. That peace which transcends all understanding. I pray that all your children are reminded that your peace transcends all understanding and will guard their hearts and minds. That they can be channels of your peace. I ask this in your son Jesus' name. Amen!

MARCH 17

All is Well... Be Cautious

ANCHOR SCRIPTURE: 1 PETER 5:8

"Be alert and of sober mind. Your enemy the devil prowls around like a roaring lion looking for someone to devour."

"Scars fade with time. And the ones that never go away, well, they build character, maturity, caution."
- Erin McCarthy

It feels so good when you get into your car to head to work, get on the highway and there is no traffic. Not one single traffic jam. Smooth sailing into the office. You arrive at work with a difference attitude. You may think, I will have a smooth ride home because all was well this morning. You don't worry about what time you leave the office because you figure all will be the same heading home.

Life sometimes is like traffic. When all is well, we feel that there is no need to be concerned because all is or has been running smoothly. We get accustomed or comfortable with the current state of things, we relax and sometimes forget that we must always remain alert. When all is well, we must not ease up on our prayer life, we must remain vigilant and not become complacent.

Today's verse is a reminder to be alert and of sober mind. Your enemy the devil prowls around like a roaring lion looking for someone to devour. Whether you are currently in a storm or you are having the time of your life, always remain alert and sober. Armor yourself with God's word. Be especially cautious when all is well.

Dear God,
Thank you for the reminder to be alert and of sober mind. That
the enemy prowls around like a roaring lion looking for someone
to devour. I pray that all your children remain alert, sober, and
anchored to your word. That they remember that their enemy,
the devil, prowls around like a roaring lion looking for someone
to devour. That they be cautious especially when all is well. I ask
this in your son Jesus' name. Amen!

MARCH 18

No Greater Love

ANCHOR SCRIPTURE: JOHN 3:16

"For God so loved the world that he gave his one and only
Son, that whoever believes in him shall not perish but
have eternal life."

"A true friend knows your weaknesses but shows you your
strengths; feels your fears but fortifies your faith; sees your
anxieties but frees your spirit; recognizes your disabilities
but emphasizes your possibilities."
-William Arthur Ward

Have you ever been in a situation where you tried to tell or show
someone that they are loved or you love them more than anything in
this world and they simply did not believe you? You jumped over hurdles, skydive (although you are afraid of heights) and possible trained

with them for a marathon, even though you were not participating in the race and they simply did not get it. That you did it all for the unconditional love you have for them.

Today's verse, in my view, is the greatest verse in the Bible. It sums up the Bible and the love that God has for each of us. There is no sin that can change this love. Whenever I am in doubt, I simply reflect on this verse and it reminds me of the great love that God has for us. No one or nothing can change this.

God loves us so much; he wants us to come to Him just as we are. He wants to have a personal relationship with us and longs for us to talk to Him freely about our sins and our needs. This relationship should be just as going to your best friend. Speak truthfully, open, and honest with God and he will always respond with love. There is no greater love.

--------- PRAYER FOR THE DAY: ---------

Dear God,
Thank you for giving your one and only Son, that whoever believes in you shall not perish but have eternal life. Today I pray that we all simply remember this; God loves us just the way we are. I ask this all in your son's Jesus name. Amen.

Know Better, Do Better

ANCHOR SCRIPTURE: JAMES 4:17

*"Remember, it is sin to know what you ought to do
and then not do it."*

Do the best you can until you know better.
Then when you know better, do better.

- Maya Angelou

Doing the right thing is not easy, emotions get in the way. Fear, ego, pride, rebellion, lack of knowledge and the urge to belong get in the way of our decision making. A while back I had a conversation with a group of teens and asked how they felt about skipping school. They said it was wrong, they were cheating themselves out of learning, and one even said it was deceitful. I asked who has skipped school at least once and most raised their hands. I asked if you know better, why don't you do better? They all looked puzzled, one honestly said because I feel like it. Another said, I do not know.

Have you ever thought about why when we know better, we still don't do better? At an earlier age we do things because we don't know better. You may touch the hot stove when you are two years old because you are curious and want to know if it is hot. Once you touch the stove and find out that it is truly hot through the burn you sustain, you should learn the lesson. You should understand never to touch a hot stove again. However, as we mature, many of us know better but don't do better.

Today's verse is a reminder that it is sin to know what you ought to do and then not do it. If you know better, you should do better. No excuses. Is there an area in your life where you know better but refuse to do better? I encourage you to dig deep and be honest with yourself.

Dear God,
Thank you for the reminder that it is sin to know what I ought to
do and then not do it. I pray that all your children take to heart
this reminder that it is sin to know what you ought to do and
then not do it. I ask this in your son Jesus' name. Amen

MARCH 20

Detachment

ANCHOR SCRIPTURE: PROVERBS 23:4

"Do not wear yourself out to get rich;
have the wisdom to show restraint."

"Rich people have small TVs and big libraries, and poor
people have small libraries and big TVs."
- Zig Ziglar

So many of us are working hard to make ends meets, some are working hard to attain one thing, to "say" they are rich and famous. Some
believe money will solve all their problems. I learned from several
wise mentors that you can have all the money in the world and if you
don't manage it properly it does no good. It may create more problems
than solve anything.

I see so many attain that status "rich and famous" and have no joy.
And he said to them, "Take care, and be on your guard against all
covetousness, for one's life does not consist in the abundance of his

122

possessions." (Luke 12:15.) I am not saying having money is wrong. In fact, a friend shared this, "much of God's work relies on charitable and responsible people with the means to help. It's when we begin grasping at wealth and desire it above all that it poisons us."

Today's scripture is a reminder to not wear yourself out to get rich; have the wisdom to show restraint. Continue to trust God's plans for you.

—————————————— **PRAYER FOR THE DAY:** ——————————————

Dear God,
Thank you for the reminder that there is no need to wear myself out to get rich; to have the wisdom to show restraint. Most importantly to trust you and your plans for me. I pray that all your children will not wear themselves out to get rich; that they will have wisdom to show restraints and trust you and your plans for their life. I ask this in your son Jesus' name. Amen!

Face the Pain

ANCHOR SCRIPTURE: PSALM 147:3

"He heals the brokenhearted and binds up their wounds."

Real pain offers only two possible responses:
we can deal with it...or we can refuse to deal with it.
- *Matt Keller*

Dealing with pain day in and day out is not easy. It is the one thing we avoid as humans. We often try to cover the pain, put a smile over it, bury the pain, pretend it is not happening or even run away from the pain.

I am reading a book entitled- The Key to Everything by Matt Keller. Mr. Keller discusses that all the tactics we use to avoid or refuse to deal with pain is hardly the healthy choice. He adds that unprocessed pain cuts short our joy, our relationships, our careers, and even potentially our lives. He ends the chapter with this statement: "Anyone who has ever stalled out, burned out, or flakes out has done so because of some pain in their life that was ignored or denied."

Today's scripture is a reminder that God heals the brokenhearted and binds up their wounds. He will wipe every tear from your eyes. If you are ignoring your pain, ask God to help you deal with the pain in a healthy way. He will wipe every tear; he will heal your broken-heart and bind your wounds.

Dear God,
Thank you for the reminder that you heal broken-hearts and bind up wounds. I pray that all your children turn to you to deal with their pain in a healthy way. That they trust you will heal their broken heart and bind their wounds. I ask this in your son Jesus' name. Amen!

MARCH 22

Servant Leadership

ANCHOR SCRIPTURE: MARK 10:45

"Reminds us, for even the Son of Man came not to be served but to serve, and to give his life as a ransom for many."

"I have found that among its other benefits,
giving liberates the soul of the giver.
– *Dr. Maya Angelou*"

The phrase "servant leadership" was coined by Robert K. Greenleaf in The Servant as Leader, an essay that he first published in 1970. In that essay, Greenleaf said: "The servant-leader is servant first... It begins with the natural feeling that one wants to serve, to serve first. Then conscious choice brings one to aspire to lead. His organization describes

Servant leadership as a philosophy and set of practices that enriches the lives of individuals, builds better organizations, and ultimately creates a more just and caring world.

Today's verse reminds us, for even the Son of Man came not to be served but to serve, and to give his life as a ransom for many." Jesus served as the exemplary "servant leader." He washed the feet of his disciples. Are you willing to wash the feet of those you lead? What is your choice, to serve or be served?

Dear God,
Thank you for the reminder that I am here to serve, not to be served. I pray that all your children remember that your Son came not to be served but to serve, and to give his life as a ransom for many. I ask this in your son Jesus' name. Amen!

MARCH 23

No Sacrifice, No Success

ANCHOR SCRIPTURE: ROMANS: 5:8

"But God demonstrates his own Love for us in this: while we were still sinners, Christ died for us."

Great achievement is usually born of great sacrifice
and is never the result of selfishness.
- Napoleon Hill

Can you imagine someone loving you so much that they sacrifice their life for your sin? A sin not yet committed. If that is not love, then

I don't know what love is. We are all loved by God no matter what we have done or will do. As you celebrate, reflect, and connect today, may you experience gratitude, peace, joy, and love.

Not everyone believes their truth, knows their worth or even embrace their power. God wants all of us to embrace the freedom and power he has given each of us. He doesn't want us to remain prisoners to our past or our current sins.

The scripture says, "Whoever calls upon the name of the Lord will be saved. If you would like to know Christ, all you must do is pray this aloud, Lord Jesus, I repent of my sins. Come into my heart. Wash me clean. I make you my Lord and Savior, Amen"

Today's scripture serves as a reminder that God demonstrates his own Love for us in this: while we were still sinners, Christ died for us. Thank you, Lord, for sacrificing your life for us.

─────────────── **PRAYER FOR THE DAY:** ───────────────

Dear God,
Thank you for the reminder that you demonstrated your love by dying for us. That you long to save, free and empower all of us. I pray that all your children accept your love, the freedom, and the power you offer by dying for us all. I ask this in your son Jesus' name. Amen!

Unique

ANCHOR SCRIPTURE: PSALM 139:14

"I praise you, for I am fearfully and wonderfully made.
Wonderful are your works; my soul knows it very well."

What sets you apart can sometimes feel like a burden
and it's not. And a lot of the time, it's what makes you great."
- Emma Stone

I recently observed a few children playing. They were all doing their
own thing. No one was trying to do what the other was doing. It seems
they knew something we tend to forget; they are each unique and are
created for their own purpose.

Merriam Webster defines unique as being the only one; being without a like or equal. There is no need to try to be like someone else.
Each of us are here on earth to serve a specific and unique purpose.
There is no need to be distracted or jealous of what others have, that
is uniquely designed for that person, not for you. When we step away
from the unique purpose for which we are created to be like someone
else, there is a void in the universe. A purpose God intended to be
filled, not filled.

Today's verse is a reminder that we are all fearfully and wonderfully
made. Wonderful are your works; my soul knows it very well. I
encourage you today to embrace that you are indeed fearfully and
wonderfully made just the way you are. Love you, be you.

Dear God,
Thank you for the reminder that I am fearfully and wonderful-
ly made. I pray that all your children remember that you made
them unique. That you were intentional in your design...Won-
derful are your works; their soul knows it very well. I pray this in
your son Jesus' name. Amen!

MARCH 25

Live, Laugh, Love

ANCHOR SCRIPTURE: PSALM 126:2-3

"Our mouths were filled with laughter, our tongues with
songs of joy. Then it was said among the nations, "The Lord
has done great things for them." The Lord has done great things
for us, and we are filled with joy."

"Our attitude toward life determines life's attitude towards us"
- John N. Mitchell

What is your attitude towards your life? Do you start your day with
gratitude, laughter, living and loving life or do you start your day with
worry, ingratitude, a frown, regret, and un-forgiveness? I met this
young man that shared his decision to accept life as it comes, good
or bad he would be grateful. He understood that life would be good
and bad but ultimately it is all for our good. My thought was simply
what wisdom at such a tender age of 18. I also thought, I wish I had
the same wisdom at his age. However, this is his story not mine. (LOL)

Yes, troubles come our way time and time again. However, I realize that our attitude toward life determines life's attitude towards us. I am intentional in paying attention to how I and others around me embrace life. It even happened this morning, as I was running late for the train, I decided that God was in control and if I made the train or not, it was his decision. I let go and let God... I made it to train with 30 seconds to spare (LOL.) Yes, a small example. We must trust God in the small and the big things... in all. What I mighty God we serve. Today's verse is a reminder to fill our mouths with laughter, our tongues with songs of joy.

Then it was said among the nations, "The Lord has done great things for them." The Lord has done great things for us, and we are filled with joy. I encourage you today to live, laugh, love and be grateful.

———————————— **PRAYER FOR THE DAY:** ————————————

Dear God,
Thank you for the reminder to fill my mouth with laughter and our tongues with songs of joy. I pray that all your children fill their mouths with laughter and their tongues with songs of joy. Then they will say among the nations, The Lord has done great things for them. The Lord has done great things for us, and we are filled with joy. That they live, laugh and love. I ask this in your son Jesus's name. Amen!

Planted from Greatness

ANCHOR SCRIPTURE: PSALM 1:3

"He shall be like a tree Planted by the rivers of water, That brings forth its fruit in its season, Whose leaf also shall not wither; And whatever he does shall prosper."

Don't judge each day by the harvest you reap but
by the seeds that you plant.
– Robert Louis Stevenson

Psalm 1:3 reminds us that person is like a tree planted by streams of water, which yields its fruit in season and whose leaf does not wither—whatever they do prospers.

We are all planted from the seed of greatness. We sometimes forget this truth. We were created by the great creator. The choice is yours to claim this inheritance. I frequently refer to my children as my fruit. I remind them that they are planted from the seed of greatness and should live by this truth.

Imagine if we all claim this truth, what a different world this would be. We would not have depression, sadness, envy and all the other emotions that comes with not claiming this inheritance...we would all know who we are.

Today's scripture is a reminder that person is like a tree planted by streams of water, which yields its fruit in season and whose leaf does not wither—whatever they do prospers.

Can you imagine, no matter how long it takes, every seed you plant will prosper. Because you are planted from the seed of greatness, your fruits will be great. You are destined for victory. I encourage you to read Psalm 1 in its entirety.

Dear God,
Thank you for the reminder that I like the tree planted by the streams of water, which yields its fruit in season and whose leaf does not wither- whatever they do prospers. I pray that all your children remember this truth, that they will yield fruits in season, whose leaf does not wither and whatever they do prospers. They are free to claim their inheritance. I ask this in your son Jesus' name. Amen!

MARCH 27

Get Out Of Your Own Way

ANCHOR SCRIPTURE: 2 TIMOTHY 1:7

"For God has not given us a spirit of fear and timidity, but of power, love, and self-discipline."

"The secret of change is to focus all of your energy
not on fighting the old, but on building the new."
- Socrates

Do you ever wonder what gets in the way of you doing the next great thing? Can you imagine wanting to know the world and you are afraid to fly? Do you ask how can I get over the fear of flying or do you give up on knowing the world?

I admit it, it is simpler to do the easiest thing, not face the fear and give up on the idea of ever getting to know the world. Think about that. What if you decided to challenge that thought of "fear to fly" to the greater desire to know the world. Think about what thoughts, true or false, may be preventing you from taking the steps you need to reach your goals.

Today's verse is a reminder that for God has not given us a spirit of fear and timidity, but of power, love, and self-discipline. I encourage you today to consider if your thoughts, beliefs, and fears are getting in the way of you attaining your next greatest goal. Remember the spirit of fear and timidity were not given to you.

PRAYER FOR THE DAY:

Dear God,
Thank you for the reminder that you did not give me a spirit of fear and timidity, but of power, love, and self-discipline. I pray that all your children embrace the power, love, and self-discipline you gave them. That they let go of the spirit of fear and timidity. That they get out of their own way. I ask this in your son Jesus' name. Amen!

Right or Kind

ANCHOR SCRIPTURE: COLOSSIANS 3:12

"Therefore, as God's chosen people, holy and dearly loved, clothe yourselves with compassion, kindness, humility, gentleness and patience."

Courage. Kindness. Friendship. Character. These are the qualities that define us as human beings, and propel us, on occasion, to greatness."
- R.J. Palacio

When confronted with the decision to be right or kind which do you choose? Being right gives a feeling of satisfaction. Keeping things real, it feels good to say, "I told you so." What do we gain from being right... to wear the badge of honor of the ego being stroked, "I am right, and you were wrong"? It seems proven right or wrong has overshadowed being kind.

Imagine choosing being kind over being right, opting to operate from the heart (from a place of love) in everything you do. To simply release all judgement and choose love and kindness every time. To fix your heart condition by deleting your ego from your decision making. Proverbs 3:3 instructs to not let kindness and truth leave you; Bind them around your neck, Write them on the tablet of your heart.

As you move forward with your day, pay attention to your decisions, are you choosing being right over being kind? Today's scripture is a reminder that as God's chosen people, holy and dearly loved, clothe yourselves with compassion, kindness, humility, gentleness, and patience.

Dear God,
Thank you for the reminder to not let kindness and truth leave me. I pray that all your children do not let kindness and truth leave them. That they remember that as God's chosen people, holy and dearly loved, that they clothe themselves with compassion, kindness, humility, gentleness, and patience. I ask this in your son Jesus' name. Amen!

MARCH 29

Growing up is Hard to Do

ANCHOR SCRIPTURE: ECCLESIASTES 3:2

"A time to give birth and a time to die; A time to plant a nd a time to uproot what is planted."

"Life can only be understood backwards;
but it must be lived forward."
- Soren Kierkegaard

Has anyone ever said these words to you, "Grow up!" Growing up is not simple. There is a lot of pain that accompanies growth, hence the term "growing pains." Growing is uncomfortable because physical and emotional pain accompanies our growth.

Would you rather remain in a pain free state with no worries, no bills, and no major life decisions to make? I asked this question to a friend recently and the answer was yes. I asked why, the honest answer was "I am comfortable." I thought, if we remain comfortable are, we growing? In reflecting on my life, the only time growth occurred was during discomfort...in the uncomfortable zone...Moving to an unknown country, leaving friends behind, and making new friends. This took faith and commitment to growing. Rick Warren says, "We grow when we commit to grow."

Today's verse is a reminder that there is a time to give birth and a time to die; A time to plant and a time to uproot what is planted. Are you committed to embracing your growing pains? Sometimes we get stuck holding onto the comfort, to the fun times in our life, to what is easy. There is a time for everything. We must continue to grow. Grow on!

PRAYER FOR THE DAY:

Dear God,
Thank you for the reminder that there is a time for everything. That you created us to grow, grow in your likeness. I pray that all your children remember that there is a time for everything, even a time to grow. That although there is "pain with growth", you created us to grow in your likeness. I ask this in your son Jesus' name. Amen!

Obedience

ANCHOR SCRIPTURE: PHILIPPIANS 4:6-7

*"Don't worry about anything; instead, pray about everything.
Tell God what you need and thank him for all he has done.
Then you will experience God's peace, which exceeds
anything we can understand. His peace will guard
your hearts and minds as you live in Christ Jesus"*

Obedience is an act of faith; disobedience is the result of unbelief
-*Edwin Louis Cole*

Have you ever prayed for obedience? I never thought in my adult life I would have to pray for obedience. Keeping things real, rebellion always feels better but wisdom teaches it leads down the wrong path. Well, guess what, prayers answered... Ask and you shall receive... early this morning I receive today's Daily Hope with Pastor Rick Warren with the following title "Obedience leads to Peace." Some of you already guessed what I said, "You can't make this stuff up." (Smile.)

Reflecting on this title, when praying for obedience are, we asking for strength to obey, to not worry or simply for peace? The text that followed in today's Daily Hope devotional touched on a key point. It talked about "if you feel overwhelmed or confused about a decision that you're pondering; you're probably caught up in yourself and not listening to God's voice. The text continued to remind me that God is not a God of disorder but of peace (1 Corinthians 14:33 NIV.) He is not the author of confusion. So, if you're feeling confused, guess what? It's not God's voice speaking in your life." Can someone say "OUCH" with me! Yep, God is full of jokes. (Feel free to check out today's Daily Hope with Rick Warren to read the rest of today's message http://pastorrick.com/devotional)

It seems the takeaway message is, to truly obey; we must decrease "me and I" and increase God. Consider this anytime you are feeling confused or overwhelmed, whose voice are you hearing; yours, someone else's, or God's? Today's scripture is a reminder to not worry about anything; instead, pray about everything. Tell God what you need and thank him for all he has done. Then you will experience God's peace, which exceeds anything we can understand. His peace will guard your hearts and minds as you live in Christ Jesus.

--- **PRAYER FOR THE DAY:** ---

Dear God,
Thank you for the reminder to not worry about anything, instead, pray about everything. To decrease me and increase you. I pray that all your children rest easy and seek no other voice but yours. That they experience no confusion, no overwhelmed feeling, and your peace that surpasses all understanding. I ask this in your son Jesus' name. AMEN!

Patience is Understanding

ANCHOR SCRIPTURE: PROVERBS 14:29

"Whoever is patient has great understanding,
but one who is quick-tempered displays folly."
Patience is not the ability to wait, but the ability
to keep a good attitude

As I sat in traffic one day, I became aware of the importance of patience. We all have experienced impatience at some point in our lives. If you don't believe me, think of babies. If you delay their feedings, they will become impatient and will not hesitate to let you know about it. Patience is sometimes defined as the capacity to accept or tolerate delay, trouble, or suffering without getting angry or upset.

Yes, I can imagine that promotion you have been waiting to receive has not come through, so you are leaving your job. That business you are starting is taking too long to take off. It requires too much work and sleepless nights and you are tired. That relationship you are trying to repair, the other party is not cooperating. That project you are working on, there is another daily. So many reasons to become impatient daily.

Today's verse is a reminder whoever is patient has great understanding, but one who is quick-tempered displays folly. I encourage you today, to practice patience. Patience is truly a virtue and if today's verse is a fact, whoever is patient has great understanding.

Dear God,
Thank you for the reminder that patience is a sign of great understanding. I chose not to display folly. I pray that all your children remember that lack of patience displays folly.

That practicing patience demonstrates their great understanding. That patient is indeed a virtue. I ask this in your son Jesus' name. Amen!

Reflections

_____

_____

_____

_____

_____

_____

_____

_____

_____

_____

_____

April

Harmony

ANCHOR SCRIPTURE: ROMANS 12:16

*"Live in harmony with one another. Do not be proud
but be willing to associate with people of low position.
Do not be conceited."*

"Harmony makes small things grow;
lack of it makes great things decay."
-Sallust

Living in harmony is not an easy task. You and I are different. No one is the same make or model. You are each unique and wonderfully made. Sometimes, conflict ensues when you try to get everyone to be in accord with your thoughts or to do things the way you want them done. If we all did things the same way, can you imagine how uninteresting your life would be?

Harmony is described as "a combination of simultaneously sounded musical notes to produce chords and chord progressions having a pleasing effect." Note the word "pleasing." Sometimes finding harmony requires complete surrender or as I sometimes say, it requires you "playing only when your instrument is required." Remove "self" and watch how living in harmony becomes easier.

Today's verse instructs us to live in harmony with one another. To not be proud but be willing to associate with people of low position. Do not be conceited. Living in harmony requires courage to navigate life in ease. I have a dear friend who shared that when she wanted to be reminded of this, she would play the song "Pata." For those not familiar with the song, here is the link https://youtu.be/gsDfHvIFwiU (I do not have rights to this song.) I encourage each of you to live in harmony every day.

Dear God,
Thank you for the reminder to live in harmony with one another. To not be proud but be willing to associate with people of low position. To not be conceited. I pray that all your children heed your instructions to live in harmony with one another; that they should not be proud, but willing to associate with people of low position. To not be conceited. I ask this in your son Jesus' name. Amen!

APRIL 2

Keep things simple

ANCHOR SCRIPTURE: LUKE 9:3

He said, "Don't load yourselves up with equipment. Keep it simple; you are the equipment."

Simplicity is ultimately a matter of focus.
-Ann Voskamp

Do you ever wonder why we put so much on our plates before we travel? There is always much to do, ensuring the pets are cared for, things at home and work are in order, shopping, getting your hair done (yes, this applies to men and women) and many other things we add to our list to escape for five days of rest. Some of these tasks are necessary but many are unnecessary.

Yep, I would be the first to confess, I have paid overweight charges. I keep stating, this should not be this complicated. The best advice that I apply now is "keep it simple silly or keep it simple sweetie aka KISS." It seems we unnecessarily complicate and burden our lives when keeping things simple is the key.

Today's verse is a reminder to not load yourselves up with equipment. Keep it simple; you are the equipment. Enough said. Keep it simple! I encourage you to read all of Luke 9.

PRAYER FOR THE DAY:

Dear God,
Thank you for the reminder to keep things simple. No need to load myself up with equipment. To keep it simple because I am the equipment. I pray that all your children keep things simple. That they realize there is no need to load themselves with equipment because they are the equipment. I ask this in your son Jesus' name. Amen!

Lesson Learned

ANCHOR SCRIPTURE: PROVERBS 22:6

"Direct your children onto the right path, and when they are older, they will not leave it."

"More is taught than caught"

I recently read an article by Rachel Cruze that stated the following: "I truly believe more is caught than taught . . . that what your kids see you do is a lot more powerful than what they hear you say. Words can be strong, but actions are stronger. The strongest impact on children, though, is when they hear and see a consistent message from their parents. When the parents' words and actions come together, it forms a powerful statement about that family's value system." This suggestion is not just for parents.

There is not enough emphasis that can be placed on the power that comes from aligning your words and actions. I also believe rather than more is "caught than taught", "more is taught than caught." There are so many lessons learned through life and somewhere along the journey it is either forgotten or the choice is made to ignore the lessons learned.

Proverbs 22:6 is a reminder to "direct your children onto the right path, and when they are older, they will not leave it." I encourage you today to be mindful of aligning your words and actions. Anchor on your family values, your inheritance.

Dear God,
Thank you for the reminder that you direct me on the right path
by your teachings. Thank you for ordering my steps. I pray that
all your children learn and capture the teachings and lessons
you want all of us to learn. That they allow you to order their
steps. I ask this in your son Jesus' name. Amen!

APRIL 4

Life with hope

ANCHOR SCRIPTURE: PSALM 34:18

"The Lord is close to the brokenhearted and saves those
who are crushed in spirit."

"He who does not hope to win has already lost."
- Jose Joaquin Olmedo

Merriam Webster defines hope as to cherish a desire with anticipation; to want something to happen or be true; to desire with expectation. It is said that "Man can live about 40 days without food, about three days without water, about eight minutes without air, but only for one second without hope." If this is the case, I wonder why lose hope? The time you lost the bid for your perfect home, when you were abandoned, when you lost a loved one, when you didn't get the job you wanted, when those near and dear to you disappointed you, all these events may have caused you to lose hope.

George Weinberg was quoted as saying "hope never abandons you. You abandon it." Things may seem dark now, as though the sun may never shine again for you. Today's verse is a reminder that the Lord is close to the brokenhearted and saves those who are crushed in spirit. No matter how tough things may get, I encourage you not to abandon hope. Hope anchors your soul. Consider how hope is anchoring you today and each day.

PRAYER FOR THE DAY:

Dear God,
Thank you for the reminder that you are close to the broken-hearted and you save those who are crushed in spirit. I pray that all your children rest in the assurance that you are close to the brokenhearted and you save those who are crushed in spirit; that they anchor on your hope and promises. I ask this in your son Jesus' name. Amen.

Innovation in Action

ANCHOR SCRIPTURE: JAMES 1:4

*"Let perseverance finish its work so that you may
be mature and complete, not lacking anything."*

"Success is just a pile of failures you are standing on"
- Dave Ramsey

You may have heard this phrase before, "failure is not an option." That phrase has been linked to NASA and their space program. "The makers of a documentary interviewed NASA officials about the problems that arose out of the Apollo 13 mission. When asked, one of the officials stated that when there were problems that needed to be addressed, they would lay out possible solutions and that failure was never one of them."

I like to think of failure as "innovation in action... if one thing doesn't work, keep trying till you find what works." Yes, our thoughts and sometimes those close to you will tell you to stop at your first attempt that doesn't work. Thomas A. Edison was quoted saying, "I have not failed. I've just found 10,000 ways that won't work."

Today's verse serves as a reminder to let perseverance finish its work so that you may be mature and complete, not lacking anything. Are you working on something new, a new business, a new relationship, a new project? Whatever is your "new" thing, I encourage you to keep going, keep growing. Persevere!

Dear God,
Thank you for the reminder to let perseverance finish its work
so that I may be mature and complete, not lacking anything. I
pray that all your children experience success in all that do. That
they let perseverance finish its work so that they may be mature
and complete, not lacking anything. I ask this in your son Jesus'
name. Amen!

APRIL 6

Intentional

ANCHOR SCRIPTURE: PSALM 139:16

"Your eyes saw my unformed body; all the days ordained for
me were written in your book before one of them came to be."

Commitment with accountability closes the gap
between intention and results.
-Sandra Gallagher

Have you ever wondered what living on purpose looks like? I read a message contributed by Rob Culler (March 21, 2001) on "living an intentional life." He formed the following statement about living an intentional life, "An intentional life is one with purpose. The purpose is followed with a bold and steady determination until the desired outcome is realized." To me, this is clear... to live on purpose will require you to be BOLD, exert steady determination to realize the desired outcome.

I had a kid in my life (I reserve the name to protect the innocent-smile,) who woke up every morning and asked, "What is our intention for today?" Once he knew the intention for the day, he ensured it was completed. He held me accountable. If there wasn't an agenda, he would suggest one. (He started this at age two.) I learned from this two-year-old that if you do not have an intention for the day, one would be created for you. That intention or agenda could have nothing to do with your purpose.

I found that continuing to grow my relationship with God helps me fulfill the purpose and intention he has for my life. Today's verse reminds us, "Your eyes saw my unformed body.

All the days ordained for me were written in your book before one of them came to be." Ah!!!...our stories were written before we were formed. Based on this verse, it seems to make sense to align with God's purpose for our lives than pursue our own purpose. What is your intention today?

_____ PRAYER FOR THE DAY: _____

Dear God,
Thank you for the reminder to live an intentional life. That you wrote my story before I was formed. I pray that all your children live an intentional life with purpose. That they remember that your eyes saw their unformed body and you ordained all their days. I ask this in your son Jesus' name. Amen!

Soar on Wings Like Eagles

ANCHOR SCRIPTURE: ISAIAH 40:31

"But those who hope in the LORD will renew their strength. They will soar on wings like eagles; they will run and not grow weary; they will walk and not be faint."

"Your wings are not broken. You already know how to fly."

Imagine going to the skating rink after not skating for a few decades (yep haven't skated since those skates that used keys to adjust to size. Remember those? Smiles.) Sometimes we forget that we already learned certain things and all we need is to remember to strengthen those muscles to do it again.

There is a song by Martina MacBride entitled "A Broken Wing." The words to the chorus say "And with a broken wing she still sings, she keeps an eye over the sky with a broken wing she carries her dreams. Man, you ought to see her fly."

A broken or injured wing can sometimes be deceptive. It sometimes leaves you believing that you can no longer fly. Today's verse reminds us but those who hope in the LORD will renew their strength. They will soar on wings like eagles; they will run and not grow weary; they will walk and not be faint. I encourage you to remember, you already know how to fly. Fly high...Soar on wings like eagles.

Dear God,
Thank you for the reminder to fly high. That those who hope in you will renew their strength. They will soar on wings like eagles; they will run and not grow weary; they will walk and not be faint. I pray that all your children remember that those who hope in you, will renew their strength. They will soar on wings like eagles; they will run and not grow weary; they will walk and not be faint. I ask this in your son Jesus' name. Amen!

APRIL 8

What's Your Priority?

ANCHOR SCRIPTURE: MATTHEW 6:33

"But seek first his kingdom and his righteousness, and
all these things will be given to you as well."

Discipline is choosing between what you want now and what you want most. It is the start of a new week. You create your plan for the week. This plan entails the 3-4 top priorities of things to accomplish each day. Then an unexpected visitor stops by, a friend asked you to go shopping, a "true" emergency occurs, someone else's emergency suddenly becomes your emergency, or you simply don't feel like working on that particular priority...these are just a few examples of things/excuses that interfere with sticking to your priorities.

The book First Things First by Stephen R. Covey talks about the process of shifting from urgency to importance. I recently re-read this book and was reminded that for many of us, there is a gap between the compass and the clock - between what's deeply important to us and the way we spend our time. The reference in the book to the clock and the compass states that the clock represents commitments, appointments, schedules, goals, and activities. The compass represents the vision, values, principles, mission, conscience, direction- what we feel is important and how we lead our lives.

How and what is leading your life? What is the first thing on your list of priorities? What is important, not urgent, for to you? Is the clock or the compass setting your priorities? Today's verse is a reminder to seek first God's kingdom and his righteousness, and all these things will be given to you as well. I encourage you to revisit your priorities and determine are you keeping first things first?

——————————— **PRAYER FOR THE DAY:** ———————————

Dear God,
Thank you for the reminder to keep first things first. To seek first your kingdom and your righteousness. I pray that all your children keep first things first. That they first seek your kingdom and your righteousness. I ask this in your son Jesus' name. Amen!

Take Charge of Your Thoughts

ANCHOR SCRIPTURE: EPHESIANS 4:23-24

"To be made new in the attitude of your minds; and to put on the new self, created to be like God in true righteousness and holiness."

Happiness doesn't depend on who you are or what you have; it depends solely on what you think
- *Dale Carnegie*

Our thoughts are powerful. They dictate whether we will have a great or bad day. As I pay attention to my thoughts, it is interesting to note that our thoughts are triggered mostly by external factors than what is happening internally. However, these external factors begin to affect our internal being. Marcus Aurelius said "The soul becomes dyed with the colors of its thoughts. Can you imagine that your thoughts have an impact on your soul?

Our thoughts affect so much whether we are happy, are afraid, get angry, are jealous, have lustful thoughts and too many other emotions to mention. What if you decide to take control of the many thoughts that fly through your head? To decide that you will not let your thoughts run wild. You make the decision to take charge of your thoughts. Mahatma Ghandi said your beliefs become your thoughts, your thoughts become your words, your words become your actions, your actions become your habits, your habits become your values, and your values become your destiny. Should your thoughts become your values and your destiny?

Today's verse is a reminder to be made new in the attitude of your minds; and to put on the new self, created to be like God in true righteousness and holiness. What's your choice, to put on the new self, created to be like God in true righteousness and holiness or continue to let your thoughts run wild? The choice is yours.

Dear God,
Thank you for the reminder that you have given me the power to
make new the attitude of my mind. To put on my new self-created
to be like you in true righteousness and holiness. I pray that all
your children embrace the power you have given them to make
new the attitude of their minds. To put on the new self-created to
be like you in true righteousness and holiness. I ask this in your
son Jesus' name. Amen!

APRIL 10

Unfinished

ANCHOR SCRIPTURE: COLOSSIANS 4:17

And say to Archippus, "Be sure to carry out the ministry
the Lord gave you."

"Two things rob people of their peace of mind;
work unfinished and work not yet begun."
– *Anonymous*

Do you recall being given an assignment or chore as a child and not be allowed outdoors to play with your friends until the chore was completed? I think this was a great lesson learned in preparation for adult life. Finish the work you are assigned to receive your reward.

Each of us have our very own assignment to complete here on earth. Some take longer to complete than others. An assignment may even require repetition until the lesson is learned. However, we must complete the task given to us. You may get tired, weary, and want to quit or change course. That is our human nature.

It is easier to quit or change course however, doing that will leave you with unfinished business. If the lesson learned as a child is true, unfinished business yields no rewards. The parable of the talents (see Matthew 25:14-30) serves as a reminder to always be aware that in the end, we will answer to God for how we used the talents, gifts and blessings He gave to us. Today's verse is a reminder to be sure to carry out the ministry the Lord gave you. I encourage you today to focus on "your purpose not your problems."

--------------- **PRAYER FOR THE DAY:** ---------------

Dear God,
Thank you for the reminder to carry out the ministry you gave me. That although quitting may be easier, that is not what you called me to do. I pray that all your children heed the advice to carry out the ministry you gave to each of us. That we don't get weary or change course while working on the assignment. I ask this in your son Jesus' name. Amen!

Freedom from Fear

ANCHOR SCRIPTURE: ISAIAH 41:10

"Reminds us, don't be afraid, for I am with you. Don't be discouraged, for I am your God. I will strengthen you and help you. I will hold you up with my victorious right hand."

"Fear is the glue that keeps you stuck.
Faith is the solvent that sets you free."
- Shannon L. Alder

You may remember as a child, when your friends, older siblings or even parents wanted to insight fear they would say "the boogeyman will get you." Have any of you met the boogeyman? Boogeyman is defined as a common allusion to a mythical creature in many cultures used by adults to frighten children into good behavior.

Do you have any fears? The more I look at the short list of things that I fear, the more courage I must face them. I think this "fear thing" is designed to keep us on the run. Running away from our destiny, running from the truth, or running away from things that are not real. Fear is sometimes described as false expressions appearing real. Apparently fear keeps us from facing our reality. How many of you are allowing fear to keep you from confrontation, from living your purpose, from mending a friendship or relationship?

Today's verse is a reminder to not be afraid, for "I AM" is with you. Don't be discouraged, for I am your God. I will strengthen you and help you. I will hold you up with my victorious right hand. If God is with you, who can be against you? As you take time today to write down all your fears, I encourage you to reflect on this promise from God.

Dear God,
Thank you for the reminder to not be afraid, that you are with
me. To not be discouraged that you are my God. That you will
strengthen and help me. That you will hold me up with your
victorious right hand. I pray that all your children remember to
not be afraid, that you are always with them. To not be discour-
aged and that you will strengthen and help them. That you will
hold them up with your victorious right hand. That they walk by
faith and not by fear. I ask this in your son Jesus' name. Amen!

APRIL 12

The Blame Waltz

ANCHOR SCRIPTURE: GALATIANS 6:5

"For we are each responsible for our own conduct."

"Blaming others for your mess ups reflects on you"

It is hard to accept blame. It is easier to shift the blame to others or to something else, so you feel justified. It's a defense mechanism to keep you from having to deal honestly with your mistakes, mess ups, or the part you played in a situation. It is easy to fall prey to shifting blame from you to another. I am sure many of you are familiar with blaming the dog for eating your homework, some of you may be familiar with blaming your sibling for eating the last cookie in the pantry, or blaming the traffic for arriving late to an appointment. If I left home 30 minutes earlier, I would be on time. I am the first to say, guilty.

157

There comes a time in your life when you must take responsibility for your actions. A time to stop enabling others and yourself in what I call "the Blame Waltz" because you don't want to accept the role you played in the situation. I wonder, are we conditioned to shift blame? It appears it is natural and acceptable that the blame waltz is enabled rather than disabled. I wonder how different this world would be if instead of dancing "the blame waltz" we look to forgive and heal one another. Maturity teaches that no one wins playing the blame game aka dancing the blame waltz.

Today's verse is a reminder that we are each responsible for our own conduct. I encourage you today to pay attention to the times you make a conscious effort to forgive and heal rather than to point the finger. Let me know how you do with this exercise.

——————— **PRAYER FOR THE DAY:** ———————

Dear God,
Thank you for the reminder that we are each responsible for our conduct. I pray that all your children are reminded that they are each responsible for their own action. I ask this in your son Jesus' name. Amen

The Power of Prayer

ANCHOR SCRIPTURE: ROMANS 12:12

"Be joyful in hope, patient in affliction, faithful in prayer."

"Prayer does not change God, but it changes him who prays."
- Soren Kierkegaard

It is sometimes difficult to believe that your prayers are being heard. You continue to pray and the answers are delayed, you receive an answer you do not like or the answer may be a resounding no. I have learned to find peace with the answers I receive to my prayers. There is power in prayer.

Sure, disappointment will set in and it seems as a natural first reaction. However, when you look back at your life you see where the answer you received to your prayers were meant for your good. The plans for your life were already laid out for you. That what is destined to happen will happen. I also now know that each of us are designed and equipped to live an extraordinary life. That prayer still works.

Today's verse serves as a reminder to be joyful in hope, patient in affliction, and faithful in prayer. Keep asking, keep praying, never give up, and be thankful. God will never give up on you!

Dear God,
Thank you for the reminder that prayer still work. To be joyful in hope, patient in affliction, faithful in prayer. I pray that all your children believe that prayer still works. That they continue to pray without ceasing. That they remain joyful in hope, patient in affliction, and faithful in prayer. I ask this in your son Jesus' name. Amen!

APRIL 14

The Power of Appreciation

ANCHOR SCRIPTURE: PSALMS 92:1

"It is a good thing to give thanks unto the LORD, and to sing praises unto thy name, O most High"

Gratitude is a spiritual force that empowers you to scale higher.
You can't change to higher level without it.
- Bishop Dr. Julius Soyinka

I often wonder if lack of appreciation for what we have gets in the way of our growth. Is ingratitude causing stagnation in our life? It is not simple to remain laser focused on being grateful that you are alive, that you had a meal this morning, that you can see and read this message. It seems easier to focus on what you don't have despite all the many opportunities that blessed you the first hour of this day. Appreciation can be defined as to judge with heightened perception or understanding, be fully aware of; must see it to appreciate it; to recognize with gratitude. It was fascinating to be reminded that to appreciate is to "judge with a heightened perception or understanding." A friend shared a sermon with me a few years ago by Bishop Dr. Julius Soyinka. In this sermon, Bishop Dr. Soyinka shares many things about appreciation that I jotted down as wisdom points. I share three here:

1- A person who does not give thanks does not move forward no matter how much he prays. Yes, God expects you to show appreciation. He values our praise and thanksgiving and is motivated by it! When we judge with a heightened perception or understanding, it yields thanksgiving and appreciation instead of ingratitude and negativity.

2- Thank the people whom God has used to bring the blessings to you. We must not take the people God has surrounded us with for granted, but they must be greatly appreciated for the various roles they play in our lives. As human beings we must learn to appreciate and show gratitude to one another unconditionally. A heart of gratitude and appreciation does not harbor offenses and never seeks opportunity to take revenge for evil.

3-Your struggles will reduce, and your glory will show when you live a life of gratitude. Every time the devil reminds you of what God has not done, show him what God has already done.

Today's verse is a reminder - It is a good thing to give thanks unto the LORD, and to sing praises unto thy name, O most High. It is a reminder of the power of appreciation.

──────────────── PRAYER FOR THE DAY: ────────────────

Dear God,
Thank you for the reminder that it is a good thing to give thanks to you and to sing your praise. That there is power in appreciation. I pray that all your children remember that it is a good thing to give thanks to you and to sing your praise. That there is power in appreciation. I ask this in your son Jesus' name. Amen!

The Gift of Grace

ANCHOR SCRIPTURE: EPHESIANS 2:8

*"For it is by grace you have been saved, through faith--
and this is not from yourselves, it is the gift of God."*

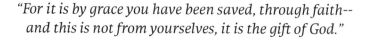

Life is measured in love and positive contributions
and moments of grace.
- Carly Fiorina

Why is grace given by some and never by others? Is it that some remember the grace given to them often and other forget? A lesson I learned in parenting is to allow grace to flow. I remember saying I told you so, in so many ways, so many times. I realized looking for opportunities to prove others wrong was not what was expected of me.

As I searched for answers to be a better parent and spouse, I was awakened to the grace that was given to me so often by God. That without the gift of grace, I would be nothing, accomplishing nothing. I awakened to the reality that the same grace extended to me; I must extend to others. I reflected that extending grace was akin to extending forgiveness. There is no maximum amount of grace that can be dished out. I remembered that no matter how hard it was to do, that we should encourage and build one another up (1 Thessalonians 5:11.) That grace is a gift that I must pass on.

Today's verse is a reminder that for it is by grace you have been saved, through faith--and this is not from yourselves, it is the gift of God. Next time you are tempted to withhold grace consider the grace offered to you and ask what would Jesus do? Would he withhold the gifting of grace?

Dear God,
Thank you for the reminder that it is by grace you have saved
me, through faith--and this is not from yourselves, it is the gift
of God. I pray that all your children remember that it is by grace
they have been saved, through faith--and this is not from them-
selves elves, it is the gift of God. That same gift given should be
passed on, not withheld. I ask this in your son Jesus' name. Amen!

APRIL 16

Your Focus

ANCHOR SCRIPTURE: PHILIPPIANS 4:8

"Finally, brothers and sisters, whatever is true, whatever
is noble, whatever is right, whatever is pure, whatever
is lovely, whatever is admirable--if anything is excellent
or praiseworthy--think about such things."

I always want to stay focused on who I am,
even as I'm discovering who I am.
- *Alicia Keys*

Do you find yourself spending too much time with your inner critic?
Believing all the lies it tells you. I have a friend who every time she
finishes a presentation she walks over and starts criticizing her
presentation. I spoke too long (even though she used the time allot-
ted); I didn't do a good job. The audience didn't seem to enjoy my talk

(even though she got a standing ovation); or I should have done something. I share with you; she has decades of experience speaking.

It seems while she is on stage, she can tame the negative thoughts that plague her often. However, once she departs the stage, she loses her focus. Despite all the evidence that she did well, she still convinces herself that she didn't do so well. You may have heard the saying, "what you focus on grows." I realize that her choice was to focus on the negative instead of the many positive things. That the positive ways others see her conflicted with the way she sees herself.

If we could only see ourselves the way God sees us. Perfectly and wonderfully made. Made to bear good and lasting fruit. That if we fix our thoughts on Jesus, we could see that we are all perfectly and wonderfully made. That the thoughts and things we focus on may not be serving us well. Today's verse is a reminder to think of such things, whatever is true, whatever is noble, whatever is right, whatever is pure, whatever is lovely, whatever is admirable and anything that is excellent or praiseworthy. To focus on your word that you are the way, the truth, and the life. Be honest with yourselves, are your troubles caused by your focus? I encourage you to consider your focus today.

─────────── **PRAYER FOR THE DAY:** ───────────

Dear God,
Thank you for the reminder to fix my thoughts on you. To seize dwelling on things that are not true. I pray that all your children fix their eyes on you. That they seize believing the lies of this world and they believe the truth you bring. That they remember that you are the way and the truth and the life. I ask this in your son Jesus' name. Amen!

Faith, Love, Grace, and Wisdom

ANCHOR SCRIPTURE: EPHESIANS 6:2

"Honor your father and mother", which is the first command-ment with a promise "so that it may go well with you and that you may enjoy long life on the earth."

"Mothers are faith, love, grace and wisdom in action"

Who is MOM to you? Is she the woman who spent many hours bringing you into this world? Is she the one who raised you even though she didn't bring you into this world? Is she your protector and anchor gone too soon; Is she the person praying for you when you couldn't pray for yourself. Is she the one who taught you the values on which you are anchored today? Is she the only person who stands by you even when you mess up royally? She is the woman you call Mom, Momma, Mama, Mother, Ma, and many other names.

She is the one person who showed you courage time and time again. Enduring hours of painful labor to deliver you into this world, to putting up with hurt to protect you, to shuttling you everywhere, to deciding to raise you with or without. There is so much that can be said about Mothers. To me being a MOM is faith, love, grace, and wisdom in action. Proverbs 1:8-9 says to listen to our Father's instructions and do not forsake your mother's teaching. They are a garland to grace your head and a chain to adorn your neck.

Today's verse is a reminder to honor your father and mother "which is the first commandment with a promise" so that it may go well with you and that you may enjoy long life on the earth." Here is a clear commandment with a promise. Many may find it difficult to adhere to this commandment. You decide if you want things to go well with you and enjoy a long life on the earth.

Dear God,
Thank you for the reminder to honor my father and mother so that it may go well with me. That I may enjoy long life on the earth. That your word, not a national holiday, dictates to honor your mother, to honor your parents. I pray that all your children honor their mothers and fathers not just on their special holiday but every day so that it may go well with them. That they may enjoy long life on earth. I ask this in Jesus' name. Amen!

APRIL 18

Redemption

ANCHOR SCRIPTURE: EPHESIANS 1:7

"In him we have redemption through his blood, the forgiveness of sins, in accordance with the riches of God's grace."

Redemption is not perfection. The redeemed
must realize their imperfections.
- John Piper

Merriam Webster defines redemption as to buy back, to get or win back; to free from what distresses or harms; to release from blame or debt; to free from the consequences of sin; to change for the better. I sum these definitions as redemption offers freedom and forgiveness from the guilt, curse, and the punishment mindset this world lays on us.

Walking around with negative thoughts, remaining prisoners to addictions, owning and living the lies of past experiences and inability to forgive yourself from errors and sins keeps one in the dark. I admire Bob Marley's song lyrics as they are filled with wisdom. I am thinking of one song in particular "Redemption Song." A line in this song goes like this, "Emancipate yourselves from mental slavery, none but ourselves can free our minds." Mental slavery does not have to be. We can all free ourselves from mental slavery. Seek the light, seek the truth, and set yourself free.

Today's verse reminds us we have redemption through Jesus' blood, the forgiveness of sins, in accordance with the riches of God's grace. If we are redeemed, our sins are forgiven. The riches of God's grace are ours, why insist to remain imprisoned? It seems each of us hold the key to our freedom. What is your choice?

———————————— **PRAYER FOR THE DAY:** ————————————

Dear God,
Thank you for the reminder that we are redeemed through the blood of your son Jesus. That through your grace my sins are forgiving. That I am free. I pray that all your children remember that they are redeemed through the blood of your son Jesus. That their sins can be forgiven through the riches of your grace. That they can be redeem. I ask this in your son Jesus' name. Amen!

17

Refocus and Rise

ANCHOR SCRIPTURE: COLOSSIANS 3:2-

*"Set your minds on things that are above,
not on things that are on earth"*

"You must learn a new way of thinking
before you can master a new way to be."
-Marianne Williamson

Have you ever been in situations where it seems that everything that could go wrong happens, aka Murphy's Law? You sometimes resort to think that you are "Bad lucky", that things will never change, that you will never win. Every time you make a leap forward, soon after there comes the setback. You then turn to lost faith and hope.

Plainly put when what we see as problems piling up is just a test. A test to see how we handle tribulations. First, let me clarify that no one is bad lucky. We are all blessed. We must own it! Setting one's thoughts on eternity, not on the temporary, helps to refocus. Refocus on the long-term plan and not look at every step taken to get to your destination. The reminder to be joyful in hope, patient in affliction, and faithful in prayer helps to get through.

During the test will you faint or become fervent? Will you do the work to past the test, take the test and have faith you will pass or will you give up and not stand through the test. I remind you of the story of Shadrach, Meshach, and Abednego (see the book of Daniel chapter 6.) Today's verse is a reminder to set your minds on things that are above, not on things that are on earth. I encourage you today to refocus and rise. Refocus on eternity and rise to your calling.

Dear God,
Thank you for the reminder to set my mind on the things that are above, not on things that are on earth. To be joyful in hope, patient in affliction, and faithful in prayer. I pray that all your children set their minds on the things that are above, not on things that are on earth. That they refocus on eternity and rise to your calling. I ask this in your son Jesus' name. Amen!

APRIL 20

Give What You Get

ANCHOR SCRIPTURE: MATTHEW 5:7

"Blessed are the merciful, for they will be shown mercy."

"The finer things in life cannot be purchased.
They can only be discovered through generosity."
- Jeff Goins

Have you ever driven up to the drive thru and were pleasantly surprised that the person in the car ahead paid for your meal? Or while driving on a toll road, the car ahead or someone paid for your toll. How did you feel? What did you do? Did you pay it forward or just said thank you Lord took your gift and carried on?

Do you feel that you give what you get? Do you focus more on receiving than giving? Let's take understanding and respect. Are you giving the same understanding and respect you seek? Answer honestly. I learned from a very young age that it is more blessed to give than to receive. You are blessed to receive however your blessing is augmented by giving.

Giving generously gives meaning to your life. You see that life is not about your possessions. You see that you are giving from what was given to you. Some people may feel that they worked hard for the things they have and give but none of this is possible without life. Who gives life? Today's verse is a reminder blessed are the merciful, for they will be shown mercy. God gives grace and mercy. It seems he gives to us to pay it forward or pass it on, not to keep for ourselves. Give what you get.

—————————— PRAYER FOR THE DAY: ——————————

Dear God,
Thank you for the reminder that blessed are the merciful, for they will be shown mercy. That you give me so much not to keep for myself but to pass on. I pray that all your children remember that blessed are the merciful, that you provide so much so they in turn can share with others. That they give what they get. I ask this in your son Jesus' name. Amen!

The Sweet Embrace of Life

ANCHOR SCRIPTURE: ECCLESIASTES 3:1

"There is a time for everything, and a season for every activity under the heavens."

Focus on the endless possibilities life is embracing you with at this very moment. Say YES to the next version of yourself

~ Roxana

Life can be sweet if we learn to embrace and not resist life's seasons. Can you imagine enduring six days of torrential rain, five days of snow-covered streets, the brisk wind that comes in the fall, and the scorching sun in the prime of summer or a perfect spring day? You may have experienced one or all of these during life's journey.

I recently had a conversation with a young woman near and dear to me about embracing her new shift in schedule. She was concerned about making it through the first overnight shift. I explained that this was just a new experience to embrace not resist. This new shift experience is meant to enjoy. That this schedule was temporary as the seasons of life. To enjoy the sweet embrace of life and the seasons that come with it.

Different experiences accompany different seasons. Embracing and enjoying the experience each season brings is one way to peace. Today's verse is a reminder that there is a time for everything, and a season for every activity under the heavens. I encourage you today to read Ecclesiastes 3 in its entirety. To embrace whatever season, you may be experiencing right now. Enjoy the sweet embrace of life.

Dear God,
Thank you for the reminder that there is a time for everything, and a season for every activity under the heavens. That embracing not resisting life brings peace. I pray that all your children remember that there is a time for everything, and a season for every activity under the heavens. That they find peace in embracing life. The life you created for them. I ask this in your son Jesus' name. Amen!

●

APRIL 22

The Gift of Laughter

ANCHOR SCRIPTURE: PSALM 126:2

"Our mouths were filled with laughter, our tongues with songs of joy. Then it was said among the nations, "The Lord has done great things for them."

That ability to laugh at myself takes me from being
a victim to being a victor.
- Annie Keys

When was the last time you laugh so hard your stomachache? Do you agree that laughter is good for your heart and soul? Do you notice when you are around "positive energy" you have no choice but to create moments of laughter and even shed a tear or two of joy and gratitude?

Sometimes life shows up and we forget that there is a remedy easily and freely available to all of us, the gift of laughter. Laughter is the best medicine. It can be triggered by a funny memory, by sharing with others, it can even be triggered by you. Why not laugh at your situation or yourself? My children laugh at me because I crack up at my own jokes. You don't need a crowd to laugh. Yep, laughing at yourself is okay in my book. I have learned not to take life so seriously and enjoy every moment no matter how tough things may be or get. I encourage to find a way to bring laughter into your day and into difficult situations.

Today's verse is a reminder to let your mouths be filled with laughter, your tongues with songs of joy. Then it was said among the nations, "The Lord has done great things for them."

PRAYER FOR THE DAY:

Dear God,
Thank you for the reminder to let my mouth be filled with laughter and my tongue with songs of joy. That you have done great things for me. I pray that all your children remember to fill their mouths with laughter and their tongues with songs of joy. That you have done great things for them. That they bring laughter into their day. I ask this in your son Jesus' name. Amen!

Resilience

ANCHOR SCRIPTURE: MATTHEW 7:24

"Therefore everyone who hears these words of mine and puts them into practice is like a wise man who built his house on the rock."

"The difference between the wise and the foolish is resilience."

I believe the difference between the wise and the foolish is resiliency. Resilience is defined in Merriam Webster as the capability of a strained body to recover its size and shape after deformation caused especially by compressive stress or the ability to recover from adjust easily to misfortune or change.

I recalled reading a daily devotion a couple years ago that briefly discussed what leads to human resilience. The devotion spoke about "a research by Psychologist Martin Seligman which suggests four main factors that lead to resilience: Emotional fitness: having the ability to amplify positive emotions like peace, gratitude, hope, or love while managing bitterness, sadness, or anger. Family fitness: having strong relationships by building trust and extending forgiveness. Social fitness: having good friendships and work relations by developing empathy and emotional intelligence. Spiritual fitness: having a sense of purpose by serving something greater than ourselves." (Excerpt from the Daily Journal, April 19, 2016.)

Consider these four fitness areas: Emotional, family, social and spiritual. How are you doing in these areas? What gives you strength to persevere, to be resilient? Today's verse reminds us that everyone who hears the words of the Lord and puts them into practice is like a wise man who built his house on the rock. It seems that listening and practicing God's word is key to resilience. What have you built your house on? Are you resilient?

Dear God,
Thank you for the reminder that everyone who hears your words
and puts them into practice is like a wise man who built his house
on the rock. Builds their house on the truth. I pray that all your
children remember to practice what they hear. To be wise and
build their house on a rock. That they are resilient and thrive.
I ask this in your son Jesus' name. Amen!

———————————————— ● ————————————————

APRIL 24

The Abundant Life

ANCHOR SCRIPTURE: JOHN 10:10

"The thief comes only to steal and kill and destroy;
I came that they may have life and have it abundantly."

———————————————

So much has been given to me; I have no time
to ponder over that, which has been denied.
- Helen Keller

———————————————

Have you ever been upset because you were denied something? You
threw a tantrum because you received an answer that was no or not
yet. Sometimes a delay or denial is part of your protection. You may
not be ready for the promotion, maybe the position is not part of the
plan for you, or maybe you just have more to learn before assuming
the position.

Instead of focusing on the denial or the "no", focus on the abundance you have, focus on all the "Yes" that surrounds you. Yes, you are living an abundant life. You have plenty, never believe you lack. I remind you that God has a plan for you, and you are exactly at the phase he intended. You have been given much!

Today's verse is a reminder that the thief comes only to steal and kill and destroy; I came that they may have life and have it abundantly. I encourage you to not give the thief a foothold in your life. Focus on the second part of this verse, I came that they may have life, and have it abundantly. Lack or abundance? The choice is yours.

—————————— **PRAYER FOR THE DAY:** ——————————

Dear God,
Thank you for the reminder that there is a thief that comes to steal and kill and destroy; that you sent your son that I may have life and have it abundantly. I pray that all your children do not give power to the thief who comes to steal and kill and destroy. That they remember you sent your son for them to have life and have it abundantly. I ask this in your son Jesus' name. Amen!

Judging

ANCHOR SCRIPTURE: JOHN 4:11-12

"Brothers and sisters do not slander one another. Anyone who speaks against a brother or sister or judges them speaks against the law and judges it. When you judge the law, you are not keeping it, but sitting in judgment on it. There is only one Lawgiver and Judge, the one who is able to save and destroy. But you—who are you to judge your neighbor?"

"You judge someone not when you assess their position, but when you dismiss them as a person"
- Pastor J.D. Greer

Do you believe it is easy to judge someone else? I always wonder what it would be like to walk in the shoes of a homeless person. To truly know of their stories. I have a friend that shares her story of a period where her family was homeless. It is amazing to hear the details of how she survived and how many strangers judged her. Without knowing her story, she was judged.

How many times have you judged someone or their behavior and later felt horrible because you found out what you unfairly judge had a story behind it? I recalled a devotional that was shared with me by Pastor J.D. Greear a few years ago that made two critical points about judging: 1- "You have to love the person more than you love your position on a particular issue. 2- Don't judge others by withholding the truth. But don't judge them by speaking the truth without grace.

Today's verse is a reminder that anyone who speaks against a brother or sister or judges them speaks against the law and judges it. When you judge the law, you are not keeping it, but sitting in judgment on it. There is only one Lawgiver and Judge, the one who can save and destroy. But you—who are you to judge your neighbor? Today I encourage you to speak the truth in love and grace.

—————————————— **PRAYER FOR THE DAY:** ——————————————

Dear God,
Thank you for the reminder to carry out the ministry you gave me. That although quitting may be easier, that is not what you called me to do. I pray that all your children heed the advice to carry out the ministry you gave to each of us. That we don't get weary or change course while working on the assignment. I ask this in your son Jesus' name. Amen!

●

APRIL 26

Purity of Motives

ANCHOR SCRIPTURE: PSALM 139:23-24

"Search me, God, and know my heart; test me and know my anxious thoughts. See if there is any offensive way in me and lead me in the way everlasting."

Many of our deepest motives come, not from an adult logic of how things work in the world, but out of something that is frozen from childhood.
- Kazuo Ishiguro

Do you feel you work hard to impress others, pretend to be whom you are not simply to be liked by others or make decisions that are not aligned with your values to gain favor? Relationships are complicated. I wonder if authenticity is the missing link. Is it that our motives lack purity?

Image building relationship showing up always authentically you and with pure motives. No mask, no imitation, no lies, no pretense. The weight that would be lifted off your shoulder. Whew! Impure motives and lack of authenticity causes unnecessary complication when building relationships, personal, business and even our relationship with God.

When was the last time you evaluated the purity of your motives when engaged in a relationship? No need to pretend to be someone else as a sacrifice to build a relationship. Be who you are, love who you are and remove the mask. Don't cheat the world of the value you offer. Today's verse is a reminder to seek the Lord always. Ask, search me, God, and know my heart; test me and know my anxious thoughts. See if there is any offensive way in me and lead me in the way everlasting. Check the purity of your motives.

—————————— **PRAYER FOR THE DAY:** ——————————

Dear God,
Thank you for the reminder to seek you in all I do. You know my heart and my anxious thoughts. Purify my heart. I pray that all your children seek you in all they do. Remove all offensive ways in them and lead them in the way everlasting. Purify their hearts. I ask this in your son Jesus' name. Amen!

Doing Good

ANCHOR SCRIPTURE: ROMANS 2:7

"To those who by perseverance in doing good seek for glory and honor and immortality, eternal life"

I alone cannot change the world, but I can cast a stone
across the water to create many ripples
- Mother Theresa

As leaders we must never seize doing good. Our tribe is always watching. Our character determines their character. Doing good all the time is difficult. Temptation always lurks. We must however think of the legacy we will leave. Pause and think before you act. It just takes one negative action to weaken our character which in turn can also weaken the character of those in our tribe. Doing good even when you don't feel like it, strengthens you and your tribe.

Some of you may say, well I am always doing good, why can't "they" also do their part?

Luke 6 reminds us "But I say to you who hear, love your enemies, do good to those who hate you, bless those who curse you, pray for those who mistreat you. (I remind you that what others do is none of your business. What you do is what counts...Yep, sharing an intimate moment here. Yikes)

Today's verse is a reminder to perseverance in doing good seek God's glory, honor, and immortality, seek eternal life. What do you say, will you be the ripple starter? Never render evil for evil but do good. There is power in doing good. The ripple starts with you.

Dear God,
Thank you for the reminder to persevere in doing good. Seek your glory, your honor and eternal life. I pray that all your children do not tire in doing good. That they seek your honor, glory, and focus on eternity. That they embrace their power to start the ripple. I ask this in your son Jesus' name. Amen!

APRIL 28

A New Thing

ANCHOR SCRIPTURE: ISAIAH 43:18-19

"Forget the former things; do not dwell on the past. See, I am doing a new thing! Now it springs up; do you not perceive it? I am making a way in the wilderness and streams in the wasteland."

A new day: Be open enough to see opporunities. Be wise enough to be grateful. Be courageous enough to be happy.
- Steve

Do you embrace the blessing of a new day or a new thing? It is easy to mindlessly merge today and yesterday, treating them like run-on sentences. Today is not yesterday nor is it tomorrow. It is brand new, never seen before and will never return. Have you ever tried starting each day on a new page? Deciding to write a new and better story each day instead of bringing yesterday's story with you today.

You are given the opportunity every day to start new. Do you take advantage of this unique opportunity? Shift your mind to today, be present in the now! What happened yesterday is gone. Nothing you can change about yesterday but plenty good you can do today. What do you say about starting today fresh, create a new thing today!

Today's scripture reminds us to forget the former things; do not dwell on the past. See, I am doing a new thing! Now it springs up; do you not perceive it? I am making a way in the wilderness and streams in the wasteland. Write your best story today. The now is all that is promised.

--------------------- PRAYER FOR THE DAY: ---------------------

Dear God,
Thank you for the reminder to remain in the now, to embrace the opportunity to start new. To forget the former things; and do not dwell on the past. That you are doing a new thing. I pray that all your children forget the former things and do not dwell on the past. That they see that you are doing a new thing! That they embrace the opportunity to start a new thing. To start fresh each day. I ask this in your son Jesus' name. Amen!

Your Best Version!

ANCHOR SCRIPTURE: 2 TIMOTHY 2:15

"Do your best to present yourself to God as one approved,
a worker who has no need to be ashamed, rightly handling
the word of truth."

Excellence is when who you are equals the best of who you can be.

- Peng Joon

Are you the best version of yourself? Is conceit, selfishness, and lack of humility, the need to be always right or always in control dimming your best self? Each day, you are presented with the opportunity to create a better you. Are you intentionally working on becoming your best version each day? Can you imagine what the best version of you looks like? Some may say I have arrived; some may know they are a work in progress.

Quality Improvement is an intricate part of the growth process. Sidney Poitier is quoted as saying, I always wanted to be someone better the next day than I was the day before. Today's verse is a reminder to do your best to present yourself to God as one approved, a worker who has no need to be ashamed, rightly handling the word of truth. I encourage you to be the best you today and even better tomorrow.

Dear God,
Thank you for the reminder to continue to improve each day. To do my best to present as one approved by God. I am a work in progress. I pray that all your children strive to be someone better each new day. That they do their best to present as one approved by God, a worker who has no need to be ashamed, rightly handling the word of truth. I ask this in your son Jesus' name. Amen!

●

APRIL 30

In the Midst of Tragedy

ANCHOR SCRIPTURE: JOHN 11:35

"Jesus wept."

"There is a saying in Tibetan, 'Tragedy should be utilized as a source of strength.' No matter what sort of difficulties, how painful experience is, if we lose our hope, that's our real disaster."
- Dalai Lama

Please join me today in praying for our sisters and brothers in Guatemala. May they find comfort amid tragedy and remember these words in John 11:35: Jesus wept.

I stumbled across this message written by Debbie McDaniel-Fresh Day Ahead and decided to share her message today.

"Sometimes in this crazy, mixed up world, when our hearts are grieving and we've suffered devastating blows, when loss feels too deep, and the battle seems fierce, the most comforting words of all are just these 2: "Jesus wept." John 11:35. The shortest verse in the Bible, yet one that holds such great power. That allows us to see straight into the very heart of our God whose heart beats for us. Into the compassion of our Savior who is acquainted with grief and understands deep sorrow. Into the very Spirit of God who covers us, is with us constantly, and breathes life into our innermost being. He wept. He hurt. He grieved. He experienced loss. He felt compassion. He understood this path of suffering."

It is difficult to understand why tragedy occurs in our world. Amid confusion, sorrow, and tragedy may it bring comfort that Jesus was acquainted with grief and understands deep sorrow, that he is present amid tragedy. May hope be restored to our sisters and brothers in knowing that God still reigns

---

PRAYER FOR THE DAY:

Dear God,
I pray that hope is restored in our brothers and sisters amid this tragedy they face today. Thank you for the reminder that you are acquainted with grief and understand deep sorrow. That you still reign. I pray that all your children remember that you are acquainted with grief and understand deep sorrow. That in knowing you still reign, hope is restored. I ask this in your son Jesus' name. Amen.

Reflections

May

Honesty, the Best Policy

ANCHOR SCRIPTURE: COLOSSIANS 3:9

*"Do not lie to each other, since you have taken off
your old self with its practices."*

Honesty is the first chapter in the book of wisdom. - Thomas Jefferson
I recently conversed with a young adult that struggled with telling the
truth to their parent. This young adult expressed their preference of
telling a lie rather than the truth in fear of the consequences. (I recall
been in a similar situation.) I thought out loud of a lesson learned, if
it is truth, why fear. The truth is the truth. We discussed how telling
an untruth would lead to a tangled web that could last decades. Being
transparent and telling the truth with love is what matters most. It
matters being honest with yourself and others as it shows maturity.

Sure, you have free will to tell lies and no one can tell you what to
choose. You can be taught the truth and you ultimately decide what
you do with it. Does it make sense to lie to make yourself look good
or pretend to be someone you think someone else wants you to be?
What is done in the dark will come to light.

Today's verse is a reminder to not lie to each other, since you have
taken off your old self with its practices. I recalled the quote attributed
to Benjamin Franklin, "Honesty is the best policy." Do you believe
honesty is the best policy? Will your legacy be one of honesty? Be
honest with yourself and the rest will come easy.

Dear God,
Thank you for the reminder that honesty is the best policy. To not lie to each other. I pray that all your children be honest with themselves and others. That they remember, honesty is the best policy. I ask this in your son Jesus' name. Amen!

●

MAY 2

Loyalty

ANCHOR SCRIPTURE: PROVERBS 3:3

"Let love and faithfulness never leave you; bind them around your neck, write them on the tablet of your heart."

The foundation stones for a balanced success are honesty, character, integrity, faith, love, and loyalty.
-Zig Ziglar

Friendships and relationships are tested daily. When you enter a relationship do you enter with the hope that the other person would be trustworthy, faithful, and loyal? If you have doubts about someone's ability to be loyal and faithful or you have evidence that their character is not one that demonstrates loyalty yet, would you enter the relationship?

A few synonyms of loyalty include allegiance, fidelity, fealty, and commitment. I sometimes wonder, has the world become so self-absorbed that loyalty no longer matters? It is funny to note that some expect loyalty and never intend to reciprocate the loyalty. It may exist for a while and at the first opportunity to exit, they don't have their way, or another shinier object shows up, there goes the loyalty.

Loyalty requires undivided attention, focus and the ability to not allow anything or anyone (even behaviors) to stray you away. I think of how our level of loyalty and faithfulness forms our character. If you are loyal, then you can be faithful. A person who is loyal is one in whom complete confidence may be placed. That no matter what, they will never leave you or forsake you.

Today's verse serves as a reminder to let love and faithfulness never leave you; bind them around your neck, write them on the tablet of your heart. Wow, this reminder and instructions are clear, bind love and faithfulness around our neck and write this on the tablets of our hearts. Mind your character not that of others.

———————————— PRAYER FOR THE DAY: ————————————

Dear God,
Thank you for the reminder that your loyalty to me is real. That you will never abandon me, seize your love and faithfulness towards me. I pray that all your children heed your advice to let love and faithfulness never leave them. To bind them around their necks and write them on the tablets of their heart. That they remember these instructions are to build their character. I ask this in your son Jesus' name. Amen!

Maturation

ANCHOR SCRIPTURE: HOSEA 14:4

"I will heal their waywardness and love them freely,
for my anger has turned away from them."

Some people see scars, and it is wounding they remember.
To me they are proof of the fact that there is healing.
-Linda Hogan

Have you had a wound that tarried in healing? It is interesting the intricate process that occurs for the skin to repair itself from injury, to complete heal. The healing process is very delicate and perplexed a times and many factors could slow or interrupt the healing process. The final step of the healing process is described as maturation or remodeling.

It is interesting to compare the way our skin heals and the way our heart and soul heal. It is a process. Like the healing of the skin, the complexity of your life can determine the length of time it takes for your heart and soul to heal. For the maturation or remodeling to occur. Maturation will eventually occur, sometimes not as rapidly as we would like it to happen.

Today's verse serves as a reminder that the Lord will heal your waywardness and love you freely, for his anger has turned away. Note, the verse did not say "may" heal it says l "will" heal. There is hope, fret not, as God's healing power shall make you whole. I encourage you to read Hosea 14 in its entirety today.

Dear God,
Thank you for the reminder that you will heal my waywardness
and love me freely. That your anger has turned away. I pray that
all your children believe that you will heal their waywardness
and love them freely. That your anger has turned away. That
they believe your healing power shall make them whole. I ask
this in your son Jesus' name. Amen!

MAY 4

Teamwork

ANCHOR SCRIPTURE: ECCLESIASTES 4:9-10

"Two are better than one because they have a good return for
their labor: If either of them falls down; one can help the other
up. But pity anyone who falls and has no one to help them up."

Talent wins games, but teamwork and intelligence
wins championships.
- Michael Jordan

Did you watch the final games of hockey and basketball this past
season? Are you watching the FIFA World Cup games? There are
many leadership lessons to learn from team sports. It is interesting to
note, how each game, the winning team is assigned a most valuable
player either because they scored the most point in the game, worked
hardest on defense or offense or demonstrated true leadership

throughout that one game. I wonder if assigning an MVP diminishes the importance of the role the entire team played in the win. Is this conditioning our minds to be the one outstanding player and forget that without the other players there would be no reward of the championship?

In team sports, is it that each player is assigned a role on the team based on their strengths for the team to win not just one game but to win the championship? Let's face it, every superstar will have a bad day. And even when they have a bad day, the team can still win. I wonder if we treated our family, customers, neighbors, and others as teammates, how could each of us individually change this world?

How about standing in the gap when they have bad days or covering for them when they are absent. If we lived as one nucleus, one team, can you imagine the harmony that could exist in this world? Can you imagine the championships that would be won?

Today's verse reminds us that two are better than one because they have a good return for their labor: If either of them falls; one can help the other up. But pity anyone who falls and has no one to help them up. I encourage you to read Ecclesiastes 4 in its entirety.

———————————— PRAYER FOR THE DAY: ————————————

Dear God,
Thank you for the reminder that teamwork is essential as when one falls; one can help the other up. I pray that all your children learn the value of teamwork. That if either of them falls; one can help the other up. I ask this in Jesus' name. Amen

Traveling Mercies

ANCHOR SCRIPTURE: PSALM 71:6

"From birth I have relied on you; you brought me forth from my mother's womb."

Twenty years from now you will be more disappointed by the things that you didn't do than by the ones you did do, so throw off the bowlines, sail away from safe harbor, catch the trade winds in your sails. Explore, Dream, Discover.

- Mark Twain

I recalled browsing through a book entitled: Traveling Mercies: Some Thoughts on Faith written by Anne Lamott (this is on my list of books to read.) As I flipped through the book, a certain paragraph jumped out at me. I wrote it down for safe keeping as it resonated as true and tried advice. A keeper.

I share Anne Lamott's words with you today: "It's funny: I always imagined when I was a kid that adults had some kind of inner toolbox full of shiny tools: the saw of discernment, the hammer of wisdom, the sandpaper of patience. But then when I grew up I found that life handed you these rusty bent old tools -- friendships, prayer, conscience, honesty -- and said 'do the best you can with these, they will have to do'. And mostly, against all odds, they do."

Friendships, prayer, conscience, and honesty are tools that we all can access to make it through each day. No matter what comes our way, these are true and tried tools that no matter how old and rusty they get, they still work. These tools give hope. As psalm 71 says; "as for me, I will always have hope; I will praise you more and more". These tools are gifts that keep on giving. Friendships that never die, no matter the time that passes. Prayers that sustain in good times and bad. Conscience and honesty keep us present and true.

As you journey through life, may traveling mercies accompany you. May you reach for tools in your "inner toolbox". Do the best you can with them, even if they are rusty, they still work. Today's verse is a reminder from birth I have relied on you; you brought me forth from my mother's womb.

----------------- **PRAYER FOR THE DAY:** -----------------

Dear God,
Thank you for the reminder of the mercies you bring through this journey called life. I pray that all your children utilize the tools you give and see the many mercies you bring through their journey called life. The traveling mercies. I ask this in Jesus' name. Amen!

Titles

ANCHOR SCRIPTURE: JONAH 2:8

*"Those who pay regard to vain idols forsake
their hope of steadfast love."*

A boss loves power; a leader loves people.
- Amit Kalantri

Are you defined or diminished by your job title, position, or financial status? What if the titles placed next to your name were permanently removed? You are no longer defined by what you do or the position you hold. Instead you are known only by the name given to you. You are accepted for who you are. Rather than a title, you represent your true purpose. T.F. Hodge said, it is more substantial to represent a purpose rather than just a title.

Imagine leading others without a title. Just your name and your purpose. Could you check your ego and lead with no ceremonial titles or expectations that others treat you in a ceremonial manner? No need to idolize yourself or another. (This begs the reminder that there is a fine line between admiration and idolization.) To lead as yourself rather than leading from the expectations of others or the expectations that come with a title. Can you imagine the freedom you would experience; the many lives you could impact?

The pressures of titles and positions are real. It seems focusing on purpose in humility rather than rank produces much more impact. Today's verse is a reminder that those who pay regard to vain idols forsake their hope of steadfast love. I encourage you to read Jonah 2 in its entirety.

Dear God,
Thank you for the reminder that to pay attention to vain idols forsake their hope of steadfast love. I pray that all your children remember that those who pay regard to vain idols forsake their hope of steadfast love. That they are freed from all idols including titles. I ask this in your son Jesus' name. Amen!

MAY 7

Assumptions

ANCHOR SCRIPTURE: PROVERBS 18:13

"Spouting off before listening to the facts is both shameful and foolish."

Assumptions are the termites of relationships.
- Henry Winkler

Merriam Webster defines assumptions as a taking on to or upon oneself; an assuming that something is true. Have you ever assumed about something that proved to be false or detrimental to someone? How did you feel after finding out the truth? I wonder why, making assumptions seems easier than seeking the truth.

Are you in a conflict right now because you made assumptions? How many of you now know that the assumptions you made were false but are afraid to admit your wrong and the detriment you caused another? Let's face it, being misunderstood or to misunderstand is difficult. Maturity requires having the courage to admit that you misunderstood, made assumptions, and clarifying assumptions when given the opportunity.

As the leader of your tribe, it seems important to provide opportunities to foster an environment that reduces misunderstandings and does not feed or water assumptions. This applies to leading at work, in your community and in your family. It is said that "the worst distance between two people is misunderstanding" and I add, "The worst distance between two people is "assuming"

Today's scripture is a reminder that spouting off before listening to the facts is both shameful and foolish. I encourage you to read Proverbs 18, mind your assumptions and resolve your misunderstandings.

—————————— **PRAYER FOR THE DAY:** ——————————

Dear God,
Thank you for the reminder that spouting off before listening to the facts is both shameful and foolish. I pray that all your children listen to the facts before spouting off. That they starve assumptions and resolve misunderstanding. I ask this in Jesus' name. Amen!

MAY 8

What you focus on grows

ANCHOR SCRIPTURE: PROVERBS 23:7

"For as he thinks in his heart, so is he..."

What you focus on grows, what you think about expands,
and what you dwell upon determines your destiny.
-Robin Sharma

Our thoughts, the information we allow into our heart, eyes and ears is very important. It seems easy to lose focus on how thoughts that are planted by others hijack our very own thoughts and focus. Have you heard the saying what you focus on grows or expands? If one waters external thoughts, messages and ideas that is what will grow. We all have free will and chose which thoughts to dwell on.

Yes, the choice is yours. The type of person you become in this life may be determined by what you choose to think about and dwell on. Look at those that surround you daily; are these people who are unhappy, unfulfilled, depressed, pessimistic, and negative towards all or always has a "bad luck" story? Do you believe they are choosing to focus on the negative side of life or like Joyce Meyers dubbed, they choose "Stinking thinking?" On the flip side are the people that surround you always happy, fulfilled, dwelling on the positive, have positive and uplifting words to share with you and intentionally chose to think positive and guard what they allow into their minds and thoughts?

I heard someone say a while back, one must guard their" thought life." I guess the difference between a positive and negative person is their "thought life." I wonder if one pays closer attention to guarding their "thought life" how many illnesses could be cured. Proverbs 23:7 reminds us that for as he thinks in his heart, so is he. I encourage you today to check in on your "thought life" and recognize what you are watering. Are you growing flowers or weeds? "Our way of thinking determines good or bad outcomes."

──────────── **PRAYER FOR THE DAY:** ────────────

Dear God,
Thank you for the reminder to check my thought life. That as I think in my heart, so am I. I pray that all your children remember that as they think in their heart, so they are. That they take time out to check-in on their "thought life" and remove the weeds. That they make room for the flowers you long for them to grow. I ask this in your son Jesus' name. AMEN!

──────────────── ● ────────────────

MAY 9

Unplugged

ANCHOR SCRIPTURE: JOHN 15:5

"Yes, I am the vine; you are the branches. Those who remain in me, and I in them, will produce much fruit. For apart from me you can do nothing."

───────────────────

"Sometimes we need to disconnect in order to reconnect with what matters."

───────────────────

Unplug is sometimes defined as to take a plug out of or to remove an obstruction from. Sometimes life requires you to unplug to realize that you weren't properly connected. That something or someone may have been obstructing your connection.

Think about it, quiet time, vacation, retreats, meditations provide the space for you to realign with self, to pause for a moment aka unplug, then reconnect. How do you feel when you intentionally take the time to recharge? To consciously remove things that may have been obstructing your connection or to simply recharge.

It is impossible to continue to produce good fruit without checking your connections. It is in the manufacturers' manual. Just like your car, most manufactures require that you bring your car in for a 30/60/90K mile check-up to ensure efficient and effective operation of your vehicle. As leaders, are you checking your connections to continue to produce good fruit?

Today's scripture serves as a reminder.... Yes, I am the vine; you are the branches. Those who remain in me, and I in them, will produce much fruit. For apart from me you can do nothing. "Almost everything will work again if you unplug it for a few minutes, including you!"

───────────── PRAYER FOR THE DAY: ─────────────

Dear God,
Thank you for the reminder to check-up on my connections to you. That you are the vine; and I am the branch. I pray that all your children check-in on their connection to you. That they remember that you are the vine, and they are the branches. Those who remain in you and you in them, will (not may) produce much fruit. For apart from you, they can do nothing. I ask this in your son Jesus' name. Amen!

Conflict in Compromise

ANCHOR SCRIPTURE: 2 TIMOTHY 2:4

"No soldier gets entangled in civilian pursuits, since his aim is to please the one who enlisted him."

Conflict cannot survive without your participation.
-Wayne Dyer

I recently uncovered an old article I kept on conflict management written in Mediate.com by Dale Eilerman. The article was title Agree to Disagree- The Use of Compromise in Conflict Management. The article discussed that although compromise may produce an agreement, compromise does not always resolve problems that contain underlying interpersonal or organizational conflicts. This is because compromise is frequently a "settled" resolution to a problem and not typically the optimal solution sought by either party.

Compromise may generate a functional or material solution but not resolve emotional or behavioral issues associated with the disagreement. As a result, lingering anger, resentment, or dissatisfaction may trigger subsequent conflicts. History provides many examples of this. Have you ever experienced conflict in compromising? Is the compromise causing anger, resentment, regret, dissatisfaction to plague your existence?

Today's verse is a reminder that no soldier gets entangled in civilian pursuits, since his aim is to please the one who enlisted him. Facing the remnants of hurt and doing the work to resolve and repair the hurt is necessary for growth to occur. It also may be the best gift you could give to your spirit, heart, and soul. No need to remain entangled in civilian pursuit. I encourage you to read 2nd Timothy 2 in its entirety.

Dear God,
Thank you for the reminder that no soldier gets entangled in
civilian pursuits, since the aim is to please the one who enlisted
me. Allowing conflicts and compromise to plague my existence
does no good. I pray that all your children remember that no
soldier gets entangled in civilian pursuits. That they remember
the aim is to please the one who enlisted him or her. I ask this in
your son Jesus' name. Amen!

MAY 11

Short Sighted

ANCHOR SCRIPTURE: 2 PETER 1:9

"For he who lacks these things is short sighted, even to blind-
ness, and has forgotten that he was cleansed from his old sins."

"A short-sighted vision leads to missed blessings"

Have you ever experienced blurred vision? Sometimes you recognized the change or someone else may have brought to your attention that you are squinting. This change may have caused you to now wear spectacles to see clearly.

A blurred vision doesn't always apply to sight. It could also apply to the vision you have for your life. You may have given up on your studies, careers, family or dreams due to exhaustion, lack of patience and lack of belief in your vision. "Life showed up" and blurred your vision. You may have become weary, chosen a shorter route to arrive faster, or just lost the faith necessary to cross the finish line. Completing the task before you just seemed impossible.

It is easy to forget that all we need to finish the race is already within us. The daily grind, the shiny objects and many other distractions blur our vision. Sometimes I think it is good to have the things that are nearby blurry and solely focus on the things that are far away, the things that you yet cannot see or feel. This may keep many in the race. Today's verse is a reminder that for he who lacks these things is short sighted, even to blindness, and has forgotten that he was cleansed from his old sins. If you read 2 Peter 1, it seems to say that many fall preys to blindness in the present moment, shortsightedness about the future, and forgetfulness of God's grace in the past. Learning to grow in grace may be the missing piece. I encourage you to read 2 Peter 1 in its' entity.

———————————— PRAYER FOR THE DAY: ————————————

Dear God,
Thank you for the reminder of the things that I must not lack. For he who lacks these things mentioned in 2 Peter 1 is short sighted, even to blindness, and has forgotten that he was cleansed from his old sins. I pray that all your children do not become short sighted, blind, or forget that you have cleansed them from their old sins. I ask this in your son Jesus' name. Amen!

People Pleasing

ANCHOR SCRIPTURE: GALATIANS 1:10

"Am I now trying to win the approval of human beings, or of God? Or am I trying to please people? If I were still trying to please people, I would not be a servant of Christ."

The key to failure is trying to please everybody.
- Bill Cosby

Are you willing to admit that you are or were a people pleaser? I will go first. I guarantee that from the time you opened your eyes this morning, you have many to please. If you are being supervised, you are aiming to please your supervisor; if you work in the service industry, you have customers to please; if you are a spouse or parent, you have your family to please; if you are a leader, you have your tribe to please. This is just a small drop in the bucket of all the people on the list to please. We are always on task to please someone.

Think about it, you may clean up your house or space for guest but not for yourself. You may do extra for others but not for yourself. You work all day, run home to take the children to activities, then head home to cook, then have nothing left for you. I am by no means saying that this is wrong. I am saying that all the people pleasing that you are on task to do from dawn to dust will eventually wear you out and will ruin your chances at succeeding to please everyone.

Scripture shares this, "You are worried and upset about many things, but few things are needed—or indeed only one." (Luke 10:41-42) The fastest way to forget who you are is to focus on who others say you are. Beware of those you aim to please especially those who idolize or criticize you as they may contribute to your demise. Are you choosing what is better? Are you prioritizing the "one" to please? The questions in today's verse (Am I now trying to win the approval of human beings, or of God? Or am I trying to please people?), serve as a reminder that if I were still trying to please people, I would not be a servant of Christ.

PRAYER FOR THE DAY:

Dear God,
Thank you for the reminder that pleasing people prevents me from serving you. I pray that all your children yield this warning that if they are still trying to please people, they would not be your servants. I ask this in your son Jesus' name. Amen!

MAY 13

Pay It Forward

ANCHOR SCRIPTURE: GALATIANS 6:9

"Let us not become weary in doing good, for at the proper time we will reap a harvest if we do not give up."

"Our actions are like ships which we may watch set out to sea, and not know when or with what cargo they will return to port."
- Iris Murdoch

Do you wake up each morning looking for multiple opportunities to do good? To share your blessing with others. Blessing others doesn't require much. You could share a smile, a "good morning", a positive word, a brief phone call to say hello or tell someone "I love you" or share a heart to heart hug to make someone's day. No money required to pay these acts of kindness forward.

Benjamin Franklin modeled "paying it forward" in a letter to Benjamin Webb in 1784. He closed the letter stating this: "This is a trick of mine for doing a deal of good with a little money. I am not rich enough to afford much in good works, and so am obliged to be cunning and make the most of little." Can you think of ways you do much with the little you have or the little you do with the much you have? James 1 reminds us to not be deceived, that every good and perfect gift is from above, coming down from the Father of the heavenly lights, who does not change like shifting shadows.

Today's verse is a reminder to let us not become weary in doing good, for at the proper time we will reap a harvest if we do not give up. No matter what transpired in the past, never allow a single or multiple negative event get in the way of remembering that you are blessed to be a blessing. Remain relentless in doing good and paying your blessings forward. You will soon reap a harvest!

───────────────── PRAYER FOR THE DAY: ─────────────────

Dear God,
Thank you for the reminder to always pay your blessings forward. To not become weary in doing good, for at the proper time we will reap a harvest if we do not give up. I pray that all your children pay their blessings forward. That they not become weary in doing good, for at the proper time, they will reap a harvest if they do not give up. I ask this in Jesus' name. Amen!

Seek Wisdom

ANCHOR SCRIPTURE: PROVERBS 4:6

*"Do not forsake wisdom, and she will protect you;
love her, and she will watch over you."*

Don't gain the world and lose your soul; wisdom is better
than silver or gold.
- Bob Marley

Can you recall the many times your parents repeated advice that you
did not follow or just didn't understand? You may have decided that it
made no sense because you had no understanding, or you consciously
made the choice to disobey. As you matured, you now recall the
advice and awakened to the wisdom that was shared.

In conversation with a dear friend about the importance of wisdom
and understanding he shared this excerpt from one of his readings
for me to consider (not sure of the source and profound); "Why would
God give wisdom and wait to give understanding? Sometimes we're
just not ready to handle it, sometimes we aren't prepared to use it, and
sometimes we're not mature enough. Whenever the Lord chooses
to give us an understanding is the best time. We must wait and be
patient." I thought wow, sound learning.

Understanding is the ability to perceive and discern a situation to
apply wisdom. As you get wisdom, understanding follows. Lacking
understanding leads you to the wilderness. Lack of wisdom yields
defeat, a life filled with bad decisions, and focused solely on the
problem. Wisdom provides the ability to see beyond the problem.
Wisdom helps you cope.

Today's verse is a reminder, do not forsake wisdom, and she will protect you; love her, and she will watch over you. I encourage you to read Proverbs 4 in its entirety. Get wisdom at any cost!

——————————— PRAYER FOR THE DAY: ———————————

Dear God,
Thank you for the reminder to not forsake wisdom, and she will protect me; love her, and she will watch over me. I pray that all your children do not forsake wisdom. That they remember wisdom will protect and watch over them. I ask this in Jesus' name. Amen!

MAY 15

Condemnation

ANCHOR SCRIPTURE: ROMANS 8:1

"Therefore, there is now no condemnation for those who are in Christ Jesus."

Don't be in a hurry to condemn because he doesn't do what you do or think as you think or as fast. There was a time when you didn't know what you know today.
-Malcolm X

Are you unconsciously or consciously condemning yourself and/ or others? Merriam Webster defines condemn as declare to be reprehensible, wrong, or evil usually after weighing evidence and without reservation. Condemnation is the act of judicially. Condemnation of ourselves and others seems to surface as the root of our internal struggles and problems in general.

I think about how the law was created to direct us on the right path. To guide us to the way and the truth and the life we should live. To admonish not convict or condemn us. Sometimes world views and that of the flesh set, redirect, or paralyzes our agenda. These views often persecute us. I remember a wise man shared with me (in his own words) to beware of condemnation as it is rarely detected. Look for it and it may be the key to your freedom. It is funny how you are taught so much and as you make the choice to live in truth or mature enough to understand the lesson, then the teachings magically return to your remembrance. Thank you, Dad.

Psalm 34 is a "go to" psalm for me and reminds us that affliction will slay the wicked, and those who hate the righteous will be condemned. The Lord redeems the life of his servants; none of those who take refuge in him will be condemned (v21-22.) Today's verse is a reminder that there is now no condemnation for those who are in Christ Jesus. Compassion instead of condemnation changes everything. Wishing you freedom from condemnation.

PRAYER FOR THE DAY:

Dear God,
Thank you for the reminder that there is now no condemnation for those who are in Christ Jesus. I pray that all your children remember that your laws were not created to condemn or convict. It is direction to the way and the truth and the life to live. That there is now no condemnation for those who are in Christ Jesus. I ask this in your son Jesus' name. Amen!

The Vicious Cycle of Greener

ANCHOR SCRIPTURE: PHILIPPIANS 4:11-13

"I am not saying this because I am in need, for I have learned to be content whatever the circumstances. I know what it is to be in need, and I know what it is to have plenty. I have learned the secret of being content in any and every situation, whether well fed or hungry, whether living in plenty or in want. I can do all this through him who gives me strength."

Get busy watering your own grass so as not to notice whether it's greener elsewhere.
- Karon Waddell

Imagine living your entire life saying if only I had a bigger house, if only I had a fancier car, if only I had a better job, if only I had a "trophy" husband or wife, if only I wasn't ill, If only I had more time and the many more millions of "if only" that visit your thoughts often. "If only" is a trap that keeps you in a vicious cycle of always wanting what you don't have rather than been content with every single possession, who you are and where you are at the present moment. (Note: by no means am I saying not to dream or pursue YOUR aspiration. Pursue YOURS not someone else's.)

More is not always good and less is not always bad. A greener lawn does not mean that the home is impeccable inside. The same applies, a brown or burnt lawn does not mean that the home is messy inside. Sometimes what you have is just what you are meant to have or need for your season. Envy, jealousy or long for the same or better lawn than your neighbors takes you nowhere. (Remember that none of it goes with you when you leave this earth.) Maybe you are so focused on your neighbor's lawn you forgot to water your own hence yours is not greener. Stay focused on what you have and your purpose.

Today's verse reminds us to be content with whatever our circumstances. To learn the secret of being content in any and every situation, whether well fed or hungry, whether living in plenty or in want. Free yourself from the vicious cycle of "greener." You can do all this through him who gives you strength.

Dear God,
Thank you for the reminder that whatever my circumstances, the grass is not greener on the other side. To free myself from this vicious cycle of "greener." I pray that all your children learn the secret of being content in any and every situation, whether well fed or hungry, whether living in plenty or in want. That they are freed from the vicious cycle of "greener." That they remember they can do all through him who gives them strength. I ask this in your son Jesus' name. Amen!

In Living Color

ANCHOR SCRIPTURE: GENESIS 9:13-14

"I have placed my rainbow in the clouds. It is the sign of my covenant with you and with all the earth. When I send clouds over the earth, the rainbow will appear in the clouds."

"Life is full of beautiful colors. It is up to us to know how to enjoy each of them."

Do you feel a sense of hope and promise when you see a rainbow after a storm? The rainbow is an arch of colors formed in the sky in certain circumstances, caused by the refraction and dispersion of the sun's light by rain. I recalled after a recent storm, witnessing a double rainbow.

The assortment of colors painted in the sky was truly breathtaking. It reminded me that the sky is not always blue with white or dark clouds. That there are many colors to enjoy. As I said this out loud someone (I do not know) said "the double rainbow signifies a transformation in life." I thought how wearing bright colors transform how you feel. How bright color breathes new life into your being. How living in color brings you out of the darkness.

Today's verse is a reminder that "I have placed my rainbow in the clouds. It is the sign of my covenant with you and with all the earth. When I send clouds over the earth, the rainbow will appear in the clouds." Wow! The dark clouds are only temporary, the rainbow will, not may appear in the clouds. Hold on to the promise and the hope. Enjoy your life in living color!

Dear God,
Thank you for the reminder of your promise and hope that when you send clouds, rainbows will appear. That the rainbow is a sign of your covenant with me and with all the earth. I pray that all your children, remember that when you send clouds, rainbows will appear. That this is a sign of your covenant with each of them and with all the earth. That they live life in living color. I ask this in your son Jesus' name. Amen!

MAY 18

Selective Hearing

ANCHOR SCRIPTURE: ISAIAH 50:4

"The Sovereign LORD has given me a well-instructed tongue, to know the word that sustains the weary. He wakens me morning by morning, wakens my ear to listen like one being instructed."

Hearing is listening to what is said. Listening is hearing
what isn't said."
- Simon Sinek

Have you ever referred to someone as hard of hearing or having select hearing (non-medically diagnosed?) This reference usually implies that the person selects what they want to hear instead of what is being communicated. At times these individuals in questions may hear what is said and changes the message to adjust either to their current desire or what is currently consuming the space in their brain.

How many of you know, live, work and are surrounded by people with select hearing? I bet many of you if you have children or spouses thought of them first. You could probably picture asking your child to friends that they selectively did not hear your request. The same applies to children making request of their parents and they selectively do not hear because they have so much on their mind. Lastly, same with a spouse making a request in the middle of the football game or in the middle of their favorite show, you can guarantee it will fall on deaf ears.

I wonder if we do the same with God's word... We selectively chose what to hear, when to hear and when to obey. Scripture in Psalms says that our ears have been opened and we are given the capacity to hear [and obey] God's word. Today's verse is a reminder that the Sovereign LORD has given me a well-instructed tongue, to know the word that sustains the weary. He wakens me morning by morning, wakens my ear to listen like one being instructed. It is interesting to note that selective hearing or selective obedience when it comes to God's word, never yields good result.

--------------------- PRAYER FOR THE DAY: ---------------------

Dear God,
Thank you for the reminder that you have given me a well-instructed tongue, to know the word that sustains the weary. You awaken me morning by morning, waken my ear to listen like one being instructed. I pray that all your children remember that you have given them a well-instructed tongue, to know the word that sustains the weary. That you awaken them morning by morning, waken their ear to listen like one being instructed. That selective hearing when it comes to your word, never yields good results. I ask this in Jesus' name. Amen!

Live in Peace

ANCHOR SCRIPTURE: ROMANS 12:18-19

"Do all that you can to live in peace with everyone.
Dear friends, never take revenge. Leave that to the righteous
anger of God. For the Scriptures say, "I will take revenge;
I will pay them back."

Peace begins with a smile.
-Mother Teresa

Do you allow circumstances to dictate how you live? Our lives are often filled with turmoil and uncertainty, sometimes self-inflicted. At times, being so wrapped up in self, gets in the way of living in peace with yourself and others. Some go through great measure to live out of peace. Others excerpt no effort, there being is peace.

A very special aunt of mine (R.I.P.) exemplified living in peace and love. Anyone who met her, in person or by phone, she would open the space with the words "Peace be with you and she mostly closed with I love you." Can you imagine short circuiting all negative circumstances by being the peace you seek? By verbalizing to others that you come in peace. Imagine setting an atmosphere of peace every place you enter or through every conversation had?

Have you done "all that you can" to be at peace with yourself and others? I would be dreaming if I told you it was easy to do good when you are wronged repeatedly. Today's verse is a reminder to do all that you can to live in peace with everyone. Dear friends, never take revenge. Leave that to the righteous anger of God. For the Scriptures say, "I will take revenge; I will pay them back. Note, the verse doesn't say to do all that you can to live in peace "with some people" it says to live in peace "with everyone." Let peace begin with you.

Dear God,
Thank you for the reminder that I must do all I can to live in
peace with everyone. No matter the circumstances, you are
always watching. I pray that all your children remember to
live in peace with everyone. That revenge is not theirs to take,
it is yours. May all your children experience peace with self and
others. I ask this in Jesus' name. Amen!

MAY 20

Taking Your Blessings for Granted

ANCHOR SCRIPTURE: ECCLESIASTES 7:1

"A good name is better than fine perfume, and the day
of death better than the day of birth."

Not what we say about our blessings, but how we use them,
is the true measure of our thanksgiving.
- *W.T. Purkiser*

Have you wondered why we are sad when someone dies and joyful
when a child is born? Each act is a blessing and an opportunity to
celebrate. In both, we celebrate life. Sometimes, through the pain of
childbirth and the pain of death, we lose sight of the blessings. There
is a blessing in it all.

The blessings of a new life to care for, nurture and raise. In death, the gratitude of the time and moments gifted with a loved one, even crazy moments spent with those we have lost. The single moments that may now be just wonderful memories. The dash between birth and death is the opportunity to build a legacy. I think about how this is sometimes taken for granted. Spending so much time focusing on what is wrong, focusing on ourselves instead of how to correct the wrong, improve the lives of others, share our blessings, and grow.

You may have heard this before... "It is not how you start that matters, it is how you finish." Many walks around gloating about all the great things they did when they do wrong. (Note the past tense.) I ask, which matters most, what you did then or what you do now? Ecclesiastes 7 is filled with many reminders including to never to take our blessings for granted. It also specifically reminds us that your death date tells more than your birth date. Think about this, how would you like to be remembered? Are you living the legacy you would like to leave? I encourage you to read Ecclesiastes 7 in its entirety.

─────────────── **PRAYER FOR THE DAY:** ───────────────

Dear God,
Thank you for the reminder that the day of my death tells more than my birth date. I pray that all your children take heed to the wisdom shared in Ecclesiastes 7. That they never take their blessings for granted. That they remember that the day of death tells more than the day of birth. That a good name is better than fine perfume. I ask this in your son, Jesus' name. Amen!

Journey

ANCHOR SCRIPTURE: ROMANS 5:3-5

"Not only so, but we also glory in our sufferings, because we know that suffering produces perseverance; perseverance, character; and character, hope. And hope does not put us to shame, because God's love has been poured out into our hearts through the Holy Spirit, who has been given to us."

Difficult roads often lead to beautiful destinations.
The best is yet to come.
- Zig Ziglar

This weekend I received a pleasant surprise visit from my cousin and her dear friend. They are on a road trip. It was interesting to note, as they shared their story, all the hurdles and delays they experienced before they even began their journey. They knew what, that they would go on this journey, however they did not have clarity on how it would be done.

Plan A fell through at the last minute, so did plan B. They finally found an option that worked. They started their journey and ran into major thunderstorms. They however continued moving forward on their journey. This experienced they shared, reminded me that sometimes all you need to know is "what" you should do, the how comes through the journey. I am grateful for the visit and that they shared their story. Today's verse is a reminder to glorify in our sufferings, knowing that suffering produces endurance, endurance produces character, and character produces hope. Now this hope does not disappoint us, because God's love has been poured out into our hearts by the Holy Spirit, who has been given to us. When your plans are delayed or interrupted, do you get annoyed or simply ease into the process? Enjoy the journey! Don't stop, the best is yet to come.

Dear God,
Thank you for the reminder that as I journey through life,
suffering will come. However, I must know that suffering
produces endurance, endurance produces character, and char-
acter produces hope. I pray that all your children remember that
whatever delay, suffering, or set back they may experience, and
that it produces endurance, character, and hope. I ask this in
your son Jesus' name. Amen!

MAY 22

Excuses, Excuses, Excuses

ANCHOR SCRIPTURE: PROVERBS 6:4

"Don't put it off; do it now! Don't rest until you do."

Your breakthrough begins where your excuses end.
- Pastor Steven Furtick

Do you think making excuses, helps, or hinders you? We sometimes
make excuses for ourselves and even make excuses for others. I realize that making excuses keeps us from growing. Yes, the timing may
not be right, or we may rather sit in our comfort zone. Which makes
you feel better, making changes or making excuses? Adjustments may

always include been honest with yourself. Yes, telling your bestie that I don't want to see the movie instead of paying and sitting through a movie you didn't want to see in the first place.

It is holding yourself accountable for not keeping your end of the bargain instead of making excuses. It may even be trying something that stretches or scares you instead of saying I can't. It takes courage to quit making excuses. To decide to take risks and enjoy the ride. Not making excuses may be the only challenge you need to overcome to make it to your next big break. Benjamin Franklin once said, "He who is good for making excuses is seldom good for anything else."

Excuses may be the tool used to shift responsibility, to block accountability, or to simply do what you want to do, remain the same, instead of growing. Think about it?

If you were brutally honest with yourself what is one thing you have used as an excuse or a crutch to delay doing something? Having enough time is an excuse I am working on eliminating. Don't go looking for time, create it. Yep, talking to myself as well. Imagine pausing to identify all the excuses you use that get in the way of your growth? Some you may have used your entire life.

Sometimes fear inspires you to make excuses. Yep, I too made excuses to remain in the same space because with excuses I remain comfortable and the same. Today's verse is a reminder, don't put it off; do it now! Don't rest until you do. Remember, excuses will always be there for you, opportunity won't. I encourage you today to "Be stronger than your excuses."

Dear God,
Thank you for the reminder to make changes, not excuses. To
not put off the things you have guided me to do, to do it now! To
be stronger than my excuses. I pray that all your children make
changes and quit making excuses. That they do not put things
off any longer, that they obey now. That they become stronger
than their excuses. I ask this in your son Jesus' name. Amen!

MAY 23

Work in Progress (WIP)

ANCHOR SCRIPTURE: PHILIPPIANS 1:6

"Being confident of this, that he who began a good work in you
will carry it on to completion until the day of Christ Jesus."

Every strike brings me closer to the next home run
- Babe Ruth

I love baseball. It teaches so many life lessons... it teaches humility,
finesse, and dignity. No showing off when you win because one day
you will lose. Keep your dignity when you lose and show finesse when
you win. It teaches perseverance and be resiliency. Keeping it real,
it is a long game. I however enjoy the patience and resiliency it teaches
children at a young age. Imagine being on a losing streak at the

start of the season and winning the World Series at the end, that is perseverance.

One thing for sure, this game equips you to keep your eye on the ball. Taking your eye off the ball a split second will mess up your swing. Stay focused even when you miss, eventually you will make contact. Stay focused on the prize. It is easy to get discouraged when you constantly strike out. Ephesians 6:10 reminds us to be strong in the Lord and in the strength of his power.

Today's verse is a reminder that being confident of this, that he who began a good work in you will carry it on to completion until the day of Christ Jesus. You are a work in progress (WIP.) Keep swinging, you are closer to a home run than you think.

—————————— **PRAYER FOR THE DAY:** ——————————

Dear God,
Thank you for the reminder that I am a work in progress. Constantly being perfected! That you began a good work in me, and you will carry it to completion. I pray that all your children remember that they are a work in progress (WIP.) That you will bring to completion the good work you began in each of them. I ask this in your son Jesus' name. Amen!

Balance

ANCHOR SCRIPTURE: EPHESIANS 5:15

"Look carefully then how you walk, not as unwise but as wise."

Life is about balance. Be kind, but don't let people abuse you.
Trust, but don't be deceived. Be content, but never stop i
mproving yourself
- Zig Ziglar

Is one of your daily battles how to achieve balance? How do you care for others and yourself at the same time? How do you fit your to do list into 16 hours (if your account for the 8 hours of sleep you should have?) Life is like walking across a balance beam. You are rarely able to walk smoothly across. It requires carefully putting one foot in front of the other. A missed step could be detrimental to successful completing the walk across the beam.

Achieving balance in life, like walking across a balance beam, requires an even distribution of weight. The goal is to avoid falling over. One way to avoid falling over is to master what to say yes to. Once you master this, you will easily learn to say no to the many things you formerly said yes to. The word no will become your best friend instead of your enemy. It will help unveil that; you do have more than enough time in your day to get the important things done.

Be aware of others filling your space with their to-do list or filling your space with things and thoughts that can be set aside for another day. Achieving balance in life is the best gift you could give yourself. Keep it real, no excuses and prioritize the important things that will keep you growing and continuously improving yourself. Today's verse is a reminder to look carefully then how you walk, not as unwise but as wise. I encourage to read Ephesians 5 in its entirety.

Dear God,
Thank you for the reminder that achieving balance is a gift. To look carefully then how I walk, not as unwise but as wise. I pray that all your children look carefully then how they walk, not as unwise but as wise. That they remember that walking wisely is key to achieving a balance life. I ask this in your son Jesus' name. Amen!

MAY 25

Secrets

ANCHOR SCRIPTURE: JOHN 8:32

"Then you will know the truth, and the truth will set you free."

Your visions will become clear only when you can look into your own heart. Who looks outside, dreams, who looks inside, awakes.
– C.G. Jung

I recently listened to a sermon by Pastor Rick Warren. He spoke about how secrets make us sick. Merriam Webster defines secret as kept from knowledge or view, hidden, or marked by the habit of discretion. It is true, no one wants to discuss the delicate subject of "secrets"...personal secrets, family secrets, company secrets. I wonder if secrets are truly ailing our world. Hmmm.

The lesson learned from the saying "what you do in the dark, will eventually come to light" is deep. Keeping secrets usually causes more harm than good although it seems to be mostly done out of a need to protect self or others. On a funny side note, my mom always says, let your "fart" be free, as that was the end of Mary Lee. The moral of the story was that Mary Lee died from holding in her urge to flatulate. It makes no sense that this naturally occurring process, emitting digestive gases from your body, would be hidden.

Although this saying gifted by my Mom is an ongoing joke in my family, it brought much wisdom... it will eventually be revealed either by sound, smell, pain or all three. Today's verse is a reminder, you will know the truth, and the truth will set you free. I once heard this statement "All secrets have an expiration date." Why hide. Don't let your secrets make you sick or expire. I encourage you to own your truth and set yourself free. Read John 8 in its entirety.

PRAYER FOR THE DAY:

Dear God,
Thank you for the reminder to learn and know my truth. It will set me free. I pray that all your children understand that secrets, although used as a protective mechanism, causes more harm than good. That they learn and embrace the truth that will set them free. I ask this in your son Jesus' name. Amen!

MAY 26

Blessings and Lessons

ANCHOR SCRIPTURE: ROMANS 8:28

"And we know that in all things God works for the good of those who love him, who have been called according to his purpose."

"Count your blessings and grow from your lesson"

Do you count your blessings each morning and evening? Many times, we miss the blessing by focusing on the lesson instead of growing through the lesson and shinning the light on the blessing brought by the lesson. (Tongue twister, uh!) Yes, we sometimes forget to count our blessings and grow from the lesson.

I recently spoke to a dear friend who said these words to me "I am sorry things didn't work out for you." He was referring to my marriage dissolution. Before I could stop myself, I responded, "Who said things didn't work out for me? Everything is working out for my good." He meant no harm and it was all in love as a brother. I then realized that it takes strong faith to see that the lesson is a blessing. That the lesson was simply an opportunity to grow to the next level.

It is funny how messages come from the least likely places. How gratitude and counting your blessings often allows you to enjoy every phase of your journey. It gives you the strength to rejoice in all circumstances. Every encounter has a purpose, a lesson, or a blessing. My friend's comment was a blessing to me. It reminded me that faith moves mountains. Today's scripture is one of my favorites and a reminder... and we know that in all things God works for the good of those who love him, who have been called according to his purpose. "Hold the vision, Trust the process."

Dear God,
Thank you for the reminder that in all things you work for the
good of those who love you, who have been called according to
your purpose. I pray that all your children remember that in all
things you work for the good of those who love you, who have
been called according to your purpose. That they "hold the vision
and trust the process." I ask this in your son Jesus' name. Amen!

MAY 27

Planting Seeds

ANCHOR SCRIPTURE: GALATIANS 6:9

"And let us not grow weary of doing good, for in due season
we will reap, if we do not give up."

Don't judge each day by the harvest you reap
but by the seeds that you plant.
- *Robert Louis Stevenson*

Does your patience get the better part of you often? Do you remember in primary school being asked to bring a bean from home then you took this bean and planted it in a paper cup filled with soil brought in by the teacher or that you collected from the school grounds? It took several weeks before you witness the first sprout after planting the seed or bean. Do you recall the feeling of hope and confidence your young soul felt when that first green leaf sprouted through the soil?

227

It is interested to note how these lessons taught long ago are often forgotten. Did you even know that this was a seed planted for you to better understand life and growing up? Yep, it may have been a simple science project that now brings great meaning. There is beauty in re-membering...Patience is the name of the game. Confidence that hard work will pay off. Hope that every seed planted will produce good fruit. Faith in things you do not control... that rain will fall, that the ideal conditions will remain for the crop to grow, that you are planting on good soil.

In life, you must trust that you have planted the seed on good soil (when you truly do.) You may have to wait a while to see the fruit from your labor. Scripture reminds us that the one who plants and the one who waters have one purpose, and they will each be rewarded accord-ing to their own labor (see 1 Corinthians 3.) At times, you may never see the crop that grew from the seed you planted. So is life. Today's verse is a reminder and let us not grow weary of doing good, for in due season we will reap, if we do not give up. Keep planting good seed on good soil and trust that a beautiful flower or fruit will eventually bloom. "Don't try to rush things that need time to grow."

─────────────── PRAYER FOR THE DAY: ───────────────

Dear God,
Thank you for the reminder to not grow weary in planting seeds and doing good. That in due season I will reap if I do not give up. I pray that all your children continue to plant good seed on good ground. That they continue to do good, for in due season they will reap, if they do not give up. I ask this in your son Jesus' name. Amen!

Take Action!

ANCHOR SCRIPTURE: JOHN 13:17

*"Now that you know these things, you will be blessed
if you do them."*

An inch of movement will bring you closer to your goals
than a mile of intention.
– *Steve Maraboli*

Are you avoiding taking action? To experience success sometimes we forget it requires taking action. Taking action is a process, one foot in front of the other. One elevation at a time. It does not mean going from 0 to 100 in one shot. Taking action is a necessary to reach your goals and quite frankly to change your ways.

Consider you want to break a habit, make a change, or achieve another level. If you don't begin the journey taking a step in the right direction, you will never achieve your goals. Sure, you may experience hesitation, temptation to remain in your comfort zone or procrastination due to fear or other factors. That is normal. Still make the first step in the right direction. Get help if you need support.

Just imagine achieving the goals you set for yourself, arriving at the next level, or finally seeing and feeling the change you want to achieve, how will you feel? 2 Timothy 2:1 reminds us to be strong through the grace that God gives you. Find the courage within and take the first step. Today's verse is a reminder that now that you know these things, you will be blessed if you do them. Take action now!

Dear God,
Thank you for the reminder that you provide the grace to be strong, now that I know these things, you will bless me if I do the things you ask. I pray that all your children remember that you provide the grace for them to be strong. That they will be blessed if they do the things you ask. That they take actions now. I ask this in your son Jesus' name. Amen!

MAY 29

Character Counts

ANCHOR SCRIPTURE: LUKE 8:17

"For there is nothing hidden that will not be disclosed, and nothing concealed that will not be known or brought out into the open."

Character is like a tree and reputation like a shadow.
The shadow is what we think of it; the tree is the real thing.

I often hear different viewpoints on or about character, the importance of character, and how as leaders this is one key area that must be continuously refined. I learned a while ago that when trouble comes there is refinement of your character that will unfold. Not on the character that you play in the movie and more on the way you handle what is given or gifted to you.

I recalled reading a book on leadership that mentioned today's quote. I was intrigued by this quote and looked a bit further into it. I discovered that there was more... President Lincoln was asked, what is a measure of a person's character? His response was "My experience is that most people think that the true measure of a person's character is how they respond to adversity. "I have found," Lincoln said, "that the real test of a person's character is to give them power. And I have been surprised how often I have been disappointed by people's character when they have been given power."

Think about this on a personal level, your shadow being what you think of something or someone and the tree being the real deal. Has this caused your own character to be shaken or have you worked on refining your own character from the experience? It is easy to turn the mirror outward. Proverbs 27 says as in water face reflects face. So, the heart of man reflects a man. Have you tried facing the mirror inward and worked on strengthening your tree instead of strengthening your shadow? Today's scripture is a reminder, for there is nothing hidden that will not be disclosed, and nothing concealed that will not be known or brought out into the open. Character counts!

--------------------------- PRAYER FOR THE DAY: ---------------------------

Dear God,
Thank you for the reminder of the importance of knowing your character to develop my own. That there is nothing hidden that will not be disclosed, and nothing concealed that will not be known or brought out into the open. I pray that all your children know and learn your character to develop their own. That they remember that there is nothing hidden that will not be disclosed, and nothing concealed that will not be known or brought out into the open. I ask this in your son Jesus' name. Amen!

Enslaved by Habits

ANCHOR SCRIPTURE: 1 CORINTHIANS 6:12 ESV

"All things are lawful for me," but not all things are helpful.
"All things are lawful for me," but I will not be enslaved
by anything."

Chains of habit are too light to be felt until they
are too heavy to be broken.
-Warren Buffett

A slave is defined as one that is totally subservient to a dominating influence. I recently read an article by Ken Wert entitled Five Enslaving Habits We Must Avoid. The article identified the following five habits we must avoid:

- Slavery to addictions: including television watching, eating junk food, gossip to mention a few;
- Slavery to the office: placing work, business or office ahead of your family;

- Slavery to success: when success becomes more important than integrity or honor or self-respect, then our subservience to the call of the dollar sign becomes self–destructive;

- Slavery to pleasure: in pursuit of pleasures that cost you or your family financially, or destroys your relationships

- Slavery to fear: fear and worry from taking the hard steps to break free from living a disingenuous life.

All I could say after reading this list of five was ouch, ouch, ouch, ouch, ouch. I immediately turned to the Lenten season. During Lent, it is customary to abstain or give up something that brings you pleasure or speaking frankly, give up something that we may or may not admit is an addiction. Harsh words to hear, huh. As I reflect on the things I have chosen or chose to give up for 40 days, it dawned on me that the choices were things I should permanently give up. Instead, I abstain for just forty days then return to the bad habit. Sometimes actually celebrating returning to the thing you gave up for 40 days. I wonder, are we celebrating being enslaved and addicted?

Mr. Werth mentioned something powerful in his article. He said that any addiction rob us of a measure of freedom and independence. It seems we must pay attention to our habits, no matter how significant or insignificant it may seem. Today's verse is a reminder, all things are lawful for me, but not all things are helpful. All things are lawful for me, but I will not be enslaved by anything. Freedom is possible.

—————————— **PRAYER FOR THE DAY:** ——————————

Dear God,
Thank you for the reminder that habits can enslave. Some may seem harmless and they still rob us from a measure of freedom. That all things are lawful for me, but not all things are helpful. To not be enslaved by anything. I pray that all your children remember that all things are lawful, but not all things are help-ful. That they are not enslaved by anything. I ask this in your son Jesus' name. Amen.

Vulnerable

2 CORINTHIANS 12:9-10 (ESV)

But he said to me, "My grace is sufficient for you, for my power is made perfect in weakness." Therefore, I will boast all the more gladly of my weaknesses, so that the power of Christ may rest upon me. For the sake of Christ, then, I am content with weaknesses, insults, hardships, persecutions, and calamities. For when I am weak, then I am strong.

"Staying vulnerable is a risk we have to take if we want to experience connection."
– Brené Brown

Do you ever wonder why connecting or remaining connected is a struggle for you? Have you been hiding or keeping secrets? We all have done or gone through one or many experiences that society or our own thoughts say, "never share this or that with anyone." Or you may hear something like this, don't embarrass yourself, the family or ruin your career and life by sharing "x."

As a leader, instead of feeling you must know it all or be the strongest person in the room, try on vulnerability for size. Work on being completely transparent and vulnerable about your weakness, your mistakes, and come out of hiding. Let your guard down and be free. You may believe that you must be stronger than those who follow you. I have learned the truth; this belief is a lie. Defenseless may be your moment of breakthrough. It may be the sweet spot where you connect with self and with your tribe. Being vulnerable may be just the antidote to your power.

Today's verse is a reminder that, but he said to me, "My Grace is sufficient for you, for my power is made perfect in weakness." Therefore,

I will boast all the more gladly of my weaknesses, so that the power of Christ may rest upon me. For when I am weak, then I am strong! Be strong in your weakness and vulnerability. Wishing you a day and week filled with massive connections!

PRAYER FOR THE DAY:

Dear Father,
Thank you for the reminder that my vulnerability and weakness perfect your power. That your grace is sufficient. I pray that all your children remember that your power is made perfect in weakness. That when they are weak, you are strong. That your grace will always be sufficient. I ask this in your son Jesus' name. Amen!

Reflections

June

Breaking Chains

ANCHOR SCRIPTURE: 1 CORINTHIANS 10:13 (ESV)

"That no temptation has overtaken you that is not common to man. God is faithful, and he will not let you be tempted beyond your ability, but with the temptation he will also provide the way of escape, that you may be able to endure it."

"Chains of habit are too light to be felt until they're
too heavy to be broken.
- *Warren Buffet*

Are you feeling imprisoned by bad habits or bad thoughts? Many times, we feel as though we are powerless to break out of routines or things that are either not good for us or that no longer serve us. Some of these are quite frankly bad habits, bad thoughts, or bad behaviors we picked up along life's journey.

What if you were made aware that you have the power to set yourself free? To escape from the things and thoughts you know are not aligned with who you truly are? To completely release the chains that has held you hostage. Would you set yourself free?

Today's verse is a reminder that no temptation has overtaken you that is not common to man. God is faithful, and he will not let you be tempted beyond your ability, but with the temptation he will also provide the way of escape, that you may be able to endure it. Be reassured, there is an escape from every temptation...You have the power to break every chain! Don't let your habits become too heavy to be broken.

Dear Father,
Thank you for the reminder that there is no temptation that has
overtaken me that is not common to man. That with every temp-
tation, you will also provide the way of escape. You are faithful. I
pray that all your children remember that there is no temptation
that has overtaken them that is not common to man. That with
every temptation, you will also provide the way of escape. You
are faithful. I ask this in your son Jesus 'name. Amen!

JUNE 2

Reset

ANCHOR SCRIPTURE: 2 CORINTHIANS 5:17

"Therefore, if anyone is in Christ, the new creation has come:
The old has gone, the new is here!"

"Every sunset is an opportunity to reset.
- *Richie Norton*

Have you ever consciously decided to reset... to go back to zero, to
start over, to simply unlearn everything you were taught? To start
fresh and live "your" truth. Yes, just start your story from a blank
piece of paper. Letting go of all the baggage and weight you thought
you had to carry and not even be tempted to pick it back up. Imagine
where you would start that story?

Sometimes in life, a reset is necessary to continue to grow, to realize that indeed you are a new creation every single day. You are not the same person you were yesterday. You are not your past. We reset often whether we notice or not. Today's verse is a reminder that if anyone is in Christ, the new creation has come: The old has gone, the new is here!" Re-set...your new is here!

Dear Father,
Thank you for the reminder that the old has gone, the new is here. I am re-set! I pray that all your children remember that that if anyone is in Christ, the new creation has come: The old has gone, the new is here! That they Re-set their minds.... the new is here! I ask this in your son Jesus' name. Amen!

Labor On Purpose

ANCHOR SCRIPTURE: 1 CORINTHIANS 15:58

"Therefore, my dear brothers and sisters, stand firm. Let nothing move you. Always give yourselves fully to the work of the Lord, because you know that your labor in the Lord is not in vain."

"Work on purpose so your labor is not in vain."

Have you ever paused and asked, why do I labor? Does my labor make a difference; does it have meaning or serve a higher purpose? Your initial purpose to labor may be to make ends meet or to pursue a career. As you mature, you may begin to think, is there more to this labor thing... It may be my opportunity to plant seeds that I or others may reap the rewards. It may be the perfect place to begin a legacy.

In looking at one of the many definitions of labor this one state, human activity that provides the goods or services in an economy. Consider that, what you do impacts an entire economy. John Locke is quoted as saying: It is labor indeed that puts the difference on everything."

Today's verse is a reminder therefore, my dear brothers and sisters, stand firm. Let nothing move you. Always give yourselves fully to the work of the Lord because you know that your labor in the Lord is not in vain. I encourage you to read 1 Corinthians 15 in its entirety. Labor on purpose!

Dear Father,
Thank for the reminder to stand firm, let nothing move me from giving myself fully to your work. That my labor for you is not in vain. I pray that all your children heed your advice to stand firm and let nothing move them from giving themselves fully to your work. That their Labor for you is not in vain. That they labor on purpose. I ask this in your son Jesus' name. Amen!

JUNE 4

Training Ground

ANCHOR SCRIPTURE: 2 TIMOTHY 3:16-17 (ESV)

"All Scripture is breathed out by God and profitable for teaching, for reproof, for correction, and for training in righteousness, that the man of God may be competent, e quipped for every good work."

"I hated every minute of training, but I said, don't quit.
Suffer now and live the rest of your life as a champion".
- Muhammad Ali

Do you regret some of the things you have gone through? Is it sometimes unexplainable and baffling? Is it sometimes too hard to handle? Imagine been in boot camp; the intense training, discipline and sacrifice that is needed to graduate is massive.

What if you simply looked at everything you go through as a boot camp. You are been refined for your next level. No matter how tough the training, it is all a requirement to graduate to the rank and file. Yes, you may protest that you were enrolled in this training without your consent.

That it is not just, or you can't handle it. You are always given just what you can handle. You simply must just trust. Hebrews 12:8 teaches if you are not disciplined--and everyone undergoes discipline--then you are not legitimate, not true sons and daughters at all.

Today's scriptures are great reminders as you continue your journey, all scriptures is breathed out by God and profitable for teaching, for reproductive, for correction, and for training in righteousness, that the man of God may be competent, equipped for every good work. The training may be tough and take more time than you like. I remind you it is all your training ground. Be resilient!

———————————— **PRAYER FOR THE DAY:** ————————————

Dear Father,
Thank you for the reminder that all scriptures is breathed out by God and profitable for teaching, for reproductive, for correction, and for training in righteousness, that the man of God may be competent, equipped for every good work. I pray that all your children embrace their training ground. That they remember you are equipping them for every good work. I ask this in your son Jesus' name. Amen!

Unbelievable

ANCHOR SCRIPTURE: HABAKKUK 1:5

"Look at the nations and watch and be utterly amazed,
for I am going to do something in your days that you would
not believe, even if you were told."

"Always remember to never forget"

Today I remember and honor all those who lost their lives 17 years ago on September 11 and those who continue to feel and live through the impact of this event.

Looking at your world and your life, are you sometimes faced with disappointment, dissolution, and even desperation when things that are happening around you don't make sense? Worry, hurt, anger, sadness, and hopelessness sometimes pursue.

Sometimes you witness so much destruction, violence, hate, and strife it leads us to say, why is all this happening? At times we even believe that our prayers will never be answered and even go to the extent of accusing God of inaction. Habakkuk 1:2 reminds us of Habakkuk's words: How long, Lord, must I call for help, but you do not listen? Or cry out to you, "Violence!" but you do not save? Can you relate to this cry?

In today's verse, God assured Habakkuk that he was going to do something in his days that he would not believe, even if he were told. Can you imagine this assurance, of things to hope for but not yet seen? Despite what things may look like or what you may have witnessed; destruction, violence, strife, and conflict, God is still working. He is working it all out for your good. Have you ever felt like Habakkuk? When you do, what actions do you take? Be encouraged, God is still working. You have favor!

Dear Father,
Thank you for the assurance that no matter what I may face or witness today, that you work all things out for the good of those who love you. I pray that all your children stand strong in this assurance that you are working behind the scenes in their favor, no matter what they face today. I pray they find favor in your sight. That they know, you are working everything out for their good. I ask this in Jesus' name. Amen!

———————————————— ● ————————————————

JUNE 6

Love Where You Are!

ANCHOR SCRIPTURE: ISAIAH 14:27

"For the Lord Almighty has purposed, and who can thwart him? His hand is stretched out, and who can turn it back?

———————————

"Do what you can, with what you have, where you are.
-Theodore Roosevelt

———————————

Recently, while riding in the car with my daughter, she played a song entitled "Where you're at" by Allen Stone. I think often of the importance of appreciating "where you are at", understanding that you are always growing. Everyone grows at a different pace. It does not make sense to compare apples and oranges. We are all different fruits even if we come from the same tree. Try comparing two apples and see if the two are identical?

As I reflect, often it is easy to focus on what is happening around you instead of appreciating what is happening in you. Imagine this, "keeping your dirt on the surface, having no reason to cover your tracks, wearing all your mistakes/sins on your collar as the lyrics of the song "Where you're at" describes. Owning that you are no angel but not so bad after all. Accepting that the best part of learning is to just "love where you are at."

Today's verse is a reminder, for the LORD Almighty has purposed, and who can thwart him? His hand is stretched out, and who can turn it back? Enjoy the process and where you're at! I encourage you to read Isaiah 14.

PRAYER FOR THE DAY:

Dear Father,
Thank you for the reminder that you have purposed, and nothing can stop your plans. I pray that all your children learn to love where they are at. That they focus on what is happening inside of them instead of around them. That they remember you remain in full control and your purpose will not be thwarted. I ask this in Jesus' name. Amen!

Carousel of Life

ANCHOR SCRIPTURE: ISAIAH 43:19 (NIV)

"See, I am doing a new thing! Now it springs up; do you not perceive it? I am making a way in the wilderness and streams in the wasteland"

"The carousel of life may have its ups and downs,
but it's still a great ride
- Unknown

Life is full of ups and downs, would you agree? Some make it through several good rounds before hitting down. Others only make it around once on a high note then hit down for some time. Consider those artists called "one hit wonders."

A friend recently shared his memory of a Charlie Brown and Lucy conversation. (Do you remember Charlie Brown cartoons?) "Charlie Brown complained to Lucy that his ball team loss all the time. Lucy replied, Charlie Brown, you learn more from your defeats than you do from your victories. Charlie Brown replied, that must make me the smartest man in the world!" That made me chuckle. Hope it make you chuckle too.

How do you handle life's ups and downs? Do you just chalk it up as one great ride; remain stuck on the down part of the ride? Imagine just taking life as a carousel ride; enjoy it all, the ups and downs. Not allowing yourself to get stuck on the down portion of the round. Today's scripture is a reminder; see, I am doing a new thing! Now it springs up; do you not perceive it? I am making a way in the wilderness and streams in the wasteland. I encourage you to read Isaiah 43. Enjoy the great ride!

Dear Father,
Thank you for the reminder that you are doing a new thing! You
are making a way in the wilderness and streams in the waste-
land. I pray that all your children remember that you are doing
a new thing. That you are making a way in the wilderness and
streams in the wasteland. That life is still a great ride in the ups
and in the downs. I ask this in your son Jesus' name. Amen!

●

JUNE 8

Change-Character-Courage

ANCHOR SCRIPTURE: TITUS 2:7-8 (NIV)

"In everything set them an example by doing what is good. In
your teaching show integrity, seriousness and soundness of
speech that cannot be condemned, so that those who oppose you
may be ashamed because they have nothing bad to say about us."

"Change makes you find your calling, your legacy, and
God's divine plan for your life. Don't run from it.
– Iman

Courage is sometimes defined as "the quality of mind or spirit that
enables a person to face difficulty, danger, pain, etc., without fear". ...
That is, if one does not experience anxiety or fear about doing something then it is easy to do and does not require courage or strength. I
love this definition of courage "being motivated from the heart to do

something brave." Think of the Tin Man and the cowardly Lion in the Wizard of Oz.

"A person's character is the sum of his or her disposition, thoughts, intentions, desires, and actions. It is good to remember that character is gauged by general tendencies, not based on a few isolated actions." To grow and to change requires courage and character. Because it is hard, we sometimes run from it. I remind you that the growth and change is yours only. When you run, you run from yourself, no one else. It is your experience, not someone else'. Embrace change, stretch your courage, and make the right choices to grow your character. Character is influenced and developed by your choices.

As you continue to lead others, (yes, you are leading someone or something) consider what legacy are your choices leaving. Is it one of courage and good character or something else? Does your legacy matter to you? No matter your age, your legacy starts now. Today's scripture is a reminder; in everything set them an example by doing what is good. In your teaching show integrity, seriousness and soundness of speech that cannot be condemned, so that those who oppose you may be ashamed because they have nothing bad to say about us. I encourage you to read Titus 2.

────────────── **PRAYER FOR THE DAY** ──────────────

Dear Father,
Thank you for the reminder to set an example by doing good. To not avoid change and growth as it strengthens my character. I pray that all your children remember to set an example by doing good. To not avoid change and growth as it strengthens their character. That they remember your teaching in Titus 2. That building character requires courage. I ask this in your son Jesus' name. Amen!

Once step at a time

ANCHOR SCRIPTURE: JAMES 1:4

"Let perseverance finish its work so that you may be mature and complete, not lacking anything"

"Sometimes the smallest step in the right direction ends up being the biggest step in your life.
- *Steve Maraboli*

Do you ever feel frustrated when you are doing your part, when you are following all the recommended steps and you see no results? You sometimes get frustrated, throw in the towel and give up after the first two or three attempts. As human this is natural.

This past Sunday at church, I was reminded of having supernatural faith and embracing the "not yet" spirit. That spirit that reminds you as long as you are taking baby steps in the right direction; you will meet your goals and arrive at your destination just in time (not too early and not too late; Right on time).

I reflected on a song I listen to when walking "Once step at a time" by Jordin Sparks. There is a part of the song that says, "You wanna show the world, but no one knows your name yet. You wonder when and where and how you're gonna make it. You know you can if you get the chance, in your face as the door keeps slamming, now you're feeling more and more frustrated and you're getting all kind of impatient, waiting."

I encourage you to breathe and remember the alphabet doesn't jump from A-Z or numbers go from 0 then 100. Today's scripture is a reminder to let perseverance finish its work so that you may be mature and complete, not lacking anything. No need to get impatient, live and learn to take one step, one day and one breathe at a time. This is progress. I encourage you to read and reflect on James 1.

─────────────── **PRAYER FOR THE DAY:** ───────────────

Dear Father,
Thank you for the reminder to strengthen my "not yet" spirit.
To let perseverance, finish its work so that I may be mature and
complete, not lacking anything. I pray that all your children de-
velop and embrace the "not yet" spirit. That they let persever-
ance finish its work so that they may be mature and complete,
not lacking anything. That they remember that taking one step
in the right direction is progress. I ask this in your son Jesus'
name. Amen!

───────────────────●───────────────────

JUNE 10

Inventory Your Habits

ANCHOR SCRIPTURE: 2 PETER 2:19 (NIV)

"For a man is a slave to whatever has mastered him"

────────────────

"People do not decide their futures, they decide their habits
and their habits decide their futures.
- *F.M. Alexander*

────────────────

Merriam Webster defines habit as a settled tendency or usual manner of behavior or an acquired mode of behavior that has become nearly

250

or completely involuntary. I recently read an article in Business Insider entitled 50 damaging habits you should break before you turn 30 by Lindsay Dodgson. Some of the habits listed are very interesting and may serve as an awakening to many. (The link to the article is below.)

You may already be aware of some of your habits/tendencies that negatively impact your life aka your controlling habits. This is where you consistently do something you wish you wouldn't do and find yourself doing it any way. Other habits may be disguised or done from your subconscious. Some habits help you upgrade, and others lead you to a downgrade.

Do you have habits you would like to change? Romans 7:15 says "I do not understand my own actions for I am as far from habitually doing what I want to do that I find myself doing the very thing that I hate." Are you willing to do the work to change and own your truth when told of a habit that needs changing or one that you know serves you no more? Do you retreat to denial and continue to practice the same bad habit? Be honest with yourself.

Today's verse is a reminder for a man is a slave to whatever has mastered him. I encourage you to inventory your habit to see what needs changing. Sometimes a bit of help or accountability is all you need to kick the habit. Have any of your habits or are currently controlling you? What steps are you taking to improving or changing your habits? Are these steps that free you or further enslave you? I encourage you to read 2nd Peter 2.

Dear Father,
Thank you for the reminder to inventory my habits. Once I do, I may realize that it is time to kick a few habits. That a man is a slave to whatever has mastered him. I pray that all your children inventory their habits and resolve to kick those habits that no longer serve them. That they remember that a man is a slave to whatever has mastered him. I ask this in your son Jesus' name. Amen!

———————————— ● ————————————

JUNE 11

Giving Up Is Not An Option

ANCHOR SCRIPTURE: 2 CHRONICLES 15:7 (NIV)

"But as for you, be strong and do not give up,
for your work will be rewarded."

———————————

"If you quit on the process, you are quitting on the result
- *Idowu Koyenikan*

———————————

October is an interesting month. It begins the last quarter of the year; it is a time the leaves begin to turn, and it is a time known to harvest. A farmer once shared this with me, "he sowed the seeds in the spring and reaped, or brought in, the harvest in the fall. Once you are sure you plant good seed in good ground, expect the harvest, expect to reap what you sow."

I hear a lot of buzz about finishing the year strong. I wonder if finishing strong depends on the seeds you sow at the start of the year? I believe that everyone sows seeds, these can be good or bad. Taking care in ensuring you sow what you want to reap is important. You can't sow cabbage and expect tomatoes. Similarly, you can't sow distrust and reap trust. Genesis 1: 12 says, "Seed after his kind"

I ask, what have you sown so far this year? Have you shown what you want to reap this last quarter of the year? My takeaway messages from my conversation with the farmer was you cannot sow greed and expect abundance and you cannot sow conditional love and expect unconditional love. Today's scripture is a reminder, "but as for you, be strong and do not give up, for your work will be rewarded." I encourage you to continue to sow what you want to reap no matter what others may sow. Giving up is not an option. Finish strong!

PRAYER FOR THE DAY:

Dear Father,
Thank you for the reminder that giving up is not an option. To continue to sow what I want to reap. To be strong as my work will be rewarded. I pray that all your children will take care in the seeds that they sow. That they sow good seed, be strong, patient, and do not give up. That they remember their good works will be rewarded. I ask this in your son Jesus' name. Amen!

Be A Lighthouse

ANCHOR SCRIPTURE: MATTHEW 5:14 (NIV)

*"You are the light of the world. A town built
on a hill cannot be hidden."*

"Lighthouses don't go running all over an island looking
for boats to save; they just stand there shining
. -Anne Lamott

It is said that one of the strongest images of standing strong in a storm is the lighthouse. The lighthouse reflects a powerful light that gives a continuous or intermittent signal to navigators to keep their ship from crashing into the shore.

It is fascinating to note that the job of a lighthouse keeper requires "repetition, precision, discipline, and ability to spend hours alone." It seems that being a lighthouse keeper is a noble and courageous career. The lighthouse keeper knew the powerful purpose of the lighthouse, to "help Mariners navigate dangerous areas by using lamps and powerful lenses", to safely bring their ship to shore.

I wonder what it would be like if each of us made a conscious choice to be a lighthouse. To simply let our light shine. To not give in to darkness and temporarily or permanently dim or out our light. To shine so brightly that our light will help others avoid crashing and make it safely through any storm. Matthew 5:14 is a reminder that you are the light of the world. A town built on a hill cannot be hidden. I encourage you to read Matthew 5 and be the lighthouse!

Dear Father,
Thank you for the reminder that I am the light of the world.
A town built on a hill cannot be hidden. I pray that all your
children chose to be a lighthouse and remember that they are
the light of the world. That a town built on a hill cannot be
hidden. I ask this in your son Jesus' name. Amen!

JUNE 13

Keep It Simple

ANCHOR SCRIPTURE: MATTHEW 6:25

"Therefore, I tell you, do not worry about your life,
what you will eat or drink; or about your body, what you
will wear. Is not life more important than food, and the body
more important than clothes?"

"Simplicity is the ultimate sophistication.
- Leonardo da Vinci

As I reflect on life, it seems the early years are focused more on accumulating stuff. Stuff simply to have stuff or maybe to assimilate having worth. It seems the legacy and patterns many follow and pass on is the more you have, the more you are worth. Maybe you can relate with this. As you age, you come to realize the opposite, the less you have, the better off you are. You long to have less "possessions" and possibly more love instead. You may long to live a simple life with as little physical possessions as possible. You may realize at a later age, that none of the material possessions matter. Could this be a sign of maturity?

Several wise people have shared with me that you come to this world with nothing and you leave with nothing. If I truly understood this concept a few decades ago, seems living a simple life would have been a good choice. The less you have, the less you have to release. The simpler your life. It seems the saying Keep It Simple Silly (KISS) are words of wisdom to pass on. Lao Tzu is quoted as saying: I have just three things to teach: simplicity, patience, compassion. These three are your greatest treasures. Today's verse is a reminder that, therefore, I tell you, do not worry about your life, what you will eat or drink; or about your body, what you will wear. Is not life more important than food, and the body more important than clothes? I encourage you to read Matthew 6. Simplify!

--------------------- PRAYER FOR THE DAY: ---------------------

Dear Father,
Thank you for the reminder to simplify. To not worry about my life. That the greatest treasures are simplicity, patience, and compassion. I pray that all your children remember that simplicity is a treasure. To keep it simple and to trust you. That they do not have a need to hold on to stuff or worry about their life. You got this! I ask this in your son Jesus' name. Amen!

Grace to the Humble

ANCHOR SCRIPTURE: PROVERBS 3:34 (GNT)

"He has no use for conceited people but shows favor to those who are humble. "

"Humility is measured by your willingness to allow others to see who you really are in your own weaknesses and in brokenness. Not what we would like for others to see."
-Bill Bright.

Humility or meekness is a quality which every leader should aspire to develop. It is almost inevitable in your leadership journey to travel without encountering people who will push your buttons and test your limits. It is your strength under control that will determine if you snap and break or succeed. A.R. Bernard is quoted as saying, humility is not weakness, but strength under control.

I wonder if intentionally working on improving your understanding of your emotions and learning to master them is vital to becoming a better leader? Understanding that you don't always have to exercise strength, instead learn to control your strength. Knowing when to exercise your strength, when to control it and when to yield to others. It takes practice, training, guidance, accountability, and humility to achieve. However, without accepting the grace that is already given to you, your growth may be stunted or even reversed.

Today's scripture is a reminder that he has no use for conceited people but shows favor to those who are humble. Are you willing to accept God's favor, his grace? Will you tap into your free gift? I encourage you to read Proverbs 3 in its entirety.

Dear Father,
Thank you for the reminder that you have no use for conceited people, and you show favor to those who are humble. I pray that all your children learn to control their strength. That they remember that you have no use for conceited people, and you show favor to those who are humble. That they understand the power in humility. I ask this in your son Jesus' name. Amen!

JUNE 15

Walk Your Talk

ANCHOR SCRIPTURE: 1 TIMOTHY 4:12

"Let no one despise you for your youth, but set the believers an example in speech, in conduct, in love, in faith, in purity."

"The world is changed by your example, not by your opinion.
-Paulo Coelho

I recently sat in on a conversation where the group, mostly baby boomers, were complaining about millennials and their so called "entitlement mindsets." I sat back, watched, and smiled to myself as I listen to this conversation. I thought, has anyone in this group paused to think how this so called "mentality" was created? Has anyone considered the role they played in nurturing this so called "entitlement mentality." Everyone wants their children to have what they didn't have however the techniques used may make or break the intent.

Those in your tribe are always watching and listening to see if what you say and what you do are congruent- - that you walk your talk. When you don't, your tribe or your children will be the first to tell you about it through verbal exchange or personal imitation. A leader of an organization once said to me, "I am implementing all these innovative ideas, and no one is buying into it." I asked candidly, are you personally implementing the things you are asking others to do? You can't ask your team to use a computer and you continue to use a typewriter. 1 Peter 5:3 says not domineering over those in your charge but being examples to the flock.

Are you great at telling others what they should be doing? Are you consistently modeling the expectations that you set for others? Take a pause to deeply examine if you are truly modeling what you want to see of others. Be honest with yourself. Your behavior earns you respect. Today's verse is a reminder let no one despise you for your youth, but set the believers an example in speech, in conduct, in love, in faith, in purity. I encourage you to read 1 Timothy 4. Walk your talk!

--------------------- **PRAYER FOR THE DAY:** ---------------------

Dear Father,
Thank you for the reminder to be the example. That I must walk my talk. I pray that all your children set the example they expect of others in speech, in conduct, in love, in faith, in purity. That they be the example they want to see. I ask this in your son Jesus' name. Amen!

The Words You Speak

ANCHOR SCRIPTURE: PROVERBS 16:24 (ESV)

*"Gracious words are like a honeycomb, sweetness
to the soul and health to the body"*

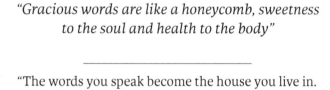

"The words you speak become the house you live in.
– *Hafiz*

Imagine saying thank you instead of saying I am sorry. Imagine thanking someone for teaching you something that may have hurt you? Yes, using gratitude versus regret as your go to attitude. My friend Helen Ober recently shared a post demonstrating the difference between saying thank you instead of I am sorry. Here are two of her suggested changes instead of saying "sorry I am late", say "thank you for waiting for me." Another suggestion shared was instead of saying "sorry for been emotional", say "thank you for loving me."

Have you thought how your words may be sabotaging your intentions? How reframing or removing certain words can either add fuel to your power or slow you down. Your words can either free you or enslave you. Another dear friend recently pointed out the use of the word "just." It awakened me that the use of this word minimized what is. Small words, big impact!

Be mindful of the words you speak; they are the fuel that fills your tank. That determines how far you go. Ludwig Wittgenstein is quoted as saying, the limits of my language means the limits of my world. Today's scripture is a reminder that gracious words are like a honeycomb, sweetness to the soul and health to the body. Provide health to your body, mind the words you speak.

Dear Father,
Thank you for the reminder to mind the words of speak. That gracious words are like a honeycomb, sweetness to the soul and health to the body. I pray that all your children mind the words they speak. That they remember gracious words are like a honeycomb, sweetness to the soul and health to the body. I ask this in your son Jesus' name. Amen!

JUNE 17

Making A Living Or A Life

ANCHOR SCRIPTURE: ROMANS 12:2-(ESV)

"Do not be conformed to this world, but be transformed by the renewal of your mind, that by testing you may discern what is the will of God, what is good and acceptable and perfect."

"True masters are those who have chosen to make
a life rather than a living.
- Neale Donald Walsch

Have you ever considered whether you are making a living or a life? Annie Sumner, a commenter in a blog that I read occasionally stated this: "Almost anyone can make money and get benefits and buy a car.

Those things are a living. But a life? A life is a joyous, passionate thing of sound and challenge and exquisite opportunities for deathless love and abysmal sadness. A life is something that exists outside of time and cannot be described except by the person who is living it with all its gorgeous failure..."

Growing spiritually has awakened me to seeing the difference between making a living and a life. Yes, at a point in my journey that is all I did, make a living. Making a living to me is attached to materials things that will break down, that are temporary such as fashion, things that eventually become more of a burden than a blessing. Making a life to me is pursuing your purpose, pursuing freedom, owning less not more, changing lives without seeking reward or recognition (although you are already rewarded) and un-anchoring yourself to the things of this world and anchoring to the things of eternity. It is about your life's legacy that has nothing to do with "the things" you own. It is about the "why" you are still here on earth. Bottom line making a living, or a life is a choice. What is your choice?

Today's scripture is a reminder to not be conformed to this world, but be transformed by the renewal of your mind, that by testing you may discern what is the will of God, what is good and acceptable and perfect.

PRAYER FOR THE DAY:

Dear Father,
Thank you for the reminder of the difference between making a living and making a life. To not be conformed to this world but be transformed by the renewal of my mind. I pray that all your children do not conform to this world but be transformed by the renewal of their minds, that by testing they may discern what is your will, what is good and acceptable and perfect. That they make a life and not a living. I ask this in your son Jesus' name. Amen!

To Judge or To Love...

ANCHOR SCRIPTURE: GALATIANS 6:1 (NIV)

"Brothers and sisters, if someone is caught in a sin, you who live by the Spirit should restore that person gently. But watch yourselves, or you also may be tempted."

An individual has not started living until he can rise above the narrow confines of his individualistic concerns to the broader concerns of all humanity.
- Martin Luther King, Jr.

"The idea that you call right is the idea that someone else calls wrong. The solution that you call perfect is the solution that another calls unworkable. The position that you feel is unassailable is the very position that others assail." Neale Donald Walsch said this. He reminds us that being "right" has nothing to do with it.

Questioning and attacking others approach on how they solve a problem, attacking another's belief, or simply judging someone else's thought process never serves one well. Neither is defending your viewpoint. I wonder if focusing simply on ensuring that no one is hurt should be the goal. That right or wrong has no significance in eternity. What matters most is avoid hurt and spread love.

The kind of love that says, "It doesn't matter who is right or wrong. It only matters that you are not hurt, not judged and just are simply love. That agape love that forgives all wrong. A love that never assigns a label that forgives all wrong. A love that just is.

Today's verse is a reminder Brothers and sisters, if someone is caught in a sin, you who live by the Spirit should restore that person gently. But watch yourselves, or you also may be tempted. I encourage you to read Galatians 6 in its entirety. To judge or to love, that is the question.

Dear Father,

Thank you for the reminder that if someone is caught in a sin, those who live by the Spirit should restore that person gently. But watch myself, or I too may be tempted. I pray that all your children love more and judge less. That they remember your warning that those who live by the Spirit should restore that person gently. To be watchful or they too may be tempted. I ask this in your son Jesus' name. Amen!

●

JUNE 19

Success

ANCHOR SCRIPTURE: 1 KINGS 2:3 (NLT)

"Observe the requirements of the Lord your God and follow all his ways. Keep the decrees, commands, regulations, and laws written in the Law of Moses so that you will be successful in all you do and wherever you go"

"Success isn't just about what you accomplish in your life;
It's about what you inspire others to do.
– *Unknown*

Do you ever wonder why the word success carries so much weight on our lives? What is success to one person, may be failure to another. Waking up and walking one step may be success to one person while running a marathon and finishing is success to another. So, what is success to you and why is it so important?

Merriam Webster defines success as the attainment of wealth, favor, or eminence. An accomplishment of an aim or purpose. Do you know anyone that doesn't desire wealth, favor, and eminence? Why do we want this thing called "success" any ways? Some may say, it is how they define their worth. I wonder if success was redefined what would that look like.

I read an article a while back entitled "What is the Definition of Success Anyway" (Huffington Post, 6/17/2015) written by Anna Partridge. She did research to see what famous people said about success. In general, she noted, the things that defined their success was the life they had built for their families and themselves. "Resoundingly these famous people defined success as the ability to bounce back — to make mistakes and learn from them. Success is about building a community and those deep, solid relationships to share our lives with people who care. Success is not a destination, but a journey and really do you ever truly reach your own success or are you still searching for what success means at 80."

It seems success is a process. It is a moving target that goes deeper than wealth and courage is required. Today's scripture is a reminder to observe the requirements of the Lord your God and follow all his ways. Keep the decrees, commands, regulations, and laws written in the Law of Moses so that you will be successful in all you do and wherever you go.

—————————— **PRAYER FOR THE DAY:** ——————————

Dear Father,
Thank you for continuing to transform my mind. For the reminder to keep the decrees, commands, regulations, and laws written in the Law of Moses so that I will be successful in all I do and wherever I go. I pray that all your children remember to keep the decrees, commands, regulations, and laws written on the Law of Moses so that they will be successful in all they do and wherever they go. I ask this in your son Jesus' name. Amen!

JUNE 20

Courage

ANCHOR SCRIPTURE: 1 CORINTHIANS 16:13(NIV)

"Be on your guard; stand firm in the faith;
be courageous; be strong"

"Courage is resistance to fear, mastery of fear, not absence of fear."
- *Mark Twain*

There is a movie that I believe came out in 2011 entitled Courageous. It is about four police officers who struggle with their faith, roles as husbands and fathers after tragedy strikes close to home. Together they made a decision that changed their lives. It is not easy living up to so many expectations as parents, children and as a family. It takes courage to take a stand, lean on faith and do the right thing against all odds.

This made me think of courage. Courage is sometimes defined as bravery. It also has been defined as "fear that has said its prayers." I loved this when I saw it written by Pastor Greg Laurie some time ago. "Courage doesn't mean you don't get afraid; it means you don't let fear stop you." We all have fears and have exercised courage at one point in our lives.

Courage is required for so many aspects of our lives. Courage is needed to do the right thing every single time; it is needed to change; it is needed to always tell the truth; it is needed to live a life in integrity; it is needed to grow; it is needed to trust God's process during the good and the bad; it is needed to lead with principles and values; it is needed to make bold moves. It seems courage is necessary to make it through life. Today's verse is a reminder to be on your guard; stand firm in the faith; be courageous; be strong. I encourage you to read 1 Corinthians 16. Be courageous!

I encourage you to read 1 Corinthians 16.

—————————— **PRAYER FOR THE DAY:** ——————————

Dear God,
Thank you for the reminder that to make it through life, I must be
on my guard, stand firm in my faith, be courageous and strong. I
pray that all your children be on guard, stand firm and strong in
their faith and are courageous. That no matter how fear may try
to get in the way, that they overcome their fears with courage.
I ask this in your son Jesus' name. Amen!

●

JUNE 21

Worry Wart

Anchor Scripture: Psalm 55:22

"Cast your cares on the LORD and he will sustain you;
he will never let the righteous be shaken"

"Worrying does not empty tomorrow of its troubles,
it empties today of its strength.
-Corrie Ten Boom

Are you or do you know anyone that is a worry wart? A worry wart is sometimes defined as a person who tends to dwell unduly on difficulty or troubles. Now, why would someone unduly want to dwell or burden themselves with difficulty or troubles? You would think troubles show up on its own, why create or build others.

Do you find yourself worrying about things that have not happened yet? I became curious about the origin of this phrase "worry wart" which insinuates or provides an image of a growth or an infection on the top layer of the skin. I read that this phrase originated from a popular comic strip that ran from 1922 until 1977 entitled Out Our Way by J R Williams. It was interesting to note, this article about words, highlighted that initially the phrase didn't mean what it does now — somebody who constantly worries about everything and anything. Instead it took its sense from the cartoon — a child who annoys everyone through being a pest or nuisance.

I encourage you to not let worry become a burden, a pest or nuisance. Beware of worry. Worry causes anxiety, and anxiety weighs down the heart. Remain present and watch your anxiety minimize. Take care of your heart. Today's verse is a reminder to cast your cares on the LORD and he will sustain you; he will never let the righteous be shaken. Be worry-free!

——————————— PRAYER FOR THE DAY: ———————————

Dear Father,
Thank you for the reminder to not worry about a thing. To cast my cares on you and you will sustain me. That you will never let the righteous be shaken. I pray that all your children cast their cares on you. You can handle it all. That they remember that you will sustain them and will never let the righteous shaken. I ask this in your son Jesus' name. Amen!

The Circle of Life

ANCHOR SCRIPTURE: ECCLESIASTES 1:3-5 (GW)

"What do people gain from all their hard work under the sun? Generations come, and generations go but the earth lasts forever. The sun rises, and the sun sets and then it rushes back to the place where it will rise again"

"The more we love the more we lose. The more we lose the more we learn. The more we learn the more we love. It comes full circle. Life is the school; love is the lesson. We cannot lose."

-Kate McGahan

When you hear "circle of life" what comes to mind for you? What comes to mind for me is the Disney movie "Lion King." It is an animated movie that "follows the adventures of the young lion Simba, who is to succeed his father, Mufasa, as King of the Pride Lands. Simba's jealous uncle, Scar, plots to usurp Mufasa's throne and lures father and son into a stampede of wildebeests where Mufasa dies. His uncle then manipulates Simba into thinking he was responsible for his father's death and caused the young cub to flee into exile."

Simba is given some valuable perspective from his childhood friend, Nala, and his shaman, Rafiki, before returning to challenge Scar to end his tyranny and take his place in the Circle of Life as the rightful King. Before his death, the father shared wisdom with his young cub that there is a "circle of life" that connects to our past and reaches our present. Although this is an animated film, it breathes life into the "circle of life."

It is interesting to note how the circle of life has cycles. The theme song for this movie describes a cycle that "unwinds our path. A path where some of us fall by the wayside and some of us soar to the stars.

Others sail through troubles and some have to live with the scars." Imagine that, you live in the circle, the circle of life.

Today's scripture is a reminder, what do people gain from all their hard work under the sun? Generations come, and generations go but the earth lasts forever. The sun rises, and the sun sets and then it rushes back to the place where it will rise again. I encourage you to read Ecclesiastes 1.

PRAYER FOR THE DAY:

Dear Father,
Thank you, the reminder, what do people gain from all their hard work under the sun? Generations come, and generations go but the earth lasts forever. The sun rises, and the sun sets and then it rushes back to the place where it will rise again. I pray that all your children remember that life is an endless circle. That generations come and generations go but earth lasts forever. That the sun rises, and the sun sets and then it rushes back to the place where it will rise again. I ask this in your son Jesus' name. Amen!

Disciplined

ANCHOR SCRIPTURE: PROVERBS 3:11-12

*"My son, do not despise the Lord's discipline or be weary
of his reproof, for the Lord reproves him whom he loves,
as a father the son in whom he delights."*

"Discipline is the refining fire by which talent becomes ability."
-Roy L. Smith

Do you enjoy being disciplined? Do you know anyone that enjoys being disciplined? It seems from childhood, being disciplined was confused as punishment rather than correction. I wonder if it has anything to do with how our minds pictured the discipline. Punishment is sometimes defined as the infliction or imposition of a penalty as retribution for an offense. Correction on the other hand is sometimes defined as an action intended to rehabilitate or improve. Whether one pictures discipline as infliction or retribution versus rehabilitation or improvement is in the mind and eye of the beholder.

However, if one practices self-discipline, it reduces the chance of rebuke and retribution from outside sources. Scriptures says "like an athlete, I punish my body, treating it roughly, training it to do what it should, and not what it wants to. Otherwise I fear that after enlisting others for the race, I might be declared unfit and ordered to stand aside." Note, training it to do what it should do, not what it wants to do. Hmm, self-discipline and succeeding in leading others may be closely connected.

It seems that self-discipline is important to power. It could be the secret ingredient to achieving the next level. If self-discipline is nonexistent, self-indulgence may take over. For sure the latter will stunt your growth. It will prevent you from reaching your next level of growth.

It seems paying attention to the discipline received and making the necessary corrections leads to maturity, it propels you to your next level. If you continue to look at discipline as punishment rather than correction, you may find yourself stuck at the same level your entire life.

Today's verse is a reminder to not despise the Lord's discipline or be weary of his reproof, for the Lord reproves him whom he loves, as a father the son in whom he delights." It seems to grow, and lead in bigger things, lead at another level, one must develop an appetite for correction, for discipline.

———————————— PRAYER FOR THE DAY: ————————————

Dear Father,
Thank you for the reminder to not despise your discipline or be weary of your reproof, for you reproves him whom you love. I pray that all your children remember the importance of your discipline and of their self-discipline. That they do not despise your discipline or be weary of your reproof, for you reproves him whom you love. I ask this in your son Jesus' name. Amen!

Perfectly Broken

ANCHOR SCRIPTURE: REVELATION 21:5 (NIV)

*"He who was seated on the throne said, "I am making
everything new!" Then he said, "Write this down,
for these words are trustworthy and true"*

"Where there is ruin, there is hope for a treasure."
- Rumi

Brokenness, Broken, Broke. Are you told these things? How do you feel when you hear these words? Maybe broken is not a bad thing. Like a stable fracture, the broken ends of the bone line up and are barely out of place. Repairing is less complicated. Maybe what some call broken is a "stable break", a break perfectly lined up to be easily put back in the right place.

In Japan, there is an ancient practice called Kintsugi (the art of precious scars) where broken or cracked ceramics are repaired using gold or a precious metal. This gives a new lease of life to the prior broken or cracked pottery that becomes even more refined thanks to its "scars" and increases its value thanks to the added precious metal. "This art teaches that broken objects are not something to hide but to display with pride."

There is a song by Tasha Cobbs entitled Gracefully Broken. Part of the lyrics of this song says this; "God will break you to position YOU; Break you to promote you And break you to put you in your right place, But when He breaks you, he doesn't hurt you,

When He breaks you He doesn't destroy you, He does it with grace." Maybe the break is to put all the broken pieces gracefully and perfectly back together again. To create something completely new with increase value. Maybe it is a reminder to trust God's plans not yours. Maybe it is a reminder to not believe the "brokenness hype." Maybe you are perfectly broken to be returned to your rightful place. Today's scripture is a reminder he who was seated on the throne said, "I am making everything new!" Then he said, "Write this down, for these words are trustworthy and true.

——————————— **PRAYER FOR THE DAY:** ———————————

Dear Father,
Thank you for reminder that sometimes a break or stable fracture is part of your plan. A plan to make me much more precious than before. To promote me to another level and make everything new. To make me whole. I pray that all your children understand that your break is not to hurt, it is to align and elevate all to your plans. That they remember you are making everything new and your words are trustworthy and true. I ask this in your son Jesus' name. Amen!

Live, Laugh, Love

ANCHOR SCRIPTURE: 1 PETER 3:10-11

"Is a reminder "If you want to enjoy life and see many happy days, keep your tongue from speaking evil and your lips from telling lies. Turn away from evil and do good. Search for peace, and work to maintain it"

The more you laugh, the more you love, the more you live. Today I share this poem by Bessie Anderson Stanley entitled Success.

Success by Bessie Anderson Stanley

He has achieved success
who has lived well,
laughed often, and loved much;
who has enjoyed the trust of
pure women,

the respect of intelligent men and
the love of little children, who has filled his niche and
accomplished his task.

who has left the world better than he found it?
whether by an improved poppy,
a perfect poem or a rescued soul.

who has never lacked appreciation of Earth's beauty or failed
to express it; who has always looked for the best in others and

given them the best he had;
whose life was an inspiration;
whose memory a benediction.

Today's scripture is a reminder "If you want to enjoy life and see many happy days, keep your tongue from speaking evil and your lips from telling lies. Turn away from evil and do good. Search for peace, and work to maintain it. I dare you to Live more, laugh more and love more! And remember, love is an action not a feeling.

Dear Father,
Thank you for the reminder to live, laugh and love more. That if I want to enjoy life and see many days, keep my tongue from speaking evil and my lips from telling lies. Turn away from evil and do good. Search for peace, and work to maintain it. I pray that all your children live, laugh, and love more. That they enjoy life and see many days. That they keep their tongue from speaking evil and their lips from telling lies. That they turn away from evil and do good. I ask this in your son Jesus' name. Amen!

Tomorrow is Not Promised

ANCHOR SCRIPTURE: JOHN 5:24 (ESV)

"Truly, truly, I say to you, whoever hears my word and believes him who sent me has eternal life. He does not come into judgment, but has passed from death to life"

"The best preparation for tomorrow is doing your best today."
- H. Jackson Brown

A dear friend died suddenly yesterday. It is not easy to wrap your head around the loss of a loved one, especially when you are unprepared. I don't think we can ever be fully prepared even when anchored on faith. It makes no sense and all that makes sense is that we must continue to trust God's plans for each of us.

The why, how, why her, why now, why so suddenly may never be answered. The one thing that was answered is that tomorrow is not promised to anyone. Here today, gone tomorrow. So, for those still holding onto grudges with your loved ones, rethink if your grudge is more important than peace and love. For those promising to connect or gather with loved ones or close friends and haven't done so yet, do it now. Don't wait. For those waiting to make that call to say hello to a friend, a relative or that neighbor that lives alone, make the call now. For those searching for their purpose, do the work, make the investment now and lead your purpose.

Today's verse is a reminder whoever hears my word and believes him who sent me has eternal life. He does not come into judgment but has passed from death to life. I believe that my dear friend has passed from death into life. She will be sorely missed. I remind you; tomorrow is not promised to any of us. Live "right" now!

Dear Father,
Thank you for the reminder that tomorrow is not promised
to any of us. That we must live right and live your way now.
That whoever hears your word and believes has eternal life.
Thank you for your words that remain true. I pray that all your
children remember that tomorrow is not promised to anyone.
That they do the work to live "right" and live your way. That they
remember you are the way, the truth, and the life through it all.
I ask this in your son Jesus' name. Amen!

JUNE 27

Thank You

ANCHOR SCRIPTURE: 2 CORINTHIANS 4:15 (NIV)

"All this is for your benefit, so that the grace that is reaching
more and more people may cause thanksgiving to overflow
to the glory of God"

"Gratitude should not be just a reaction to getting what you
want, but an all-the-time gratitude, the kind where you notice
the little things and where you constantly look for the good
even in unpleasant situations."
-Marelisa Fabrega

Showing gratitude is the most powerful and yet underutilized tool
we have as humans. Yes, those two simple words "Thank You" are

so powerful and are yet still underutilized. I noticed recently how expressing gratitude by saying Thank YOU to just saying "Thanks" is a common practice. This practice to me sends a different sentiment. It seems to take away the value and sentiment of personalizing the expression of gratitude when you remove the word "You." Think about it, saying "thanks" versus saying "thank you." There is power in adding the word "you."

As a child, you may have been taught to say please and thank you. If you reflect, you may notice the difference saying thank you made to your life. Busyness, always wanting more, and lack of remaining present may cause one to forget to be grateful and at times even forget to say thank you. As I look back, I think our parents were on to something. They were teaching us the secret to happiness and everlasting joy. Sincerely remaining grateful for all and personally expressing gratitude and thanksgiving seems to give you only one option, to remain positive through all circumstances.

Today's verse is a reminder that all this is for your benefit, so that the grace that is reaching more and more people may cause thanksgiving to overflow to the glory of God. Thank you for grace.

─────────────── **PRAYER FOR THE DAY:**───────────────

Dear Father,
Thank you for the reminder of the grace you give daily. To be thankful not just on Thanksgiving Day, be thankful always. That all I go through is for my benefit, so that the grace that is reaching more and more people may cause thanksgiving to overflow to your glory. I pray that all your children are reminded of the grace you give daily. To be thankful not just on Thanksgiving Day, to be thankful always. That all they go through is for their benefit, so that the grace that is reaching more and more people may cause thanksgiving to overflow to your glory. I ask this in your son Jesus' name. Amen!

Give Thanks Always

ANCHOR SCRIPTURE: PSALM 100:4 (NIV)

"Enter his gates with thanksgiving and his courts with praise; give thanks to him and praise his name"

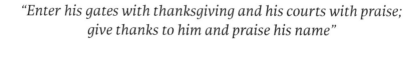

"When we focus on our gratitude, the tide of disappointment goes out and the tide of love rushes in."
-Kristin Armstrong

Every day is a day to give thanks. Today you are gifted a day, a special holiday to gather with loved ones. To pause and remember all the things and people for which you are grateful. What if you carried this same sentiment daily? To take time out of your day to thank someone special in your life. To spend time and share a meal with those who hold a special place in your heart. To pause and check your surroundings and breath in all the things that bless your life daily and for which you are grateful.

It is easy, after this holiday ends or even before it ends, to set gratitude aside. To return to focusing on what you don't have and all that disappoints you. I encourage you to hold onto gratitude and rejoicing in all. Look for the tiny things in your life that allows you to focus on gratitude. You may not be able to touch or see these things. To be grateful to God from whom all blessings flow.

Today's verse is a reminder to enter his gates with thanksgiving and his courts with praise; give thanks to him and praise his name. Give thanks always.

Dear Father,
Thank you for the reminder to give thanks always. To enter your gates and courts with praise and thanksgiving. To thank you and praise your name. I pray that all your children remember to give thanks always. To enter your gates and courts with praise and thanksgiving. To always thank you and praise your name. I ask this in your son Jesus' name. Amen!

I am truly and sincerely grateful for each of you and your daily support. Thank YOU and much love to all.

Keep Climbing

ANCHOR SCRIPTURE: 2 CHRONICLES 15:7 (NIV)

"But as for you, be strong and courageous, for your work will be rewarded."

"Every mountain top is within reach if you just keep climbing"
~ *Barry Finlay*

In honor of Small Business Saturday, I share this poem by Richard Branson with you. No matter how hard the climb gets, keep climbing!

A Poem for All Entrepreneurs
By Richard Branson

The road to success is paved with tests,
So you've got to believe in yourself above the rest.
Dream big, and let your passion shine,
If you don't, you won't end up with a dime.
Challenge the status quo, disrupt the market, and say YES!

And remember that innovation is an endless quest.
Don't forget to change business for good, if you want to change the world then you should. If you think with your head and listen to your heart, I promise you'll get off to a flying start.

Make bold moves, but always play fair,
Always say please and thank you – it's cool to care.
Do what you love and love what you do,
This advice is nothing new.
Now, stop worrying about whether your business will be a hit,
Rise to the challenge and say, 'screw it, let's do it!'

Dear Father,
Thank you for the reminder to be strong and courageous that my
work will be rewarded to keep moving, keep climbing. I pray that
no matter the mountain your children face, that they remain
strong and courageous. That they remember that the mountain
too is within reach if they keep climbing. I ask this in your son
Jesus' name. Amen!

JUNE 30

Giving Generously

ANCHOR SCRIPTURE: PROVERBS 3:27 (NIV)

"Do not withhold good from those to whom it is due,
when it is in your power to act"

"I have found that among its other benefits, giving
liberates the soul of the giver."
Maya Angelou

Do you ever pause to think about why you give? Do you give for recognition, do you give because someone gave to you, do you give out
of pity or do you simply give for no reason? I wonder if you even need
a reason to give. Wasting your life living it for yourself seems empty
when you can always give money, influence, or time. It all counts as
giving. Giving introduces those around you to generosity, to caring
for others.

Do you recall as a child going to visit your Uncle, Aunt, or Grandparents and they would always have something to give to you or would give you a few dollars just because? Or at times, they gave you a few dollars and told you to split it amongst your siblings or cousins. Did you do anything or ask for this gift? Your answer may be no. As I think about these experiences, I realize how these were small acts that taught caring is sharing. It also introduced the importance of giving and generosity.

Sometimes we worry about having so much when we can't take none of it with us when we leave this earth. Proverbs 21:26 reminds us that all day long he craves for more, but the righteous give without sparing. What if you give without sparing of your time, talent, and treasures? What if this became your legacy? It is said that it is more blessed to give than to receive. Today's verse is a reminder to not withhold good from those to whom it is due, when it is in your power to act.

───────────────── **PRAYER FOR THE DAY:** ─────────────────

Dear Father,
Thank you for the reminder of the importance of giving and generosity. To not withhold good from those to whom it is due, when it is in my power to act. I pray that all your children remember the power of generosity. That they do not withhold good from those to whom it is due, when it is in their power to act. That caring is sharing. I ask this in your son Jesus' name. Amen!

July

Hope Anyways

ANCHOR SCRIPTURE: ROMANS 5:5

*"And hope does not put us to shame, because God's love
has been poured out into our hearts through the Holy Spirit,
who has been given to us."*

"Life is a rope that swings us through hope.
Always believe that today is better than yesterday, and
tomorrow will be much better than today...
- Shermin Samuel

As the year ends, you may begin to feel disappointed that you didn't accomplish as much as you set out to do at the onset of this year. Rather than shame and disappointment, chose to hope instead. Hope that you know there is a great plan for your life. A plan for you to prosper and not fail.

I recalled a message someone shared with me that read "Having goals is not enough. One must keep getting closer to those goals, amidst all the inevitable twists and turns of life. Hope allows people to approach problems with a mindset and strategy-set suitable to success, thereby increasing the chances they will actually accomplish their goals." I keep this close and refer to it often. I have a dear sister friend that reminds us to "jot that down." "Jot that down"...that mindset and strategy is key to success.

Hope is the confident expectation of what has been promised and planted in you. Hope truly anchors your soul amidst the inevitable twists and turns of life. Today's verse is a reminder that hope does not put us to shame, because God's love has been poured out into our hearts through the Holy Spirit, who has been given to us. Keep hope alive and endure!

Dear Father,
Thank you for the reminder that hope anchors the soul. That no matter the twist and turns of life, that having hope does not put us to shame because your love has been poured out into our hearts through the Holy Spirit, who has been given to us. I pray that all your children allow hope to anchor their souls. That they remember that hope does not put us to shame, because God's love has been poured out into our hearts through the Holy Spirit, who has been given to us. That they keep hope alive. I ask this in Jesus' name. Amen!

●

JULY 2

Try or Trust

ANCHOR SCRIPTURE: JEREMIAH 7:8 NIV

"But look, you are trusting in deceptive words that are worthless."

─────────────────

"Never be afraid to trust an unknown future to a known God.
- *Corrie ten Boom*

─────────────────

Do you find yourself trying more than you are trusting? To try is defined as an effort to accomplish something. To trust is defined as reliance on the character, ability, strength, or truth of someone or something. Note to try requires effort. To trust requires reliance, no effort necessary.

Do you recall that old car, no matter what, you could always rely that it will take you from point A to point B. That trust that when you put the key in the ignition, no matter how old the car may be, you fully trusted that the car would start. No effort worry or concern would overcome you. You just trusted. I believe such a car was referred to as "old reliable." What if you applied the same trust in your skills, abilities, and strength? There would be no need to exert effort or "try," you would effortlessly do. I find that our thoughts are the culprit that separates whether you try, or you trust.

Pausing, reflecting, and quieting your thoughts allow you the opportunity to see when you should trust more than try. Today's scriptures are reminders to look, you are trusting in deceptive words that are worthless. That those who know your name trust in you, for you, LORD, have never forsaken those who seek you. Trust more! I encourage you to read Jeremiah 7 and Psalm 9.

———————————— **PRAYER FOR THE DAY:** ————————————

Dear Father,
Thank you for the reminder that I am trusting deceptive words that are worthless. That those who know your name trust in you, for you have never forsaken those who seek you. I pray that all your children look and see that they are trusting in deceptive words that are worthless. That those who know your name trust in you, for you, Father, have never forsaken those who seek you. That they trust you more. I ask this in your son Jesus' name. Amen!

Transformation

ANCHOR SCRIPTURE: 2 CORINTHIANS 5:17

"Therefore, if anyone is in Christ, the new creation has come:
The old has gone, the new is here!"

"What the caterpillar calls the end of the world,
the master calls a butterfly."
- Richard Bach

Merriam Webster defines transformation as an act, process, or instance of transforming or being transformed. Change and transformation is an ongoing part of life. For some it is subtle for others it is dramatic. Transformation usually involves some discomfort and may involve pain.

The transformation may be a new and better chapter, it may be a new way of doing things or it may be a new you. Just remember that transforming and change is a process and not a destination, some parts of the process are easy and some not so easy. Embrace the process it is not the end; it is just the beginning. Like the caterpillar, you may feel like it is the end, when it is just the beginning.

There is a shift in your focus when you understand change and transformation. You understand that nothing you do is about you, it is about those that surround you, those in your tribe and those that are coming behind you. Hebrews 10:24 says "And let us be concerned about one another in order to promote love and good works..."

Today's scripture is a reminder, therefore, if anyone is in Christ, the new creation has come: The old has gone, the new is here! Be encouraged.

Dear Father,
Thank you for the reminder that if anyone is in Christ, the
new creation has come: The old has gone, the new is here. That
transformation is a process not a destination. I pray that all your
children are patient in the process. That they remember if any-
one is in Christ, the new creation has come: The old has gone, the
new is here. I ask this in your son Jesus' name. Amen!

JULY 4

Be a Rainbow

ANCHOR SCRIPTURE: GENESIS 9:13

"I have set my rainbow in the clouds, and it will be the sign
of the covenant between me and the earth."

"Try to be a rainbow in someone else's cloud."
- Dr. Maya Angelou

This weekend, while in the mountains, I witnessed something interesting. Looking up at the sky, I saw a faint rainbow peeking through
the clouds. It was an amazing view. I thought about Maya Angelou's
wisdom when she shared this: "Try to be a rainbow in someone's
cloud." If we were still long enough to see the many rainbows that
show up in our clouds, how much brighter would our day be?

Are you prepared and willing to be a rainbow in someone else's cloud? Today's scripture is a reminder: I set my rainbow in the cloud, and it shall be for the sign of the covenant between me and the earth. Be a blessing to someone today!

───────────── **PRAYER FOR THE DAY:** ─────────────

Dear Father,
Thank you for the reminder to be a rainbow in someone else's cloud. That you set your rainbow in the cloud, and it shall be for the sign of the covenant between you and the earth. I pray that all your children remember to be a rainbow in someone else's cloud. That you set your rainbow in the cloud, and it shall be for the sign of the covenant between you and the earth. I ask this in your son Jesus' name. Amen!

Eyes on the Prize

ANCHOR SCRIPTURE: PHILIPPIANS 3:13-14 (NIV)

"Brothers and sisters, I do not consider myself yet to have taken hold of it. But one thing I do: Forgetting what is behind and straining toward what is ahead, I press on toward the goal to win the prize for which God has called me heavenward in Christ Jesus"

"Your most important work is always ahead of you, never behind you."
- *Stephen R. Covey*

Stephen Covey's 7 Habits of highly effective people teaches in habit number 2 to begin with the End in Mind. Dr. Covey states that to begin each day, task, or project with a clear vision of your desired direction and destination, and then continue by flexing your proactive muscles to make things happen.

It seems we must lock-in our destination and keep doing the one thing each day to reach that end. When you have clarity, laser focus, and believe in your vision, it seems that as long as you are doing your part, one thing each day to continue in the desired or assigned direction, you do not lose patience.

You begin to understand that the pitfalls, the delays, the things you thought kept you from your destination, are propelling you to the prize. Just continue to believe that you will arrive one step at a time. Like my dear friend Yolanda says "Pole Pole" (pronounced Polay Polay) which is Swahili for "slowly, gently, softly, quietly; be calm, take it quietly, don't excite yourself, never mind": slowly; take it easy."

Today's scripture is a reminder Brothers and sisters, I do not consider myself yet to have taken hold of it. But one thing I do: Forgetting what is behind and straining toward what is ahead, I press on toward the goal to win the prize for which God has called me heavenward in Christ Jesus. Yes, take it easy, lock your eyes on the prize and keep it moving!

---------- **PRAYER FOR THE DAY:** ----------

Dear Father,
Thank you for the reminder to start with the end in mind. To forget what is behind and strain toward what is ahead, to press toward the goal to win the prize for which you have called me heavenward in Christ Jesus. I pray that all your children start with the end in mind. That they forget what is behind and strain toward what is ahead, to press toward the goal to win the prize for which you have called them heavenward in Christ Jesus. That they remember your promises. I ask this in your son Jesus' name. Amen!

Against All Odds

ANCHOR SCRIPTURE: ROMANS 4:18 (TPT)

Against all odds, when it looked hopeless, Abraham believed the promise and expected God to fulfill it. He took God at his word, and as a result he became the father of many nations. God's declaration over him came to pass: "Your descendants will be so many that they will be impossible to count!"

"Never let the odds keep you from doing what you know in your heart you were meant to do."
- H. Jackson Brown, Jr.

Have you ever faced a situation where all odds were against you? I recently had a conversation with a dear friend. He was about to throw in the towel on his dream. I stand corrected, he was about to throw in the towel on his purpose. We talked many times and I believed the vision God gave him. He, however, temporarily lost sight of the audacious purpose that God had placed on his life.

He forgot that sometimes to fulfill your purpose, you must come against all odds. That you cannot continue to be comfortable in thinking small. That our Father' calling for us is to think and dream BIG. That the steps he gave us are simple and not so easy to follow. Those steps I simplified as 1-Give God your first (of everything), 2- Obey God's every word, then 3- Trust. Simple right, not. (LOL)

Sometimes you say you believe, and trust and you still choose to disobey when the odds are against you. I remind you; we are all descendants of Abraham. The odds were against Abraham and Sarah to conceive. Against all odds, Abraham continued to believe God's Word and remain expectant for that promise to be fulfilled way into his senior years.

If you are doing what you know in your heart you were meant to do, keep trusting. When you reach a point where it looks like all odds are against you, trust more than ever before. This is where God does his best work. Surrender all control and let God fulfill his promises to you as his child.

Today's verse is a reminder, "Against all odds, when it looked hopeless, Abraham believed the promise and expected God to fulfill it. He took God at his word, and as a result he became the father of many nations. God's declaration over him came to pass: "Your descendants will be so many that they will be impossible to count!" Don't give up. The odds, no matter how slim, are in your favor. Keep trusting!

PRAYER FOR THE DAY:

Dear Father,
Thank you for the reminder of my lineage. No matter what the odds say, you never break your promises. That I must remain expectant that you will fulfill your promises. I pray that all your children remember their lineage. That this reminder of their lineage will provide them assurance that no matter the odds, to continue to give you their first, obey and trust you to fulfill the promises you made to each of them. I ask this in your son Jesus's name. Amen!

Refocus

ANCHOR SCRIPTURE: ROMANS 8:5 ESV

*"For those who live according to the flesh set their minds
on the things of the flesh, but those who live according to the
Spirit set their minds on the things of the Spirit."*

Happy New Year, Happy New Month and Happy January!

"JANUARY, the first month of the year, A perfect time
to start all over again, changing energies and deserting
old moods, new beginnings, new attitudes"
- Charmaine J Forde

A new year and month, just like a new day, offers you the opportunity to adjust and corrections. To re-prioritize what is important, to refocus your vision. As humans, we may be led into temptation, lured by distractions, or place emphasis on the insignificant. Rather than getting entangled with trying to understand why you lost focus, why not spend your energy refocusing and getting back on track to your greater.

A new year is a great time to do so. Consistently doing the work to remain focus on your greater. Remaining present so you are not awakened six months, one year, or decades later to realize you have been operating with a blurred focus. Some of you may recall when you surrendered to the fact that you needed reading glasses. You tried everything to avoid the dreaded reading glasses. However, to see what you were signing or to read the fine print, those glasses where needed to see clearly. Treat this new year as new glasses that help you refocus to your greater.

Today's scripture is a reminder that for those who live according to the flesh set their minds on the things of the flesh, but those who live according to the Spirit set their minds on the things of the Spirit. I encourage you to read Romans 8 in its entirety. Have a consistent and focused new year.

PRAYER FOR THE DAY:

Dear Father,
Thank you for the reminder that a new year allows a new focus. That those who live according to the flesh set their minds on the things of the flesh, but those who live according to the Spirit set their minds on the things of the Spirit. I pray that all your children remember that a new year is an opportunity to adjust their focus on their greater. That those who live according to the flesh set their minds on the things of the flesh, but those who live according to the Spirit set their minds on the things of the Spirit. I ask this in your son Jesus' name. Amen

The Power of Choosing Joy

ANCHOR SCRIPTURE: JOHN 15:10-11 (NIV)

*"If you keep my commands, you will remain in my love,
just as I have kept my Father's commands and remain in his
love. I have told you this so that my joy may be in you
and that your joy may be complete"*

The joy we feel has little to do with the circumstances of our lives
and everything to do with the focus of our lives."
- *Russell M. Nelson*

Merriam Webster defines joy as the emotion evoked by well-being, success, or good fortune or by the prospect of possessing what one desires. It is interesting to note that the definition of joy includes "possessing what one desires." I wonder why someone would desire anything less than joy.

There is power in choosing joy in every circumstance. James 1:2 says, my brethren, count it all joy when you fall into various trials. Joy is a choice. "The Book of Joy: Lasting Happiness in a Changing World" helps you understand how to attain joy and teaches that you are here to thrive, not just survive. It's an empowering dialogue between the Dalia Lama and Desmond Tutu, the Archbishop of South Africa that underscores the concept that our happiness really does lie within ourselves and that we have the power to create a more blissful reality." I am not saying that living a joyful life is easy, it is however attainable. It may require, as The Book of Joy notes, "going into the wounds and feeling those uncomfortable thoughts and feelings, and then shifting your perspective to that of forgiveness, or gratitude, or compassion, or love." Today's verse is a reminder, if you keep my commands, you will remain in my love, just as I have kept my Father's commands and remain in his love. I have told you this so that my joy may be in you and that your joy may be complete. I encourage you to read John 15 in its entirety.

Dear Father,
Thank you for the reminder that there is power in choosing joy.
That if I keep your commands, you will remain in my love, just as
your son have kept your commands and remain your love. I pray
that all your children remember that there is power in choosing
joy. That if they keep your commands, you will remain in their
love. That you have told them this so that your joy may be in each
of them and that their joy may be complete. I ask this in your son
Jesus' name. Amen!

JULY 9

Healing

ANCHOR SCRIPTURE: ISAIAH 58:8

"Then your light shall break forth like the dawn,
and your healing shall spring up quickly."

"You will begin to heal when you let go of past hurts.
Forgive those who have wronged you and learn to forgive
yourself for your mistakes."
Anonymous

I recently had a conversation with a dear friend about healing. Do you ever wonder what it takes to truly heal? I am not talking about healing what you can see, a cut or a bruise. I am talking about healing what you and the world cannot see. The injured souls, hearts and minds that are held captive by untruths, half-truths, limiting beliefs, and hurtful experiences in their lives.

How can one ever heal if you can't or won't talk about the unseen pain or hurt? If you continue to ignore or pretend that it is not present? Sure, you can pretend all is well on the outside while you continue to slowly die or fall apart on the inside. As I reflect on biblical stories, many were healed by earnestly asking and seeking healing. They spoke about their pain and illness and were healed.

Today's scripture is a reminder that "Then your light shall break forth like the dawn, and your healing shall spring up quickly." Will you allow your light to break forth like the dawn to spring up your healing or continue to remain captive to the darkness, untruths, half-truths, limiting beliefs, and hurtful experiences? I encourage you to read Isaiah 58 in its entirety and consider this, are you trying to heal without talking about the root cause of your pain? Get help if you need to and let your light break forth like the dawn.

———————— PRAYER FOR THE DAY: ————————

Dear Father,
Thank you for the reminder of the biblical stories and how healing took place. That surrendering wholeheartedly to you, and your ways, my light shall break forth like the dawn, and my healing shall spring up quickly. I pray that all your children heal from the untruths, half-truths, limiting beliefs, and hurtful experiences that may be standing in the way of their freedom. That like many in the bible, they begin to talk about their pain, begin to heal and let their light break forth like the dawn. That they heed your guidance in Isaiah 58. I ask this in Jesus' name. Amen!

Piece of the Puzzle

ANCHOR SCRIPTURE: EPHESIANS 2:21 (NIV)

*"In him the whole building is joined together and rises
to become a holy temple in the Lord."*

"Without you, the puzzle is incomplete"

Merriam Webster defines a puzzle as a problem difficult to solve or a situation difficult to resolve. I wonder if solutions to problems would be made simpler if we simply saw our world as a jigsaw puzzle. That each of us represent a small irregularly cut piece that must be fitted together to form a picture. That without interlocking these irregular, small pieces, the world is incomplete.

Have you ever completed a jigsaw puzzle? Each piece that comes in the box, has an assigned location. The key is to keep searching until you find the right piece that interlocks with the other. This is the only way to move forward in completing the puzzle. Deepak Chopra is quoted as saying, "There are no extra pieces in the universe. Everyone is here because he or she has a place to fill, and every piece must fit itself into the big jigsaw puzzle."

If you have not found that place where you interlock perfectly, don't give up. Reference the big picture if you must, there is a place in the universe for your small irregular cut. Today's verse is a reminder, in him the whole building is joined and rises to become a holy temple in the Lord.

Dear Father,
Thank you for the reminder that my irregular piece of the puzzle
is significant. That without interlocking with the right pieces the
puzzle is incomplete. That in you, the whole building is joined
and rises to become a holy temple. I pray that all your children
remember that no matter the irregularity of their piece of the
puzzle, that they matter. That without interlocking with the
right pieces the puzzle is incomplete. In you, the whole building
is joined and rises to become a holy temple. I ask this in your son
Jesus' name. Amen!

JULY 11

When Trouble Comes...

ANCHOR SCRIPTURE: JAMES 1:2-4

"Reminds us, "Dear brothers and sisters, when troubles
of any kind come your way, consider it an opportunity for
great joy. For you know that when your faith is tested,
your endurance has a chance to grow...."

"Joyce Meyer reminds us that worry, doubt, confusion, depression, anger and feelings of condemnation: all are attacks on the mind. It is reassuring to know that there is guidance on how to navigate these trouble times.

When trouble comes it is easy to feel alone, have a cloudy mind, to live in the darkness, to feel trapped or stuck with no way out. We will all experience trouble in this world. It is not if but when. James 1:2-4 reminds us, "Dear brothers and sisters, when troubles of any kind come your way, consider it an opportunity for great joy. For you know that when your faith is tested, your endurance has a chance to grow. So, let it grow, for when your endurance is fully developed, you will be perfect and complete, needing nothing." Psalm 34 states, "The righteous person may have many troubles, but the Lord delivers him from them all."

I remain obedient and humbly shared these words today. These are just a few of the words that guide me and lift me during difficult times. I encourage you to keep the faith and trust God. Rise up, and lift your eyes to the mountains where does your help come from?

Your help comes from the Lord, the Maker of heaven and earth. I encourage you to read Psalm 91 and 121. May it bring you strength, peace, and courage. Be encouraged!

Praying for you!

―――――――――――― **PRAYER FOR THE DAY:** ――――――――――――

Dear Father,
Thank you for the reminder to persevere when trouble comes as you are testing the depth of my faith. I pray that all your children recognize your testing and continue to persevere and trust you more than themselves when trouble comes. I ask this in your son Jesus Jesus' name, Amen.

Resilience

ANCHOR SCRIPTURE: ISAIAH 41:10 ESV

"Fear not, for I am with you; be not dismayed, for I am your God; I will strengthen you, I will help you, I will uphold you with my righteousness right hand."

"The human capacity for burden is like bamboo-far more flexible than you'd ever believe at first glance.
-Jodi Picoult

Merriam Webster defines resiliency as the capability of a strained body to recover its size and shape after deformation caused especially by compressive stress or an ability to recover from or adjust easily to misfortune or change.

Resilience seem to be a common trait of leadership. I recalled reading an article in Forbes magazine that stated "Resilience is that feature of character that demonstrates an ability to bend but not break. Leaders need resilience because they are often faced by obstacles that can overwhelm them. Few remain defeated for long, and so examining resilience is always a good leadership lesson."

I recalled the devastation of Hurricane Katrina where resilience was demonstrated by young and old. It was as though they knew they would bend but not break. It seems resilience requires taking all that is thrown at you, moment by moment with grace to move forward. Sometimes, amid trouble, you can simply pause and reflect of the many times you bent and never broke. The many stories you could share about what I refer to as your "bamboo experience." That you are a resilience leader.

Today's verse is a reminder, "Fear not, for I am with you; be not dismayed, for I am your God; I will strengthen you, I will help you, I will

303

uphold you with my righteousness right hand." No matter what you are facing today, remember you were bent before, but not broken. God is with you and will strengthen you.

———————— PRAYER FOR THE DAY: ————————

Dear Father,
Thank you for the reminder of the importance of resilience during tough times. To fear not, for you are with me; be not dismayed for you are my God who will strengthen, help me, and uphold me with your right hand. I pray that all your children are reminded of their history of resilience. That to fear not, for you are with them, be not dismayed for you are their God who will strengthen, help them, and uphold them with your right hand. I ask this in your son Jesus' name. Amen!

Perspective

ANCHOR SCRIPTURE: ISAIAH 41:10 ESV

"Fear not, for I am with you; be not dismayed, for I am your God; I will strengthen you, I will help you, I will uphold you with my righteousness right hand."

"Empathy begins with understanding life from another person's perspective. Nobody has an objective experience of reality. It's all through our own individual prisms."
-*Sterling K. Brown*

Did you know, that although today is a federal holiday to honor presidents of the United States, nine states do not celebrate this holiday? This made me think of how being consumed in your own world, may cause you to make assumptions such as, everyone is off today or this an official holiday across the nation, when this may not be true.

This brought me to the word perspective which is sometimes defined as a particular attitude toward or way of regarding something, a point of view. It did not occur to me that some major holidays would not be celebrated nationwide...perspective. This is why I love learning, reading, and connecting with new people. You always learn something new and begin to grow and understand life from another person's perspective. Do you take the time to understand the other person's perspective before making assumptions? Leading others may require sharpening our skills in perspective taking.

Matthew 7:12 is a reminder, so whatever you wish that others would do to you, do also to them, for this is the Law and the Prophets.

Dear Father,
I thank you for the reminder about perspective. That whatever
I wish that others would do to me, do also to them, for this is
the Law and the Prophets. I pray that all your children pause
and remember the benefits of perspective taking. That whatever
they wish that others do to them, that they also do onto others,
for this is the Law and the Prophets. I ask this in your son Jesus'
name. Amen!

JULY 14

Elevated Thinking

ANCHOR SCRIPTURE: COLOSSIANS 3:2 (NIV)

"Set your minds on things above, not on earthly things."

"Your mind shines brightest when you enlighten others; your heart,
when you encourage others; your soul, when you elevate others; and
your life, when you empower others.
– *Matshona Dhilwayo*

The word elevate is sometimes defined as to lift or make higher, raise
in rank and status or to improve morally, intellectually, or culturally.
There are so many thoughts that come to mind when thinking of
these definitions for the word elevate. One thought is how to begin

living life at a higher level. Many may consider living at a higher level in relation to economic, social or education. I wonder if the focus of elevated living is blurred.

What if the elevation sought is one of setting our minds on the things above? Things that we cannot see. An elevation that allows each of us to operate with the fruits of the spirit (love, joy, peace, forbearance, kindness, goodness, faithfulness, gentleness, and self-control) constantly activated. I wonder if this is key to freedom. To freeing and renewing our minds and our hearts. To no longer hurt people because you were hurt. To lead and elevate your thoughts to things above to elevate and empower others.

Today's scripture is a reminder to set your minds on things above, not on earthly things. That attaching your thoughts to earthly things may keep you in bondage. Elevate your thoughts on things above and live in freedom every day. I encourage you to read Colossians 3 in its entirety.

───────────────── **PRAYER FOR THE DAY:** ─────────────────

Dear Father,

Thank you for the reminder to set my mind on things above, not earthly things. To elevate my thinking, to elevate my life. I pray that all your children remember to set their minds on things above, not on earthly things. That they elevate their thinking and continue to improve their lives. I ask this in Jesus' name. Amen!

Covenant

ANCHOR SCRIPTURE: DEUTERONOMY 7:13 (NIV)

*"He will love you and bless you and increase your numbers.
He will bless the fruit of your womb, the crops of your land—
your grain, new wine and olive oil—the calves of your
herds and the lambs of your flocks in the land he swore to
your ancestors to give you."*

---

*"God doesn't want us to have rigid rituals with Him. In the new
covenant, He is more interested in having a relationship with us."*
- Joseph Prince

Covenant is sometimes defined as a written agreement or promise usually under seal between two or more parties especially for the performance of some action. Have you looked at the covenants you have established? Are you keeping track of these and fulfilling each? Have you broken any covenant intentionally or unintentionally and why?

Today's scripture from Deuteronomy reminds me of a very important covenant the Lord God made with our ancestors. He will love, bless us, and increase our numbers. He will bless the fruit of our wombs and bless all. The preceding verse (V12) warns us of the following: "If you pay attention to these laws and are careful to follow them, then the LORD your God will keep his covenant of love with you, as he swore to your ancestors."

Such wonderful legacy we can easily tap into by obeying and paying attention the Lord's law. Learning, understanding, and following God's law is important to me. So are the covenants made with my brothers and sisters. I encourage you to consider your convents today and take an honest look on whether you are honoring these. It is easier said than done.

Dear God,
Thank you for honoring the covenants you made with my ances-
tors and continue to bless me and my fruits. I pray that all your
children believe that they too have inherited your love, abundant
blessing, and increase. I ask this in your son Jesus' name. Amen!

JULY 16

Refuge

ANCHOR SCRIPTURE: PSALM 46:1 (NIV)

"God is our refuge and strength, an ever-present
help in trouble."

"Education is an ornament in prosperity and a refuge in adversity."
- Aristotle

Merriam Webster defines refuge as something (as a building) that offers cover from the weather or protection from danger. Have you ever watched a young child hide behind a parent because they were afraid of a clown or some other person? Have you been caught in a rainstorm, with ferocious winds where not even an umbrella could protect you from getting soaked? Have you been stuck in making a critical and life changing choice?

For those affected by events, such as the examples mentioned above, probably fear, worry, confusion, quickly took control of your thoughts. You probably sought refuge, strength, and guidance from someplace or someone. You probably even said "God help me."

Today's verse is a clear reminder God is our refuge and strength, an ever-present help in trouble. Think about where you seek help or shelter when things get tough. Do you seek help and refuge from other places, or do you ask God to keep you from harm? I encourage you today, next time trouble presents, consider where you will seek help, protection, guidance and even strengthen.

———————————— **PRAYER FOR THE DAY:** ————————————

Dear God,
Thank you for being my refuge and strength, an ever-present help in trouble. You protect, heal, and save me time and time again. I pray that all your children seek you for refuge, guidance, and strength when trouble shows up and even if trouble is not present, they still seek your strength and protection daily. Your strength and refuge not their own. I ask this in your son Jesus' name. Amen!

Having Faith

ANCHOR SCRIPTURE: MATTHEW 17:20 (NIV)

He replied, "Because you have so little faith. Truly I tell you, if you have faith as small as a mustard seed, you can say to this mountain, 'Move from here to there,' and it will move. Nothing will be impossible for you."

"You can't control everything. Sometimes you just need to relax and have faith that things will work out. Let go a little and just let life happen."
- *Kody Keplinger*

It is funny to watch how sometimes the tiniest situations shakes our faith. I was recently at the hairdresser and I noticed he was sweating and seem uneasy. I wondered silently, what is wrong. Shortly after, he mentioned I am concerned as I don't have enough of one supply to finish your hair and at this hour, I have no idea where I will get it. I looked at him and said, you have just enough to finish. Have faith, God got you.

He looked at me and I said, "it is what it is, but it is never what it seems." Have faith! Bottom line, the one supply held out to finish styling my hair. I said you must have faith even in this tiny situation. At the end he praised God, literally. Today's verse reminds us all that with faith as small as a mustard seed, nothing, absolutely nothing will be impossible for you.

We continue to forget this reminder and worry when things become scary because our expectation has not yet been made. Sometimes God says "not yet" but we hear no and try to handle things ourselves to turn the no we heard into a yes. Or the no may mean don't take this road, take another road...follow me. We are all guilty of this. I encourage you today to examine the size of your faith.

Dear God,
Thank you for another great reminder to have faith. It doesn't take much faith to command a mountain. I pray that all your children re-member to have faith as small as the tiny mustard seed. That you keep all your promises. I ask this in your son Jesus name. Amen!

JULY 18

Fired Up

ANCHOR SCRIPTURE: 2 CHRONICLES 15:7 (NIV)

"But as for you, be strong and do not give up, for your work will be rewarded."

"The struggle you're in today is developing the strength you need for tomorrow. Don't give up."
- *Robert Tew*

Getting up every morning for work, school or even to take care of someone or a pet is no easy task. The routine of serving or working with or for others tires you. The excitement you felt when you started that new job, on the first day of school, the first few months of marriage or a relationship, or even the first time you acquired your pet, somehow dissipates. The excitement and fire of that new thing is gone.

I wonder, it would be nice to have that fire you felt on the first day on the job, school, that you brought that new pet home, every single day. The reality is that it Is no easy task. Feeling that drive day in and day out takes commitment, passion, obedience, and simply deep love. We must dig deep to be strong and not give up.

Following God's teachings is the same. It is difficult to obey God's words day in and day out. There is always something shinier (we believe) than God. "Shiny objects," more money, the next latest gadget shows up and we lose our fire for God because we are weak and not strong. We then realize, there is nothing better, nothing sweeter than being with God, serving God and his people and that reality rekindles your fire. Today's verse encourages you to keep the fire burning. Be strong and do not give up, for your work will be rewarded."

—————————— **PRAYER FOR THE DAY:** ——————————

Dear God,
Thank you for your faithfulness. You never give up on me as I gave up on you. You remain fired up for me no matter what shiny objects distract me from you. I pray that all your children remain strong, fired up and do not give up on you. That they realize serving you yields a much sweeter and lasting reward than any temporary shiny object. I ask this in your son Jesus' name. Amen!

Who Gets the Victory?

ANCHOR SCRIPTURE: PROVERBS 21:31

*"The horse is made ready for the day of battle,
but victory rests with the Lord."*

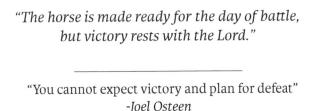

"You cannot expect victory and plan for defeat"
-Joel Osteen

Consider the work and efforts in training a horse. It should include a few basics such as teaching the horse to understand basic riding or driving aids such as slow down or stop, go, back up, turn left and right, control the hindquarter and forequarter. Some of these basics are the backbone of training a horse. If you can master the basic things, all the fancy stuff will be loads easier because of the quality of the foundation.

Many try hard to fight daily battles whether at work or in their personal lives without the basic riding or driving aids. They seek their own strength and knowledge to win these daily battles. However, they will not win if they have not established a quality foundation.

My brothers and sisters, I encourage you to seek God's help to fight and win the battle for you. Read his word and seek his guidance daily. This is where you begin to develop that quality foundation to train your thoughts and equip yourself with the tools to win the battle. Engage with a community of believers. You cannot go to war solo. As when you are weak the others are strong. They will pray with and for you.

Lean on God, he wants to fight all your battles for you. Another Proverbs 3:5-6 states "Trust in the Lord with all your heart and lean not on your own understanding; in all your ways submit to him and he will make your paths straight. God is waiting for you to rely on his strength not on your own to make your path straight. Trust that he will win the battle in his perfect timing.

──────────── PRAYER FOR THE DAY: ────────────

Dear God,
Give me the strength to seek your word and wisdom daily. Guide me to a small community to strengthen my faith in you. Lead me to always seek your will not mine. And finally help me to not sweat the battle because I know you are in command. I ask this all in your son's Jesus name. Amen

●

JULY 20
Path of Life

ANCHOR SCRIPTURE: 1 CORINTHIANS 16:1

"Watch, stand fast in the faith, be brave, be strong." - NKJV

"You will find the path of life when your inner compass is ready."
– Debasish Mridha

Every person who has ever lived has faced difficult decisions. Some decisions were obvious while others were not. For those of us who are following Christ, we have a great resource for making decisions. This resource comes through the relationship we have with Jesus. Through His Word and the direction of His Spirit, we are better equipped to walk down the path He desires for us. We can trust the path because He is leading us and loves us, even when the path gets hard.

Psalm 16:11 "You will show me the path of life; In Your presence is fullness of joy; At Your right hand are pleasures forevermore." NKJV

So how do we go about seeking the path God desires for us? First, we need to know God's Word. As we read His Word, we will be able to understand God's guidelines and promises. These will help guide our steps. In those moments where we are unsure, we should seek godly counsel as well as pray for the Holy Spirit's help in discerning where next to step. Finally, we step out in faith, trusting our Lord who can help us along the way. When we trip and fall, God's grace is there to catch us. When we face an obstacle, His strength will help us overcome. When we finally reach our destination, He will personally usher us into His presence. This is the promise we have in Jesus.

Life Lesson: God will direct our paths as we listen to Him and trust Him.

—————————— PRAYER FOR THE DAY: ——————————

Dear God,
I am so thankful for Your guiding hand. Not only have You forgiven me of my sins, but You are involved in the details of my life and desire to lead me every day. Lord, help me to be sensitive to Your Spirit and knowledgeable of Your Word so that I will make wise decisions. In Jesus' name, Amen.

Facing Trials with Joy

ANCHOR SCRIPTURE: JAMES 1:2-12

"Count it all joy, my brothers, when you meet trials of various kinds, for you know that the testing of your faith produces steadfastness"

"The severe pain and the great trials we go through teach us the real essence of great joy"
-Ernest Agyemang Yeboah

Is not if you face trials but when you face your trials how do you or will you embrace your trials? Do you choose joy, or do you give in to sin, temptation, depression, or lack of hope? Temptation to sin rather than to love. I remind you that these are all choices.

Today's Reflection brings us to James 1:2-12

"Count it all joy, my brothers, when you meet trials of various kinds, for you know that the testing of your faith produces steadfastness. And let steadfastness have its full effect, that you may be perfect and complete, lacking in nothing. If any of you lacks wisdom, let him ask God, who gives generously to all without reproach, and it will be given him. But let him ask in faith, with no doubting, for the one who doubts is like a wave of the sea that is driven and tossed by the wind. For that person must not suppose that he will receive anything from the Lord; he is a double-minded man, unstable in all his ways...Blessed is the man who remains steadfast under trial, for when he has stood the test he will receive the crown of life, which God has promised to those who love him." James 1:2-12 ESV

In summary, your trials are great blessings that are given to us to bless us, grow us, and to glorify God. The passage in James makes it easy to see that trials are good and why we should consider it all joy when we encounter them.

The next time you face trials I remind you that you will face the following two choices:

-Pursue sinful flesh desires to sin, to tear you down, to deceive you, to have no hope and for you to worship self or

-Pursue the opportunity to prove your faith, mature and grow, remain steadfast, bring about wholeness and completion, and to worship and trust God.

My prayer is that this be a helpful encouragement to you today and brings you joy as you encounter various trials. Amen

Grace, Peace and Love to you.

JULY 22

God's Grace
ANCHOR SCRIPTURE: EPHESIANS 4:7

"But to every one of us is given grace according to the measure of the gift of Christ."

"Grace is given to heal the spiritually sick,
not to decorate spiritual heroes."
- Martin Luther

Do you recall as a child, your dreams of becoming a doctor, police officer, fire fighter, famous singer, dancer, artist, lawyer, teacher or some career you envisioned pursuing when you reached a certain age? No one could change that vision (smile.)

Then as you grew older, for some, that clear visual you had as a child became blurred. You began to doubt that vision could be attained whether because you thought you couldn't achieve it; it was too hard, or life simply got in the way. You strayed from that vision.

As Christian's the same occurs when God has established our purpose and gifts. We begin to doubt if we can accomplish certain task. Ephesians 4:7 reminds us that every one of us is given grace according to the measure of the gift of Christ.

Truly understanding God's saving grace, should be our first motivation for living a godly life. In scripture Paul encourages believers to live in a way which honors the gift each of us are given by God. We are all one body, one unified family. At the same time, different believers are given different talents. Some are called to positions of leadership and authority others are called to do something else. We are, however, all called to "serve" our part in our one unified family.

Today, I encourage you to connect with God to find what you are truly called to do...what is the gift you are given by God's grace.

———————————— PRAYER FOR THE DAY: ————————————

Dear God,
I know I am alive today because you have a purpose for my life. Please help guide me to that purpose so I can fully enjoy your saving grace. I thank you for your daily grace towards me and my family. I ask this in your son's Jesus name. Amen

Making Plans

ANCHOR SCRIPTURE: JEREMIAH 29:11

"For I know the plans I have for you," declares the Lord, "plans to prosper you and not to harm you, plans to give you hope and a future.

"God's plans are always exceedingly better than your plans"
- Ilka V. Chavez

Why do we make plans? So, we can know what is going to happen; so, we can be prepared; so, life will be easier. How do you feel when everything goes as planned? Satisfied; in control; like I accomplished something good. How do you feel when things don't go as planned? Frustrated; totally helpless; it doesn't bother me too much. What role does God have in your plans? Not much, I make them without considering Him; I pray He will help my life to go well; I feel like He has let me down when my plans fail.

God said He has a plan for each of our lives. He also says His plan is to prosper us, and not to harm us. Many people think God is an angry and judgmental God who does whatever He wants even if it hurts us. This passage of Scripture says that isn't true. God does not want to harm us. He wants what is best for us.

Before Jeremiah shares this promise of prosperity, he gives the Israelites this directive from God: "seek the peace and the prosperity of the city to which I have carried you into exile. Pray to the Lord for it, because if it prospers, you too will prosper." Jeremiah 29:7. Sometimes where you are currently in life may not sit well with you. However, this uncomfortable place is exactly what will lead you to prosper.

God has a plan for each of our lives; He wants each of us to know Him. When we know Him our lives are different? Everything we do is different. When we experience His love and His forgiveness, we are free from anything that is holding us prisoner. When we allow God to oversee our lives, He promises to prosper us, give us hope and a future. We must be careful to understand when God talks about prospering it isn't material blessings He is talking about. God will provide for us, it may not be the way we would imagine, but he will provide. Nothing and nobody else in the world can really offer us these promises.

--------------------- **PRAYER FOR THE DAY:** ---------------------

Dear God,
Thank you for having a better plan than mine. Like the Israelites, it may not make sense to me. I rejoice and remain in peace knowing that you are always in control. My brothers and sisters be encouraged. I asked this all in Jesus' name. Amen

Lacking Nothing

ANCHOR SCRIPTURE: PSALM 23:1–3

"Reminds us that the shepherd meets the sheep's every need: food, water, rest, safety, and direction. When we as believers follow our Shepherd, we, too, know that we will have all we need. We will not lack the necessities of life, for He knows exactly what we need."

"Be content with what you have; rejoice in the way things are. When you realize there is nothing lacking, the whole world belongs to you."
- *Lao Tzu*

Do you sometimes feel you are lacking things what I now refer to as "stuff"? I am here to share the good news that you "lack nothing." God has provided everything you need for today!

As a reminder, I invite you to recite Psalm 23 today. The Lord is my shepherd, I shall not want. He makes me lie down in green pastures. He leads me beside still waters. He restores my soul. He leads me in paths of righteousness for his name's sake.

Even though I walk through the valley of the shadow of death, I will fear no evil, for you are with me; your rod and your staff, they comfort me. You prepare a table before me in the presence of my enemies; you anoint my head with oil; my cup overflows.

Surely goodness and mercy shall follow me all the days of my life, and I shall dwell in the house of the Lord forever. (ESV)

Dear God,
Thank you for providing everything I need. Not less, not more.
Just exactly what I need. Without you, I am, and I have nothing.
Amen

JULY 25

Fearing God

ANCHOR SCRIPTURE: PROVERBS 9:10

"The fear of the LORD is the beginning of wisdom, and knowledge of the Holy One is understanding."

"Even strength must bow to wisdom sometimes."
- Rick Riordan

Some of us have many fears. The fear of heights, the fear of the dark, the fear of flying, the fear failing, the fear of being alone, the fear of falling, the fear of God's creatures... snakes, roaches, rats just to mention a few.

Speaking of fear, do you ever wonder what is meant by "Fear the Lord your God?" This is nowhere near the fears previously mentioned. There are two meanings we could reference in respect to the word "fear." One is a feeling of being afraid or scared, and the other is a state of deep reverence and respect. When God tells us to fear Him, the word seems to draw to the second meaning. "The fear of the LORD is the beginning of knowledge.... The fear of the LORD is the beginning of wisdom..." (Prov. 1.7, 9.10). We can all gain knowledge, but the only way to have proper understanding concerning the knowledge of this world that brings true wisdom is to begin with respect and reverence for the God who created us and this world.

Fearing God is the key to true wisdom, growth and understanding. Only fools reject wisdom and instructions. Will you choose the ways of the wise or the fool?

PRAYER FOR THE DAY:

Dear God,
Thank you for the daily reminder of the words spoken by Moses in Deuteronomy 10:12-13...fear the Lord your God, walk in all his ways, love him, serve the Lord your God with all your heart and with all your soul, and keep the commandments of the Lord and his statutes which I command you today for your good. Continue to guide me to the wise life and not the fool's way. I ask this in your son Jesus' name. Amen

Be the Light!

ANCHOR SCRIPTURE: MATTHEW 5:16

"In the same way, let your light shine before others, that they may see your good deeds and glorify your Father in heaven."

"Learn to light a candle in the darkest moments of someone's life. Be the light that helps others see; it is what gives life its deepest significance."
- Roy T. Bennett

Yesterday, my church, Light of Life celebrated five years since its establishment. What an achievement. At one of the sermons, the guest Pastor spoke about Light is meant to shine. That led me to reflect on how many people you meet daily who are consciously or unconsciously dimming or blocking their light. We even meet or run across people who chose to stay in the dark because they believe the light will cause harm. They are unaware that the enemy prefers that they live in the dark as living in the light gives them life.

I pray that all get to know that every person has the power to shine their own light. God's light is in every one of us. We just simply need to seek it and free ourselves to let it shine like it was meant to do. I challenge each of you to let your light shine starting today. Sometimes you are the only light a person may see. Yes, you could be their saving light, their "Light of Life." Shine On!

PRAYER FOR THE DAY:

Dear God,
Thank you for teaching me how to let my light shine brightly and for obediently accepting to be, sometimes, the only light a home-

less person or hurting person may see. It is all for the glory of
your kingdom. I pray that everyone who reads these words also
find their power to let their light shine brightly before others. I
ask this in your son's Jesus name. Amen.

JULY 27

Taking Time

ANCHOR SCRIPTURE: MATTHEW 11:28

"Come to me, all who labor and are heavy laden,
and I will give you rest." -ESV

"It's not about 'having' time. It's about making time.
If it matters, you will make time."
- Unknown

Think of your relationship with the closest members of your family
or your best friend. When you return home from a long day at work,
or you have been working for months on a project, who takes time
out to say, you don't need to cook today or they say dinner is done;
who greets you at the door with your slippers and leads you to a warm
bath? Who says let's take time, go for a stroll or a massage?

For most, as you reflect, you will know who those people in your life
are. The very individual(s) you have developed such an intimate relationship with that you simply don't have a need to say anything. They
know. They are always there to say or simply show by their actions,
"come to me and I will give you rest.

Today, I reflect on one of the great promises of God. When I think and reflect on the words, "come to me, all who labor and are heavy laden, and I will give you rest." I think of my relationship with God. I ask is this about just saying God I am tired take this from me or is it more about establishing and continuously strengthening that intimate relationship with God. That relationship where without saying a word, he knows and feels when I am doing too much, he simply makes a way to give me rest.

Taking time out each morning to continue to strengthen my relationship with God and truly have that intimate and close bond has been one of the best decisions I made. It is no longer a one-way conversation (yes, me talking and not listening. smile.) It is now a two-way conversation. I am not saying this is what everyone should do. I am simply sharing my experience that strengthening my relationship with God has been an amazing journey. I compare it to having someone who always have your back no matter what. We all have those people in our lives who tell us or show us the truth whether we like it or not. Ultimately, we know the discipline, advise or invitation to rest is always for our good.

PRAYER FOR THE DAY:

Dear God,
Thank you for always having my back. I know sometimes I complain about your chosen method to guide or discipline me. Time and time again, you have proven that it is all for my good and my growth. I pray today that many take a few minutes out of their busy lives to develop an intimate relationship with you for their good and their growth. I ask this in your son's Jesus name, Amen.

Peace

ANCHOR SCRIPTURE: PHILIPPIANS 4:6-7

"Do not be anxious about anything, but in everything by prayer and supplication with thanksgiving let your requests be made known to God. And the peace of God, which surpasses all understanding, will guard your hearts and your minds in Christ Jesus.

"Peace cannot be kept by force, it can only be achieved
by understanding"
- *Albert Einstein*

What is peace? I looked up the definition of peace and Merriam Webster defines peace as follows: a state of quiet; especially: freedom from public disturbance or war; freedom from upsetting thoughts or feelings; harmony in personal relations; a state or period of peace between governments; and finally an agreement to end a war. Consider this definition for a minute.

Can you imagine living every day in freedom from public disturbances or war (not worried about the actions taken by government and principalities), freedom from thinking or feeling upsetting thoughts or simply living in harmony with yourself and others because you truly know who ultimately controls everything?

God promises and reminds us through Philippians 4:6-7, not to become anxious about anything but in "everything" (no matter what you are going through) by prayer and in supplication and here is the most important part with thanksgiving let your request be known to God. I encourage you today to not only pray but thank God for everything you have, everything you are going through because he will bring you the peace that surpasses ALL understanding.

Dear God,

Thank you for providing me with your book of wisdom. Your bible tells the truth and guides and reminds me daily of all your promises. As I continue to grow spiritually and truly understand obedience to your word, I hold onto to all your promises to see me through ALL situations in peace and harmony. A peace that surpasses all understanding. I pray that many take the time to establish their own relationship with you to enjoy the peace that only you can bring. I ask this all in your son's Jesus name. Amen

JULY 29

The Golden Rule

ANCHOR SCRIPTURE: LUKE 6:31

"Do to others as you would have them do to you."

""We have committed the Golden Rule to memory;
let us now commit it to life."
- Edwin Markham

As kids, we played with our friends and family all sorts of fun games. However, I am sure you can recall several occasions during that play time were on one occasion or several, someone was mean to you. They made the choice not to allow you to join in a particular game, they didn't share their toy or snack with you. You probably even remembered that at times, you were the one choosing not to share your toys, snack or play time.

It is funny as I reflect today, how some of those same behaviors still persist in us as adults. We don't want to share our knowledge, our money, our time, our love, to name a few, simply because we believe we earned it and chose not to share. We forget that God provides all and can remove all in a split second. We forget that everything we have belongs to God. It is all on loan to us or given to us for the good of God's kingdom.

I raise this simply to remind each of you that not because we disobeyed the golden rule as long as we can remember, makes it okay to continue this disobedience. To live in freedom, we must live by this rule-"do to others as you would have them do to you." Let's take this one step further, do not speak unkindly to anyone or about anyone. This requires strength to not focus on what others are doing but focusing solely on God.

Let's test ourselves to live by Luke 6:31 and "Do to others as you would have them do to you" for the next 24 hours. I am praying for each of you.

———————————— PRAYER FOR THE DAY: ————————————

Dear God,
As I continue to grow spiritually give me the strength, courage, wisdom, and integrity to live daily by Luke 6:31. I ask this all in your son's Jesus name, Amen!

Stay the Course

ANCHOR SCRIPTURE: ISAIAH 41:10 (NIV)

"So do not fear, for I am with you: do not be dismayed, for I am your God. I will strengthen you and help you; I will uphold you with my righteous right hand."

" Face fear in the face, keep moving and stay the course. Stick to plan A."
- *Ilka V. Chavez*

Today's verse is interesting. It provides us two commands to obey: Do not fear and do not be dismayed. It supplies us with two reasons why we must obey: For I am with you and for I am your God. Lastly, this verse also reminds us of three promises God will keep: I will strengthen you; I will help you, and I will uphold you with my righteous right hand.

In my study (Isaiah 40:1-2), reminds me that this verse was written to people in fear. As I reflect, God tells us here, through his instructions, that he will be with us always to free us from fear in everything we face...Job conflicts, lack of a job, the messes we create, problems from our past, or present, problems with our relationships, health concerns, concern about your future and that of your family just to mention a few. He will be there with you no matter what situation you face.

My brothers and sisters, next time fear shows up in your life in any form, shape, or manner, please remember these instructions but most importantly, please re-member God's promise that he will strengthen you, he will help you and he will uphold you with his righteous right hand. All you need to do is turn to him. He will help you. Remind yourself- "I will not live in fear because God is here." Be encouraged and stay the course. God is with you.

Dear God,
I thank you for your unconditional love, grace, mercy, and companionship through all of life's peaks and valleys. I pray that all of us rest in your strength, "face fear in the face" when it shows up and stay the course that you have set for each of us. I ask this all in your son's Jesus name. Amen

JULY 31

A Good Gift

ANCHOR SCRIPTURE: JAMES 1:17

"Every good gift and every perfect gift is from above, coming down from the Father of lights with whom there is no variation or shadow due to change."

"Health is the greatest gift, contentment the greatest wealth, faithfulness the best relationship."
-Buddha

This morning, waking up to the chirping of the birds, reminded me of God's perfect gifts that are always present for us to enjoy. From the time we open our eyes we may hear the birds chirping or roosters crowing, till we go to sleep by the sound of the crickets or gazing at the stars in the sky. Gifts such as the air we breathe, the sunlight, the ocean, wisdom, and the truth of his word. These and many more good and perfect gifts come from one source, GOD.

Some other gifts from God may not seem good at the time we receive them, but they are just as good. For example, God gave the apostle Paul a thorn in the flesh which caused him so much discomfort that he sought the Lord three times to remove it from him. But it became a tremendous blessing to him in the end, for he discovered how he can be strong even in his weakest moments through God's grace. (2 Cor. 12:7-10)

Materials things, clothing, large bank accounts, fame, etc., that we often chase as human, are nowhere as valuable as the gifts God gives us. Today I encourage you to take time out to enjoy and thank God for all his good and perfect gifts. Whether it is sitting still to smell the roses or pressing forward with "a thorn in your side." Rest assured that God's grace will see you through. God's Grace will refresh and strengthen you when you least expect.

--------------------- **PRAYER FOR THE DAY:** ---------------------

Dear God,
I thank you for all the gifts that you give me daily. I know I take these gifts for granted because the materials gifts aka "the shiny objects" seem more valuable. I thank you for my spiritual growth to understand that your simple and perfect gifts are way more valuable that the desires of my flesh. I pray for all to see your good and perfect gifts in everything they go through, they say, and they do. I ask this all in your son's Jesus name. Amen!

Reflections

August

Ohana

ANCHOR SCRIPTURE: GENESIS 12:3

"In thee [Abraham] shall all families of the earth be blessed"

Call it a clan, call it a network, call it a tribe, call it a family:
whatever you call it, whoever you are, you need one.
- Jane Howard

The urban dictionary defines family as a group of people, usually of the same blood (and do not have to be), who genuinely love, trust, care about, and look out for each other. This is not to be mistaken with relatives sharing the same household but hate each other. REAL family is a bondage that cannot be broken by any means.

As I celebrate life and birthdays, I think about the real reason for family. Family are always there for you through thick and thin. No matter what happens. As the Urban dictionary describes, family is "a group of people (not necessarily blood) who genuinely love, trust, and care about and look out for each other. "REAL" family is a bondage that can never be broken. When you simply love, there is nothing, absolutely nothing, that can break that bond.

I believe families are close to God's heart. From the beginning God said "It is not good for man to be alone." Then, He blessed them and told them," "Be fruitful, and multiply, and replenish [fill] the earth"" (Genesis 1:28). In Deuteronomy 6:6, God told the Israelites to keep His commands in their hearts and to teach them diligently unto their children, talking of them throughout the day in every circumstance of life.

"Ohana means family and family means nobody gets left behind or forgotten." Today's scripture is a reminder, "In thee [Abraham] shall all families of the earth be blessed...." The ways of the world makes it easy to forget our relationship to Abraham and the promises made to his seeds. That you and your family, as descendants of Abraham, are co-heirs of the great blessings of wealth, spiritual blessings and rulership. This bond can never be broken. Family matters!

———————————— **PRAYER FOR THE DAY:** ————————————

Dear God,
Thank you for the reminder of my relationship to Abraham and the promises made to him. I pray that all your children remember that they are heirs of the great blessings of wealth, spiritual blessings and rulership. That they awaken and embrace this power. I ask this in your son Jesus' name. Amen!

Freedom

ANCHOR SCRIPTURE: GALATIANS 5:1,13

*"So, Christ has truly set us free. Now make sure that you stay
free, and don't get tied up again in slavery to the law ...
For you have been called to live in freedom, my brothers, and
sisters. But don't use your freedom to satisfy your sinful nature.
Instead, use your freedom to serve one another in love."*

"Freeing yourself was one thing, claiming ownership
of that freed self was another."
- *Toni Morrison*

Juneteenth, also known as Juneteenth Independence Day or Freedom Day, is a holiday that commemorates the June 19, 1865 announcement of the abolition of slavery in Texas, Juneteenth.com states that Juneteenth is the oldest known celebration commemorating the ending of slavery in the United States. It took two and a half years after President Lincoln's Emancipation Proclamation - which had become official January 1, 1863, to enforce this new Executive order. However, with the surrender of General Lee in April of 1865, and the arrival of General Granger's regiment, the forces were finally strong enough to influence and overcome the resistance.

Today's celebration brings me to reflect on why it takes us so long, sometimes decades, to realize we are truly free. To realize that God gave his only son to save us. Freedom means we do not have to choose to live in sin. Today's scripture reminds us, "But don't use your freedom to satisfy your sinful nature. Instead, use your freedom to serve one another in love." If sinful ways continue to lure you into a life that enslaves you mentally, physically, and spiritually, consider connecting with a community of believers. This community can help you strengthen your faith, remain strong in the truth, and remind you daily that you are indeed free.

In Texas, it took General Lee's submission and surrender and a stronger community (the arrival of General Granger's regimen), for the abolishment of slavery to be recognized. Can you imagine the strength you can gain from connecting with a community of believers who remind you daily that you are free? You are free of mental and physical bondage. As I read about Juneteenth, I am reminded that "Jesus promised both physical and spiritual redemption. Now, both physical and spiritual freedoms are true causes to celebrate!"

————————— **PRAYER FOR THE DAY:** —————————

Dear God,
Thank you for sacrificing your only son to set me free. Free from past hurt, free from lies I believed and free from believing that I was not worthy to be part of your community of believers. We are all welcome into your family. I pray that all seek and find a community of believers that can serve as General Granger's

Global Positioning System (GPS)

ANCHOR SCRIPTURE: PSALM 16:1-2

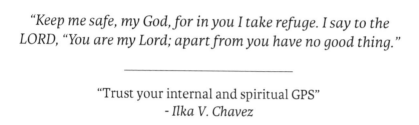

"Keep me safe, my God, for in you I take refuge. I say to the LORD, "You are my Lord; apart from you have no good thing."

"Trust your internal and spiritual GPS"
- *Ilka V. Chavez*

I noticed recently that many people do not go from point A to point B without relying on their GPS. They have become so reliant on this system, that they don't leave home without it. I digress a bit to recall that as I grew up, we had no GPS. The GPS entailed someone guiding you through every turn using a landmark such as turn right at the yellow house at the corner and then left at the corner store with the red awning etc. Some of the younger generation reading this may not relate to this memory.

We were not concerned that we didn't have a GPS then. The detailed instructions led us to our destination. Today's verse reminds us that apart from God, we have no good thing. Separated from his word, we are frequently loose our way. Can you relate? His word is our mental and spiritual GPS. If we read it and follow the detail instructions, we remain on a straight path to our destination. When we decide that, "oh I got this" and feel we no longer need to rely on God's guidance or we stray even a bit from the word, this is when we lose or way. We could be circling for decades without even realizing we lost our way.

Today I encourage you to seek God's guidance daily as that is the Global Positioning System that will ensure you reach your intended destination.

Dear God,
Thank you for providing your word to guide me on the straight path I should take daily. Apart from you, I truly have no good thing. As a matter of fact, I frequently lose my way when I depart from you. I pray that all are reminded today that you and your word are truly the Global Positioning System that will guide them to their intended destination. I ask this in your son's Jesus' name Amen.

AUGUST 4

Searching for Purpose

ANCHOR SCRIPTURE: 2 TIMOTHY 3:16-17 (NIV)

"All Scripture is God-breathed and is useful for teaching, rebuking, correcting and training in righteousness, so that the servant of God may be thoroughly equipped for every good work."

"If you can tune into your purpose and really align with it, setting goals so that your vision is an expression of that purpose, then life flows much more easily."
- *Jack Canfield*

I recently read that one in five people today struggles with depression, often rooted in feeling purposeless. In searching for purpose, you may seek what you believe is your heart's desire. The things and places you believe, or society leads you to believe is your life purpose. I wonder when it can't be found, if one will surrender to the thought that they may be searching in the wrong places.

The amazing news is that every person on this planet has a specific purpose to fulfill. The key is finding it by searching in the right place. Have you ever uttered these words: What is my purpose in life and how do I find it? I recalled asking this question and the answer I got was this: "For I know the plans I have for you," declares the LORD, "plans to prosper you and not to harm you, plans to give you hope and a future." Yes, Jeremiah 29:11. Light bulbs went off...go to the source for the answer.

Turn to your higher source, the Creator, for your answer. But first, allow the creator to transform your thinking to better understand your purpose and his will for you. I can almost guarantee, it will not align with what the world tells you and sometimes may surprise you that your heart deceived you.

Without a life purpose as the compass to guide you, your goals and action plans may not ultimately fulfill you. I encourage you to find your purpose, live it, then lead it! Let's not cheat the world of your gift and your light.

Today's verse is a reminder, "All Scripture is God-breathed and is useful for teaching, rebuking, correcting and training in righteousness, so that the servant of God may be thoroughly equipped for every good work." It may surprise you, once you are operating in your purpose, it may not feel like work. I encourage you to read 2 Timothy 3 in its entirety.

—————————— **PRAYER FOR THE DAY:** ——————————

Dear God,
Thank you for the reminder that you created my purpose. To seek you and your plans for me then I will find my purpose. I pray that all your children remember that you have the blueprint for their

life. To seek you, allow you to transform their minds and their purpose will be found. That your scriptures are useful for teaching, rebuking, correcting, and training in righteousness, so that the servant of God maybe thoroughly equipped for every good work. I ask this in your son Jesus' name. Amen!

○
··● ··

The Discipline of Solitude

ANCHOR SCRIPTURE: MARK 1:35 (NIV)

"Very early in the morning, while it was dark, Jesus got up, left the house, and went off to a solitary place, where he prayed.

"Loneliness is inner emptiness; solitude is inner fulfillment.
-Richard Foster

Recently I read a devotional about solitude. It started with this quote from philosophers Blaise Pascal- "I have discovered that all the unhappiness of men arises from one single fact, "in that they cannot stay quietly in their own chamber." Today more than ever, we are pulled by so many distractions it is almost impossible to find solitude. As I read this, I was reminded of the importance of intentionally setting aside time of solitude. Time to hear guidance from our higher source. I recently realized that even amid chaos you can practice solitude. That with all the noise at the beach, filled by summer visitors, you can tune out the noise and hear only the waves.

"Solitude is the discipline of tuning our hearts to hear nothing but the voice of God, whether it comes to us in a whisper or a roar. When we move into solitude, we seek to silence all other voices that clamor for our attention, just to be attuned to hear God's voice." Today's verse is a reminder that "very early in the morning, while it was dark, Jesus got up, left the house and went off to a solitary place, where he prayed." There is power in solitude! I encourage you to read Mark 1 in its entirety.

PRAYER FOR THE DAY:

Dear God,
Thank you for the reminder that there is a difference between solitude and loneliness. That there is power in solitude. I pray that all your children understand the power of solitude. That they remember that early in the morning, while it was dark, Jesus got up, left the house, and went off to a solitary place, where he prayed. I ask this in your son Jesus' name. Amen!

AUGUST 6

Tomorrow

ANCHOR SCRIPTURE: PROVERBS 6:4

"Don't put it off; do it now! Don't rest until you do."

The present is the ever-moving shadow that divides yesterday from tomorrow. In that lies hope.
-Frank Lloyd Wright

Are you focused on the million horrible things happening in the world or the million great things happening in the world? Are you focused on the end or today? My morning mentor this morning talked about what a decision is and how to make one properly. I thought about deciding to be present.

Do you find yourself making decisions for tomorrow? Tomorrow I will do this, I will start saving tomorrow, I will work on my calling tomorrow, I will forgive tomorrow, I will quit doing this tomorrow etc. Or fool yourself and say the timing is not right because of fear or believing someone else' truth. Someone once said, "Tomorrow must be the longest day of the week, judging by the many things that we leave until tomorrow to do..."

Back to decision-making. (LOL) The morning mentor shared that "you can never make a decision for the future. You can contemplate, consider but you cannot decide. If it is a real decision, it governs your life today. Until you have acted on it, it is only a consideration or contemplation." Action truly speaks now, not tomorrow. There is so much to relate to here on faith, belief, and trust. I will leave that for you to decide, now or tomorrow?

Today's verse is a reminder "Don't put it off; do it now! Don't rest until you do." Remember, tomorrow may never come. Decide for today, not for tomorrow. "Remember, tomorrow is promised to no one."

--------- PRAYER FOR THE DAY: ---------

Dear God,
Thank you for the reminder that a decision is to act now, not tomorrow. To not put the decision off, do it now! Don't rest until I do. I pray that all your children don't put off the decision to follow you until tomorrow. That they do it now. That they remember that you are the way, the truth, and the life. Now is all that is guaranteed. I ask this in your son Jesus' name. Amen!

God's Perfect Timing

ANCHOR SCRIPTURE: HABAKKUK 2:3

*"For still the vision awaits its appointed time; it hastens
to the end—it will not lie. If it seems slow, wait for it;
it will surely come; it will not delay."*

"The right thing at the wrong time is the wrong thing."
-Joshua Harris

Waiting, having patience and endurance are one of the most difficult tests that God allows in our lives. Can you recall a time when you stood in line for a concert ticket, for a free bonus and just at the time you were next in line, you received the news that tickets were sold out or the bonus items were all gone.

You probably felt the disappointment to your core. You simply could not understand and probably said "why me." What if you simply believed that this was all aligned with God's perfect timing. No questions asked. I am sure we can all recall a situation where at the end we saw that not attending that concert allowed you to do something better or simply that it all worked out for our good.

I understand that waiting on the perfect timing to have your prayers answered is by no means easy. Today I share three things to do while you wait for God's perfect timing.

1-Trust the Lord with all your heart and all you might. His plans and his timing are always better than ours. I remind myself often that all works together for my good and for the glory of God and his Kingdom.

2- Turn to the Lord in prayer and conversation. Yes, as you wait, things will get tough, you will get tired and weary, you will believe this is the end (like the caterpillar thought before it turned into a beautiful butterfly), and you will think unhelpful thoughts. However, when you turn to the Lord in continuous prayer and conversation, he shows you the way. He gives you the strength, his strength, not yours to persevere. A spirit of resiliency is renewed in you.

3- Thank the Lord while you wait. Thank him in advance for answered prayers. Don't wait for your prayer to be answered to thank and praise the Lord. Always thank the Lord no matter what. Trust that he wants you to learn a lesson to build your character to grow in his likeness.

I hope these help you today to persevere.

──────────────── **PRAYER FOR THE DAY:** ────────────────

Dear God,
Thank you for showing me the way and the understanding that your timing is perfect. You are never early, never late, just right on time. Thank you for the strength to endure until your perfect timing. I pray that all today truly hang on to the promise and hope that their prayers will be answered according to your perfect will and timing not theirs. That they will submit and surrender to your will and not their ways. I ask this in your son's Jesus name, Amen.

Living a Legacy

ANCHOR SCRIPTURE: PROVERBS 13:22

"A good man leaves an inheritance to his children's children."

"It's hard to say what I want my legacy to be when I'm long gone."
- *Aaliyah*

Webster's dictionary defines the word "inherit" as: "to come into possession of or receive as a right, by law, from an ancestor at his death." I often think of my Mother, Father and Grandmother when making critical decisions. I always ask, what would Mom, Dad or Grandma do? All the time, searching for the wisdom they imparted on me has always guided me to make the right decision. As I think deeper, these decisions were grounded in faith and teachings from God's words.

I recalled; my Dad subscribed to various publications that provided prayers for any situation you could encounter. He would share those with me. As I started my family, he would periodically send me new prayers by mail and say add this to your morning prayer time. My grandmother also imparted wisdom to me before she passed. We were very close. She taught me and instructed me to memorize a few, what I consider "go to" psalms when I needed guidance or God's help. I share the psalms with you, Psalms 23, 27, 91 and 121. She also said, "when all fails, go to the Lord's Prayer." They are a few others however, these are my "go to" verses inscribed in my heart.

What are your "go to" verses in the Bible? Are you teaching these to your children and your children's children? What legacy are you leaving for your family? Some of us may not have financial wealth written in our stories, however the best inheritance to leave costs you nothing. Learning and teaching the word of God to your children and your grandchildren may be the best gift you could leave your offspring. The inheritance that my Dad and grandmother left me, has stabilized my ship time and time again.

Dear God,
Thank you for leaving me the greatest inheritance there is, your word, the truth, and the light. I pray that all seek you, as our Father, for guidance and consider the legacy we are living and leaving today. I ask this in your son Jesus's name. Amen!

———————————————— ● ————————————————

AUGUST 9

Living a Legacy

ANCHOR SCRIPTURE: 2 CHRONICLES 15:7

Be strong and do not give up, for your work will be rewarded."

"Keep your face to the sunshine and you cannot see a shadow."
- Helen Keller

Have you ever tried to reach a big hairy audacious goal? This is one of those goals that every person you know (including your best friend) and even logic says it is not attainable. You continue working hard towards your goal despite what everyone says even logic.

348

Today's verse calls us to remain strong and do not give up on God because he will not give up on you. Do not cease your worship of God and avoid and root out idolatry. The same indomitable spirit you find to pursue your scary goal, you should equally find to have no other idol but God.

"This is the key to preserving yourselves from such calamities and misfortune your predecessors felt." You will face opponents, like those who say, you cannot achieve the goals you set. You are encouraged in today's' verse to not be weak- For your work shall be rewarded — "What you do for God, and for his honor and service, shall not be overlooked, or go unrewarded."

———————————— PRAYER FOR THE DAY: ————————————

Dear God,
Thank you for lighting my way to avoid and root out present and past idols. I pray that all remain constant in your word, stay focused on you, to gain the strength to worship you and have no other idols but you. I ask this all in your son Jesus' name. Amen

No Greater Love

ANCHOR SCRIPTURE: JOHN 3:16

"For God so loved the world that he gave his one and only Son, that whoever believes in him shall not perish but have eternal life." (NIV)

"A true friend knows your weaknesses but shows you your strengths; feels your fears but fortifies your faith; sees your anxieties but frees your spirit; recognizes your disabilities but emphasizes your possibilities."
-William Arthur Ward

Have you ever been in a situation where you tried to tell or show someone that they are loved or you love them more than anything in this world and they simply did not believe you? You jumped over hurdles, skydive (although you are afraid of heights) and possible trained with them for a marathon, even though you were not participating in the race and they simply did not get it. That you did it all for the unconditional love you have for them.

Today's verse, in my view, is the greatest verse in the Bible. It sums up the Bible and the love that God has for each of us. There is no sin that can change this love. Whenever I am in doubt, I simply reflect on this verse and it reminds me of the great love that God has for us. No one or nothing can change this.

God loves us so much; he wants us to come to Him just as we are. He wants to have a personal relationship with us and longs for us to talk to Him freely about our sins and our needs. This relationship should be just as going to your best friend. Speak truthfully, open, and honest with God and he will always respond with love. The is no greater love.

Dear God,
Thank you once again for giving your one and only Son, that
whoever believes in you shall not perish but have eternal life.
Today I pray that we all simply remember this; God loves us just
the way we are. I ask this all in your son's Jesus name. Amen.

●

AUGUST 11

Dominion

ANCHOR SCRIPTURE: EPHESIANS 1:19-21

I also pray that you will understand the incredible greatness
of God's power for us who believe him. This is the same mighty
power that raised Christ from the dead and seated him in the
place of honor at God's right hand in the heavenly realms.
Now he is far above any ruler or authority or power or
leader or anything else—not only in this world but also
in the world to come.

"Living a natural life is living in dominion of a darkened mind"
-Sunday Adelaja

I frequently wonder how to possess dominion over my thoughts, feelings, failures, and day to day walk. I reflected on the lamp, the television, and the toaster. None of these objects work if they are not plugged in.

When these objects are plugged in and have functioning parts such as a bulb that has not burned out, they work well. They are connected to the source, and all parts work as instructed. Being plugged is key to dominion.

I reflected on how the same applies when I am connected to the power and authority over my life. My thoughts, fears and worries over things of this world change drastically. The mighty power that raised Christ from the dead and seated him in the place of honor at God's right hand in the heavenly realm is what keeps me functioning.

Prayer and developing your own relationship with God, is key to ensuring you remain connected and that God's will be done in your daily walk. Prayer is the power that accomplishes things when all else fails. Faith gives you dominion and a person with faith walks with God.

My connection with the Heavenly Father strengthens my walk-in dominion. Our Heavenly Father gives dominion to those that believe in Him.

——————————— PRAYER FOR THE DAY: ———————————

Dear God,
Thank you for your mighty power that keeps me functioning. I pray that all understand the incredible greatness that your power brings to all those who believe in you. Our promotion is simply waiting for our daily connection with you. I ask this all in your son's Jesus name. Amen

Let Go

ANCHOR SCRIPTURE: ISAIAH 43:18-19

"Do not remember the former things, Nor consider the things of old. Behold, I will do a new thing, Now it shall spring forth; Shall you not know it? I will even make a road in the wilderness, And rivers in the desert."

"Some of us think holding on makes us strong, but sometimes it is letting go."
- *Hermann Hesse*

Holding on to the things you know is a natural reaction. Letting go of the former things is not always easy. Holding onto to the past blocks the blessings that God has in store for each of us. Holding onto our ways and not obeying God's will, prevents us from blessing others.

Today's verse helped me understand what it means to simply let go. It was freeing to understand that letting go of the things of old is abandoning what is "beyond our control to embrace what we can change."

PRAYER FOR THE DAY:

Dear God,
Thank you for reminding me that letting go of my will and trusting yours, has the power to make a road in the wilderness. I pray that all have faith in you and find the courage to let go of the former and embrace the new. In Jesus' Name, Amen.

Hope and Integrity

ANCHOR SCRIPTURE: PSALM 25:21

*"May integrity and uprightness protect me,
because my hope, Lord, is in you."*

"When I die, my integrity goes to the grave with me"
- *Ilka V. Chavez*

Recently, I pondered the relationship between hope and integrity. I wonder if losing hope and your integrity are connected. As I reflect, I could think of many stories in the Bible and in our world today, where compromising to the ways of this world brings inevitable corruption, loss of hope and integrity. For example, you may read the story of Jehoshaphat, a godly man.

Hope seems to come from knowing that the Lord is in us and he protects us daily from so much. It is important to surrender and listen to his calling. When we do, there is an ease in living with hope and walking in integrity. Never lose hope...hang on to your integrity; walk away from temptation; remain steadfast in your hope of fulfilling your dreams, in people, and in answered prayers.

PRAYER FOR THE DAY:

*Dear God,
Thank you for your constant grace and mercy. I pray for continued protection of all your children. May their hope remain in you. In Jesus' name. Amen.*

Why Worry?

ANCHOR SCRIPTURE: MATTHEW 6:27

"Can any one of you by worrying add a single hour to your life?" (NIV)

"Our fatigue is often caused not by work, but by worry, frustration and resentment."
– Dale Carnegie

Worry has a clever way of killing people. The poet Robert Frost (1874–1963) wrote, "The reason why worry kills more people than work is because more people worry than work." Have you thought about the things you worry about daily? You worry about what you are going to wear today; you worry about the day that hasn't started; you worry about your finances; you worry about your children and your grandchildren; you worry about how an event you are having will turn it. You, worry, worry, worry.

We have become a society of worry warts. It is part of our DNA. When one worry is over, we deliberately go searching for another and another. Worrying is like chasing your tail... it is useless. Worrying does more harm than good. Most importantly worrying is a sin because you are demonstrating you lack no faith in God. Why do we bother ourselves and others to worry when in Matthew 6:25-34 we are instructed "Don't worry, be hopeful."?

I leave you with today's verse, "Can any one of you by worrying add a single hour to your life?" Meditate on that today. I encourage you to create a worry jar. When worry shows up, write it down, put it in a jar and ask God to handle it. And please, don't take it back out of the jar. Trust God to handle it!

Dear God,
I thank you for the reminder of your instructions to not worry instead have hope. I pray that all your children trust you enough to handle all their worries. That they understand that you are the almighty and can handle all their worries. I ask this in Jesus' name. Amen

---

AUGUST 15

Making Plans

ANCHOR SCRIPTURE: PROVERBS 19:21

"Many are the plans in a person's heart, but it is the LORD's purpose that prevails." (NIV)

"Life is what happens to us while we are making other plans."
- Allen Saunders

What are your plans for today? Are you headed to the beach, to work, heading on a well-deserved vacation or simply taking a day at home to relax? Yes, we all make plans. Do you ever seek counsel on the plans you make?

Many people face disappointments time and time again mainly because they make plans and forget one key ingredient, to seek God's counsel. His plans and purpose for our lives will always prevail. It is interesting that all the instructions we must follow are readily available to us. Yet, we insist to rely solely on our knowledge than the clear guidance provided in the Bible (I affectionately refer to as the book of wisdom.)

The previous verse (v.20), instructs us to listen to advice and accept discipline, and at the end you will be counted among the wise. Would you rather be wise or smart? As you continue with your plans for today, I encourage you to seek God's counsel and guidance in all you say, do, and think. It will save you from disappointment. I recently saw this note of humor: "If you want to make God laugh, make plans without him."

─────────── **PRAYER FOR THE DAY:** ───────────

Dear God,
Thank you for your availability and counsel as I plan my day. I pray that all your children also recognize that you are available to them as they plan their day. That they surrender to your plans as that is the only plan that prevails. I ask this in Jesus' name.
Amen

Forgive

ANCHOR SCRIPTURE: COLOSSIANS 3:13

"Bear with each other and forgive one another if any of you has a grievance against someone. Forgive as the Lord forgave you."

"I believe that life is short, and there is too much time wasted bearing grudges, and I like to move on."
- *Sam Taylor-Johnson*

Hurt, especially by a person you never thought would cause you hurt is sometimes puzzling. This could be a family member, a neighbor, a co-worker, a supervisor, and even your own children. As humans, you will experience such hurt in your lifetime. Now you wonder, how am I supposed to forgive if I don't know how bad the hurt will be? Why should I forgive? Shouldn't I wait for an apology before forgiving? I am sure many more questions than answers come to mind.

Today's verse calls each of us to be prepared to forgive long before the hurt occurs. Yes, you must be prepared to forgive those you may have a grievance against, no matter the gravity of the hurt. Simply put "Forgive as the Lord forgave you." You may never get an apology. As I reflect, today's verse seems important to memorize and store in our hearts. It surely will bring you peace.

I leave you with words from Audrey Hepburn that were recently shared with me. "For beautiful eyes, look for the good in others; for beautiful lips, speak only words of kindness; and for poise, walk with the knowledge that you are never alone."

Dear God,
Thank you for the reminder that we must bear with each other and forgive one another. Thank you for forgiving all our sins before we committed them. I pray that all your children armor themselves with today's verse that reminds us we all have "a speck in our eyes." I ask this in Jesus' name. Amen

---

AUGUST 17

The Secret Ingredient

ANCHOR SCRIPTURE: 2 PETER 1:5-7 (NIV)

For this very reason, make every effort to add to your faith goodness; and to goodness, knowledge and to knowledge, self-control; and to self-control, perseverance; and to perseverance, godliness; and to godliness, mutual affection; and to mutual affection, love.

"A well-made salad must have a certain uniformity; it should make perfect sense for those ingredients to share a bowl."
-Yotam Ottolenghi

Preparing your favorite recipe is always fun. Everyone in your family looks forward to having your special dish. I am sure many relatives and friends ask for the recipe. Have they ever said, I tried to make your dish and it simply did not taste the same? You must add a secret ingredient when you prepare your dish. For me, my secret ingredient has always been an extra portion of love.

I reflect on our lives and how it compares to a recipe. Is there a secret ingredient we sometimes forget to add to our lives? Today's verse through Peter, tells us the exact ingredients we need to live a more fulfilling life in Christ. No secret ingredients.

The first ingredient is faith and having a personal relationship with God. Then you add 1 cup of goodness, another cup of knowledge, mix well. Then slowly add self-control and perseverance. Lastly add godliness, mutual affection, and love. Then you let it bake. God does not expect us to make this recipe perfect the first time. However, with practice, and growing your relationship with God, you can gradually perfect this recipe.

PRAYER FOR THE DAY:

Dear God,
Thank you for providing me with the exact recipe for living a fulfilling life. I pray that all your children try to practice the recipe provided by Peter so they too can live a filled life. I ask this in your son's Jesus name. Amen

Own Your Truth

ANCHOR SCRIPTURE: JOHN 8:32

"And you will know the truth, and the truth will set you free."

"Harmony makes small things grow,
lack of it makes great things decay."
-*Sallust*

Living in harmony is no easy task. You and I are different. No one is the same make or model. We are all unique and wonderfully made. Sometimes, we enter conflict as we try to get everyone to be in accord with our thoughts or to do things the way you want them done. If we all did things the same way, can you imagine how boring your life would be?

Today's verse serves as a reminder to always live in harmony. Do not be proud or conceited. Find a way to strike a chord with all those you meet and those who live and work with you. Sometimes finding that harmony requires complete surrender or as I sometimes tease, it requires you "staying in your lane." God guides us daily. When we listen and seek him, we live in peace and harmony.

PRAYER FOR THE DAY:

Dear God,
Thank you for your clear instructions to live in harmony with one another. I pray that all your children will find the courage to live in harmony with each other. The Apostle Paul prayed the following in Romans 15:5-6-"May the God of endurance and encouragement grant you to live in such harmony with one

another, in accord with Christ Jesus, that together you may with one voice glorify the God and Father of our Lord Jesus Christ." I ask this all in Jesus name, Amen.

Independence

ANCHOR SCRIPTURE: 2 CORINTHIANS 3:17

"Now the Lord is the Spirit, and where the Spirit of the Lord is, there is freedom." (NIV)

"True independence and freedom can only exist
in doing what's right."
-Brigham Young

What is independence to you? Is it self-sufficiency, self-reliance, autonomy, freedom, liberty? As humans, we long for independence. As we move from high school to college, we long for independence. Others have been hurt, they no longer trust, so they are determined not to rely on others. They live independent lives.

I wonder if independence from all is necessary to be and feel free? Maybe or maybe not. Today's scripture reminds us that there is one thing that we cannot live freely without..."the Lord is the spirit, and where the spirit of the Lord is, there is freedom." You may long for independence however, without acknowledging and relying on the spirit of the Lord, you may never be free.

I encourage you to find freedom today! "Where the Holy Spirit is, remarkable things happen."

―――――――――――― PRAYER FOR THE DAY: ――――――――――――

Dear God,
Thank you for the presence of your Holy Spirit that set me free. I pray that as your children seek their independence, they don't do it without you. I ask this in your son Jesus' name. Amen

---

AUGUST 20

Using your Freedom

ANCHOR SCRIPTURE: GALATIANS 5:13

"You, my brothers and sisters, were called to be free.
But do not use your freedom to indulge the flesh; rather,
serve one another humbly in love." (NIV)

"If you give up your freedom for safety,
you don't deserve either one."
-Benjamin Franklin

Keeping and using your freedom is like going against all odds. You must go against the flow.1 Going against the flow could include making "unpopular choices" to stay clear of sin. It could mean doing

363

something that scares you, but it is the right thing to do. Remaining free and using your freedom to do good is by no means an easy task.

In searching for answers on how to live free every day, I thought to look for ways Jesus used his freedom. He used his freedom to trust God's judgement (1 Peter 2:23). He used his freedom to redeem each of us and take on our pain (1 Peter 2:24). He did not use his freedom to deceive (1 Peter 2:22), retaliate or threaten (1 Peter 2:23.) These are just a few of the many examples. Simply, it seems the key to remain free and use your freedom as intended, is to stay focused on Jesus.

———————— PRAYER FOR THE DAY: ————————

Dear God,
Thank you for the reminder on how to use our freedom. I pray that all your children use their freedom to serve one another humbly in love and not to indulge in the desires of their flesh. I asked this in Jesus name. Amen

Cardiopulmonary Resuscitation (CPR)

ANCHOR SCRIPTURE: GALATIANS 5:13

For this is what the high and exalted One says-- he who lives forever, whose name is holy: "I live in a high and holy place, but also with the one who is contrite and lowly in spirit, to revive the spirit of the lowly and to revive the heart of the contrite.
(NIV)

"Take some time to learn first aid and CPR.
It saves lives, and it works."
- *Bobby Sherman*

I was recently reminded that it has been a while since I last took a cardiopulmonary resuscitation (CPR) class. I think knowing this skill is important because you never know when you may need it to save someone's life. I have heard some say, in previous classes that they don't know if they can breathe life into a stranger's mouth. The prophet Isaiah's words from today's scripture reminded me of CPR. He says, "to revive the spirit of the lowly and revive the heart of the contrite." Can you imagine your heart is failing and someone is ready, willing, and able to bring you back to life? No questions asked.

Many of us are walking dead people. Until we draw closer to God and his word, is when we awaken. God performs CPR often. His word awakens as it is the truth, the way, and the life. Can you recall the many times God administered CPR on you? Will you do the same for someone else?

Dear God,
Thank you for reviving my heart time and time again. You are always ready, willing, and able to breathe life back into me. I pray that all your children awaken and take time to study your word. It saves lives and it works. I asked this in Jesus' name. Amen

---

AUGUST 22

Prioritizing

ANCHOR SCRIPTURE: MATTHEW 6:33

"But seek first his kingdom and his righteousness, and all these things will be given to you as well."

"Effective leadership is putting first things first. Effective management is discipline, carrying it out."
-Stephen Covey

Yesterday in speaking to a friend, I mentioned that in my life journey, I learned to put first things first. There is always so much to do and places to be and many seeking your time. The key, I learned, to leading a disciplined life, is to put first things first. Like many, I fell many times to learn this lesson. However, once you master the lesson, it becomes a discipline.

Speaking of discipline, if I can remember, my mom and my grandmother have always awakened somewhere between 3-5 in the morning to pray. My grandmother always said, "seek first the kingdom of God."

I never understood this until I matured... Your quiet time with God and getting to know him should be the number one priority in your life. This requires discipline and ensuring nothing gets in the way. Now I understand how my grandmother led and my Mom leads a disciplined and orderly life. They learned to put first things first.

It is interesting that many say, "I don't have time to do my devotional or pray because xxxx." Pastor Rick Warren says "Put God first in your life, and you'll have more time. Whatever, you need more of in your life, give God first place in that area. You weren't put on the planet to mark things off your to-do list. You were made to spend time with God."

PRAYER FOR THE DAY:

Dear God,
Thank you for teaching me the discipline to put you and the work for your kingdom first in my day. I pray that all your children will follow your instructions to seek first your kingdom and your righteousness. I pray they discover the joy it brings you when they make time for you. I ask this in Jesus name. Amen.

Be Happy

ANCHOR SCRIPTURE: PSALM 37:4

Take delight in the Lord, and he will give you the desires of your heart. (NIV)"

"Your heart is where your treasure is, and you must find
your treasure in order to make sense of everything."
-Paulo Coelho

Life has exposed me to many people who simply are not happy. They are not happy with their job, they are not happy with their weight, they are not happy with their spouse, they are not happy with their relatives, they are not happy with themselves and the list goes on. No matter what it is, they are not happy.

Some of these people spend their entire lives seeking or chasing happiness. I compare it to a treasure hunt. If these people only knew the secret to finding their treasure, their happiness is to seek God. They don't need to go looking for happiness through someone else, through a job, waiting for something to happen, waiting for prince or princess charming to show up to be happy.

Today I encourage you and hope you encourage others to delight in the Lord. He will give you the desires of your heart. He will lead you to genuine happiness and peace. Everything else you get is a bonus.

Dear God,
Thank you for leading me to true happiness. To knowing that
you live in me and by taking delight in you, you will give me the
desires of my heart. I pray that all your children would delight
in you Lord, which is the key to finding their happiness, their
treasure, and their heart. I ask this in your son's Jesus name.
Amen

●

AUGUST 24

A Time of Rest

ANCHOR SCRIPTURE: MARK 2:27 (NLT)

"Jesus says, the Sabbath was made to meet the needs of people,
and not people to meet the requirements of the Sabbath."

"There is virtue in work and there is virtue in rest.
Use both and overlook neither."
- Alan Cohen

We all live busy lives. There is sometimes not one free minute in
the day till you lay down to sleep. I reflect today about the sabbath.
Merriam Webster defines the Sabbath as the seventh day of the week
observed from Friday evening to Saturday evening as a day of rest and

worship by Jews and some Christians; Sunday observed among Christians as a day of rest and worship; a time of rest.

I recalled growing up, Sundays were a true day of rest. You went to church in the morning, attended Sunday school, before or after church service, then headed home to have lunch. Usually we would either rest after lunch or Dad would say we are headed to the beach or a visit to grandma. We always looked forward to Sundays as it was truly a day of rest and family time.

Today's verse reminds us that the Sabbath was made to meet our needs and not for us to meet the requirement of the Sabbath. God truly is the supplier of everything we need. We all need a day a rest.

——————————— **PRAYER FOR THE DAY:** ———————————

Dear God,
Thank you for supplying me with all I need. A day of rest is key to refill my cup and replenish my soul. I pray that all your children find one day among their busy schedules to observe the sabbath to refill their cup, spend quality time with family and replenish their soul. I ask this in your son's Jesus name. Amen

AUGUST 25

Compassion

ANCHOR SCRIPTURE: EPHESIANS 4:31-32

"Get rid of all bitterness, rage and anger, brawling and slander, along with every form of malice. Be kind and compassionate to one another, forgiving each other, just as in Christ God forgave you."

"Love and compassion are necessities, not luxuries. Without them humanity cannot survive."
-Dalai Lama

Have you ever been angry and bitter about something or with someone? Do you ever wonder why you cannot shake that rage or anger? We are all humans and will flirt with prolonged anger and range.

Ephesians 4:31 says we must get rid of ALL bitterness, rage, and anger, brawling and slander, along with every form of malice. No matter what had been done to you. Verse 32 proceeds to remind us to be kind and compassionate to one another, forgiving each other, just as Christ God forgave us.

Nothing else to add to this.... God forgave all our trespasses even before we committed them. He shows grace, mercy, and compassion to you daily. He asks that we do the same to our brother and sisters, show compassion and forgive.

Dear God,
Thank you for your continued love, grace, mercy, and compassion towards me. I pray that all your children have compassion and forgive those who cause them anger and who trespass against them. I ask this in your son's Jesus name. Amen.

AUGUST 26

Seeking Happiness

ANCHOR SCRIPTURE: PSALM 37:4

"Take delight in the Lord, and he will give you the desires of your heart". (NIV)

Your heart is where your treasure is, and you must find your treasure in order to make sense of everything."
-Paulo Coelho

Life has exposed me to many people who simply are not happy. They are not happy with their job, they are not happy with their weight, they are not happy with their spouse, they are not happy with their relatives, they are not happy with themselves and the list goes on. No matter what it is, they are never happy.

Some people spend their entire lives seeking or chasing happiness. I compare it to a treasure hunt. If they only knew the secret to finding their treasure, their happiness is to seek God. They don't need to go looking for happiness through someone else, through a job, waiting for something to happen, winning the lottery, waiting for prince or princess charming to show up to be happy.

Today, I encourage you and hope you encourage others to delight in the Lord. Serve the Lord, continue strengthen your relationship with God and he will give you the desires of your heart. He will lead you to genuine happiness and peace.

———— **PRAYER FOR THE DAY:** ————

Dear God,
Thank you for leading me to true happiness, my true treasure. To know that you live in me and by taking delight in you, you give me the desires of my heart. I pray that all your children delight in you Lord and find true happiness through you. I ask this in your son's Jesus name. Amen

God Hears Your Prayers

ANCHOR SCRIPTURE: PSALM 34:15

"The eyes of the Lord are on the righteous, and his ears are attentive to their cry" (NIV)

"Never forget the three powerful resources you always have available to you: love, prayer, and forgiveness."
- *H. Jackson Brown, Jr.*

A few weeks back, I was conversing with a young adult about his plans. He informed me that he longed to be a leader of an organization. I asked what steps are you taking to achieve this goal? He paused then stated, he finished college, he worked through a few internships, he prays, he works hard but it simply is not happening.

I went on to discuss a bit about patience, perseverance and prayer. He said sometimes I am not sure God hears my prayers. I said, I am no expert and I am still learning lots about developing a strong relationship with God. However, one thing I could share with this young man is that in my life experience, sometimes when your prayers are not answered just yet, there is usually something God wants to teach you. Sometimes he is simply equipping you with the tools you will need for that next promotion.

As humans, we will experience impatience with God and sometimes get frustrated or angry with God simply because he is not answering our prayers when we expect him to do so. I encourage you today to know that every time you talk to God in prayer he is listening. He simply cannot tell you everything he is doing in your life because how else will you learn the skills you need if all the answers are giving to you? God is attentive to your cry. Prayer still works.

Dear God,
Thank you for encouraging me to continue talking to you in prayer and reminding me that indeed you do hear my cry. I pray that all your children trust you enough to answer their prayers, according to your will and your perfect timing. Give them the strength to persevere in prayer and patience to know that you will answer. I ask this in Jesus name. Amen

AUGUST 28

Faith vs. Feeling

ANCHOR SCRIPTURE: EPHESIANS 2:8

"For it is by grace you have been saved, through faith—and this is not from yourselves, it is the gift of God" (NIV)

It's hard to beat a person who never gives up."
- Babe Ruth

I tell you, writing a book got me thinking about faith vs. feeling. Some days ideas flow and other days thoughts and ideas just aren't flowing. You feel you need to take a break after weeks of writing. The break you take can easily go from a few hours to a few days to a few weeks to a few months. I realize that a writer is always writing. Whether it is a day where ideas are simply not flowing, you still exercise discipline, sit, and write at least one word or one sentence to finish writing your book. The key here is although it is baby steps, you are making progress.

As a writer, if you succumb to feeling vs. fact and faith, you will never finish one single book. You simply push as making progress is better than standing still, taking breaks, or surrendering to "feelings." Feelings are not reliable; they are generated from the heart and the heart is deceitful (Jeremiah 17:9.)

Similarly, you can't rely on feelings to pray daily, to read God's word or developing a strong relationship with God. You rely on faith. Remaining connected and committed to writing every single day is important to finish a book. The same reality applies to maintaining your faith and your relationship with God; you must read his word, pray, and talk to him often. Even when you don't "feel like it"... you must remain connected. Today's verse reminds us that faith not feelings saves.

———————————— **PRAYER FOR THE DAY:** ————————————

Dear God,
Thank you for the reminder that faith not feelings is what gets you to the finish line. I pray that all your children remember that faith not feelings will see them through their challenges. Whether it is writing a book, finishing a project, weight loss, or growing in their spiritual walk, consistent baby steps equals progress. I ask this in your son's Jesus' name. Amen

Soul Health

ANCHOR SCRIPTURE: PSALM 23:3

"He refreshes my soul. He guides me along the right paths for his name's sake."

"Don't gain the world and lose your soul;
wisdom is better than silver or gold."
- *Bob Marley*

Breakfast, lunch, and dinner. Most of us make sure we eat at least three meals a day. We eat to replenish our body, for energy and to ensure we don't starve. Sometimes the meals are good for us, other times they are not. We still eat. The meals we eat during one meal processes, is emptied then we are hungry again. Our body says it is again time to eat and the cycle continues. We eat till we are filled, we empty, then refill again.

I thought about what else needs feeding in our lives. Our minds need feeding and our soul. I thought how do you feed your soul? Why feeds your soul? Like eating to replenish and nourish our bodies, our soul also needs replenishing and nourishing. Some people take short breaks during the day to escape the daily grind. Mark 6:31 says "Come away by yourselves to a secluded place and rest a while." This does not require taking time off. Simply taking a few minutes out of your day to rest, replenish and refresh your soul is one way. Another may be spending time in God's words and reciting his promises. This helps me nourish, refill, and refresh my soul.

How do you refresh your soul? How is your soul health? God wants you to have a healthy body, mind, and soul. Today's verse from psalm 23 reminds us that the Lord is our shepherd and he refresh our soul and will guide us along the path of righteousness. He cares about not just the condition of our hearts but also the condition of our souls.

Dear God,
Thank you for the reminder that caring for my soul is as important
as caring for my heart and body. I pray that your children take
time daily to check on their "soul health", replenish and refresh
it as the soul can also run dry. I ask this in your son's Jesus name.
Amen

AUGUST 30

Changing Tunes

ANCHOR SCRIPTURE: PSALM 98:1

"Oh, sing to the Lord a new song! For He has done marvelous
things, His right hand and His holy arm have gained
Him the victory

"How cruelly sweet are the echoes that start, when memory
plays an old tune on the heart!"
-Eliza Cook

I have been on road trips with groups where it sometimes seems
impossible to please everyone with the music selection. One person
may like pop, one rock, another rap, one salsa, another classical and
the other gospel. For some, the tune selection clearly resonates with
their current journey or their current thoughts.

If you look back at your life, you could probably relate to the different tunes you listen to at different stages of your growth. As you matured, your choice of music or choice of tunes change. Taking a deeper look, those tunes changed according to what was presently going on in your heart, mind, and soul.

In the Bible changing tunes or to be exact "sing a new song" has been mentioned when God does something powerful or extraordinary. It triggers those affected to write a new song, to change tunes. Throughout life you will change your tunes however there are some tunes that no matter what is going on in your life, they still speak truth and life to you. I leave you with this one... "Jesus loves me this I know, for the Bible tells me so..." This song still speaks truth and should bring your life. Has God done something in your life for you to sing a new song today?

--- PRAYER FOR THE DAY: ---

Dear God,
Thank you for your words of wisdom that it is okay to change tunes from time to time. No matter what, you are with us. Some of these tunes will be temporary and others will always see us through. I pray that all your children recognize that you almighty God have the power to change their tunes when the time is right. In the meantime, they can rely on the tunes that endure forever. I ask this in Jesus name, Amen.

Suiting Up

ANCHOR SCRIPTURE: EPHESIANS 6:11(NIV)

"Put on the full armor of God, so that you can take your stand against the devil's schemes."

"Wear your tragedies as armor, not shackles"

Imagine the intense training it takes to be a member of the armed forces. When you enlist, you agree to defend an entire nation. Wow, that is dedicated service. This is why I always thank those who serve in the Armed Forces. I have not been a member of the armed forces and have participated in Reserved Officers Training Corps (ROTC), a training program for training high school and college students for the United States Armed Forces.

I recall in the 10th grade going to jungle training as part of the ROTC program. The test you took was just as real as though you were training for actual enlisted service. You suited up with the complete war gear and grind through very tough courses; climbed over very tall barriers, scuttled yourself in the mud to crawl under barbed wire, jumped across a very deep ditch and ran to the finish line despite being exhausted. All wearing the full war gear. I however finished the test. What a joy to receive that jungle training certificate.

Today's verse reminds us to put on the full armor of God, so that you can take your stand against the scheme of the enemy. (Read Ephesians 6:10-18.) This, to me, is suiting up daily for battle, for spiritual warfare. Suiting up with God's words and all his promises to prepare for warfare. So, we don't fall prey to the schemes of the enemy. We will all face warfare and you never know when it will hit. Are you preparing, are you suiting up daily?

Dear God,
Thank you for providing us with a reminder in Ephesians 6:10-18
to suit up daily. The reminder that if we don't learn the truth, we
will fall prey to the lies of the enemy. I pray that all your children
seek your word and your truth daily to prepare themselves and
their family for warfare. I pray they all know that they are part
of your army. I ask this in Jesus name. Amen

Reflections

_____

_____

_____

_____

_____

_____

_____

_____

_____

_____

_____

September

Fruitful Hearing

ANCHOR SCRIPTURE: MARK 4:20 (NIV)

"Others, like seed sown on good soil, hear the word, accept it, and produce a crop-some thirty, some sixty, some a hundred times what was sown."

"We must stay connected to vine to keep bearing fruits."
- Lailah Gifty Akita

As parents, grandparents, aunts, uncles, brothers, and sisters do you sometimes feel you speak in parables? You try to share your experiences, your wisdom, your knowledge on a particular life situation with your children, grandchildren, nieces, nephews, siblings, colleagues and even your spouses. The advice or story you share is to help guide them on a fruitful path. Even though you may explain in a complex manner, your hope is that it falls on good soil. Sometimes the seed sown, falls along a path, on shallow ground, among thorns or simply on deaf ears.

In Matthew 13, "the disciples asked Jesus, "Why do you speak to the people in parables?" He replied, "Because the knowledge of the secrets of the kingdom of heaven has been given to you, but not to them." This to me is powerful. To have "the knowledge of the secrets of heaven." Isn't that what we hope for all those we love? For all our brothers and sisters?

Today's verse, Mark 4:20, to me brings hope, that many will hear, accept, and obey God's word. Although you may not see that you have sown a seed in good soil, you trust that the seed you plant will yield a hundred times what was sown. Continue to speak and share your parables. Those choosing to hear will eventually yield good fruit. Don't give up!

—————————————— **PRAYER FOR THE DAY:** ——————————————

Dear God,
Thank you for ears to hear your word and guidance. Jesus says, "He who has ears to hear, let him hear." I pray that all your children will be like a seed sown on good soil. That they will hear your word, accept it, and produce a crop that is not just thirty, sixty, but it is a hundred times what they sow. I asked this in Jesus name. Amen!

God is Love

ANCHOR SCRIPTURE: 1 JOHN 4:8 (NIV)

*"Whoever does not love does not know God,
because God is love."*

"When all fails, simply love"
- *Ilka V. Chavez*

I sometimes tease some of family members that I didn't have a choice in selecting them to be part of my family. However, I will still love them as they are. Have you ever wondered how you managed to be relatives with certain people? Let's keep it real, all of us have that one relative that when they show up to the family reunion or a family function we say, Lord, why did I have to be related to him or her? Or you say what a shame or embarrassment. I wonder if some say that about me. (LOL)

However, the reality is we must love everyone despite if they embarrass you, they hurt you and always acting up. We must simply love. My Mom always says, "God is love." As these thoughts enter my mind about certain members of the family, I simply remember this, God is love. God created us to be one body, one family, one church, one love. I once read this (can't recall the source) and have kept it close by when I simply don't feel to love someone. "With power and authority in the family of God also comes the requirement that all must be done in love, not in selfishness, pride, greed or arrogance. We must become like God in character and nature if we are to become like Him in being!"

Today's verse is a simple reminder to love all the same as God loves you. Think about the times you ignored God, think about the times you were embarrassed to claim your relationship with God, think about all the times you hurt God by your disobedience. Through it all, he loved you and today he still loves you because God is love.

Dear God,
Thank you for loving me just the way I am. For never being embarrassed by me or to claim me as your child. I pray that all your children recognize that to know you is to love because you are love. That they each search their hearts and find the strength to love despite the hurt, shame and embarrassment. I ask this all in your son's Jesus name. Amen.

SEPTEMBER 3

Loving Choices

ANCHOR SCRIPTURE: 1 THESSALONIANS 5:14

"Admonish the idle, encourage the fainthearted,
help the weak, be patient with them all"

"This life is for loving, sharing, learning, smiling, caring, forgiving, laughing, hugging, helping, dancing, wondering, healing, and even more loving..."
- Steve Maraboli

It is easier to talk about someone's mistakes, their downfall, or their imperfections with others than directly with the person. This is sometimes known as gossip. I wonder why gossip is more pleasing or simpler than facing the person with whom you may find a conflict or that may be committing an offense? Is it easier to talk about the speck in someone's eyes rather than removing your own? Is it fear or simply uncomfortable? Or does it bring joy to simply focus on others than yourself?

Let's face it, it is painful and uncomfortable to talk with a friend, a loved one, a neighbor and even a stranger about self-righteousness or some other fault. The safe route may be to look the other way, pretend it is not happening, leave well enough alone or talk "about" rather than "to" that person. The Bible tells about many examples were Jesus spoke directly to those committing an offense. He sometimes spoke in parables, but he spoke to them, eye to eye, not about them.

God calls us to make loving not safe choices. His word teaches us the truth so we can share this truth with others. Today's verse reminds us to "admonish the idle, encourage the fainthearted, help the weak, be patient with them all." Is there someone you have been talking about instead of talking to about something? It may be uncomfortable, but you never know if you will encourage that person by speaking the truth directly than continuing to talk about them or remain silent. Will you take the safe or the loving choice today?

———————————— **PRAYER FOR THE DAY:** ————————————

Dear God,
Thank you for teaching me the way and the truth. For lovingly admonishing me yet still encouraging me when I walk away from your truth. I pray that like you, all your children make loving rather than safe choices. It may hurt to tell the truth eye to eye but in the long run, it will do good. I ask this in Jesus name. Amen

More or Less

ANCHOR SCRIPTURE: JOHN 3:30 (NIV)

"He must become greater; I must become less."

"Less is more."
- Ludwig Mies van der Rohe

More or less can sometimes means vagueness or uncertainty. These words can also mean you get more, or you get less. Who doesn't love a sale or bargain? You buy two and get three free. In this case, you get more items for a lesser price. As I reflect on a deeper meaning of more or less, it has nothing to do with material things, if you feel like a million bucks in a particular outfit or car, if you have a large home or a small home or if you acquire fame.

As your relationship with God increases, he becomes more, and you become less. Everything you do, think, and say is about God and his truth. It is inevitable, he becomes greater and you become less. Like the song says, "It is not about you, it is about Jesus." There is no vagueness and there is no bargaining.

To me, when you grow in your relationship with God, your joy increases, your desires, wants, and needs becomes his desires, wants, and needs. John the Baptist said (see John 3:27-30) his joy is now complete. "He must become greater and I become less." This is the purpose and plan of Jesus himself, simply love, live his truth, and have joy!

Dear God,
Thank you for teaching me that materials things, no matter the
value, is having less. It weighs you down. That having you in
my life has more value that all the material riches in the world.
Those are simply bonus if that is your will for us. I pray that as
all your children increase their relationship with you, that you
increase, and they decrease.

SEPTEMBER 5

Endurance

ANCHOR SCRIPTURE: HEBREWS 10:26

"If we deliberately keep on sinning after we have received the
knowledge of the truth, no sacrifice for sins is left,"

"The sky is not my limit...I am."
-T.F. Hodge

Merriam Webster defines the word endurance as the ability to with-
stand hardship or adversity; the ability to sustain a prolonged stressful
effort or activity. As I talk to many young and older people a consistent theme has recently surfaced. The theme is how does one endure
through difficult times?

As I reflect on this, I thought about some of the key things necessary
to endure through hard times. Here is a short list that came to mind:

it is necessary to have discipline, focus, patience, ability to persevere, renewing your thoughts often, continued movement, trust, integrity, remain true and live the truth, prayer, faith and a community to sustain you through it all. These are just a few of many things you need to endure.

I thought, if many didn't have these things, they would constantly fall prey to sin and negative thoughts. They would simply give up and chose sin rather than the truth to help them endure. The apostle John says: "If we walk in the light as He is in the light, we have fellowship with one another, and the blood of Jesus Christ His Son cleanses us from all sin." (1 John 1) To endure, choose to walk in the light, in fellowship with one another rather than hiding in dark places and in sin.

PRAYER FOR THE DAY:

Dear God,
Thank you for providing your words, the truth to endure and as a reminder to keep shinning. I pray that all your children realize that they too have choices, to shine or to dim their light through sin. I pray you place warriors in their midst so they will know the joy that comes with endurance. In Jesus name, Amen.

Prudence

ANCHOR SCRIPTURE: PROVERBS 14:15 (NIV)

*"The simple believe anything, but the prudent
give thoughts to their steps."*

"Wisdom at the mountain-foot sees farther than intelligence
at the mountaintop."
- *Matshona Dhliwayo*

You may have heard the tale of the Emperor's new clothes. This Emperor loved to wear fine clothing and spent all his people's money on his clothes. Two swindlers claiming to be weavers came to the Emperor's City. They claimed to make the finest, lightest, and most spectacular cloth the world has seen. It was invisible to anyone who was incompetent or stupid. Of course, the Emperor had to have it.

He paid lots of money to have it made for him. He sent his advisors to check on the progress. They saw nothing. However, not wanting to say they saw nothing at all, the advisors reported that the cloth was magnificent, when the cloth didn't exist! The day came for the Emperor to showcase his new clothes. "While expressing admiration at their Emperor's new "invisible" clothes, a small boy cried out... "But the Emperor has no clothes!" "

Some would say the advisors demonstrated prudence and the child did not. However, the child spoke the truth. Everyone faces situations where they must give thought to their words and steps. Today's verse reminds us not to be simple like the Emperor. We must mind our steps. Sometimes the decision may be to remain quite for a while, other times it may be that you speak the truth in love.

Dear God,
Thank you for your words of wisdom.

"The simple believe anything, but the prudent give thoughts to their steps." Sometimes this prudent and truthful step may be silence other times not. I pray that all your children will give thoughts to their steps while remaining truthful to your words. In Jesus name Amen.

SEPTEMBER 7

In Pursuit of Dreams

ANCHOR SCRIPTURE: MATTHEW 7:7-8 (NIV)

Ask and it will be given to you; seek and you will find; knock and the door will be opened to you. For everyone who asks receives; the one who seeks finds; and to the one who knocks, the door will be opened.

Dreams crystallize into reality when they are pursued.
- Mary Morrissey

A Dream is defined in Merriam Webster as a series of thoughts, images, or emotions occurring during sleep; an experience of waking life having the characteristics of a dream: such as a visionary. Some say never dream, others say be a dreamer. I say dream on, you are not the only one. When you dream and add pursuit to that dream there is an energy that is exchanged to concur that which you desire. Keep seeking as your dream can be yours.

Imagine your dreams becoming a reality.There are two quotes by Walt Disney that makes me smile at dreams:

1-"If you can dream it, you can do it. Always remember that this whole thing was started by a mouse."

2- "All our dreams can come true, if we have the courage to pursue them."

We all have dreams. Sometimes it is hard to keep the dream alive. "Start where you are. Use what you have. Do what you can." and keep the dream alive.

Today's verse is a reminder, "Ask and it will be given to you; seek and you will find; knock and the door will be opened to you. For everyone who asks receives; the one who seeks finds; and to the one who knocks, the door will be opened." Will you have the courage to pursue your dreams? Go for it. I encourage you to read Matthew 7 in its entirety.

───────────────── PRAYER FOR THE DAY: ─────────────────

Dear Father,
Thank you for the reminder to pursue my dreams. To ask and it will be given to me; seek and I will find; knock and the door will be opened to me. To have the courage to pursue my dreams. I pray that all your children have the courage to pursue their dreams. That they remember to ask and it will be given to them; seek and they will find; knock and the door will be opened to them. I ask this in your son Jesus' name, Amen.

Wheat and Weeds

ANCHOR SCRIPTURE: MATTHEW 13:29

"No, he answered, 'because while you are pulling the weeds, you may uproot the wheat with them."

"Until maturity, we can't tell wheat apart from weeds"

I have a very dear friend who would always say, "I don't go to church because it is filled with hypocrites. They have biases, they smile and grin in my face and as soon as I walk away, they start talking about me and try to discredit who I am." I thought to myself, am I going to let others stop me from growing in my faith? Will I let the weeds stifle my opportunity to grow and live in freedom?

I suppose God intended weeds to mix with the wheat to help us grow. Possibly, to ensure that we recognize the weed from the wheat...ultimately to recognize and carefully remove the weeds from our own crop before trying to remove from another's crop. Possibly to grow our character.

I eventually said to that friend, you are welcome to join me to church when you are ready. I realized the choice was not mine. I continued and still continue to remove the weed from my crop, improve my relationship with God, pray for this friend and leave the rest in God's capable hands. (Read - Matthew 13 - The parable of the Sower.)

Dear God,
Thank you for the reminder that sometimes your intention is
to have the weed grow with the wheat. That separation of the
two requires a careful process. I pray that all your children
understand and trust that although they may have weed grow-
ing alongside their wheat, that in the time of harvest, you will
guide them on the process to separate the two. I ask this in Jesus
name. Amen.

SEPTEMBER 9

Thrown to the Wolves

ANCHOR SCRIPTURE: LUKE 10:3 (NIV)

"Go! I am sending you out like lambs among wolves"

"Throw me to the wolves & I'll return leading the pack"
-Unknown

Have you ever been in a situation where you felt like someone "threw
you to the wolves?" The idiom "throw somebody to the wolves" is to
put someone in a situation where there is nothing to protect them. Do
you recall the feeling? You probably felt helpless, disappointed, fear
and anger.

Have you watched someone being thrown to the wolves or have you been the one to throw someone to the wolves? How did you feel after doing such act? Can you imagine how the 72 Jesus appointed felt when they were told: " Go! I am sending you out like lambs among wolves."(Read Luke 10) A similar message was given to the 12 disciples in Matthew 10:16 "I am sending you out like sheep among wolves. Therefore, be as shrewd as snakes and as innocent as doves." (Read Matthew 10.) It is no secret, wolves eat lambs.

Jesus however provided clear instructions on how to avoid been eaten by the wolves. He said, " be as shrewd as snakes and innocent as doves." Some balancing act. In Luke 10:19-20 Jesus says "I have given you authority to trample on snakes and scorpions and to overcome all the power of the enemy; nothing will harm you. However, do not rejoice that the spirits submit to you, but rejoice that your names are written in heaven." These are important promises to remember, the authority given to you to trample on snakes and scorpions... your name is written in heaven. Jesus equipped you to be powerful not powerless.

—————————— **PRAYER FOR THE DAY:** ——————————

Dear God,
Thank you for the daily reminder of your promises. That you equipped me with the tools and prudence to be a sheep among wolves. I pray that all your children suit-up and plug-in daily to your truth so they may remain protected and powerful. They will walk like sheep among wolves and not be eaten. I ask this in your son's Jesus name. Amen

Wisdom and Wealth

ANCHOR SCRIPTURE: PSALM 49:20 (NIV)

"People who have wealth but lack understanding are like the beast that perish."

"The real measure of your wealth is how much you'd be worth if you lost all your money."
- Unknown

I once read an article and it is said, "life is about righteousness not riches." In this day and age many people focus on getting rich. Everyone wants to be rich and famous. In pursuing this dream some focus simply on getting rich. Many never pause to think that nothing they possess right now goes to eternity with them.

I recently met an actress who shared her story of having wealth for some time. Somewhere along the way, she lost her gigs, became depressed and loss all her wealth. She admits that she lacked wisdom and the foundation to manage her wealth. I am sure you have heard many stories of recording artist, actors and millionaires who went from rags to riches back to rags.

Is it that they lack wisdom and the tools to manage their wealth or simply they lose sight of the bigger picture? Today's verse warns that people who have wealth but lack understanding are like the beast that perish. Understanding the facts of life, God's word, and his truth, seeking righteousness, seeking wisdom, and understanding provides the greatest wealth for our internal life.

Dear God,
Thank you for your guidance on what I need for my life in your
kingdom. I pray that all your children have wealth with under-
standing. That they remember "It's not the riches, it's the riches
without the foundation that comes from earning those riches"
that truly matters. I ask this in your son's Jesus name. Amen!

SEPTEMBER 11

Help Wanted

ANCHOR SCRIPTURE: PSALM 121:2

"My help comes from the LORD, the Maker of heaven
and earth."

"Always seek out the seed of triumph in every adversity."
- Og Mandino

As I walked through the small downtown area in my neighborhood, I
see a couple stores with help wanted signs. I start to think of someone
who may be seeking employment to let them know of places that are
seeking help. Sometimes they are open to the information and other
times they are not.

It is perplexing that here is a place needing help and here is a person
needing a job to help themselves and there is no connection. Is it that

the person believes this position cannot fill their needs? Is it that they believe this is not the type of help they want? Is it that they seek help in all the wrong places? One never knows.

One thing clearly stated in today's verse is that our help comes from the Lord, the Maker of heaven and earth. We each have access to the creator of heaven and earth to help us with all our wants and needs. Wow! Remember this the next time you seek help. Start your "help wanted" search with the creator of heaven and earth. Your help comes from him.

─────────────── **PRAYER FOR THE DAY:** ───────────────

Dear God,
Thank you for always answering my call for help. I sometimes search for help in all the wrong places and then you remind me, my help comes from you. I pray that all your children remember that when "help is wanted" they should turn to you. You will guide them; you will help them. I ask this in your son's Jesus name. Amen!

Created to Create

ANCHOR SCRIPTURE: GENESIS 1:27

"So, God created mankind in his own image, in the image of God he created them; male and female he created them."

"Life isn't about finding yourself. Life is about creating yourself."
- *George Bernard Shaw*

I recently attended a networking meeting and met a very interesting woman. She caught my attention. After the meeting we engaged in conversation. She indicated that she loved to write... that writing brought out her creativity. She also shared that her ten-year old daughter just became an author. She created a story about two sisters in Africa and was inspired to publish this story into a book.

As I left the meeting, I thought wow, we are all truly created to create. The greatest creator created us in his likeness, in his image to do the same. I thought, a ten-year old figured that out early. From our birth, we are all created with the innate ability to create. However, some-where along our journey called life, we lose our way and forget this truth, "We've been made in the image and likeness of God."

I wonder what stops us from fully tapping into our creativity. Is it that we don't believe we have the ability? Is it that as we grow older, we are exposed to sin and feel un-worthy? Today, I encourage each of you to tap into your God given creativity, your gift. No matter your age, if you have been thinking about creating something, create it now, if you have been thinking about starting something, start working on it today. We are God's work, God's image, God's family.

Dear God,
Thank you for creating me in your own image. For given me the greatest gift of spirit within to help me be creative. To help me remember that even if I sin, I should not allow that to block my creativity. Your son already paid the price. I pray that all your children re-member that they were created to create and are members of your family. I ask this in Jesus' name. Amen!

SEPTEMBER 13

Do Not Enter

ANCHOR SCRIPTURE: PSALM 112:1 (NIV)

Praise the LORD. Blessed are those who fear the LORD,
who find great delight in his commands.

"Fear God and you need not fear anyone else."
- *Woodrow Wilson*

During the course of life, we are instructed by our parents, teachers, guides, elders, and others who influence us, on the way to go. They also provide us with guidance on the things we should not do. I refer to these as "do not enter" guidance.

Many of us when warned (despite receiving clear evidence from experience), still make the choice to defy wisdom. We do what we want to do. We enter or flirt with the "do not enter" warnings. We simply become stubborn because we feel we are been robbed of some joy by these warnings.

Today's verse reminds us that blessed are those who fear the Lord, who find great delight in his commands. Obeying and living according to God's guidance, his words, truly brings joy, peace, and God's blessing. Trespassing the "do not enter" sign, is the beginning of temptation. The fear of the Lord is the beginning of wisdom. Which do you choose?

PRAYER FOR THE DAY:

Dear God,
Thank you for lighting my path to understand that fearing and obeying you, is truly the key to long lasting joy, peace, and receiving your blessings. I pray that all your children fear you and follow your clear guidance. That they stay clear of the "do not enter" signs. I ask this in Jesus name. Amen!

Misplaced Praise

ANCHOR SCRIPTURE: PSALM 118:28-29 (NIV)

You are my God, and I will praise you; you are my God, and I will exalt you. Give thanks to the Lord, for he is good: his love endures forever.

"Don't work for recognition but do work worthy of recognition."
- *H. Jackson Brown, Jr.*

Everyone loves to receive praise for a job well done. Our eyes gleam with pride when we finish our first big race, we pass a critical exam, we do something good for someone else, and even when we take our first steps. Some of the praise you receive may be, "I am so proud of you, congratulations, yeah, you did it, job well done, or high five."

I reflected on these praise moments. I thought, it is great to praise someone for their accomplishments but sometimes we forget to share that praise or honor with the one who created us to do all these things. We sometimes don't acknowledge his part not to be held accountable to his word and his truth. We instead take all the credit, all the praise and honor for ourselves and to satisfy our ego. We simply misplaced the praise.

Today's verse reminds us that we must always praise the Lord. For me, it is not only to praise him always with my lips. It is to be obedient to his word. It is to honor who he is in my life; he is my God. He deserves all the honor, all the praise, all the glory and all the thanksgiving simply because he loves us. He gave his son's life for our sins even before we committed them. He provides everything we have.

Dear God,
I thank you and praise you for all your daily provisions. I am
nothing without you. I pray that all your children remember
that you created them, that you provide everything they have
and that they rightfully praise you for all you do for them daily.
I ask this in Jesus name. Amen

SEPTEMBER 15

Serene

ANCHOR SCRIPTURE: COLOSSIANS 3:15 (NIV)

Let the peace of Christ rule in your hearts, since as members
of one body you were called to peace. And be thankful.

"Peace cannot be kept by force. It can only be
achieved by understanding."
- Albert Einstein

The word serenity is sometimes defined as the state of being calm, peaceful, and untroubled. There is a church him that begins with the words "Let there be peace on earth and let it begin with me." Little did I understand as I sung this hymn, as a small child and still sing as an adult, the power in those words.

When you achieve peace, (when you are serene no matter what "the noise" around you may want you to believe) it is a sign of true and deep understanding. An understanding that I achieved by diving deeper into God's words and believing God's truth. It is an understanding that God would never "leave junk" for his children. That his peace, your serenity, is the most "prized possession" he left for you.

Today's verse reminds us of this inheritance gifted to each of us by God, "Let the peace of Christ rule in your hearts, since as members of one body, you were called to peace. "I read in one of my daily devotionals the following "learn the combination to the safe (submission to the Holy Spirit) and choose to withdraw peace from your "trust account" daily." The power that these words project is incredible. We have the power to choose peace.

PRAYER FOR THE DAY:

Dear God,
Thank you for leaving me such a powerful inheritance, your peace. Your steadfast guidance has provided me with "the combination to the safe." I pray that all your children listen to your guidance, inscribe the combination in their hearts so they too can choose serenity. Choose the peace that surpasses all understanding. I ask this all in your son's Jesus name. Amen.

How is Your Faith?

ANCHOR SCRIPTURE: MATTHEW 9:22 (NIV)

Jesus turned and saw her. "Take heart, daughter," he said, "your faith has healed you." And the woman was healed at that moment.

"Worrying is arrogant because God knows what He's doing."
-Barbara Cameron

Longstanding problems with health, personal, and work are sometimes unbearable. All we can see is the problem. The solution seems so farfetched. I thought about healing as I meditated on today's verse.

We sometimes think that doctors and medicine heal us. The reality that came to mind is that doctors "take care" of us, the medicine keeps things stabilized but they do not "heal us." This statement is by no means an intent to take away from the wonders that doctors perform. It is simply to think about how you begin to truly heal from longstanding problems.

Do you maintain all your focus on the problem instead of the solution and healing? Do you surrender and walk by faith and not by sight? Today's verse is a great example of a woman whose faith was unshakeable. She ailed for a long while but remained focused on the solution instead of the problem. She knew, by faith, that Jesus could heal her and found a way to be healed. She simply touched Jesus' garment.

Dear God,
Thank you for the reminder that my faith has healed me time
and time again. To always walk by faith and not by sight. I pray
that all your children walk by faith and not by what they see.
That they trust you and surrender to your will for their lives. By
their strong faith, you will heal their longstanding problems. I
ask this in your son Jesus name. Amen!

●

SEPTEMBER 17

Ears to Hear

ANCHOR SCRIPTURE: MARK 4:9 (NIV)

Then Jesus said, "Whoever has ears to hear, let them hear."

"Listening is a positive act: you have to put yourself out to do it."
- David Hockney

"Who Can't Hear, Must Feel." I am sure some of you remembered
this being echoed from your parents. This usually meant you have
been warned.... you overlooked the negative consequences of your
actions and proceeded despite warning, simply to have things your way.
Usually, a short while later, you came home with a gash in your head

407

with blood all over seeking sympathy. You wished you had heeded the warning to not climb that tree. Instead of rushing to your aid first, your parent would say, since you can't hear, then feel.

Same as our parent, today's verse yields a warning, "whoever has ears to hear, let them hear." Are you listening to God, the Father, when he whispers to you? Are you listening to the guidance and warnings he gives you in making your choices? Can you even hear him? Be still and hear his voice. Many of us simply are not still long enough to hear God speak. He is saying pssst "can you hear me."

Jesus warns us in today's verse to listen. This is such an important warning, to not simply listen but also seek for the meaning behind the warning. If we do this, we may save ourselves from one too many gashes and scars.

———————————— PRAYER FOR THE DAY: ————————————

Dear God,
Thank you for the reminder of this important teaching. To listen for your voice that simply wants to guide me because you love me so much. I pray that all your children find a quiet time and space to hear you talk to them. Even more important, for them to enjoy this special relationship with you. I ask this in your son Jesus's name. Amen!

Personal Greatness

ANCHOR SCRIPTURE: PHILIPPIANS 2:3

Do nothing out of selfish ambition or vain conceit.
Rather, in humility value others above yourselves

"The person who clears the path ultimately controls its direction,
just as the canvas shapes the painting."
- Ryan Holiday

Selfishness, seeking personal greatness, and what I refer to as the "Mine, Me, and I" syndrome seems to be increasing in our society. I have worked for bosses who care nothing about the team. All they are concerned with is how they look, what they can get "out of the deal," and self-praise. I have even had bosses receive awards that clearly a team helped him/her achieve and they don't, at a minimum, express gratitude to all those who helped them achieve their greatness.

As humans, the temptation to choose selfishness over selflessness will always be present. Selfish people take it all for themselves. The ego takes control of their life and they seek personal greatness. Selfless people share and give from the heart. To me, the more selfless you are, the clearer your path. Matthew 23:12, reminds us "Whoever exalts himself will be humbled, and whoever humbles himself will be exalted."

Today's verse is one that no matter your age, it is probably still a struggle. It is the struggle all humans face from time to time. This verse tugs at my heart and is present in my daily walk. Do nothing out of selfish ambition or vain conceit. It reminds me daily to humble myself and value others above myself.

Dear God,
Thank you for teaching me to do nothing out of selfish ambition or vanity. To always value others above myself. I pray that all your children take this teaching to heart and continue striving to obey this command daily. I ask this in your son Jesus' name. Amen!

SEPTEMBER 19

Temptation

ANCHOR SCRIPTURE: HEBREWS 2:18 (NIV)

Because he himself suffered when he was tempted, he is able to help those who are being tempted.

"Opportunity may knock once, but temptation
leans on the doorbell."
- Unknown

Can you imagine been on a diet and going to a party. All the foods you shouldn't eat may be there to temp you. You, however, say, I have the will power and will not be tempted. However, when you show up to the party, the first thing you see is your favorite chocolate cake.

410

You wonder how can I avoid that? Then your thoughts take over and before you know it, you have eaten a sliver or two of the cake. There goes the diet. You simply did not resist the temptation.

Have you given into temptation recently? Have you suffered because you were lured and gave in to something you should not have or do? Each one of us have given into temptation at some point in our lives. Jesus suffered every temptation imaginable. Can you imagine, he never gave in. Because he himself suffered when he was tempted, he knows what you are going through and wants to help you. Will you seek his help now or before you are tempted next?

PRAYER FOR THE DAY:

Dear God,
Thank you for showing me through your words how not to give in to temptation. As a human, I know I will be tempted and may fall. But I am reassured that you are here to help guide and strengthen me to keep from temptation. I pray that all your children trust you enough to seek your guidance to help strengthen their will power and increasingly lead them away from temptation. I ask this in your son Jesus' name. Amen!

Stand Firm

ANCHOR SCRIPTURE: EPHESIANS 6:10

Finally, be strong in the Lord and in his mighty power.

"It is not the beauty of a building you should look at; it's the
construction of the foundation that will stand the test of time."
- David Allan Coe

Have you ever lost everything you have and own? Your home, your
family, your health, and nothing left fighting for? Look at Job, he lost
everything, and when he did, he said: "We bring nothing with us at
birth; we take nothing with us at death. The Lord alone gives and
takes. Praise the name of the Lord." Despite such devastation and
tough trial, he continued to trust God's purpose for his life and trust
that God would fight for him. (Read Job) Job did not sin or accuse God
of doing wrong. He stood strong in the Lord's mighty power.

Going through any difficult season is not easy. We want to fight for
ourselves, sometimes we feel alone, other times we simply deny it is
happening but sometimes we raise the white flag and surrender it all
to God, trust him, praise him and thank him through it all. You trust
that he will fight the battle for you. Deuteronomy 3:22 reminds us "Do
not be afraid of them; the LORD your God himself will fight for you."
Will you trust God to fight ALL your battles for you? Trust him, hang
on to his promises, stand strong and keep pressing forward.

Dear God,
Thank you for teaching me to trust you during trials and battles.
For the reminder that you stand ready to fight the battle for me.
I pray that no matter what battle your children currently face,
that they stand strong, trust you, remember your promises and
have faith that you are fighting the battle for them. Victory is
always yours. I ask this in Jesus' mighty name. Amen!

SEPTEMBER 21

Parked in Pain

ANCHOR SCRIPTURE: ISAIAH 48:17 (AMPC)

Thus says the LORD, your Redeemer, the Holy One of Israel:
I am the LORD your God, who teaches you to profit,
who leads you in the way that you should go.

Your pain is not your identity. Press forward and be free.
The choice is yours.

I recently read a devotional by Joyce Meyer on moving forward. It reminded me that "An important aspect of the healing of our soul is finding the courage to move beyond our pain."

In the devotional, Ms. Meyer mentioned a movie she saw about a talented woman so deeply wounded that she withdrew from life, people, and landed in a mental health facility. After a brief stay, she was released. After her release, she drove her van onto someone's driveway, parked and lived there the rest of her life. Imagine not knowing how to, or choosing not to deal with the wounds and deep pain that ails you? Imagine living the rest of your life in a parked position.

One telling sign you know you are remaining parked in your pain is un-forgiveness of yourself and others. If you are not moving, you cannot heal, you cannot push from pain to power. Feeling sorry for yourself should simply be a temporary stop, not a permanent place. Move through the phases of grief, loss, pain with help, prayer, and accountability. God wants you to move forward, be free and fulfill your highest potential.

I have a dear friend, Dr. Melida Harris who wrote a book titled, "Unveiling the Illusion: Know who you are." The book talks about how pain can keep you trapped in a mentality that impedes your God-given potential. I encourage you not to let your pain keep you in a parked position, become your identity or your dwelling place. It's time to move from park to drive. Move forward and be free.

Isaiah 48:17 is a reminder that, "Thus says the LORD, your Redeemer, the Holy One of Israel: I am the LORD your God, who teaches you to profit, who leads you in the way that you should go. Seek the Lord and he will show you and lead you in the way you should go. Release the pain and move forward to your power. I encourage you to read Isaiah 48 in its entirety.

--------- PRAYER FOR THE DAY: ---------

Dear Father,
Thank you for the reminder that pain is not my dwelling place. To seek you, my Redeemer and you will lead me in the way that I should go. The power is in moving from parked to drive. You drive and lead me Father. I pray that all your children find the

courage, help, and seek guidance to move from park to drive. That they forgive those who may have caused them pain or forgive themselves for causing pain to others. That no matter the depth of the wound and pain, they can rise up and move forward seeking you Lord. I ask this in your son Jesus' name, Amen.

———————————————●———————————————

Live in the Moment

ANCHOR SCRIPTURE: DANIEL 2:21 (NIV)

He changes times and seasons; he deposed kings and raises up others. He gives wisdom to the wise and knowledge to the discerning."

———————————

Be present in all things and thankful for all things."
- Maya Angelou

———————————

We are blessed to experience different seasons. Seasons are for a purpose. In the summer we are privileged to enjoy the beauty of the flowers, the butterflies, the ocean waves, the fullness of trees and simply God's creation outdoors. In the fall we observe the transition of the tree losing it leaves, the birds flying from north to south for warmer weather and the beaches too frigid to enjoy. We are, however, able to see the beauty in every season.

Today's verse reminds us that God changes times and seasons. He created everything to go through change. He deposes kings and raises up others. He gives wisdom to wise and knowledge to the discerning. That is powerful. It seems important that whatever time or season we are in, we should enjoy. God is in control of the climate changes as well as the changes in season we all go through.

It is not always easy to enjoy every season of life. If you reflect on your seasons you may find one common thread. That thread is probably growth. Every season we encounter is to help prepare us for the next season, to strengthen our character and to prepare us for life eternal. I encourage you today to live in the moment. Enjoy whatever season you are in, no matter how painful it may be. God is still in control. Live in the moment!

--------- **PRAYER FOR THE DAY:** ---------

Dear God,
Thank you for providing me with different seasons to help me grow. Life sure would be boring not having the experience of different seasons. I pray that all your children enjoy their current season and remember that you have the power to deposed kings and raise up others. To give wisdom to the wise and knowledge to the discerning. I ask this all in Jesus' mighty name. Amen!

Rebuild

ANCHOR SCRIPTURE: GALATIANS 2:18 (ESV)

*For if I rebuild what I tore down, I prove myself
to be a transgressor.*

It is the neglect of timely repair that makes rebuilding necessary.
- Richard Whately

Merriam Webster defines rebuild as to make extensive repairs (recon-
struct); to restore to a previous state (rebuild); or to make extensive
changes (remodel.) My church (Light of Life Church) is teaching a
series on "rebuilding." It has led me to ask, why would something
or someone need rebuilding? Is it because of wear and tear, bad or
defective construction, or perhaps neglect or lack of maintenance
and upkeep.

Imagine these scenarios: Building or constructing something yourself (for selfish reasons) and then realizing a major defect for lack of
consulting another with the proper expertise; having a car and never
taking it for the recommended oil change and tune up; leading a team
and never providing training, evaluation, or coaching as each member grows; or being in any relationship and not pausing to see or say
how is it going (assess); or purchasing a home and doing no repairs,
upgrades or replace worn items for 20 years. These scenarios are just
a short list of possible reasons why things, people, relationships may
be weakened, destroyed, or fall apart and require rebuilding.

"It is the neglect of timely repair that makes rebuilding necessary?"
Timing, vulnerability, transparency, and humility are key to prevent a
total rebuilt. This relates so closely to leadership. To avoid demolishing
things built, destroying those we lead, or constantly rebuilding relationships and organizations, we must constantly check-in, tune-up,

417

and establish consistent and frequent checkpoints to ensure we are sustaining what was built. To timely repair rather than require rebuilding.

Galatians 2:18 reminds us, "For if I rebuild what I tore down, I prove myself to be a transgressor." I encourage you to read Galatians 2 in its entirety.

PRAYER FOR THE DAY:

Dear Father,
Thank you for the reminder of the importance of timely repair. That if I rebuild what I tore down, I prove myself to be a transgressors. I pray that all your children pay attention and perform timely repairs on their minds, bodies, and souls rather than waiting to rebuild. That they assess and repair their relationship with you now. I ask this in your son Jesus' name, Amen.

418

Mistakes

1 THESSALONIANS 5:19 (NIV)

Do not quench the Spirit;

"There is nothing wrong with making mistakes,
but one should always make new ones. Repeating mistakes
is a hallmark of dim consciousness."
-Dave Sim

I recently read an article written by Alice Boy on "How to Overcome Your Fear of Making Mistakes." In the article Ms. Boy mentioned how making a mistake can be paralyzing in normal times and even worsened during times of heightened uncertainty.

In the article Ms. Boy proceeds to provide a few tips to help get one unstuck. Two of the tips she provided resonantes with me . One is to "try to accept reality by making a list of truths you might need to come to grips with, such as: I understand that people will not always behave in ideal ways." Finally, think about how you can act on your values to address the situation. Let's say one conscientiousness is important to you. You might apply that value by making sure your employees have masks that fit them well and easy access to hand sanitizer."

The article also reminded that each of us have tools to "help us learn to tolerate uncertainty without worrying too much about making a mistake." The reality is we will make mistakes in life. The key is tapping into wisdom to minimize these mistakes.

Today's verse is a reminder, to not quench the Spirit. Yielding and tapping into the helper, the Holy Spirit, gifted to you, can minimize your mistakes. Take heed and yield. I encourage you to read 1 Thessalonians 5 in it's entirety.

Dear Father,
Thank you for the gift of the Holy Spirit, my helper, to minimize the multitude of mistakes I will make. May I grow in learning to yield to my present help in times of trouble and confusion. May I never quench the Spirit. I pray that all your children grow in learning to yield and obey the Spirit to minimize their mistakes. That they do not quench the spirit, their present help in times of trouble and confusion. I ask this in your son Jesus' name, Amen!

SEPTEMBER 25

Showers of Blessings

ANCHOR SCRIPTURE: EZEKIEL 34:26

"I will make them and the places surrounding my hill a blessing. I will send down showers in season; there will be showers of blessing."

" Our prayers should be for blessings in general, for God knows best what is good for us."
- Socrates

A lot of rain has fallen lately. I had a colleague stop by my office to say hello and said, I don't like the rain. I asked why, he said I wear glasses and when it rains, my glasses fog, my lens get wet and I have issues with my vision. My response was, we need everything including the rain to grow. Can you imagine the world without rain? How would we replenish the water we drink; how would the flowers and the grass grow; how would we wash away the pollen and dust? To me, the rain is a blessing. He said, you made your point and walked away. I simply smiled.

Ezekiel 34 is filled with promises. It reminds us that the Lord is our shepherd and we shall not want. He provides everything we need in due time. Including the storms of life. We, however, must trust that is it all for our good despite the inconvenience or discomfort. He promises, "I will make them and the places surrounding my hill a blessing. I will send down showers in season; there will be showers of blessing." Wow, showers of blessings. Last, I remember a blessing is a good thing. Abundant blessing is even a better thing.

1st Thessalonians 5:18 says: "In everything give thanks." To me, today's verse is a reminder to give thanks for everything, including the rain and the storms of life. Rest in the hope and comfort that there shall be showers of blessings. You shall prosper. Count your blessings today.

—————— PRAYER FOR THE DAY: ——————

Dear God,
Thank you for the reminder that you will send down showers in season, and they will be showers of blessings. This brings hope for a new prosperity. I pray that all your children trust that you will send down showers of blessings for their prosperity. I ask this in your son Jesus' name. Amen!

SEPTEMBER 26

Ask

ANCHOR SCRIPTURE: JOHN 16:24(NIV)

*Until now you have not asked for anything in my name.
Ask and you will receive, and your joy will be complete."*

"If they can get you asking the wrong questions,
they don't have to worry about answers."
- *Thomas Pynchon*

Do you sometimes feel like your prayers are never answered? Or you simply give up because you are not receiving immediate results? You lose hope. I recently overheard a conversation where two people were discussing their prayer life. One said to the other, praying and believing is not for "Sissy's." That led me to think, consider how you are asking and how you are praying for what you desire. Are you strengthening your relationship with the Father? Are you believing with courage that your prayers will be answered or are you been a Sissy?

Today's verse reminds us to ask for anything in Jesus' name and you will receive, your joy will be complete. The preceding two verses (v22-23) reminds us what Jesus said to his disciples, "So with you: Now is your time of grief, but I will see you again and you will rejoice, and no one will take away your joy. In that day you will no longer ask me anything. Very truly I tell you, my Father will give you whatever you ask in my name."

Note to self, Jesus did not say my Father "may" give you, he said my Father "will" give you whatever you ask in my name. I always remind myself that whatever I ask for, that it is in line with God's will as that is all I want to be granted. Be encouraged, your grief will only last a short while. Keep praying, with courage, for God's will in your life and ask in his son Jesus' name and you will rejoice. No one or nothing will take away your joy.

Dear God,
Thank you for the reminder that praying and believing is not for Sissy's. That if I ask for anything in Jesus' name and I will receive, my joy will be complete. I pray that all your children have courage and believe that their prayers will be answered. That they remember that whatever they ask, to ask in our son Jesus' name. Then be patient until you answer. I ask this in your son's Jesus name. Amen!

SEPTEMBER 27

Let It Be

ANCHOR SCRIPTURE: JOHN 14:27 (ESV)

Peace I leave with you; my peace I give to you. Not as the world gives do I give to you. Let not your hearts be troubled, neither let them be afraid.

There will be an answer, let it be"
– *The Beatles."*

Do you recall the song written by Paul McCartney entitled Let it be? I recently listened to this song and realized the wisdom shared by its lyrics almost five decades ago. The words of the second verse say "And when the brokenhearted people living in the world agree, there will be an answer Let it be. For though they may be parted, there is still a chance that they will see, there will be an answer... Let it be, let it be, let it be, let it be. Yeah, there will be an answer let it be let it be, let it be, let it be, let it be whisper words of wisdom let it be."

Let it be, imagine if you just let things be. To let the process be and seek words of wisdom through the process. Let things be as they may is sometimes wise. You may realize that no matter what you do, your actions may have nothing to do with the outcome. Seeking wisdom may save you a lot of heartache and give you the peace to let whatever troubles you may face simply be. Let the peace of the Lord be with you.

Today's scripture is a reminder that "Peace I leave with you; my peace I give to you. Not as the world gives do I give to you. Let not your hearts be troubled, neither let them be afraid." Seek peace and LET IT BE!

—————————— **PRAYER FOR THE DAY:** ——————————

Dear Father,
Thank you for the reminder to seek the peace that you left for me. Not as the world gives but as you give. To not let my heart be troubled or be afraid. To "let it be" your will. I pray that all your children head your words of wisdom to seek the peace you left for each of them, not the peace that the world gives but peace as you give. That their hearts may not be troubles or be afraid. To let your will be. I ask this in your son Jesus' name. Amen!

Stay In The Ring

ANCHOR SCRIPTURE: 2 CORINTHIANS 12:9

"But he said to me, My grace is sufficient for you, for my power is made perfect in weakness. Therefore, I will boast all the more gladly about my weaknesses, so that Christ's power may rest on me."

"God doesn't cancel the fight; he gives you what it takes to win!"
- *Dr. Derek Grier*

I recently listened to a sermon by Bishop Derek Grier entitled The Vision and the Thorn. I reflected on this sermon and how often it is easy to take credit for so much when there is a bigger source behind our accomplishments. The source behind our victory when we are weak or think we are done. I was reminded that no matter the thorn in our side we are equipped with what we need to keep moving. Just when we want to tap out, we are re-energized by our source.

Sometimes in the midst of the battleground it seems as if you are surrounded and there is no way out but to "raise the white flag" and tap out because you feel you have lost the battle. What if what seem like a loss to you is a step in the right direction to your next victory. To winning the war. What if you look passed what is in front of you, give up relying on yourself, and allow God to be who he is meant to be in your life. What if God's grace alone would keep you in the ring and prevent you from tapping out too soon?

Today's scripture reminds us, "But he said to me, "My grace is sufficient for you, for my power is made perfect in weakness." Therefore, I will boast all the more gladly about my weaknesses, so that Christ's power may rest on me." I encourage you to read 2 Corinthians in its entirety. Do not tap out, you are winning.

Dear Father,
Thank you for the reminder to stay in the ring no matter what things look like. Do not tap out yet. Your grace is sufficient, for your power is made perfect in weakness. Don't believe the hype, what may look like a total loss is your next big move to victory. I pray that all your children stay in the ring even when things get tough. That they remember your grace is sufficient to see them to their next victory. I ask this in Jesus' name. Amen!

SEPTEMBER 29

Trials are Temporary

ANCHOR SCRIPTURE: 2 CORINTHIANS 4:18 (NIV)

"So, we fix our eyes not on what is seen, but on what is unseen, since what is seen is temporary, but what is unseen is eternal."

"The closer you are to the end of your temporal trials, the louder the voice of critics. Close your ears to the heavy downpours of their discouragements. God whispers: "I am with you"!"
-Israelmore Ayivor

Have you ever looked back on your life and wondered how on earth you made it through some of the things you did, was done to you, or were done for you? Somethings may have felt unbearable at the

426

time, some you couldn't understand and still trying to make sense of it, others you simply accept the grace that is given and moved on. You now know and admit it was tough to see through the end of those trials.

Consider a seed just planted or the caterpillar in a cocoon. Do you recall as a kindergartener doing a project where you brought a pea or bean from home, your teacher brought soil and you planted that pea or bean in a paper cup filled with soil? You either placed it on the windowsill of your classroom or took it home to patiently watch it grow into a plant or tree. Oh, the wait. A few weeks went by before that first sprout protruded the soil. Remember that feeling of excitement? Finally, a sign...Or like some of us may have heard, just when the caterpillar thought it would die, it became a butterfly.

Temporary trials sometimes feel like they will never end or that you will not make it. Somehow, you either find the strength to see that it is all temporary or you focus further than what you are currently facing. Today's scripture is a reminder "So we fix our eyes not on what is seen, but on what is unseen, since what is seen is temporary, but what is unseen is eternal." Nothing, absolutely nothing, last forever. Look to eternity and hang in there.

PRAYER FOR THE DAY:

Dear Father,
Thank you for the reminder that what is unseen is eternal. To fix my eyes not on what is seen, but on what is unseen, since what is seen is temporary, but what is unseen is eternal. I pray that all your children, no matter what they may be going through at this moment, fix their eyes on not what is seen, but on what is unseen, since what is seen is temporary, but what is unseen is eternal. I ask this in your son Jesus' name. Amen!

The Truth Frees

ANCHOR SCRIPTURE: JOHN 8:32 (NIV)

"Then you will know the truth, and the truth will set you free."

"The truth was always the truth, but until I knew the truth
for myself, I couldn't be free."
-Shelley Hendrix

Telling and Living the truth is not easy. It comes with all sorts of battles between the flesh and the spirit. I recently saw a post that said:

Truth: Accept it

Faith: Speak it

Hope: Hold onto it

Love: Live it

This post spoke power, truth, and freedom to me. Imagine accepting what is real, the truth, and not fantasy and a lie. Imagine speaking with faith. Imagine always holding onto to hope and allowing hope to anchor your soul. Imagine being and living love. Remembering that Greater is he that is in me than he who is in the world. (1 John 4:4)

Imagine finally being free of the untruths you were told or that you told yourself. Imagine finally living in freedom every day. Today's verse is a reminder, "Then you will know the truth, and the truth will set you free." "So, if the Son sets you free, you will be free indeed." Will you accept the truth and set yourself free?

Dear Father,
Thank you for the reminder of the freedom brought by truth,
faith, hope, and love. That if I remain in your word, then I am
truly your disciple, I will know the truth and the truth will set
me FREE. I pray that all your children remain in your word, that
they learn the truth and that they are set free. I ask this in your
son Jesus' name. Amen!

Reflections

_____

_____

_____

_____

_____

_____

_____

_____

_____

_____

_____

October

Enslaved by Habits

ANCHOR SCRIPTURE: 1 CORINTHIANS 6:12 ESV

"All things are lawful for me," but not all things are helpful. "All things are lawful for me," but I will not be enslaved by anything.

"Chains of habit are too light to be felt until they are too heavy to be broken . -Warren Buffett

---

Merriam Webster defines enslaved as to reduce to or as if to slavery. Slave is defined as one that is totally subservient to a dominating influence. I recently read an article by Ken Wert entitled "Five Enslaving Habits We Must Avoid." The article identified the following five habits we must avoid:

- slavery to addictions including tv watching, eating junk food, gossip to mention a few.

- slavery to the office, placing work, business, or office ahead of your family.

- slavery to success, when success becomes more important than integrity or honor or self-respect, then our subservience to the call of the dollar sign becomes self–destructive.

- slavery to pleasure, in pursuit of pleasures that cost you or your family financially, or destroys your relationships

- Slavery to fear, fear and worry from taking or making the hard steps to break you free from living a disingenuous life.

431

All I could say after reading the list of five was ouch, ouch, ouch, ouch, ouch. I immediately turned to the Lenten season. During lent, it is customary to abstain or give up something that brings you pleasure or speaking frankly, give up something that we may or may not admit, is an addiction. Harsh words to hear, huh. As I reflect on the things I have chosen or chose to give up for 40 days, it dawned on me that the choices were things I should permanently give up. Instead, I abstain for just forty days then return to the bad habit. Sometimes actually celebrating returning to the thing you gave up for 40 days. I wonder are we celebrating being enslaved and addicted. Something to think about.

Mr. Werth mentioned something powerful in his article. He said that any addiction robs us of a measure of freedom and independence. It seems we must pay attention to our habits, no matter how significant or insignificant it may seem. Today's verse is a reminder, all things are lawful for me," but not all things are helpful. "All things are lawful for me," but I will not be enslaved by anything. Freedom is possible.

PRAYER FOR THE DAY:

Dear Father,
Thank you for the reminder that habits can enslave. Some may seem harmless and they still rob us from a measure of freedom. That all things are lawful for me, but not all things are helpful. To not be enslaved by anything. I pray that all your children remember that all things are lawful, but not all things are helpful. That they not enslaved by anything. I ask this in your son Jesus' name. Amen.

Glow to Glow

ANCHOR SCRIPTURE: PSALM 43:3 (ESV)

"Send out your light and your truth; let them lead me;
let them bring me to your holy hill and to your dwelling!"

"A candle loses nothing by lighting another candle.
-James Keller

Have you ever participated in a candlelight vigil? The peace and beauty experienced are calming. To watch one candle, lightning the other and the other till all are lit.

If we as humans would consider this. Rather than trying to extinguish each other's light, why not go the extra mile to re-light another's extinguished light. Why not fan another's dimming flame. The beauty is none of these actions will impact your light. If anything, your light may shine brighter. Remember, someone re-lit or fanned your candle when it was dimmed or out. It is an experience no one can escape.

Today's verse is a reminder, "Send out your light and your truth; let them lead me; let them bring me to your holy hill and to your dwelling!"

Would you help others shine their light? Glow and help others glow.

Dear Father,
Thank you for the reminder to send out your light and your truth; let them lead me; let them bring me to your holy hill and to your dwelling!"

I pray that your children continue to shine their light and help others shine theirs. To let your light and your truth lead them and bring them to your holy hill and to your dwelling! I ask this in your son Jesus' name. Amen!

OCTOBER 3

Reclaim Your Peace

ANCHOR SCRIPTURE: MATTHEW 10:13

If the home is deserving, let your peace rest on it;
if it is not, let your peace return to you.

"You can't shake hands with a clenched fist"
– Indira Gandhi

I recently saw a post on social media that quoted Bishop T.D. Jakes as saying "The hardest person to help is someone who has become comfortable in their dysfunction. Shortly after a seeing this post, a friend sent me a message by Pastor Dharius Daniels on five types of people you can't help. 1. People who don't think they need it 2. People who know they need it and don't want it 3. People who don't want it yet 4. People who don't want it from you 5. People who aren't willing to do what it takes to get it. It is frustrating when you know where they may be headed however you have to at some point reclaim your peace. You must know what yours is to handle and what is God's to handle. Many "fixers" (you know who you are) walk around frustrated because no. I love this quote and what I think is great advice by Pastor Daniels: "Give them UP to God but don't give up on them." Imagine it is this simple, Let go and let God handle it. Then you can reclaim your peace that surpasses all understanding. It is by no means easy. You will simply have to trust God.

Have you ever given someone a gift and they either return it or say no, thank you? The gift could be a million dollars and the person still refuses the gift. Many times, we try to change others or try to bring them to the truth. Although it may hurt as you may believe you are trying to help or share your gift, you may need to understand that sometimes all are not always ready to receive the gift you have to offer. That person may not yet understand the value of your gift. At that point you have a decision to make, do you continue to force the acceptance of the gift or do you walk away.

Today's scripture is a reminder, "if the home is deserving, let your peace rest on it; if it is not, let your peace return to you.

––––––––––––– PRAYER FOR THE DAY: –––––––––––––

Dear Father,
Thank you for the reminder that I can't shake hands with a clenched fist. That if the home is deserving, let your peace rest on it; If it is not, let your peace return to you. To reclaim the peace you left with me. I pray that all your children remember that they cannot shake hands with a clenched fist. That if the home is deserving, let your peace rest on it; if it is not, let your peace return to you. That they reclaim the peace you left for each of them. I ask this in your son, Jesus' name, Amen.

435

Hands Off

ANCHOR SCRIPTURE: MATTHEW 10:13

"He says, "Be Still, and know that I am God; I will be exalted among the nations, I will be exalted in the earth"

Learning to let go is not giving up! It is simply passing the burden to a better fighter, so you can fight another day. (God) -Shannon L. Alder Hands off is sometimes used to alert or warn not to touch or interfere with something. It may also mean your direct control or intervention is not required. Fixers are people known to want to fix everything or believe that they can fix everything. The thought of seeing a problem and not intervening is not part of their DNA.

Fixing everything can be exhausting. Imagine constantly living with the urge to fix, control, push or pull something. It may make sense to activate discernment to know what yours is to fix and what belongs to another. Sometimes it is best to know when to keep your hands off. "Word to the wise": 1- everything and everyone is not your assignment or yours to fix. 2- God will always be in control.

Today's scripture is a reminder, "Be Still, and know that I am God; I will be exalted among the nations, I will be exalted in the earth." Consider what situations or people are your hands on when they should be off? I encourage you to read Psalm 46 in its entirety.

Dear Father,
Thank you for the reminder to keep my hands off what con-
cerns you. To be still and know that you are God; that you will be
exalted among the nations and the earth. I pray that all your
children grow in discernment to keep their hands off what con-
cerns you. That they learn to be still and know that you are God;
that you will be exalted among the nations and the earth. I ask
this in your son Jesus' name. Amen!

OCTOBER 5

Limited Vision

ANCHOR SCRIPTURE: EPHESIANS 1:18-20

I pray that the eyes of your heart may be enlightened in order that you may know the hope to which he has called you, the riches of his glorious inheritance in his holy people, and his incomparably great power for us who believe. That power is the same as the mighty strength he exerted when he raised Christ from the dead and seated him at his right hand in the heavenly realms.

Before making a promise, do you consider if you really want and can help? Do you consider if you can keep the promise for the duration that is defined? A promise can be defined as to pledge to do, bring about, or provide. It is sometimes defined as a reason to expect something.

Some say promises are not to be taken lightly and in general should be kept unless compelling circumstances exists. Speaking of compelling circumstances, I had a conversation recently with a friend who doubted a few promises made. As this friend spoke, I could see the loss of hope, faith, and power. This seemed to be impacted by their limited vision. Because the pain overpowered their belief, this friend could not hold onto the promise and reminder of the promise keeper.

Yes, that the one who made the promise would never leave or forsake. The conversation led to the reminder that the promise keeper never breaks promises. The promise will be kept. It may take time and endurance required. Seek understanding and exercise patience.

Today's verse is a reminder that you may know the hope to which he has called you, the riches of his glorious inheritance in his holy people, and his incomparably great power for us who believe. That power is the same as the mighty strength he exerted when he raised Christ from the dead and seated him at his right hand in the heavenly realms. Don't limit your vision.

———————————— PRAYER FOR THE DAY: ————————————

Dear Father,
Thank you for the reminder of the hope to which you have called me, the riches of your glorious inheritance, and your incomparable great power for us who believe. That this power is the same as when you raised Christ from the dead and seated him at your right hand in the heavenly realms. I pray that all your children remember this hope for which they too are called, the riches of your glorious inheritance, the incomparable great power you you give to all who believe. The same power used to raise Christ from the dead and seat him at your right hand in the heavenly realms. That they remove all limits form your vision. I ask this in your son Jesus' name, Amen. What a mighty God we serve.

438

A Clean Slate

ANCHOR SCRIPTURE: PSALM 32:5 (NLT)

Finally, I confessed all my sins to you and stopped trying to hide my guilt. I said to myself, "I will confess my rebellion to the Lord." And you forgave me! All my guilt is gone.

At some point in your life, you will go through a period of rebellion. You may even experience a period of guilt for your thoughts, words, or actions. Can you imagine the severity of this pain? Such a severe pain you begin to lose yourself.

I have a dear friend who walked around decades feeling guilty. To drown out the guilty feelings, this friend tried to please everyone. Can you imagine carrying so much guilt that it pains? Trying to draw at so many straws to hide or cover the pain only you can feel and see.

If you knew of an easy solution to relieve your pain, would you try this solution? Today's verse is a reminder, finally, I confessed all my sins to you and stopped trying to hide my guilt. I said to myself, "I will confess my rebellion to the Lord." And you forgave me! All my guilt is gone. Imagine you unnecessarily walked around with guilt that pained so much when all was needed was a confession for the guilt to be gone. Yes, for you to have a clean slate. I encourage you to read Psalms 32 in its entirety.

Dear Father,
Thank you for the reminder that by confessing my transgressions, small or big, the guilt can be gone, and I can have a clean slate. I pray that all your children have the courage to confess their transgression and rebellion. To release all guilt and start over with a clean slate. I ask this in your son Jesus' name. Amen.

OCTOBER 7

To Judge Or To Love...

ANCHOR SCRIPTURE: GALATIANS 6:1 (NIV)

Brothers and sisters, if someone is caught in a sin, you who live by the Spirit should restore that person gently. But watch yourselves, or you also may be tempted.

An individual has not started living until he can rise
above the narrow confines of his individualistic concerns to the
broader concerns of all humanity.
- Martin Luther King, Jr.

"The idea that you call right is the idea that someone else calls wrong. The solution that you call perfect is the solution that other calls unworkable. The position that you feel is unassailable is the very position that others assail." Neale Donald Walsch said this. He reminds us that being "right" has nothing to do with it.

Questioning and attacking others approach on how they solve a problem, attacking another's belief, or simply judging someone else's thought process never serves one well. Neither is defending your viewpoint. I wonder if focusing simply on ensuring that no one is hurt should be the goal. That right or wrong has no significance in eternity. What matters most is avoid hurt and spread love.

The kind of love that says, "It doesn't matter who is right or wrong. It only matters that you are not hurt, not judged and just are simply love. That agape love that forgives all wrong. A love that never assigns a label that forgives all wrong. A love that just is.

Today's verse is a reminder Brothers and sisters, if someone is caught in a sin, you who live by the Spirit should restore that person gently. But watch yourselves, or you also may be tempted. I encourage you to read Galatians 6 in its entirety. To judge or to love, that is the question.

-------------------- PRAYER FOR THE DAY: --------------------

Dear Father,
Thank you for the reminder that if someone is caught in a sin, those who live by the Spirit should restore that person gently. But watch myself, or I too may be tempted. I pray that all your children love more and judge less. That they remember your warning that those who live by the Spirit should restore that person gently. To be watchful or they too may be tempted. I ask this in your son Jesus' name. Amen!

Embrace Your Power

ANCHOR SCRIPTURE: PSALM 139:14 (NIV)

"I praise you because I am fearfully and wonderfully made.
your works are wonderful, I know that full well"

"No one is you and that is your power."
-Anonymous

"People always think that the most painful thing in life is losing the one you value. The truth is the most painful thing is losing yourself in the process of valuing someone too much and forgetting that you are special too."

Embracing your power begins with knowing who and whose you are. Clearly understanding that you are unique (yes, there is only one of you. No replicas), you are worthy, you are valuable, you are wonderfully made. The awakening to this truth, awakens a power like no other. A power that came with us upon birth, and somehow, we lost along the way.

Today's scripture is a reminder "I praise you because I am fearfully and wonderfully made; your works are wonderful; I know that full well." Once you remember that our Father does not make junk (no matter who you are or what you did), he made you. Wake up and embrace your power.

Dear Father,
Thank you for the reminder that I am fearfully and wonder-
fully made. That I know full well, your works are wonderful. I
pray that all your children remember that they are fearfully and
wonderfully made. That know full well, your works are wonder-
ful. I ask this in your son Jesus' name. Amen!

OCTOBER 9

Ignite your Day

ANCHOR SCRIPTURE: JOHN 8:12

"Then Jesus again spoke to them, saying, "I am the Light
of the world; he who follows Me will not walk in the darkness,
but will have the Light of life."

"Just in case no one told you today... You are good enough."

Do you wake –up each morning and give yourself a high-five or thumbs up? Do you awaken with thumbs down, head low attitude? When I awaken, I say thank you. On most days, I immediately go into prayer and gratitude. Once I am done with that quiet time, I make myself smile by saying aloud "time to make the donuts." If you know about the donut business, most must be at work way before the sun-rises. I encourage you to remain present and check-in with yourself.

Are you embracing each new day with gratitude, new creativity, with excitement and ready to see what greatness appears this day? Leaders in Excellence start their day with giving themselves a high five and saying, "Thumbs up To Life." Then you can pass that onto to your tribe. What do you say? Drag what happened yesterday into today and future weeks, months or years or let it go and start fresh and bright each day? Pay attention when you awake tomorrow and the rest of this week? Are you igniting or dimming your own day?

Today's verse is a reminder, "Then Jesus again spoke to them, saying, "I am the Light of the world; he who follows Me will not walk in the darkness, but will have the Light of life." Will you be the light for yourself and others? Walk in the light. You are good enough!

––––––––––––––––– **PRAYER FOR THE DAY:** –––––––––––––––––

Dear Father,
Thank you for the reminder that your son is the light of the world; those who follow him will not walk in darkness but will have the Light of life. I pray that all your children seek and find the Light of life. That they walk out of darkness and into the light. I ask this in your son Jesus name. Amen!

Up Level Your Thinking

ANCHOR SCRIPTURE: PSALM 19:14 (ESV)

Let the words of my mouth and the meditation of my heart
be acceptable in your sight, O Lord, my rock, and my redeemer.

"You have the capacity to leave a lasting impact and indelible impression upon this world.... Claim the sacred spaces of your minds, nurture and cultivate a vision of fulfillment, and move toward that destiny with patience, perseverance, and prayer."
-Mahershala Ali

Leading in excellence requires an elevated way of thinking. You must not see as the world sees things. BIG vision requires BIG faith. When leading others to a truth they yet cannot see, what tools do you use to help bring them along? Do you tap into their imagination, do you celebrate the small successes along the way, do you help them see what is in it for them, or do you share often what success looks like? As you lead in excellence, you will have to decide how your character with help your tribe up level their thinking as you up level yours. Master your thinking, Master your emotions!

Continue to lead in excellence!

PRAYER FOR THE DAY:

Dear Father,
Thank you for the reminder to let the words of my mouth and the meditation of my heart be acceptable in your sight. I pray that all your children let the words of their mouth and the meditation of their heart be acceptable in your sight. That they think and lead in excellence. I ask this in your son Jesus' name, Amen.

Help Others Win

ANCHOR SCRIPTURE: JOHN 3:30

"He must become greater; I must become less."

---

*"The way to achieve your own success is to be willing
to help somebody else get it first."*
-Iyanla Vanzant

Leading others may require you to be willing to help somebody else achieve success before you. Are you willing to help someone on your team achieve success before you? One thing comes to mind is selfless vs. selfish leadership and why you lead? (See my book What Leaders Say and Do.) Is it always about what is in it for me (WIIIFM) or what is in it for us (WIIIFU?) Reflect on the purpose of your actions each day. Be honest with yourself.

Growing requires you to understand that nothing you do is about you. It is always about a greater purpose. If you become less, and allow God to become greater, you will find the strength to help others win before you win. Today's scripture is a reminder, "He must become greater; I must become less."

--- **PRAYER FOR THE DAY:** ---

Dear Father,
Thank you for the reminder that every assignment given to me is about a greater purpose. Nothing is about me and all is about your kingdom. That you must become greater; I must become less. I pray that all your children remember that everything is for a greater good. That you must become greater; and they must become less. I ask this in your son Jesus' name. Amen!

Disappointment

ANCHOR SCRIPTURE: 1 PETER 5:6-8

"So humble yourselves under the mighty power of God, and at the right time he will lift you up in honor. Give all your worries and cares to God, for he cares about you. Stay alert! Watch out for your great enemy, the devil. He prowls around like a roaring lion, looking for someone to devour."

"Blessed is he who expects nothing, for he shall never be disappointed."
-Alexander Pope

At some point in your life, you will face disappointment. Disappointment is sometimes defined as to be discouraged or sad because of an unmet expectation regarding someone or something. You may be expecting something without verbalizing it or expecting the impossible. Many disappointments come from a need that you have and may or may not have expressed this need, want, or expectation out loud or clearly.

Imagine awakening to the reality that someone or something did not disappoint you. Instead, you created this disappointment and the feelings you now experience. You may be carrying these feelings for decades without acknowledging the part you played in the disappointment. Whew, that was even too much for me. LOL. Maturity and wisdom teach to not expect anything and you will never be disappointed. Much harder said than done. There is a quote I recently saw that said, "When you release expectations, you are free to enjoy things for what they are instead of what you think they should be."

Today's scripture is a reminder, "So humble yourselves under the mighty power of God, and at the right time he will lift you up in honor.

Give all your worries and cares to God, for he cares about you. Stay alert! Watch out for your great enemy, the devil. He prowls around like a roaring lion, looking for someone to devour."

Dear Father,
Thank you for the reminder to release expectations so I may be free to enjoy things for what they are instead of what I think they should be. To be humble under your mighty power and at the right time you will lift me up in your honor. I pray that all your children release all disappointments. That they be free to enjoy things for what they are instead of what they think it should be. That they remember to humble themselves under your mighty power and at the right time you will lift them up in your honor. That they stay alert, and give all their worries, disappointments, and cares to you for you care about each of them. I ask this in your son Jesus' name. Amen!

Serenity- The Power of Peace

ANCHOR SCRIPTURE: COLOSSIANS 3:15

Let the peace of Christ rule in your hearts since as members of one body you were called to peace and be thankful."

"You are called to peace, be grateful"

I was recently reminded on why one of my favorite sayings is "God is in control" so take everything one day at a time. As I was doing my nails, my nail technician noticed a bracelet I was wearing and asked where did I get that bracelet? He said it was a simple but powerful bracelet. He inquired on where I received it. We talked about the bracelet then I was reminded that this bracelet was given to me for serenity, to be in peace.

The inscription on this bracelet was written by the theologian-philosopher Reinhold Niebuhr and it is known as the Serenity Prayer. It is commonly quoted as follows:

God grant me the serenity
to accept the things, I cannot change;
courage to change the things I can;
and wisdom to know the difference.
Living one day at a time;
Enjoying one moment at a time;
Accepting hardships as the pathway to peace; Taking, as He did, this sinful world
as it is, not as I would have it;
Trusting that He will make all things right
if I surrender to His Will;
That I may be reasonably happy in this life
and supremely happy with Him
Forever in the next. Amen

Today's scripture is a reminder, let the peace of Christ rule in your hearts since as members of one body you were called to peace and be thankful. May those who seek peace today remember this prayer. Although it is used for many twelve steps programs such as Alcoholics Anonymous and others, it can be used for the day to day person struggling to find peace in a daily situation. May the peace of the Lord be with you and may this remind you that you are not in control, God is in control.

─────── **PRAYER FOR THE DAY:** ───────

Dear Father,
Thank you for the reminder to be at peace. That you remain in control of everything, every day, and all life happenings. To let the peace of Christ rule in your hearts since as members of one body you were called to peace and be thankful. I pray that all your children remember that you are in control. To let the peace of Christ rule in their hearts since as members of one body they were called to peace and be thankful. I ask this in Jesus' name. Amen!

Flow Versus Force

ANCHOR SCRIPTURE: PHILIPPIANS 2:13

*"That energy is God's energy, an energy deep within you,
God himself willing and working at what will give him
the most pleasure.*

"May what I do flow from me like a river, no forcing
and no holding back, the way it is with children."
-Rainer Maria Rilke

Consciously making the choice to flow or force is an everyday task.
Flow could refer to a flow caused by a natural source such as wind
or the natural power created in a river that allows the water to move
along. Force is using unnatural sources such as machines or human
force to move something along. One definition of flow in Merriam
Webster is a smooth uninterrupted movement or progress. One definition of force in Merriam Webster is to impose or thrust urgently,
importunately, or inexorably.

I recalled going canoeing and being taught when to paddle and when
to let the force of the river in particular locations help the canoe move
along. At times in this journey, one side of the canoe was
required to paddle while the other needed to either hold or raise the
paddle in other to ensure the canoe remained stable and continue to
move smoothly along the river.

Sometimes in life, we try to force certain behaviors and actions that
are unnatural. Rather than letting things flow, we may try to force
flow. When this happens, things may not turn out quite the way you
intend for things to happen. Do you consciously pay attention at the
times when you try to force something that should just flow? Simply
allow things to happen at their intended time. This could apply to

goals you set for yourself, or things that you believe you should. Instead, allow it all to flow and it all will happen at the exact time.

Today's verse is a reminder that energy is God's energy, an energy deep within you, God himself willing and working at what will give him the most pleasure. No need to force, just flow. God's got you!

—————————— PRAYER FOR THE DAY: ——————————

Dear Father,
Thank you for the reminder to flow and never force. That the energy is your energy, an energy deep within me that you are working at to give you the most pleasure. I pray that all your children remember to flow. That the energy is your energy, an energy deep within them that you are working at to give you the most pleasure. I ask this in your son Jesus' name. Amen!

452

OCTOBER 15

Blessed

ANCHOR SCRIPTURE: PHILIPPIANS 2:13

*Blessed is the one who does not walk in step with the wicked
or stand in the way that sinners take or sit in the company of
mockers, but whose delight is in the law of the Lord, and who
meditates on his law day and night. That person is like a tree
planted by streams of water, which yields its fruit in season and
whose leaf does not wither— whatever they do prospers"*

"Blessed are they who see beautiful things in humble places
where other people see nothing."
- *Camille Pissarro*

I once heard someone say, "that if they didn't have bad luck, they
would not have any luck at all." Can you imagine walking around
believing that all comes to you is bad luck? All I could think when I
heard this statement was "little could you see the blessings and abundance that surrounds you."

I wonder if lack of gratitude, perspective, or deception by the
definition this world places on people and things causes our brothers
and sisters to bring these unhealthy thoughts to mind. Imagine being
able to see, feel and believe that you are blessed in all things and at
all times.

Today's scripture is a reminder, "Blessed is the one who does not walk
in step with the wicked or stand in the way that sinners take or sit in
the company of mockers, but whose delight is in the law of the Lord,
and who meditates on his law day and night. That person is like a
tree planted by streams of water, which yields its fruit in season and
whose leaf does not wither—whatever they do prospers. You are not
bad lucky, you are blessed!

Dear Father,
Thank you for the reminder that I am blessed. That blessed is
the one whose delight is in your law and meditates on it day and
night. That person is like a tree planted by streams of water,
which yields its fruit in season and whose leaf does not wither
-whatever they do prospers. I pray that all your children medi-
tate and delight on your Law day and night. That they remem-
ber that person is like a tree planted by the streams of water,
which yields its fruit in season and whose leaf does not wither
-whatever they do prospers. That they are blessed. I ask this in
your son Jesus' name. Amen!

OCTOBER 16

What Do You Think?

ANCHOR SCRIPTURE: MATTHEW 6:21

"For where your treasure is, there your heart will be also"

"Leading from your heart doesn't diminish your power.
It is your power.
- *Christine Arylo*

Leading from the heart may not be a bad thing. There are some
precautions one must take such as guarding your heart (Proverbs
4:23), Ensure you periodically check your heart and its condition to
ensure it is healthy and does not deceive or mislead. (1 Corinthians 15:33)

Seems setting your heart on the things above and storing your treasure there fuels and empowers one to lead from the heart. (See Colossians 3:1)

As leaders, (Yes, we are all leaders) do you ever consider how much of your light you share daily. Have you paused to take note that despite sharing your light, you lose nothing? By sharing your knowledge, wisdom, helping others achieve their goals and dreams does nothing to your light. It allows others to glow too.

I encourage you to be careful not to feed a culture than encourages "light dimming" rather a culture than encourages "light fanning." There is enough space for all lights to shine.

--- **PRAYER FOR THE DAY:** ---

Dear Father,
Thank you for the reminder that leading from my heart doesn't diminish my power. It is my power. That where my treasure is, there my heart will be also. I pray that all your children remember that leading from the heart doesn't diminish their power, it is their power. That where their treasure is, there their heart will be also. That they remember, there is enough space for their light to shine. I ask this in your Son Jesus' name, Amen

Observe vs. Watch

ANCHOR SCRIPTURE: HABAKKUK 1:5 (CSB)

"Look at the nations and observe--be utterly astounded!
For I am doing something in your days that you will not believe
when you hear about it."

To sail successfully, you need to observe with great care. You need to identify what the wind and the water are telling you and then find a way to execute, to reach whatever goal you've set, be that simply making it home or winning a race.
-Diane Greene

To observe or to watch, that is the question. To observe is sometimes defined as to notice or perceive (something) and register it as being significant. To watch is sometimes defined as to act as a spectator; look on.

It is interesting, as I thought of these two words, I thought of the impact on our learning styles. We may all have experienced how two people see the same thing, but observe something completely different.

"Observation is where real learning comes from. When we observe we see something on a deeper level." We look pass the surface. Watching seems more of the "physical process" were we spectate and add our own thoughts without diving deeper. As you continue on your day, pay attention to the difference it makes to observe vs. watch.

Habakkuk 1:5 is a reminder, "Look at the nations and observe--be utterly astounded! For I am doing something in your days that you will not believe when you hear about it." Observe, as what you see, is not what is. Observe and be amazed!

Dear Father,
Thank you for the reminder to observe what you are doing. I will be amazed. I pray that all your children observe what you are doing in the nations and in their lives. They will be utterly astounded. That they remember what they see, is not what is. I ask this in your son Jesus' name. Amen!

OCTOBER 18

Leading with Courage

ANCHOR SCRIPTURE: JOSHUA 1:9

"Have I not commanded you? Be strong and courageous. Do not be afraid; do not be discouraged, for the lord your God will be with you wherever you go.

Courage is not the lack of fear, it is acting despite the fear

Everyone experiences fear at some point in their life. Some fear making decisions and never make up their minds. Others make up their mind and by doing so, do away with fear. Leadership requires diminishing or dismissing fear, to make hard decisions. It also helps you to not be paralyzed in the decision-making process. Know what you must do, make the best decision you can based on where you want to go, not where you are, and then move on. (See Joshua 1:9)

Dear Father,
Thank you for the reminder that you have commanded me to be strong and courageous. To not be afraid or discouraged for you will be wherever I go. I pray that all your children remember your command to be strong, courageous, to not fear, or be discouraged for you will be with them wherever they go. I ask this in your son Jesus' name. Amen.

OCTOBER 19

Blessings or Curses

ANCHOR SCRIPTURE: DEUTERONOMY 30:19 (NLT)

Today I have given you the choice between life and death,
between blessings and curses. Now I call on heaven and earth
to witness the choice you make. Oh, that you would choose life,
so that you and your descendants might live!

"What you focus on grows, what you think about expands,
and what you dwell upon determines your destiny."
- Robin S.

I recently had a conversation with someone about aging as I wished them a Happy Birthday. She said she was in her 60s and felt like she was in her 50s. I said enjoy your youth as age is just a number. She commented that her knee pain often reminds her of the additional decade that is added to the age she currently feels.

I shared with her how my almost 81-year old mother says in her own way "I don't pay attention to this pain. If I follow it, I get nothing done" and keeps it moving. My interpretation is "You can empower or disempower your pain." Because often, as Mary Morrissey says, "Pay attention to what you are paying attention to." What you focus on grows.

Sometimes, focusing too much attention on the problem, keeps us from seeing the solution. From seeing the blessing. Yes, there is blessings in the pain. The problem continues to grow because we speak it, think about it all the time, and give it a life of its own. Pausing frequently to pay attention to what we say and do or listen to what others around us say and do can be a game changer. Listen for chatter and thoughts that empower or disempowers you. What are you growing, problems or opportunities? Focusing on your blessings or curses? Today, you get to decide if you are ready to change the game.

Today's verse is a reminder, "Today I have given you the choice between life and death, between blessings and curses. Now I call on heaven and earth to witness the choice you make. Oh, that you would choose life, so that you and your descendants might live!" Pay attention to what you empower. I encourage you to read Deuteronomy 30 in its entirety.

Dear Father,
Thank you for the reminder to pay attention to what I empower.
That today you have given me the choice between life and
death, between blessings and curses. That you call on heaven
and earth to witness the choice I make. Oh, that I would
choose life, so that I and my descendants might live! I pray
that all your children pay attention to what they give power.
That they remember that you have given them choices
and that you have called heaven and earth to witness the choice
they make. That your hope is they choose life, so that they and their
descendants might live. I ask this in your son Jesus' name. Amen!

Stay the Course

ANCHOR SCRIPTURE: HEBREWS 12:1-2 (ESV)

Therefore, since we are surrounded by so great a cloud of witnesses, let us also lay aside every weight, and sin which clings so closely, and let us run with endurance the race that is set before us, looking to Jesus, the founder and perfecter of our faith, who for the joy that was set before him endured the cross, despising the shame, and is seated at the right hand of the throne of God.

"The only way to finish is to stay the course."
- *Ilka V. Chavez*

When, not if, life presents hurdles, excuses, bumpy roads, will you stay the course? Stay the course is an idiom that is describe as "To persevere with as much determination, energy, or fortitude as one can until the end of a race, competition, or contest." Let's face it, staying the course is not easy, especially when you are in the middle of your journey or even the start of your journey and you are hit with a pandemic, crisis, major losses and other legitimate reasons to quit. At the start you have all the energy in the world, in the middle you may start to lose steam then something major shows up, what will you do? Will you find a way to finish despite everything that presents? I was reminded of this at my work out today. It is easy to make excuses rather than adjust. Adjustment may look like changing your speed, take a short break, doing what you can from where you are, recalculating to take a different route but ultimately deciding to stay the course at all cost to finish the race.

Think about this in these four areas of your life: health and wellness, your vocation, your relationships and your time and money freedom. You know what you would love aka you know the destination, are you willing to stay the course to get to the destination? I know it is taking too long, you don't have the energy, you are not in my shoes, it is too hard etc. Not because it hasn't happened yet, means it won't happen. Today's verse is a reminder, "Therefore, since we are surrounded by so great a cloud of witnesses, let us also lay aside every weight, and sin which clings so closely, and let us run with endurance the race that is set before us, looking to Jesus, the founder and perfecter of our faith, who for the joy that was set before him endured the cross, despising the shame, and is seated at the right hand of the throne of God." Keep the faith, stay the course.

--- **PRAYER FOR THE DAY:** ---

Dear Father,
Thank you for the reminder to stay the course you have set for me. To set aside every weight, and sin which clings so closely and run with endurance the race that is set before me. Thank you for sending your son Jesus to perfect my faith to finish the race. I pray that all your children stay the course set for each of them. That they set aside every weight, and sin which clings so closely and run the race that is set before them. That they look to Jesus, the founder and perfected of faith to endure, stay the course, and finish the race. I ask this in your son Jesus' name. Amen!

Seize the Moment

ANCHOR SCRIPTURE: EPHESIANS 5: 15-17 (MSG)

*"So, watch your step. Use your head. Make the most of
every chance you get. These are desperate times!
Don't live carelessly, unthinkingly. Make sure you
understand what the Master wants."*

"Stop acting as if life is a rehearsal. Live this day as if it were your
last. The past is over and gone. The future is not guaranteed. "
- Wayne Dyer

Are you allowing opportunities to pass you by, or do you seize the
moment? To seize the moment means to "take full advantage of life's
opportunities whenever and wherever they present themselves; to
live life to one's full potential." Imagine being laid off. The devastation
is real. The personal feeling of rejection is real. What do you do? Do
you sit and waddle with these emotions or do you shake it off and
make the best of where you are? With every devastating situation
there is an opportunity to be seized. Will you be bold to seek and
seize the opportunity in the midst of the devastation? Don't let it slip
you by.

The book of Ecclesiastes reminds us that "whatever turns up, grab
it and do it. And heartily! This is your last and only chance at it, for
there's neither work to do nor thoughts to think in the company
of the dead, where you're most certainly headed." Be encouraged,
remain present in the very moment you are given, don't waste it,
notice what you are noticing, and take nothing for granted.

Today's verse is a reminder, "So watch your step. Use your head. Make
the most of every chance you get. These are desperate times! Don't

live carelessly, unthinkingly. Make sure you understand what the Master wants." I encourage you to read Ephesians 5 in its entirety. Carpe Diem Seize the moment!

_____ **PRAYER FOR THE DAY:** _____

Dear Father,
Thank you for the reminder to seize every moment, Carpe Diem. Notice what I am noticing. To watch my step, use my head, and make the most of every chance I get. To not live carelessly, un-thinkingly. To make sure I understand what you want. I pray that all your children seize every moment, and every day. That they awaken and notice what they are noticing. That they watch their step, use their head, and make the most of every chance they get. That they do not live carelessly, unthinkingly and they understand what you want. I ask this in your son Jesus' mighty name. Amen!

Mistakes

ANCHOR SCRIPTURE: 1 THESSALONIANS 5:19 (NIV)

"Do not quench the Spirit;"

"There is nothing wrong with making mistakes,
but one should always make new ones. Repeating mistakes
is a hallmark of dim consciousness."
-Dave Sim

I recently read an article written by Alice Boy on "How to Overcome Your Fear of Making Mistakes." In the article, Ms. Boy mentioned how making a mistake can be paralyzing in normal times and even worsened during times of heightened uncertainty.

In the article, Ms. Boy proceeds to provide a few tips to help get one unstuck. Two of the tips she provided resonates with me. One is to "try to accept reality by making a list of truths you might need to come to grips with, such as: I understand that people will not always behave in ideal ways." Finally, think about how you can act on your values to address the situation. Let's say one conscientiousness is important to you. You might apply that value by making sure your employees have masks that fit them well and easy access to hand sanitizer."

The article also reminded that each of us have tools to "help us learn to tolerate uncertainty without worrying too much about making a mistake." The reality is we will make mistakes in life. The key is tapping into wisdom to minimize these mistakes.

Today's verse is a reminder, to not quench the Spirit. Yielding and tapping into the helper, the Holy Spirit, gifted to you, can minimize your mistakes. Take heed and yield. I encourage you to read 1 Thessalonians 5 in its entirety.

Dear Father,
Thank you for the gift of the Holy Spirit, my helper, to minimize
the multitude of mistakes I will make. May I grow in learning to
yield to my present help in times of trouble and confusion. May
I never quench the Spirit. I pray that all your children grow in
learning to yield and obey the Spirit to minimize their mistakes.
That they do not quench the spirit, their present help in times of
trouble and confusion. I ask this in your son Jesus' name, Amen!

●

OCTOBER 23

Readiness

ANCHOR SCRIPTURE: PROVERBS 13:10

"Where there is strife, there is pride, but wisdom
is found in those who take advice.

———————————

"When the student is ready the teacher appears.
When the student is truly ready the teacher disappears."
- Lao Tzu

———————————

Readiness is sometimes defined as the state of being fully prepared
for something. As a leader and parent have you found that you can
advise your children, students, and those you mentor however if the
student is not ready to learn they will not listen. Go a bit further and
think about the first-time guidance given to you some time ago finally
clicked. I bet it made you smile.

It is easy to forget how you learned a lesson and expect others to learn it by just verbally sharing the lesson or warning. At times, the only way for the lesson to be absorbed is when the student is prepared to receive the teaching or is open to learning. This may require a journey to releasing ties to the ego, arrogance, pride, hard-headedness or what I refer to as "doing what you feel like doing."

The intention for providing advice or guidance is usually a good one. To prevent another loved one from bumps, bruises, or scars. However, this is not always the way their story is written or the road they must travel. God is in control. When they are prepared to receive the lesson, they will learn and even master the lesson enough to lead the lesson on their own. "When the student is ready the teacher appears. When the student is truly ready the teacher disappears."

Today's verse is a reminder: "Where there is strife, there is pride, but wisdom is found in those who take advice. Keep learning, living, teaching, leading, and growing. The teacher awaits. Remember the teacher is not always a person. I encourage you to read Proverbs 13 in its entirety.

——————————— PRAYER FOR THE DAY:———————————

Dear Father,
Thank you for the reminder that when the student is ready the teacher appears and when the student is truly ready the teacher disappears. Thank you for sending your helper and teacher to aid us as we grow. That wisdom is found in those who take advice. I pray that all your children remove strife and pride from their life. That they accept the help and aid of the helper you placed in each of us. I ask this in your son Jesus' name. Amen!

Freed by Grace

ANCHOR SCRIPTURE: ROMANS 7:6

*"But now, by dying to what once bound us, we have been
released from the law so that we serve in the new way of the
Spirit, and not in the old way of the written code."*

"Grace is the voice that calls us to change and then gives
us the power to pull it off."
– *Max Lucado*

Grace is defined as unmerited divine assistance given to humans for
their regeneration or sanctification; a virtue coming from God; a state
of sanctification enjoyed through divine assistance; a special favor;
or disposition to or an act or instance of kindness, courtesy, or clemency. If each of us truly understood the favor that surrounds us and
stands ready to set us free, oh what a world it would be.

Dr. Charles Stanley reminds us that believers stand upon the
immovable foundation of God's grace. It covers us like a canopy and
surrounds like a protective wall. Imagine surrounded by a protective
wall, standing on an immovable foundation that sets you free. No
condemnation for those who are in Christ Jesus. We mess up time
and time again, yet Christ' unfailing amazing grace frees us. Self-
imprisoned and acquitted by God's Grace. It truly is amazing.

Today's verse is a reminder, "But now, by dying to what once bound
us, we have been released from the law so that we serve in the new
way of the Spirit, and not in the old way of the written code. "Courage
is grace under pressure." You are released and freed by God's Grace. I
encourage you to read Romans 7 in its entirety.

Dear Father,
Thank you for helping me to die to what once bound me. For free-
ing me through your amazing grace so that I may serve in the
new way of the Spirit. I pray that all your children die to what
bounds them. That they accept the freedom you offer through
your amazing grace. This way they can serve in the new way of
the Spirit, and not in the old way of the written code. I ask this in
your son Jesus' name, Amen.

OCTOBER 25

All My Children

ANCHOR SCRIPTURE: 1 JOHN 3:1 (NIV)

See what great love the Father has lavished on us, that we
should be called children of God! And that is what we are! The
reason the world does not know us is that it did not know him.

"What it's like to be a parent: It's one of the hardest things
you'll ever do but in exchange it teaches you the meaning
of unconditional love."
-Nicholas Sparks

All My Children is an "American televised soap opera that depicts
intertwined relationships and secrets of several families." Its topics
deals with controversial yet socially relevant topics and the rise and
fall of power. Some of you may remember this soap opera.

469

Imagine the controversies faced by all the children of these families, same as all of God's children. They face controversial issues, decisions, and the rise and fall of power and prestige. Although depicted in a soap opera, these are everyday occurrences God's children face. However, through it all, God remains faithful to all his children whether they notice it or not. He is a good Father. He gave his only begotten son for each of us.

Today's verse is a reminder, "See what great love the Father has lavished on us, that we should be called children of God! And that is what we are! The reason the world does not know us is that it did not know him." I encourage you to read 1 John 3.

————————— **PRAYER FOR THE DAY:** —————————

Dear Father,
Thank you for the reminder of the great love you have lavished on me. Such an honor to be called your child. I pray that all your children awaken and recognize the great love you have lavished on them. That they remember they are your children and they are loved. I asked this in your son Jesus' name, Amen.

Trust

ANCHOR SCRIPTURE: PSALM 56:9-11 (ESV)

*"Then my enemies will turn back in the day when I call. This
I know, that God is for me. In God, whose word I praise, in the
Lord, whose word I praise, in God I trust; I shall not be afraid.
What can man do to me?"*

" Never be afraid to trust an unknown future to a known God."
-Corrie ten Boom

Trust is not a natural occurrence. Some claim you have to earn it; others say it comes with time, and some say never do it. The issues with trust are real. Yes, that one-word trust, to believe in the reliability, truth, ability, or strength of something or someone.

Sometimes you are asked to trust without seeing. Look at our pledge of allegiance, our money, and our national anthem, "In God We Trust." Everything around you and that you may handle daily says trust. So why is it so hard to do this thing called trust? Maybe it was a deception you experienced, a deep hurt, that is just who you are... don't trust a thing, or you fear. It however seems important to "Trust God" if these words are placed on and in so many important symbols and things.

"For God has said, 'I will never fail you. I will never abandon you.' So, we can say with confidence, 'The LORD is my helper, so I will have no fear. What can mere people do to me?'" (Hebrews 13:5-6) Is God's word and promises not sufficient to trust? To trust that he remains in control of all things whether they make sense or not to you. To trust that he loves you unconditionally. [Note to self: most things of God make no sense to our flesh or the human mind. Think higher thoughts, stay focused on Jesus, and keep trusting God.]

Today's verse is a reminder, "Then my enemies will turn back in the day when I call. This I know that God is for me. In God, whose word I praise, in the Lord, whose word I praise, in God I trust; I shall not be afraid. What can man do to me?" Is there anything you're having a hard time trusting God with? Seek God about that thing. I encourage you to read Psalm 56 in its entirety.

PRAYER FOR THE DAY:

Dear Father,
Thank you for the reminder to put my trust in you. I will praise your name; trust you and I shall not be afraid. I pray that all your children put their trust in you. "In God we Trust." That they trust you more than they trust themselves. That they remember you are their helper, to not be afraid, and to continue to praise your holy name. I ask this in your son Jesus' name. Amen.

OCTOBER 27

Teachable

ANCHOR SCRIPTURE: PSALM 32:8- (NIV)

*"I will instruct you and teach you in the way you should go;
I will counsel you with my loving eye on you."*

"If you are not willing to learn, no one can help you.
If you are determined to learn, no one can stop you."
-Zig Ziglar

Being Teachable is described as being able and willing to learn; capable of being taught; allowing something to be taught or learned easily. Teachability is critical to leading yourself and others. It requires a will to admit you do not know everything. Yes, humility plays a key part in being a lifelong learner. It also leaves margin for others to instruct and teach you on the way to go regardless of their position or age.

I recently had a conversation with a young woman (who could be my daughter and even granddaughter.) We spoke about social media on how best to maximize its use to advance one's purpose in life. She clearly had more knowledge than I about this area and I listened excited to learn more. It was fascinating to be the student of twenty-year-old. She was clearly surprised at my childlike reaction in learning from her expertise.

Sometimes conceit and arrogance can be barriers to teachability and can impact your leadership of others and self. Proverbs 15:12, "Conceited people do not like to be corrected; they never ask for advice from those who are wiser." Of note is that conceit and arrogance stems from fear and insecurity.

Today's verse is a reminder, "I will instruct you and teach you in the way you should go; I will counsel you with my loving eye on you."

473

Will you allow arrogance, conceit, fear, and insecurity keep you from learning and leading your best life?

---—— **PRAYER FOR THE DAY:** ———

Dear Father,
Thank you for the reminder that you will instruct and teach me on the way I should go; you will counsel me with your loving eye on me. To not let arrogance and conceit keep me from being teachable. I pray that all your children remember that you will instruct and teach them on the way they should go; you will counsel them with your loving eye. That they do not allow conceit, arrogance, fear, or insecurity to get in the way of your teachings and instructions. I ask this in your son Jesus' name. Amen!

Stewardship

ANCHOR SCRIPTURE: PHILIPPIANS 3:12 (NLT)

"I don't mean to say that I have already achieved these things or that I have already reached perfection. But I press on to possess that perfection for which Christ Jesus first possessed me."

"A leader must be a good listener. He must be willing to take counsel. He must show a genuine concern and love for those under his stewardship."
- *James E. Faust*

Stewardship is sometimes defined as the job of supervising or taking care of something, such as an organization or property. Including in charge of something or someone that lives.

Fathers are placed in a position to not just be responsible for one human being but a family and sometimes a tribe of human beings. Overseeing anything can be a heavy burden, especially something or a group of things or people that live, breathe, and grow. The gift of stewardship of another is a constant and evolving journey. Not easy, always evolving, and worth it.

Today, I honor all Fathers those living and those in heaven. Being a Father is not easy and it is worthy. Joyce Meyer wrote that "Fathers have hearts toward God by genuinely wanting His will and doing all they can to work with Him toward that goal. God knows your heart, and He sees you as perfect even while you're still making the journey toward perfection."

Today's verse is a reminder, "I don't mean to say that I have already achieved these things or that I have already reached perfection. But I press on to possess that perfection for which Christ Jesus first possessed me." Fathers, as you press on to possess that perfection, remember that God word says, "Come to me, all you who are weary and burdened, and I will give you rest. For my yoke is easy and my burden is light." I encourage you to read Philippians 3 in its entirety. Happy Father's Day to all Dads.

PRAYER FOR THE DAY:

Dear Father,
Happy Father's Day. Thank you for the reminder of the Father's journey. That it is a constant journey to possess perfection. I pray that all your children, especially Fathers press on to possess that perfection for which Christ Jesus first possessed. I ask this in your son Jesus' name. Amen!

Learn it. Live it. Lead it.

ANCHOR SCRIPTURE: PHILIPPIANS 4:9 (NIV)

"Whatever you have learned or received or heard from me or seen in me—put it into practice. And the God of peace will be with you."

"The past is where you learned the lesson. The future is where you apply the lesson, don't give up in the middle."

~ Dhiraj Raj

I recently saw this quote by Dhiraj Raj- "Life is the fusion of past and present which gives birth to future. In fact, past is just like shadow of your own shadow which doesn't determines your quality of life rather it gives life shifting lesson for discovering your best present. Once you discover your best present then it paves a solid highway for your quality future. So, live your present designing it in your best way as life is too short to live with your past pain and hurts. As you are the best architect of your destiny and responsible in charge of your life, never give up despite of stormy adversities. Just celebrate every fraction of second in a deserving way."

~ Dhir

Imagine celebrating every fraction or second of your life no matter how easy or tough it may have been. Understanding that it is all a lesson for your future. Understanding that the lesson is not to be kept a secret but to share and help someone else grow. Your past doesn't determine your future, it simply gives "life shifting lesson for discovering your best present." No need to hide it, just learn from it and share the lessons with others. Reyna Aburto is quoted as saying, "Our path is not about what we have done or where we have been; it is about where we are going and what we are becoming."

Today's verse is a reminder that, "Whatever you have learned or received or heard from me or seen in me—put it into practice. And the God of peace will be with you." Keep putting in practice and sharing your lessons learned. Never give up in the middle of becoming. Your future is greater than your past. Learn it. Live it. Lead it. I encourage you to read Philippians 4 in its entirety.

--------------------- **PRAYER FOR THE DAY:** ---------------------

Dear Father,
Thank you for the reminder that, "Whatever I have learned or received or heard from you or seen in you, put it into practice. And you will be with me. To share the lessons learned and never give up in the middle of becoming. I pray that all your children put into practice and share what they have learned, receive, heard and seen from you. That they don't give up amid becoming. That they remember their future is much greater than their past. I ask this in your son Jesus' mighty name. Amen!

Diligence

ANCHOR SCRIPTURE: 1 TIMOTHY 4:15–16 (NIV)

"Be diligent in these matters; give yourself wholly to them, so that everyone may see your progress. Watch your life and doctrine closely. Persevere in them, because if you do, you will save both yourself and your hearers."

The expectations of life depend upon diligence; the mechanic that would perfect his work must first sharpen his tools.
-Confucius

Merriam Webster defines diligence as steady, earnest, and energetic effort: persevering application. It seems to persevere in anything requires diligence. Think about when you set a goal to accomplish something, when you attain a goal without much effort. The goal is either attained because you value it, want a certain feeling or result, or it is something you would love to attain. At some point after setting that goal for yourself, you may realize that if you don't work at it every day you will not reach your goal.

The only way to achieve your goal is through diligently working towards it each day. Doing at least one thing to inch you closer to your goal. The size doesn't matter, one step, one bite at time to reach the finish line. If a tool that requires sharpening is not sharpened frequently, then it eventually will not function properly. Think of a pencil. Diligently do the work, allow the sharpening, and watch how you will persevere.

Today's verse is a reminder, "Be diligent in these matters; give yourself wholly to them, so that everyone may see your progress. Watch your life and doctrine closely. Persevere in them, because if you do, you will save both yourself and your hearers." I encourage you to read 1 Timothy 4 in its entirety. Be diligent and persevere!

Dear Father,
Thank you for the reminder to be diligent in all matters; give
myself wholly to them, so that everyone may see my progress.
Watch your life and doctrine closely. Persevere in them, because
if I do, I will save both myself and my hearers. I pray that all your
children are diligent in their matters, so that everyone may see
their progress. That they watch their life and doctrine closely.
Persevere in them, because if they do, they will save both them-
selves and their hearers. I ask this in your son Jesus' name. Amen

OCTOBER 31

Open Doors

ANCHOR SCRIPTURE: REVELATIONS 3:7 (NIV)

"To the angel of the church in Philadelphia write:
These are the words of him who is holy and true, who holds
the key of David. What he opens no one can shut, and what he
shuts no one can open."

"Personality can open doors, but only an upright
character keeps them open."
-*Elmer G. Letterman*

Your personality can open doors for you, but will you manage to keep
them open? Your character is a very important detail in ensuring that
the doors that are opened for you are kept open. Character is said

to be the "sum of our choices." It is who you are. Choosing to make the most of your circumstances, standing tall through them and not allowing your circumstances or situations to define or shake you, helps to develop your character.

Many times, we find ourselves in situations where we choose to react emotionally, or we make the choice to consult with our character and values before reacting. It is all a choice. Despite the adversities or circumstances try to keep your thoughts, words and actions aligned to your character and values. God is interested in your character; it keeps the doors open.

What seems impossible for man is possible with God. Will you allow God to develop your character, to open the doors for you? Today's verse is a reminder, "To the angel of the church in Philadelphia write: These are the words of him who is holy and true, who holds the key of David. What he opens no one can shut, and what he shuts no one can open." I encourage you to read Revelations 3 in its entirety.

──────────────── **PRAYER FOR THE DAY:** ────────────────

Dear Father,
Thanks for the reminder, that the doors that you close nobody can open and the one that you open nobody can close. That if we continue to trust you, you will keep the right doors opened. I pray that all your children remember that the doors that you close nobody can open and the one that you open nobody can close. That they remain firm in their integrity and character. You will take care of the rest. I ask this in your son Jesus' name. Amen!

Reflections

November

Sacrifice

ANCHOR SCRIPTURE: JOHN 15:13 (TPT)

*"For the greatest love of all is a love that sacrifices all.
And this great love is demonstrated when
a person sacrifices his life for his friends"*

---

*"Sacrifice is a part of life. It's supposed to be.
It's not something to regret. It's something*

Merriam Webster defines sacrifice as destruction or surrender of something for the sake of something else or something offered in sacrifice. Imagine setting aside all your selfish desires to give your life or surrendering your liberty for something bigger or greater, for someone else. Could you do that?

You may have met soldiers who tell their stories of being on the battleground. Of watching their fellow soldiers lose their life or turning back to help bring another wounded soldier to safety. You may have also heard or witness for yourself, the mental and physical wounds still being experienced by those who sacrificed or surrendered their freedom for a larger cause. It is important to never forget these sacrifices made by many both living and dead. Honor, remember and acknowledge what others have sacrifice for you.

Today' verse is a reminder, "For the greatest love of all is a love that sacrifices all. And this great love is demonstrated when a person sacrifices his life for his friends." Jesus made the ultimately sacrifice, he gave his life for us. On this Memorial Day, let us honor, remember and salute all who made great sacrifice.

483

Dear Father,
Thank you for the reminder, that the greatest love of all is a love that sacrifices all. And this great love is demonstrated when a person sacrifices his life for his friends. I pray that all your children remember that the greatest love of all is a love that sacrifices all. And this great love is demonstrated when a person sacrifices his life for his friends. That they never forget those who made great sacrifices for them to have life and have life abundantly. Thank you, Jesus. I ask this in your son Jesus' name. Amen!

NOVEMBER 2

Unwavering

ANCHOR SCRIPTURE: ISAIAH 40:31 (AMP)

"But those who wait for the Lord [who expect, look for, and hope in Him] Will gain new strength and renew their power; They will lift up their wings [and rise up close to God] like eagles [rising toward the sun]; They will run and not become weary, They will walk and not grow tired."

"Once you are clear about what you wish to create, you can maintain a steady stream of thoughts – unwavering, resolute, and focused."
-Dr Prem Jagyasi

When something is unwavering, it is firm or unshakable. It will not waver, wander, or stray from its foundation. Have you ever seen a movie or live report that shows the disaster after a storm or earthquake? Everything surrounding the impacted area may be destroyed. However, if you look closer, there may be one thing that survived the disaster. That one thing seemed to be unwavering, unshakable, untouchable amidst disaster. It just miraculously remains intact through it all.

I think of Shadrach, Meshach, and Abednego (Daniel 3) who went through the fire unwavering and came out untouched. I think of the front-line workers who during today's pandemic (some call it war) continue to show up time and time again unselfishly and unwavering despite fear. Despite all, they remain steady, unwavering, resolute, and focused." (no matter the internal wounds.)

Today's verse is a reminder, "But those who wait for the Lord [who expect, look for, and hope in Him] Will gain new strength and renew their power; They will lift up their wings [and rise up close to God] like eagles [rising toward the sun]; They will run and not become weary, They will walk and not grow tired." I encourage you to read Isaiah 40 in its entirety. Become unwavering!

———————— **PRAYER FOR THE DAY:** ————————

Dear Father,
Thank you for the reminder that those who hope in you will renew their strength. They will soar on wings like eagles; they will run and not grow weary; they will walk and not be faint. I pray that all your children hold their hope in you. That they remember that when they do, they will renew their strength, they will soar on wings like eagles; they will run and not grow weary, they walk and not be faint. I ask this in your son Jesus' name, Amen!

NOVEMBER 3

Happy International Mother's Day to all Moms!

ANCHOR SCRIPTURE: PROVERBS 31:31 (NIV)

"Honor her for all that her hands have done, and let her works bring her praise at the city gate."

"Motherhood is a choice you make every day, to put someone else's happiness and well-being ahead of your own, to teach the hard lessons, to do the right thing even when you're not sure what the right thing is...and to forgive yourself, over and over again, for doing everything wrong."
- Donna Ball

Thank you to all Moms for putting others ahead of yourselves, for teaching the hard lessons, for establishing strong foundations in each of your children, for doing the right thing even when unsure if it is the right thing. It truly takes a tribe to raise children.

Proverbs 22:6(NIV)- "Start children off on the way they should go, and even when they are old, they will not turn from it."

I honor all Mothers today. May your day be as special as you.
Peace and blessings.

Dear Father,
Thank you for the reminder that we are blessed to have or have had a mother. That I must honor her for all that her hands have done, and let her works bring her praise at the city gate. I pray that all your children remember that they are blessed to have or to have had a mother. That they must recognize and honor her for all that her hands have done, and let her works bring her praise at the city gate. I ask this in your son Jesus' name, Amen.

NOVEMBER 4

Inner Peace (Peace of Mind)

ANCHOR SCRIPTURE: JOHN 14:27 (AMP)

Peace I leave with you; My [perfect] peace I give to you; not as the world gives do I give to you. Do not let your heart be troubled, nor let it be afraid. [Let My perfect peace calms you in every circumstance and give you courage and s trength for every challenge.]

"Peace is the result of retraining your mind to process life as it is, rather than as you think it should be."
-Wayne W. Dyer

Inner peace or peace of mind is sometimes referred to as a "deliberate state of psychological or spiritual calm despite the potential presence of stressors. Being at peace is considered by many to be healthy and the opposite of being stressed or anxious and is a state where our mind performs at an optimal level with a positive outcome. Peace of mind is thus generally associated with bliss, happiness and contentment."

Inner peace cannot be found through another's action or the world. That peace is temporary. There is a peace that if you seek it in faith, it can soothe the troubles or fears you face daily. It may require some work as it is retraining your thoughts and ridding yourself of paradigms to experience that inner peace. It is a peace that surpasses all understanding. Marvin Gaye is cited with saying "If you cannot find peace within yourself, you will never find it anywhere else."

Today's verse is a reminder, "Peace I leave with you; My [perfect] peace I give to you; not as the world gives do I give to you. Do not let your heart be troubled, nor let it be afraid. [Let My perfect peace calms you in every circumstance and give you courage and strength for every challenge.]" I encourage you to read John 14 in its entirety. May you find inner peace.

──────────── **PRAYER FOR THE DAY:** ────────────

Dear Father,
Thank you for the reminder that the peace I seek is within me. That you left that perfect peace with me. I pray that all your children remember that you give them perfect peace; not as the world gives. That they do not let their heart be troubled, nor let it be afraid. That they let your perfect peace calm them in every circumstance and give them courage and strength for every challenge. I ask this in your son Jesus' name. Amen!

Orchestrate

ANCHOR SCRIPTURE: COLOSSIANS 1:17

He is before all things, and in him all things hold together.

"The perfect orchestration of the symphony of life is one of
the Creator's greatest and most beautiful miracles."
-Suzy Kassem

To orchestrate could mean to arrange or direct the elements of (a situation) to produce a desired effect, especially surreptitiously. Imagine that your entire life was orchestrated? That everything that has transpired in your life was carefully planned out, the comfortable and the uncomfortable.

I recently held a conversation with a dear friend about the intricate details of directing an orchestra. In the conversation she explained that as every instrument warms up separately, it sounds like a "hot mess." However, when the conductor shows up, he/she takes the "hot mess" and makes sweet melody.

She also explained that being a conductor is no easy task and requires heightened skills to orchestrate every musician in the orchestra. It is said that "conducting an orchestra requires musical skills and education beyond most mortals' abilities." Imagine every detail of your life is a single note into a beautiful harmony. It produces the perfect orchestration of the symphony of your life. For it was you who formed my inward parts; you knit me together in my mother's womb. I praise you, for I am fearfully and wonderfully made. Wonderful are your works; that I know very well. (Psalm 139:13-14)

Today's verse is a reminder, "He is before all things, and in him all things hold together." Wonderful works that creates sweet harmony. I encourage you to read Colossians 1 in its entirety.

Dear Father,
Thank you for orchestrating every detail of my life. Thank you for being before all things and for holding all things together. I pray that all your children see your wonderful works as you orchestrate every detail of their lives. That they remember you are before all things and hold all things together. I ask this in your son Jesus' name. Amen!

NOVEMBER 6

When Scared Love

ANCHOR SCRIPTURE: 1 JOHN 4:18

There is no fear in love. But perfect love drives out fear because fear has to do with punishment. The one who fears is not made perfect in love.

If light is love, then fear is its shadow
- L.J. Vanier

Imagine choosing light over darkness, love over fear. Think about it, when you are scared, are you able to freely love or shine your light? Fear may even threaten your ability to be compassionate to yourself and others. Fear is even capable of taking you to a dark and shameful place.

A study from the University of Exeter found that being reminded of being loved and cared for dampens the threat response. I recalled seeing this statement that stayed with me, "Fear is an emotion, love is not an emotion, it is a decision." When in a threatening situation or you are overcome by fear, try consciously choosing love. Decide to love over being scared. Love repels fear and shame.

Today's verse is a reminder, "There is no fear in love. But perfect love drives out fear because fear has to do with punishment. The one who fears is not made perfect in love." Love cast out fear. I encourage you to read 1 John 4 in its entirety.

—————————— **PRAYER FOR THE DAY:** ——————————

Dear Father,

Thank you for the reminder that love repels fear. That there is no fear in love. But perfect love drives out fear because fear has to do with punishment. The one who fears is not made perfect in love. I pray that all your children choose love over fear. That they remember that there is no fear in love. That perfect love drives out fear because fear has to do with punishment. The one who fears is not made perfect in love. I ask this in your son Jesus' name. Amen!

The Road Less Traveled

ANCHOR SCRIPTURE: ISAIAH 26:3 - (AMP)

"You will keep in perfect and constant peace the one whose mind is steadfast [that is, committed and focused on You—in both inclination and character], Because he trusts and takes refuge in You [with hope and confident expectation]."

"Two roads diverged in a wood and I - I took the one less traveled by, and that has made all the difference."
- Robert Frost

The "Road Not Taken" is a well-known poem written by Robert Frost in 1916, that although it is sometimes referred to as complicated, it brings you to think about choices in life. It highlights that one must make the choice on whether to go with the mainstream or become a trailblazer. "If life is a journey, this poem highlights those times in life when a decision has to be made."

At some point in our lives we must make very tough choices. Go with the status quo or branch out on a different path. Think about it, from the time you entered school and for some earlier, you made choices to be with the more popular classmates even though you had nothing in common. They were popular and you wanted to be labeled as that, popular. As you became older, you may have made decisions that were not aligned with your values but because society accepts it, you broke your own rules. These are imaginable views of arriving at the fork in the road. Wouldn't it be nice to have peace sticking to the unpopular and anchoring on your values when you are faced with the choice of taken the road most traveled or heading down a road not yet built?

Today's verse is a reminder, "You will keep in perfect and constant peace the one whose mind is steadfast [that is, committed and focused on You—in both inclination and character], Because he trusts and takes refuge in You [with hope and confident expectation]. Maybe choosing the road less traveled is a way to make a difference, choosing commitment, character, and trust.

PRAYER FOR THE DAY:

Dear Father,
Thank you for the reminder that you will keep in perfect and constant peace the one whose mind is steadfast on you, because he trusts and takes refuge in you with hope and confident expectation. That even traveling on the road less taken, you are there with me. I pray that all your children seek you as they make choices when they arrive at the fork in the road. That they trust and seek refuge in you with hope and confident expectations especially when the road they choose is less traveled. I ask this in your son Jesus' name. Amen!

Extravagant Love

ANCHOR SCRIPTURE: 1 JOHN 4:10

"This is love: not that we loved God, but that he loved us and sent his Son as an atoning sacrifice for our sins."

"That's what love does- It pursues blindly, unflinchingly, and without end. Even if it costs everything."

- Bob Goff

Merriam Webster defines extravagant as spending much more than is necessary; excessively high: extravagant expenses; extravagant prices; exceeding the bounds of reason, as actions, demands, opinions, or passions; going beyond what is deserved or justifiable; extravagant praise.

Extravagant love gives without needing or expecting a return. Sometimes it feels undeserving because it is excessive and goes beyond one's own imagination. Imagine a love that flows despite what you have done. A love that forgives the worst thing you think you could do. It probably grows more, the more errors you commit. No sense in trying to reject it because nothing, absolutely nothing, will stop this extravagant love from flowing to you. Surrender to it.

The Apostle Paul reminds us that God commands his love towards us, in that while we were yet sinners, Christ died for us. How could such love not capture your heart and draw you near? How could such extravagant love not give you hope that anchors your soul?

Today's verse is a reminder: "This is love: not that we loved God, but that he loved us and sent his Son as an atoning sacrifice for our sins." This is love, un-describable, undeniably extravagant love.

Dear Father,
Thank you for sending your Son to die for my sins. For the reminder that this is love: not that I loved you, but that you loved me and sent your Son as an atoning sacrifice for my sins. I pray that all your children are reminded of your extravagant love. Not that they loved you, but that you loved them and sent your Son as an atoning sacrifice for their sins. Thank you, Father, for your extravagant love. I asked this in your son Jesus' name. Amen!

NOVEMBER 9

Extra Grace Required (EGR)

ANCHOR SCRIPTURE: COLOSSIANS 3:13- (AMP)

"Bearing graciously with one another, and willingly forgiving each other if one has a cause for complaint against another; just as the Lord has forgiven you, so should you forgive."

"A thought to help us through these difficult times: Be kind, for everyone you meet is fighting a hard battle."
-Ian MacLaren

When you are suffering and in pain, it is difficult to think of anyone but yourself. You may be so preoccupied with your own problems and struggles there is room for nothing else. Extending compassion and sympathy when in this state may seem unattainable. But Ian MacLaren

495

noted wisely, "Let us be kind to one another, for most of us are fighting a hard battle."

This weekend I attended a very intense training that required many hours on the computer with limited breaks. The organizers had to quickly pivot and move an in-person live training to a virtual training in less than three weeks. It was interesting that they kicked off the training asking for extra grace. Acknowledging that things may not be perfect, that there may be gaps or struggles along the training, but by grace, we all got through the weekend. I noticed, when some felt frustrated by delays in receiving a response to a question or noticing a typo on a slide, there was an immediate shift to grace.

What an awakening. By the simple reminder to ask for grace, it was given. Imagine awakening each morning and planting these words in your spirit and thought, EXTRA GRACE REQUIRED (EGR), you could change the trajectory of your entire day and possibly someone else's day. Today's verse is a reminder: "bearing graciously with one another, and willingly forgiving each other if one has a cause for complaint against another; just as the Lord has forgiven you, so should you forgive." As you continue to navigate this unprecedented and difficult time, remind yourself daily, extra grace required. Note, EGR is a two-way street, it is not just given to others, it is given to self as well.

───────────── **PRAYER FOR THE DAY:** ─────────────

Dear Father,
Thank you for the reminder, bearing graciously with one another, and willingly forgiving each other if one has a cause for complaint against another; just as the Lord has forgiven you, so should you forgive. Extra grace required. I pray that all your children remember the grace you have given and that they pass this on to others and self. That they bear graciously with one another, and willingly forgiving each other if one has a cause for complaint against another; just as you have forgiven them, so should they forgive. I ask this in your son Jesus' name. Amen!

The Gift of Hope

ANCHOR SCRIPTURE: HEBREWS 6:19 (AMP)

"This hope [this confident assurance] we have as an anchor of the soul [it cannot slip and it cannot break down under whatever pressure bears upon it]—a safe and steadfast hope that enters within the veil [of the heavenly temple, that most Holy Place in which the very presence of God dwells]"

"The greatest gift leaders can give their people is HOPE"
- *Unknown*

Ray Johnston wrote in "The Hope Quotient" that "Some wise person once said that we can live about forty days without food, about three days without water, about eight minutes without air- but not a single second without hope."

Why hope? I looked up acronyms for the word HOPE as I took it many likely existed for this word. Here are a few that I found: "Have Only Positive Expectations"; "Hold On Pain Ends"; "Honor, Obey, Pray, Encourage"; "Holding On to your Promises Each day"; "Helping Others Pursue Excellence" just to mention a few. You can choose which resonates for your current season.

Without hope you are lost, without hope you give up on everything you have, without hope you quit just before you cross the finish line. To have hope requires courage, to have hope demands that you make hard choices during turmoil, to have hope allows you to lead your tribe from victims to victors. And this is probably why, the greatest gift leaders can give their people is HOPE.

Today's verse is a reminder that "This hope [this confident assurance] we have as an anchor of the soul [it cannot slip and it cannot break down under whatever pressure bears upon it]—a safe and steadfast hope that enters within the veil [of the heavenly temple, that most Holy Place in which the very presence of God dwells.]" "Be diligent so that what you hope for may be fully realized." Never lose hope!

—————————————— **PRAYER FOR THE DAY:** ——————————————

Dear Father,
Thank you for the reminder to lead with hope. That hope is my confident assurance, safe and steadfast to anchor my soul. I must never lose hope. I pray that all your children never lose hope. That they remain diligent in hope and remember the assurance and anchor it brings to their soul. I ask this in your son Jesus' name. Amen!

Devoted to Prayer

ANCHOR SCRIPTURE: COLOSSIANS 4:2 (AMP)

Be persistent and devoted to prayer, being alert and focused on your prayer life with an attitude of thanksgiving.

"Our prayers may be awkward. Our attempts may be feeble. But since the power of prayer is in the one who hears it and not in the one who says it, our prayers do make a difference."

- Max Lucado

"I don't know how to pray." These were the words echoed from a dear friend who was in a very desperate and dark situation. My heart ached in hearing these words. It reminded me of very early in my faith walk when I clumsily tried to pray to God. As a child, you "Keep It Simple." The way you said your prayer at night, the way you blessed your food, the way you asked for that bike you really wanted for Christmas. You kept it simple, said it with a grateful heart, used the words you knew, and believed the prayer was heard. I said just talk to God as you would talk to a friend and when the words don't come to you, simply say the words HELP ME GOD will suffice. God will help you. James 5 is a reminder that the effectual fervent prayer of a righteous man availed much.

Do you remember this bedtime prayer you may have said as a child? Now I lay me down to sleep, I pray the Lord my soul to keep. If I should die before I wake, I pray to God my soul to take. If I should live for other days, I pray the Lord to guide my ways. This quote from Charles Spurgeon, "If you believe in prayer at all, expect God to hear you. If you do not expect, you will not have. God will not hear you unless you believe He will hear you; but if you believe He will, He will be as good as your faith", is a reminder of the importance of believing. Believe that God hears every single prayer no matter how awkward you think it may be.

Today's verse is a reminder: "Be persistent and devoted to prayer, being alert and focused in your prayer life with an attitude of thanksgiving." I encourage you to read Colossians 4 in its entirety. Prayers do make a difference.

———————————— **PRAYER FOR THE DAY:** ————————————

Dear Father,
Thank you for the reminder to be persistent and devoted to prayer, no matter how awkward, being alert and focused on my prayer life with an attitude of Thanksgiving. I pray that all your children remember to be persistent and devoted to prayer, no matter how awkward, being alert and focused on their prayer life with an attitude of Thanksgiving. That the "power of prayer is in the one who hears it and not in the one who says it, our prayers do make a difference." I ask this in Jesus' name. Amen!

Fear or Faith?
The choice is yours

ANCHOR SCRIPTURE: ISAIAH 41:10 (MSG)

"Don't panic. I'm with you. There's no need to fear for I'm your God. I'll give you strength. I'll help you. I'll hold you steady, keep a firm grip on you."

There are two primary forces in this world, fear, and faith. Fear can move you to destructiveness or sickness or failure. Only in rare instances will it motivate you to accomplishment. But faith is a greater force. Faith can drive itself into your consciousness and set you free from fear forever
-Norman Vincent Peale

Fear and faith both demand that you believe in something you cannot see says Bob Proctor. A friend recently told me about two elderly cousins living together one is a cancer survivor and the other is about 15 years younger and have a few complications but none like the cancer survivor. The cancer survivor refused to stay quiet and is out and about everyday although been told to stay in. The other is afraid and concerned for both. She was asking for help in keeping the higher risk cousin in the house.

It begs to think is the high-risk cancer survivor operating at a different level than the cousin with the lesser risk. Her faith maybe stronger than her fear. They are both believing in something they cannot see but one constricts, pulls you in (fear) while one is freeing (faith). This is not to say the high-risk person should not obey instructions or guidance. It just makes one think about where strong or as some say "crazy" faith could take you.

Today's verse is a reminder: "Don't panic. I'm with you. There's no need to fear for I'm your God. I'll give you strength. I'll help you. I'll hold you steady, keep a firm grip on you." I encourage you to read Isaiah 41 in its entirety. Be at peace, don't panic.

--------------------------- **PRAYER FOR THE DAY:** ---------------------------

Dear Father,
Thank you for the reminder to not panic that you will help me. That you are here with me and you are my God. You will hold me steady and keep me firm on your grip. I pray that all your children remember not to panic, that you are there with them and will help them all. You are their God and will hold them steady and keep them firm on your grip. I ask this in your son Jesus' name. Amen!

NOVEMBER 13

Preparation

ANCHOR SCRIPTURE: PROVERBS 6:6-8 NASB

*Go to the ant, O sluggard, observe her ways and be wise,
which, having no chief, officer or ruler, prepares her food
in the summer and gathers her provision in the harvest."*

"Success is where preparation and opportunity meet."
-Bobby Unser

The most recent pandemic COVID-19 makes it inevitable not to consider preparedness. One never knows when such event may hit, panic sets in, and you may be left feeling unprepared. There is so much to prepare for and so many other areas where preparedness may be lacking.

I recently read a devotional by Inspiration Ministries that talked about the sluggards. A sluggard usual refers to a habitually lazy person. The devotional reminded that "although sluggards tend to be wasteful, they still have a huge appetite. They love to consume the resources they have, yet they aren't ready for the future. They don't plan or think ahead. They don't plow their fields or sow seeds when they have the opportunity."

During chaos, you may think you have missed the opportunity to prepare especially if you don't have what you need. However, there is the present and there is a future. You can begin now, preparing for the long haul. Gathering just enough of what you need to sustain you through this and the next season. No need to remain stuck, in slumber or sluggish. Wake up and start doing what you can, with what you have, from where you are. You still have an opportunity to prepare for the future. Start now.

Today's verse is a reminder: "Go to the ant, O sluggard, observe her ways and be wise, which, having no chief, officer or ruler, prepares her food in the summer and gathers her provision in the harvest." I encourage you to read Proverbs 6 in its entirety. When preparedness and opportunity meet, it yields success.

———————————————— **PRAYER FOR THE DAY:** ————————————————

Dear Father,
Thank you for the reminder to go observe the ways of the ant and be wise, without a chief or ruler, she prepares her food in the summer and gathers her provision in the harvest. I pray that all your children shed any sluggish spirit and prepare. That they observe the ant, be wise, and prepare now for the future. That as they do their part, you will handle the rest. You are present and are with each of them. I ask this in your son Jesus' name. Amen!

Humility

ANCHOR SCRIPTURE: PROVERBS 22:4

Humility is the fear of the Lord; its wages are riches and honor and life."

Mastery begins with humility.
-Robin Sharma

Humility is said to be a good trait to develop. I have heard it said that "Being a parent can be a very humble job, wiping noses, changing diapers, and meeting a child's every need for years without thinking of self." Other forms of humility could be helping an employee complete their task even though you are the owner of the company. Is this something you would consider doing? Or when you make a huge profit, would you share it with those who helped you gain the profit? God's word states do nothing out of selfish ambition or vain conceit. Rather, in humility value others above yourselves, not looking to your own interest but each of you to the interest of the others. Zig Ziglar is quoted as saying: "Humility will open more doors than arrogance ever will." Mother Teresa was a great example of humility. She had everything she needed in the convent where she lived. She however chose to give up her life to live with the poor on the streets of Calcutta caring for the sick and dying. Is this something you could or would do?

Being humble is not easy especially with something called ego as part of our being. It is also difficult to surrender control or give credit where credit is due when attention strokes one's ego. Today's verse is a reminder that humility is the fear of the Lord; its wages are riches and honor and life. Proverbs 15 adds that wisdom's instruction is to fear the Lord, and humility comes before honor. It seems humility and wisdom are connected. I encourage you to read Proverbs 22 in its entirety. Be humble.

Dear Father,
Thank you for the reminder that humility and wisdom's instructions are to fear you. That humility opens more doors than arrogance. I pray that all your children take heed to your word that humility and wisdom's instructions are to fear you. That they remember that humility comes before honor. I ask this in your son Jesus' name. Amen!

NOVEMBER 15

Victory Walk

ANCHOR SCRIPTURE: PSALM 37:23-24 (NIV)

The Lord makes firm the steps of the one who delights in him;
though he may stumble, he will not fall, for the Lord upholds
him with his hand.

Once you hear the details of victory, it is hard
to distinguish it from a defeat.
- Jean-Paul Sartre

"As a man sow, shall he reap. and I know that talk is cheap. But the heat of the battle is as sweet as the victory" -Bob Marley. Merriam Webster defines victory as the overcoming of an enemy or antagonist, achievement of mastery or success in a struggle or endeavor against odds or difficulties. Think about the efforts a soldier must undergo to prepare for war; the preparation required to participate in the Olympics, the daily struggles to resist the flesh, worldly things, and your enemies. The struggle is part of the victory walk.

You will encounter potholes, detours, major falls, and losses on the road to victory. Savoring the victory may allow you to handle the agony of defeat as you walk. Remember God's promises. "God will let you into the battlefield, so you can understand the meaning of victory." Without heat you will never understand victory.

"But thanks be to God! He gives us the victory through our Lord Jesus Christ." Set your mind on Jesus, victory, and hope. What you sow, you shall reap. Today's verse is a reminder, "The Lord makes firm the steps of the one who delights in him; though he may stumble, he will not fall, for the Lord upholds him with his hand." I encourage you to read Psalm 37 in its entirety. Walk in Victory!

—————————— PRAYER FOR THE DAY: ——————————

Dear Father,
Thank you for the reminder to set my mind on Jesus, victory, and hope. That you make firm the steps of the one who delights in you; though I may stumble, I will not fall, for you uphold me with your hand. I pray that all your children set their mind on Jesus, victory, and hope. That they remember that you make firm the steps of the one who delights in you; though they may stumble, they will not fall, for you uphold them with your hand." I ask this in your son Jesus' name. Amen!

Ears Wide Open

ANCHOR SCRIPTURE: ISAIAH 50:4 (AMP)

"The Lord God has given Me [His [a]Servant] the tongue of disciples [as One who is taught], That I may know how to sustain the weary with a word. He awakens Me morning by morning; He awakens My ear to listen as a disciple [as One who is taught]."

Keep your eyes and ears wide open— and your mouth closed if you wish to acquire the habit of prompt decision.
- Napoleon Hill

Have you ever referred to someone as hard of hearing or having select hearing (non-medically diagnosed?) This reference usually implies that the person selects what they want to hear instead of what is being communicated. At times these individuals in questions may hear what is said and change the message to adjust either to their current desire or what is currently consuming the space in their brain or their spirit.

How many of you know, live, work and are surrounded by people with select hearing? I bet many of you if you have children or spouses thought of them first. You could probably picture asking your child to do a task and one hour later it is not done because they were so preoccupied with their games or texting with friends that they selectively did not hear your request. The same applies to children making request of their parents and they selectively do not hear because they have so much on their mind. Lastly, same with a spouse making a request in the middle of the football game or in the middle of their favorite show, you can guarantee it will fall on deaf ears.

What if one took extra caution to have "ears wide open", that is, to pay attention to what is happening, especially to find out something or make a prompt decision? Today's verse is a reminder, "The Lord God has given Me [His [a]Servant] the tongue of disciples [as One who is taught], That I may know how to sustain the weary with a word. He awakens Me morning by morning,

He awakens My ear to listen as a disciple [as One who is taught]. It is interesting to note, not having ears wide open, or having selective hearing or selective obedience seldom yields good results. I encourage you to read Isaiah 50 in its entirety. Remain with ears wide open to acquire the habit of prompt decision.

PRAYER FOR THE DAY

Dear Father,
Thank you for the reminder to remain with ears wide open. That you awaken me morning by morning, you awaken my ear to listen as a disciple. I pray that all your children remain with ears wide open. To hear your guidance and instructions clearly. That they remember you awaken them morning by morning; you awaken their ear to listen as a disciple. I pray they remain with ears wide open to hear your voice. I ask this in your son Jesus' name. Amen!

Redemption

ANCHOR SCRIPTURE: EPHESIANS 1:7 (AMP)

"In Him we have redemption [that is, our deliverance and salvation] through His blood, [which paid the penalty for our sin and resulted in] the forgiveness and complete pardon of our sin, in accordance with the riches of His grace."

Redemption is not perfection. The redeemed must realize their imperfections.

- John Piper

Walking around with negative thoughts, remaining prisoners to addictions, owning and living the lies of past experiences and inability to forgive yourself from errors and sins keeps one in the dark. "Darkness tries to steal redemption, mercy and grace says no."

Merriam Webster defines redemption as to buy back, to get or win back; to free from what distresses or harms: to release from blame or debt; to free from the consequences of sin: to change for the better. I sum these definitions as redemption offers freedom and forgiveness from the guilt, curse, punishment mindset this world lays on you.

I admire Bob Marley's song lyrics as they are filled with wisdom. I am thinking of one song in particular "Redemption Song." A line in this song goes like this, "Emancipate yourselves from mental slavery, none but us can free our minds." Mental slavery does not have to be. We can all free ourselves from mental slavery. Seek the light, seek the truth, and set yourself free. What is your choice, mental slavery, or freedom?

Today's verse is a reminder, "In Him we have redemption [that is, our deliverance and salvation] through His blood, [which paid the penalty for our sin and resulted in] the forgiveness and complete pardon of our sin, in accordance with the riches of His grace."

I encourage you to read Ephesians 1 in its entirety. Redemption is yours!

─────────── **PRAYER FOR THE DAY:** ───────────

Dear Father,
Thank you for the reminder that we have redemption, complete pardon of our sin in accordance with the riches of your grace. I pray that all your children accept the redemption you offer through the riches of your grace. That they are freed from mental slavery. I ask this in your son Jesus' name. Amen!

Unshakable

ANCHOR SCRIPTURE: HEBREWS 12:27 (NLT)

Therefore, since we are surrounded by so great a cloud of witnesses, let us also lay aside every weight, and sin which clings so closely, and let us run with endurance the race that is set before us, looking to Jesus, the founder and perfecter of our faith, who for the joy that was set before him endured the cross, despising the shame, and is seated at the right hand of the throne of God.

"Those who have not found their true wealth, which is the radiant joy of being and the deep, unshakable peace that comes with it, are beggars, even if they have great material wealth. They are looking outside for scraps of pleasure or fulfillment, for validation, security, or love, while they have a treasure within that not only includes all those things but is infinitely greater than anything the world can offer. "
-Eckhart Tolle

I always wondered what it takes to be "unshakable" ... "not possible to weaken or get rid of, not able to be shaken." Does it require grit, courage, relying on yourself or relying on something else? Possibly many of you reading this may have experienced some situation or life event that may have shaken your foundation or "you thought" it shook your foundation.

I say "thought" because at the moment of the shock it may have felt unstable, it may have felt as you and your foundation were shattered. However, you may have been reminded that you were built on a rock that cannot be shaken. You may have realized that your faith is stronger than the event. Or you may have recalled these words from Psalm 32 "I will guide you along the best pathway for your life. I will advise you and watch over you." That event you dreaded or lost you suffered may have been the best pathway for your life, even though it shocked you and you still don't understand. This is a great reminder that "God's thoughts are not your thoughts, neither are your ways God's ways." Maybe understanding this aka having strong faith is one way to be unshakable. Trusting that God knows best and will prune you knowing what is best for you.

Today's verse is a reminder, "This means that all of creation will be shaken and removed, so that only unshakable things will remain." Shaken to only preserve the unshakable. I encourage you to read Hebrews 12 in its entirety.

―――――――――――― **PRAYER FOR THE DAY:** ――――――――――――

Dear Father,
Thank you for the reminder that all creation will be shaken and removed, so that only unshakable things remain. I pray that all your children develop strong faith and trust in you. That they remember you are the rock. That all creation will be shaken and removed, so that only unshakable things remain. I ask this in your son Jesus' name. Amen!

Perfect Peace

ANCHOR SCRIPTURE: ISAIAH 26:3 (NKJV)

"You will keep him in perfect peace, whose mind is stayed on You, because he trusts in You."

"Peace cannot be kept by force. It can only be achieved by understanding."
-*Albert Einstein*

Merriam Webster defines peace as a state of tranquility or quiet: such as freedom from civil disturbance or freedom from disquieting or oppressive thoughts or emotions. I recalled listening to a teaching that mentioned the Hebrew version of perfect peace is "Shalom Shalom."

Peace is a gift that sometimes remains unopened. Everyone has access to open this gift, that brings strength and freedom. Remaining true to yourself and keeping your mind stayed on the Lord seems to be key ingredients to enjoying the gift of peace.

Perfect peace because you put your trust in God not in man or yourself. "Trust in the Lord forever, for the Lord, the Lord himself, is the Rock eternal." (Isaiah 26:4)

It seems the battle for perfect peace starts in the mind. Keeping your mind steadfast on other things may lead to disquieting or oppressive thoughts or emotions. Caring for your mind and its focus daily may keep you in perfect peace. Today's verse is a reminder, you will keep him in perfect peace, whose mind is stayed on You, because he trusts in You." I encourage you to read Isaiah 26 in its entirety. Shalom, Shalom.

Dear Father,
Thank you for the reminder that you will keep him in perfect
peace, whose mind is stayed on you. To trust in you forever for
you are the rock. I pray that all your children keep their minds
stayed on you and that they find the gift of perfect peace. That
they trust in you forever for you are the rock. I ask this in your
son Jesus' name. Amen!

NOVEMBER 20

Give Goodness

ANCHOR SCRIPTURE: PSALM 23:6

Surely, goodness and mercy shall follow me all the days of my
life, and I shall dwell in the house of the Lord forever.

"Life is an echo. What you send out, comes back. What you sow,
you reap. What you give, you get. What you see in others, exists
in you. Remember, life is an echo. It always gets back to you.
So, give goodness."
-Unknown

Do good, be good, it is good. Good is a word that is not foreign to many.
Why good, "to be desired or approved of, to do that which is morally
right; to be righteous; to empathize with and sacrifice for others." In
the beginning God saw all that he had made, and it was "very good."

515

I recently observed a group of people come together in a supermarket to help a woman with small children pay for all the groceries she had planned to purchase without realizing she did not have enough funds to complete the purchase. I also recently viewed a video where a judge pardons an elderly man of a traffic citation because he listened to this man's story and saw that he was a "good" man. At approximately 94 years of age, he is still caring for his disabled son. This to me was goodness in action. Henry David Thoreau said, "Goodness is the only investment which never fails."

Beloved, do not imitate evil but imitate good. Whoever does good is from God. (3 John 1:11) Today's verse is a reminder, "Surely goodness and mercy shall follow me all the days of my life, and I shall dwell in the house of the Lord forever." I encourage you to read Psalm 23 in its entirety. Do the right thing, for the right reason, for goodness sake. One act of kindness, one ounce of goodness can change the world.

PRAYER FOR THE DAY:

Dear Father,
Thank you for the reminder to do the right thing for the right reason for goodness sake. That surely goodness and mercy shall follow me all the days of my life, and I shall dwell in your house forever. I pray that all your children do the right thing for the right reason for goodness sake. That they remember that surely goodness and mercy shall follow them all the days of their life and they shall dwell in your house forever. I ask this in your son Jesus' name. Amen.

Patience

ANCHOR SCRIPTURE: GALATIANS 6:9

"Let's not get tired of doing what is good, for at the right time we will reap a harvest—if we do not give up."

"Patience, persistence and perspiration make
an unbeatable combination for success."
- Napoleon Hill

What is patience? Merriam Webster defines patience as bearing pains or trials calmly or without complaint, manifesting forbearance under provocation or strain, not hasty or impetuous steadfast despite opposition, difficulty, or adversity. I have heard some people define patience as "easier said than done."

It is one of the hardest behaviors to practice in a "Microwave Society" (where everything is expected RIGHT NOW.) You want change right now, you want your children to behave right now, you want the latest fashion item right now, you want that promotion right now, you want your problems to be fixed right now. The "right now" conditioning hampers our growth.

Do you recall cooking a meal that took several hours or days to prepare? It may have required several phases before putting it all together. Anyone remembers a slow cooker? The slow cooker taught patience and at the end, you probably said it was worth the wait. The love and care you put into serving that perfectly prepared meal did not go unnoticed by those consuming the meal.

What in your life right now requires that you practice patience? That you understand that whatever you await may be slow cooking and will be worth the wait. Today's verse is a reminder, "Let's not get tired of doing what is good, for at the right time we will reap a harvest—if we do not give up." I encourage you to read Galatians 6 in its entirety. Keep practicing patience. It remains a virtue.

───────────── PRAYER FOR THE DAY: ─────────────

Dear Father,
Thank you for the reminder that patience is a virtue. To not get tired of doing what is good, for at the right time we will reap a harvest- if we do not give up. I pray that all your children remember that patience is a virtue. To not get tired of doing what is good, for at the right time they will reap a harvest- if they do not give up. I ask this in your son Jesus' name. Amen!

Gentleness

ANCHOR SCRIPTURE: PHILIPPIANS 4:5 (AMP)

"Let your gentle spirit [your graciousness, unselfishness, mercy, tolerance, and patience] be known to all people. The Lord is near."

I learned that it is the weak who are cruel, and that gentleness is to be expected only from the strong.
-*Leo Rosten*

Humility brings it to life. Pride and shame silence, it. It breathes through compassion for others and whispers in the presence of temptation. Sweet gentleness, how could such softness be so strong?

If we only knew the power of this fruit known as gentleness...it tames the tongue and guides to do no harm. Imagine leading your life with this superpower. No need to show off behind a title or hide behind doing wrong. Patience can persuade a prince, and soft speech can break bones (Proverb 25:15.) I wonder if this is the reason gentleness is sometimes described as strength under control. Why the weak are cruel and the gentle are strong. Something to ponder as you grow.

Today's verse is a reminder, "Let your gentle spirit [your graciousness, unselfishness, mercy, tolerance, and patience] be known to all people. The Lord is near." I encourage you to read Philippians 4 in its entirety. Be gentle to self and others.

Dear Father,
Thank you for the reminder of the power in gentleness. To look beyond what is in front of me and let my gentle spirit be known to all people. I pray that all your children let their gentle spirit be known to all people. That they remember there is power in gentleness and that you are near. I ask this in your son Jesus' name. Amen!

●

NOVEMBER 23

Love Love

ANCHOR SCRIPTURE: 1 JOHN 4:7 (AMP)

"Beloved, let us [unselfishly] love and seek the best for one another, for love is from God; and everyone who loves [others] is born of God and knows God [through personal experience]

The ultimate lesson all of us have to learn is unconditional love, which includes not only others but ourselves as well.
- Elisabeth Kubler-Ross

Do you recall learning to ride a bike, learning to swim, or watching a toddler learning to take their first step? At first, it is scary, disconcerting, or you may even experience anxiety. To master anything requires that you do it repeatedly.

The same applies with love. If you have never experienced unconditional love, how would you know to give it? The first time you realize that such a thing exists, it may seem surreal. You may even reject it because it feels uncomfortable. Once you begin to practice, to love love, you may find it easier to love unconditionally. Through the cracks, imperfections, hurt, you still love love and find that you are capable of unconditional love. "Unconditional love is loving someone beyond their limits and yours." "It is hard to compete with unconditional love." Learn it. Live it. Lead it.

Today's verse is a reminder to unselfishly love and seek the best for one another, for love is from God; and everyone who loves [others] is born of God and knows God [through personal experience.] Keep practicing loving love and soon you will love you self and others unconditionally and God loves you. I encourage you to read 1 John 4 in its entirety. Love Love.

―――――――――― **PRAYER FOR THE DAY:** ――――――――――

Dear Father,
Thank you for the reminder of your unconditional love. That the same love you grant me, I must learn to grant to others. I pray that all your children continue to practice till they master the art of unconditional love. That they remember to love unselfishly, unconditionally and seek the best for one another, for love is from you. I ask this in your son Jesus' name. Amen!

Faithfulness

ANCHOR SCRIPTURE: 1 THESSALONIANS 5:24 (AMP)

*Faithful and absolutely trustworthy is He who is calling you
[to Himself for your salvation], and He will do it [He will fulfill
His call by making you holy, guarding you, watching over you,
and protecting you as His own].*

Health is the greatest gift, contentment the greatest wealth,
faithfulness the best relationship.

- Buddha

I recently read an article by Dr. Richard J. Krejcir on the character of faithfulness. Dr. Krejcir describes faithfulness as the "'gluing' fruit that will preserve our faith and the other characters of the Spirit and identify God's will so we can be dependable and trusting to God and others. It is the one fruit that we give to God, whereas the others are from the Spirit working in us!" Losing our trust and hope that God is in control is where we lose the fruit of faithfulness.

Being faithful is tricky especially when leading yourself and others. In his article, Dr. Krejcir makes note that faithfulness goes against modern psychology and societies thinking, as it requires us to move beyond ourselves, whereas psychology tells us to be selfness putting the "me" first, rearranging the world to our needs, which creates self-destruction and broken relationships. The fruit of faithfulness seems to be very important in maintaining and building one's character. Without it one will doubt everything including God's promises.

Today's verse is a reminder, "Faithful and absolutely trustworthy is He who is calling you [to Himself for your salvation], and He will do it [He will fulfill His call by making you holy, guarding you, watching over you, and protecting you as His own]." Imagine, you are loved so much that you are made holy, you are guarded, watched over and protected by the highest. God is faithful, are you faithful to God? I encourage you to read 1 Thessalonians 5 in its entirety.

─────────── **PRAYER FOR THE DAY:** ───────────

Dear Father,
Thank you for the reminder of the importance of the fruit of faithfulness and for your faithfulness. I pray that all your children look at how they can activate the fruit of faithfulness daily. That they remember, "Faithful and absolutely trustworthy is He who is calling you [to Himself for your salvation], and He will do it [He will fulfill His call by making you holy, guarding you, watching over you, and protecting you as His own]." I ask this in your son Jesus' name. Amen!

Joy

ANCHOR SCRIPTURE: PSALM 16:11- (NIV)

"You make known to me the path of life; you will fill me with joy in your presence, with eternal pleasures at your right hand."

"If you carry joy in your heart, you can heal any moment."
-Carlos Santana

Do you know anyone that does not want to experience joy or happiness? It is interesting to note that the difference between both is profound. I recently read in a 2015 issue of Psychologies that "Joy is more consistent and is cultivated internally. It comes when you make peace with who you are, why you are and how you are, whereas happiness tends to be externally triggered and is based on other people, things, places, thoughts and events."

Lamentation 3:17 describes the temporary nature of "happiness" as it is forgotten when trouble appears... "My soul is bereft of peace; I have forgotten what happiness is." Scripture also reminds us "So also you have sorrow now, but I will see you again, and your hearts will rejoice, and no one will take your joy from you."

Seeking the fruit of joy may be more beneficial than limiting ourselves to happiness. What would you rather, something lasting or temporary? Today's verse is a reminder, "you make known to me the path of life; you will fill me with joy in your presence, with eternal pleasures at your right hand." I encourage you to read Psalm 16 in its entirety. Here's wishing you true and deep joy today and always.

Dear Father,
Thank you for the reminder of the difference between joy and happiness. That you will fill me with joy in your presence, with eternal pleasures at your right hand. I pray that all your children remember that happiness is temporary, joy is long lasting. That you will fill them with joy in your presence, with eternal pleasures at your right hand. May they experience the everlasting joy you bring. I ask this in your son Jesus' name. Amen!

NOVEMBER 26

Self-Control

ANCHOR SCRIPTURE: PROVERBS 25:28 (NIV)

"Like a city whose walls are broken through is a person who lacks self-control."

"Self-control is the chief element in self-respect, and self-respect is the chief element in courage."
-*Thucydides*

The ability to control oneself, one's emotions and desires or the expression of them in one's behavior, especially in difficult situations is defined as self-control. Self-control is one of the primary factors that stand in the way of reaching your goals says the American Psychological Association (2011.)

Obeying the word is never easy especially when you want to do what you "feel" like doing. Knowing the word and acting on or "doing" the word requires lots of self-control. Doing the right thing also requires self-control and self-respect. Living in the world, we lose sight of the importance of self-control. Maybe this is the reason it is one of the hardest fruits to master.

Today's verse is a reminder that "like a city whose walls are broken through is a person who lacks self-control. Word to the wise, "Never let your emotions overpower your intelligence." I encourage you to read Proverbs 25 in its entirety. Be masters of self-control.

———————————— **PRAYER FOR THE DAY:** ————————————

Dear Father,
Thank you the reminder to the importance of self-control. That like a city whose walls are broken through is a person who lacks self-control. I pray that all your children remember the importance of self-control. That like a city whose walls are broken through is a person who lacks self-control. I ask this in your son Jesus' name. Amen!

Kindness

ANCHOR SCRIPTURE: EPHESIANS 4:32

"Be kind and compassionate to one another, forgiving each other, just as in Christ God forgave you."

"Kindness in words creates confidence. Kindness in thinking creates profoundness. Kindness in giving creates love."

-Lao Tzu

Kindness and compassion seem to be scarce nowadays. Could the culprit be the bad wrap given to kindness and compassion as a sign of weakness rather than what it is, a sign of strength? Imagine, the concern is so grave, a Kindness Institute was established at UCLA "to support world-class research on kindness, create opportunities to translate that research into real-world practices, and serve as a global platform to educate and communicate its findings. Among its principal goals are to empower citizens and inspire leaders to build more humane societies."

One of the investors shared that the vision for the institute is "that we will all live in a world where humanity discovers and practices the kindness that exists in all of us." Imagine investing $20 million to address the issue of kindness... Kindness is one of the fruits of the spirit God wishes to develop and activate in each of us. Against this there is no law. You have the power to be kind, use it!

Today's verse is a reminder "Be kind and compassionate to one another, forgiving each other, just as in Christ God forgave you." The word is true and serves as guidance, obey and be kind.

Dear Father,
Thank you for the reminder to be kind and compassionate to one another, forgiving each other, just as you forgave me. Your word empowers and inspires. I pray that all your children are empowered and inspired by your word. To be kind and compassionate to one another, forgiving each other, just as you forgave them. I ask this in your son Jesus' name. Amen!

NOVEMBER 28

The Beauty of Grace

ANCHOR SCRIPTURE: JOHN 1:16 (ESV)

"For from his fullness we have all received, grace upon grace..."

Grace isn't a little prayer you chant before receiving a meal.
It's a way to live. The law tells me how crooked I am.
Grace comes along and straightens me out.
- Dwight Lyman Moody

Grace is defined as simple elegance or refinement of movement. A biblical definition I once found and jotted down for reflection said grace is an enabling power and spiritual l healing offered through the mercy and love of Jesus Christ... No one can return to the presence of God without divine grace.

Thinking of grace, I see the simple elegance of a ballet dancer or a swan floating along in the water. No matter what may have happened before that dance or float, grace takes over as the dance or float begins. An enabling power that changes and transform everything... from crooked to straight. Ahhh... the beauty of grace.

Today's verse is a reminder," For from his fullness we have all received, grace upon grace." John F. MacArthur Jr. reminds us in this quote, "If I'm not showing grace...have I forgotten the grace I've been shown." I encourage you to read John 1 in its entirety.

--- **PRAYER FOR THE DAY:** ---

Dear Father,
Thank you for the reminder that from your fullness I have received, grace upon grace. That if I'm not showing grace, I have forgotten the grace I've been shown. I pray that all your children remember that from your fullness we have all received, grace upon grace. That they never forget the grace that they've been shown. I ask this in your son Jesus' name. Amen!

Gratitude Changes Everything

ANCHOR SCRIPTURE: 1 TIMOTHY 4:4-5 (ESV)

"For everything created by God is good, and nothing is to be rejected if it is received with thanksgiving, for it is made holy by the word of God and prayer."

"Gratitude is a spiritual force that empowers you to scale higher. You can't change to higher level without it."
- Bishop Dr. Julius Soyinka

I often wonder if lack of appreciation for what we have gets in the way of our growth. Is ingratitude causing stagnation in our life? It is not simple to remain laser focused on being grateful that you are alive, that you had a meal this morning, that you can see and read this message. It seems easier to focus on what you don't have despite the many blessings that greeted you the first hour of this day.

Appreciation can be defined as to judge with heightened perception or understanding, be fully aware of; must see it to appreciate it; to recognize with gratitude. It was fascinating to be reminded that to appreciate is to "judge with a heightened perception or understanding." Are you judging with a heightened perception or understanding? Are you seeing all your blessings, things, and people for which you must express appreciation? There is power in appreciation.

Today's verse is a reminder, "For everything created by God is good, and nothing is to be rejected if it is received with thanksgiving, for it is made holy by the word of God and prayer." I encourage you to read 1 Timothy 4 in its entirety.

Dear Father,
Thank you for the reminder that gratitude changes everything.
That everything created by you is good and nothing is to be
rejected. I pray that all your children remember that gratitude
changes everything. That everything created by you is good and
nothing is to be rejected if it is received with thanksgiving, for it
is made holy by the word of God and prayer. I ask this in Jesus'
name Amen.

NOVEMBER 30

Lean Not On Your Own Understanding

ANCHOR SCRIPTURE: PROVERBS 3:5-6

"Trust in the LORD with all your heart; and lean not on your
own understanding. In all thy ways acknowledge him, and he
shall direct thy paths."

"Your mind is finite, lean not on it."
- Loraine Angela Dixon

Experiencing any loss is not easy. Developing a habit of trusting, is
also not easy. There are so many things we cannot and will never understand as our minds are finite.

It is natural to want to find an explanation for something that makes no sense. To have a rational or wrap your mind around something that may hit you by surprise. Surrender to not lean on your own understanding admittedly is where the struggle resides.

Isaiah 55:8-9 is a powerful reminder that "For my thoughts are not your thoughts, neither are your ways my ways," declares the Lord. "As the heavens are higher than the earth, so are my ways higher than your ways and my thoughts than your thoughts."

Proverbs 3:5 reminds us to do two exclusive things- "Trust in the LORD with all our heart; and lean not on our own understanding." Proverbs 3:6 reminds us, in all thy ways acknowledge him, and he shall direct thy paths. I encourage you to read Proverbs 3 in its entirety. Keep trusting and loving even when it makes no sense.

─────────── **PRAYER FOR THE DAY:** ───────────

Dear Father,
Thank you for this reminder to trust you with all my heart and lean not on my own understanding. You are our refuge and strength, an ever-present help in trouble. I pray that all your children continue to trust you and lean not on their own understanding. That they remember you are our refuge and strength an ever-present help in trouble. May your strength abound in all families experiencing loss and are in mourning. I ask this in your son Jesus' name. Amen!

December

DECEMBER 1

Idols in Your Heart

ANCHOR SCRIPTURE: EZEKIEL 14:3 (NLT)

Son of man, these leaders have set up idols in their hearts. They have embraced things that will make them fall into sin. Why should I listen to their requests?

"People worship what they value most."
-*Pastor Jimmy Rollins*

As a former workaholic, I never thought about how working all the time, even after hours could be a form of idolatry. I truly thought it was the right thing to do and to show my loyalty to my employer. I even recalled putting work in front of my prayer time and my family. I made the choice to have work consume most of the hours in my day that there was only time for the required hour of Sunday church service and the five to ten minutes daily for devotion.

For me, one of the idols in my heart was work. There are so many idols that we allow or crave in our heart's money, power, things, titles, people, pleasures to name a few. Some of these idols are birth and defined by worldly desires. We allow these idols to take over our hearts and become more important than our relationship with God. If we continue to embrace things that are not of God and continue to invite "idols" in our hearts, how can we make room to develop a strong relationship with God?

Today's verse is a reminder of Ezekiel's revelation when "leaders came insincerely seeking God's counsel, their facade was revealed, and they were indicted for determining to pursue their evil way and defy God's will. They had set up idols in their hearts." A reminder, you shall have no other gods before me. (Exodus 20:3) What idols are you storing in your heart that is preventing you from developing a rich and intimate relationship with God? I encourage you to read Ezekiel 14 in its entirety.

──────────── **PRAYER FOR THE DAY:** ────────────

Dear Father,
Thank you for the reminder that I have set-up idols in my heart. That I must repent and turn away from my idols. I pray that all your children recognize the idols they have stored in their heart, that they repent and turn away from all idols. That they place their relationship with you as their priority. I ask this in your son Jesus' name. Amen!

DECEMBER 2

Change the Channel

ANCHOR SCRIPTURE: PHILIPPIANS 4:8(NIV)

Finally, brothers and sisters, whatever is true, whatever is noble, whatever is right, whatever is pure, whatever is lovely, whatever is admirable—if anything is excellent or praiseworthy—think about such things.

"What you focus on grows, what you think about expands, and what you dwell upon determines your destiny."
- Robin S. Sharma

You may have heard a certain television channel referred to as "constant negative news" because it is said that is all that is seen in that channel. Do you have friends or colleagues you consider bearers of constant negative news? How do you handle this? Do you sit and entertain the negative thoughts or messages, or do you change the subject?

Sometimes the same happens when something negative interrupts our day or flow. Instead of letting it go, we may spend the entire day replaying the incidence instead of moving on. Which is not productive and takes up much of your time. Changing the channel or thought may be the best gift you could give yourself.

Today's verse is a reminder, "Finally, brothers and sisters, whatever is true, whatever is noble, whatever is right, whatever is pure, whatever is lovely, whatever is admirable—if anything is excellent or praiseworthy—think about such things." Next time you find yourself stuck on replay, simply change the channel.

Dear Father,
Thank you for the reminder to think about whatever is true,
noble, right, pure, lovely, excellent, and praiseworthy. If these
are not my thoughts, change the channel. I pray that all your
children change the channel when their thoughts are not true,
noble, right, pure, lovely, excellent, and praiseworthy. I ask this
in your son Jesus' name. Amen!

DECEMBER 3

Serve One Another

ANCHOR SCRIPTURE: 1 PETER 4:10 (ESV)

"As each has received a gift, use it to serve one another, as good
stewards of God's varied grace"

"Life's most persistent and urgent question is,
'What are you doing for others?"
- Dr. Martin Luther King, Jr.

"On the third Monday in January of each year, the Day of Service is
observed as a "day on, not a day off." MLK Day of Service is intended
to empower individuals, strengthen communities, bridge barriers,
create solutions to social problems, and move us closer to Dr. King's
vision of a "Beloved Community."

As I reflect on this day of service, I think about how God truly did not make us to live for ourselves. Service allows us the opportunity to set ourselves aside and focus on the needs of others. Mark 10:45 reminds us that "even the Son of Man came not to be served but to serve others and to give his life as a ransom for many." Imagine intentionally finding ways to serve others every day or even to give your life as a ransom for many?

Jesus died for everyone so that those who receive his new life will no longer live for themselves. Instead, they will live for Christ, who died and was raised for them. Today's verse is a reminder, "As each has received a gift, use it to serve one another, as good stewards of God's varied grace." What are you doing for others with the gift(s) you received? I encourage you to read 1 Peter 4 in its entirety.

————————— **PRAYER FOR THE DAY:** —————————

Dear Father,
Thank you for the reminder that I am here to serve others not self. That as I received a gift, use it to serve others as a good steward of God's varied grace. I pray that all your children remember that they are here to serve others, not self. That as they each received a gift, that they use it to serve one another, as good stewards of God's varied grace. I ask this in your son Jesus' name. Amen!

Being Vulnerable

ANCHOR SCRIPTURE: HEBREWS 12:1-2 (ESV)

"I came to you in weakness and fear, and with much trembling and my speech and my message were not in plausible words of wisdom, but in demonstration of the Spirit and of power.

Vulnerability is the language of the soul and the voice of the heart.
- *Virginia Burges*

"Courage starts with showing up and letting ourselves be seen." "Because true belonging only happens when we present our authentic, imperfect selves to the world, our sense of belonging can never be greater than our level of self-acceptance." "Vulnerability sounds like truth and feels like courage." These are the words of Brené Brown.

Let's face it, being vulnerable is one of the hardest things to be. To display all your imperfections. To live and walk in your truth. Vulnerability comes from the Latin word for "wound," vulnus. Vulnerability is the state of being open to injury or appearing as if you are. Vulnerability can be physical, emotional, social, economic, or environmental. Vulnerability does more good than harm. If leaders could see this, they may heal rather than destroy their tribe. 1 John 1:9 says, "if we confess our sins, he is faithful and just and will forgive us our sins and purify us from all unrighteousness."

Today's verse is a reminder, ""I came to you in weakness and fear, and with much trembling and my speech and my message were not in plausible words of wisdom, but in demonstration of the Spirit and of power. I encourage you to read 1 Corinthians 2 in its entirety. How about letting yourself be seen. Be vulnerable!

Dear Father,
Thank you for the reminder that my vulnerability demonstrates power. That vulnerability is the language of the soul and the voice of the heart. I pray that all your children remember that vulnerability demonstrates power. That vulnerability sounds like truth and feels like courage. That they remember the words of 1 Corinthians 2:3-4. I ask this in your son Jesus' name. Amen!

DECEMBER 5

Seek Wisdom

ANCHOR SCRIPTURE: PROVERBS 4:6 (NIV)

Do not forsake wisdom, and she will protect you;
love her, and she will watch over you.

Don't gain the world and lose your soul;
wisdom is better than silver or gold.
-Bob Marley

Can you recall the many times your parents repeated advice that you did not follow or just didn't understand? You may have decided that it made no sense because you had no understanding, or you consciously made the choice to disobey. As you matured, you now recall the advice and awakened to the wisdom that was shared.

539

In conversation with a dear friend about the importance of wisdom and understanding he shared this excerpt from one of his readings for me to consider (not sure of the source and profound); "Why would God give wisdom and wait to give understanding? Sometimes we're just not ready to handle it, sometimes we aren't prepared to use it, and sometimes we're not mature enough. Whenever the Lord chooses to give us an understanding is the best time. We must wait and be patient." I thought wow, sound learning.

Understanding is the ability to perceive and discern a situation to apply wisdom. As you get wisdom, understanding follows. Lacking understanding leads you to the wilderness. Lack of wisdom yields defeat, a life filled with bad decisions, and focused solely on the problem. Wisdom provides the ability to see beyond the problem. Wisdom helps you cope.

Today's verse is a reminder, do not forsake wisdom, and she will protect you; love her, and she will watch over you. I encourage you to read Proverbs 4 in its entirety. Get wisdom at any cost!

———————————— PRAYER FOR THE DAY: ————————————

Dear Father,
Thank you for the reminder to not forsake wisdom, and she will protect me; love her, and she will watch over me. I pray that all your children do not forsake wisdom. That they remember wisdom will protect and watch over them. I ask this in Jesus' name. Amen!

Habit of Trust

ANCHOR SCRIPTURE: ISAIAH 26:4

*"Trust in the LORD forever, for the LORD GOD is
an everlasting rock."*

"When the trust account is high, communication
is easy, instant, and effective."
- *Stephen R. Covey*

Trust is not easy to establish or even something one could fathom making a habit. Trust is sometimes defined as firm belief in the reliability, truth, ability, or strength of someone or something. Can you imagine developing a habit of trust?

A habit of trust may allow you to see past your circumstances, good and bad. It may be hard to develop a habit of trust when all you have experienced is loss of trust your entire life. I recalled someone saying to me, how on earth do you expect me to trust someone I can't see when I can't even trust those I see? I said, maybe you have been placing your trust on the wrong source. Just something to consider.

Imaging learning a new habit, to simply say I trust you Lord, regardless of your circumstances and really mean it. Investing your energy in trusting God's promises instead of trusting the promises you made to yourself or that someone else made to you. Reflecting on the miracles that happened in your life when you exercised trust rather than doubt. Which habit will you develop, trust or doubt? Be reminded, "we are what we repeatedly do!"

Today's verse is a reminder, "Trust in the Lord forever, for the Lord God is an everlasting rock."

Dear Father,
Thank you for the reminder to develop a new habit of trust. Trust in you forever, for you are my everlasting rock. I pray that all your children develop a new or renewed habit of trust. Trust in you forever, for you are their everlasting rock. I ask this in your son Jesus' name. Amen!

DECEMBER 7

Staying Power

ANCHOR SCRIPTURE: 1 CORINTHIANS 15:58 (ESV)

"Therefore, my beloved brothers, be steadfast, immovable, always abounding in the work of the Lord, knowing that in the Lord your labor is not in vain."

"Burning desire to be or do something gives us staying power -
a reason to get up every morning or to pick ourselves up and start
in again after a disappointment."
- Marsha Sinetar

Has anyone ever asked you this question, how do you do it? How do you keep pressing forward during what seems like disappointment after disappointment or storm after storm? Have you noticed trees in your community that remain firm through rain, snow, earthquakes, and other disasters? It seems they may have roots that are sufficiently deep to keep them from uprooting and blowing around.

I wonder if this is the same for those who are constantly asked, how do you do it? That they are deeply rooted in strong faith, trusting God through all, remaining steadfast in their work for the Kingdom. It is said, "If someone has staying power that person always manages to continue doing what they have to do until it is finished."

Today's verse is a reminder, "Therefore, my beloved brothers, be steadfast, immovable, always abounding in the work of the Lord, knowing that in the Lord your labor is not in vain." I encourage you to read 1 Corinthians 15 in its entirety. Find your staying power.

——————————— PRAYER FOR THE DAY: ———————————

Dear Father,
Thank you for the reminder to have staying power. To be stead-
fast, immovable, always abounding in your work, knowing that
in you my labor is not in vain. I pray that all your children have
staying power. That they remain steadfast, immovable, always
abounding in your work, knowing that in you their labor is not
in vain. I ask this in your son Jesus' name. Amen!

Worry or Pray

ANCHOR SCRIPTURE: PHILIPPIANS 4:6(NLT)

"Don't worry about anything; instead, pray about everything. Tell God what you need and thank him for all he has done."

"Worry Changes Nothing, Prayer Changes Everything."

It is said that "worry negates prayer." It is also said that worrying is a sin as when we do, we are not trusting God with a situation, we are trusting ourselves. Does this mean that there is no way we can do both? We must make a choice, pray, or worry. Trust God or call God a liar. Wow...that whip me right into shape when I heard this.

It is our human and flesh nature to worry and have concern especially when there is so much devastation, many threats (natural and not natural) unexplained loss, and events that baffle our minds. Joyce Meyer often reminds us that the battlefield is in our minds. We can continue to entertain the battle in our minds or pray. Think about it, has worrying solved or changed anything in your life? Has praying without ceasing changed anything in your life? Now, your answers to these questions should help you choose how to spend your days, praying or worrying.

Isaiah 26:3 reminds us "you will keep in perfect peace those whose minds are steadfast, because they trust in you." Today's verse gives us clear instructions, "Don't worry about anything; instead, pray about everything. Tell God what you need and thank him for all he has done." The choice is now yours.

Dear Father,
Thank you for the reminder not to worry about anything; in-
stead, pray about everything. Tell you what I need and thank you
for all you have done. That you will keep in perfect peace those
whose minds are steadfast because they trust you. I pray that all
your children remember not to worry about anything; instead,
pray about everything. That you will keep in perfect peace those
whose minds are steadfast because they trust in you. That they
continue to pray without ceasing. I ask this in your son Jesus'
name. Amen!

Clear Vision

ANCHOR SCRIPTURE: HABAKKUK 2:2-3 (NKJV)

"Then the LORD answered me and said: "Write the vision And make it plain on tablets, That he may run who reads it. For the vision is yet for an appointed time, But at the end it shall speak, and not lie: though it tarries, wait for it; Because it will surely come, it will not tarry."

"You cannot separate good leadership from clear vision."
- *John Maxwell*

Vision is sometimes defined as the ability to think about or plan the future with imagination or wisdom. It could also be described as writing, seeing, and believing before something happens.

With the start of a new year, many prepare vision boards, write plans, establish dreams and goals. Remaining focused on the vision long term is not easy. Distractions show up, life shows up, competition show up and even envy show up. These things will always get one off track the vision if it is not clear and made plain.

Once the vision is established, one should anchor on the vision and not alter frequently... A key to leadership. Yes, this part requires a lot of faith, perseverance, and belief by the author of the vision. Otherwise, it is easy to fall prey to the distractions. A clear vision serves to discipline your actions and aligns with your values. Lacking good values will cause lack in your vision. Proverbs 29:18 reminds us that where there is no vision, the people perish: but he that keepers the law, happy is he.

Today's verse is a reminder, "...Write the vision and make it plain on tablets, that he may run who reads it. For the vision is yet for an appointed time, but at the end it shall speak, and not lie: Though it tarries, wait for it; Because it will surely come, it will not tarry. Write your vision clearly, stick with it, have faith, and believe.

--------------------------------- PRAYER FOR THE DAY: ---------------------------------

Dear Father,
Thank you for the reminder to write the vision and make it plain. That the vision is yet for an appointed time. But at the end it shall speak and not lie. Though it tarry, wait for it. I pray that all your children seek you as they prepare their vision. That as you guide, they write their vision and make it plain. That they remember that the vision is yet for an appointed time. But at the end it shall speak and not lie. Though it tarry, wait for it. Because it will surely come, it will not tarry. I ask this in your son Jesus' name. Amen!

The Best For Last

ANCHOR SCRIPTURE: JOHN 2:10

Everyone brings out the choice wine first and then the cheaper wine . . . but you have saved the best till now."

"Sometimes the very thing you're looking for,
is the one thing you can't see."

As this year comes to an end, many may be reflecting on their wins and losses and planning or looking for what's next. Some may be simply counting their blessings and grateful despite losses or wins.

What if even with a few hours left in the year, you have yet to see the best God has to offer. That your biggest "win" is not even close to the "win" God has in store for you. Not much time is needed, all is needed is faith as little as a mustard seed. It is easy to lose hope when you see all the choice prizes taken. Or only expect the cheap wine to be served when the choice wine is finished. But what if the best is still yet to come. That it was left till now, till today.

Today's verse is a reminder "Everyone brings out the choice wine first and then the cheaper wine . . . but you have saved the best till now." God saves the best for last.

Dear Father,
Thank you for the reminder that you save the best for last. That sometimes the very thing we are looking for, is the one thing we can't see." I pray that all your children do not lose hope despite the year they have had. That they remember you are still in the miracle-working business and you often save the best for last. I ask this in your son Jesus' name. Amen!

DECEMBER 11

Generosity

ANCHOR SCRIPTURE: PROVERBS 11:25 (NIV)

A generous person will prosper; whoever refreshes others will be refreshed.

"Every man must decide whether he will walk in the light of creative altruism or in the darkness of destructive selfishness."
-*Martin Luther King, Jr.*

Generosity is sometimes characterized by a noble or kind spirit. A spirit that is always willing to share everything it has. A profound act of kindness.

Have you ever received a compliment about something you wore or have and thought, "I will give it to the person since they like it so much."? Do you recall any occasions when someone would say, "I like your outfit, earring, necklace, shirt or hat you are wearing and you immediately removed the item and gave it to that person? Or on the other hand, been the recipient of someone immediately gifting you something they wore that you really liked.

Kindness or generosity is something we think about all the time, however many times we manage to talk ourselves out of acting on sharing. Judgement of self or the proposed recipient may be part of the self-talk. What if the minute you think to be generous you simply act on it, no over thinking, devaluing what you want to gift or judging the recipient?

2 Corinthians 9:7 instructs that "each of you should give what you have decided in your heart to give, not reluctantly or under compulsion, for God loves a cheerful giver." In this season of generosity consider all the gifts that are freely in you to give. You may realize that generosity is not solely for a season but for a lifetime. Today's verse is a reminder "A generous person will prosper; whoever refreshes others will be refreshed."

PRAYER FOR THE DAY:

Dear Father,
Thank you for the reminder to immediately act on kindness and generosity. Do not hesitate or second guess when prompted to be generous. That a generous person will prosper; whoever refreshes others will be refreshed. I pray that all your children remember that a generous person will prosper; whoever refreshes others will be refreshed. That generosity is not just for a season but for a lifetime. I ask this in your son Jesus' name. Amen!

Branched Off

ANCHOR SCRIPTURE: JOHN 15:5 (NIV)

*"I am the vine; you are the branches. If you remain in me
and I in you, you will bear much fruit; apart from me
you can do nothing."*

You will always be a branch, never a vine.

When you see a branch withered, limp or brown standing out amongst other green or healthy branches what comes to mind? If you asked anyone that grows grapes, they may know exactly the problem...the branch has become separated from the vine. I once heard this while visiting a vineyard.

Becoming strong and growing an abundance of fruit on your tree or seeking freedom should not be sufficient justification to separate from the vine. Forgetting or disconnecting from the source that helped you produce what you have, that brought you this far may not be such a good idea. Think about it, pause, and check out your surroundings, can you identify those who have been deceived to believe they are vines and not branches?

It is interesting to note, that the vine is the source and sustenance of life for the branch, but the branch is prone to wander. To continue to bear fruit in your old age, stay fresh and green, remain connected. Disconnecting, even if you have much fruit now, you will eventually wither and cease producing fruit. You will always be a branch, never a vine. Today's verse is a reminder, "I am the vine; you are the branches. Whoever abides in me and I in him, he it is that bears much fruit, for apart from me you can do nothing." I encourage you to read John 15 in its entirety.

Dear Father,
Thank you for the reminder that you are the vine and I am the
branch. That apart from you, I can do nothing. I pray that all
your children remember to stay connected to you and not wan-
der. That you are the vine and they are the branches. That apart
from you they can do nothing. I ask this in your son Jesus's name.
Amen!

DECEMBER 13

The Great Sabotage

ANCHOR SCRIPTURE: JOHN 10:10 (NKJV)

"The thief does not come except to steal, and to kill,
and to destroy. I have come that they may have life,
and that they may have it more abundantly."

"I crafted most of my own tragedies without ever having even
the remotest understanding that it is myself who
have done the crafting."
- Craig D. Lounsbrough

Sabotage is sometimes defined as deliberate destruction or damage of something or obstructive action carried on by someone to hinder, hamper or hurt a process. Can you imagine being your worst enemy? Because you are not in touch with your worth, you seek to steal, kill, and destroy your blessings.

Withholding love is one way we sabotage ourselves. Marianne Williamson said withholding love is a form of self-sabotage, as what we withhold from others, we are withholding from ourselves. What things or feelings are you withholding from yourself and others that may be blocking the blessings that are already yours or preventing you from having life more abundant? From living an abundant life.

Today's verse is a reminder, "The thief does not come except to steal, and to kill, and to destroy. I have come that they may have life, and that they may have it more abundantly." I encourage you to read John 10 in its entirety and end the great sabotage.

─────────────── **PRAYER FOR THE DAY:** ───────────────

Dear Father,
Thank you for the reminder that the thief does not come except to steal, and to kill, and to destroy. That you have come so I may have life and have it more abundantly. To seize being the author of my own demise. I pray that all your children remember that the thief does not come except to steal, and to kill, and to destroy. That you have come that they may life, and that they may have it more abundantly." That sometimes they are the authors of their own demise. That they end the great sabotage. I ask this in your son Jesus' name. Amen!

Refreshment

ANCHOR SCRIPTURE: PSALM 23.3

He refreshes my soul.
He guides me along the right paths for his name's sake.

Love is the greatest refreshment in life.
-Pablo Picasso

Refreshment is sometimes described as the giving of fresh mental or physical strength or energy. Think about when you are provided refreshment during an event. It may provide you with nourishment or a boost to get you through an event or in between meals.

When I think about refresh, I think about a peace lily plant whose leaves wither when it is not watered timely. However, as soon as water is added, in short order, the leaves are again vibrant and new flowers begin to bloom. The withered leaves are simply a sign that the plant is thirsty and needs a refreshment.

Do you pay attention to when your body, mind or soul needs a refreshing, or do you allow one or all to go without quench for a long time and become dry? If you allow it to go dry, it may take longer to bounce back once refreshment is supplied. Today's verse is a reminder, "he refreshes my soul. He guides me along the right paths for his name's sake." Take time often to refresh your mind, body, and soul. The Lord will provide. I encourage you to read psalm 23 in its entirety.

Dear Father,
Thank you for the reminder of the importance to refresh. That
you stand ready to refresh my mind, body, soul and will guide
me along the right paths for your name sake. I pray that all your
children remember the importance of frequent refreshing. That
you stand ready to refresh their body, mind, and soul and you
will guide them along the right paths for your name sake. That
they continue to trust you. I ask this in Jesus' name. Amen!

DECEMBER 15

Perpetual Thanksgiving

ANCHOR SCRIPTURE: 1 THESSALONIANS 5:18

In everything give thanks: for this is the will of God in Christ
Jesus concerning you.

I am grateful for what I am and have. My thanksgiving is perpetual."
- Henry David Thoreau

Is your gratitude limited to feelings and circumstances? Are you only grateful in the good times, when things are going your way, or is your gratitude perpetual?

Imagine repeatedly and frequently being grateful. Having uninterrupted gratitude. That no matter your circumstance or feeling you remain grateful. Walt Disney is quoted as saying, "The more you are in a state of gratitude, the more you will attract things to be grateful for." I once read that some people resist living a life of gratitude in fear that saying, "thank you" implies responsibility or that they need to pay something back." Wow!

Imagine someone doing something for you simply out of the goodness of their heart, never even flirting with the thought that you owe them anything. That they are so grateful for what they have, they do not mind sharing. I have witnessed a homeless person sharing a meal with a bird or their pets. I have witnessed, a mother feed her children first and leave nothing for herself, and yet she says thank you. These events are reminders that it is possible to live in perpetual thanksgiving.

Today's verse is a reminder, "In everything give thanks: for this is the will of God in Christ Jesus concerning you." Happy Thanksgiving. Hope it is perpetual!

———————————— **PRAYER FOR THE DAY:** ————————————

Dear Father,
Thank you for the reminder that in everything give thanks: for this is your will concerning me. To have perpetual Thanksgiving. Not just one day of the year. I pray that all your children remember that in everything give thanks: for this is your will concerning each of them. That they remember that Thanksgiving is not just one day of the year, but every day. That they exercise perpetual thanksgiving. I ask this in your son Jesus' name. Amen!

Grateful for Grace

ANCHOR SCRIPTURE: EPHESIANS 2:8 (NLT)

*God saved you by his grace when you believed. And you can't
take credit for this; it is a gift from God.*

"In order to experience grace, we must first heal
the parts of ourselves that resist it."
— Dr. Debra L. Rebel

Grace is sometimes defined as unmerited divine assistance given to
humans for their regeneration or sanctification or disposition to or
an act or instance of kindness, courtesy, or clemency. Have you ever
thought about the importance that grace plays in your life?

Grace may show up when you continuously trip over yourself, repeat
past mistakes and are still forgiven. Sometimes grace shows up as
strength when you have none left. It shows up as beauty and unconditional love. Yes, grace shows up in so many ways and yet we still
forget to say thank you.

Imagine writing down all the times you experience grace. You may find
it is numerous in just one day. The grace experienced daily is amazing.
Today's verse is a reminder, God saved you by his grace when you believed. And you can't take credit for this; it is a gift from God. Embrace
rather than resist the grace offered to you. Be grateful for grace.

Dear Father,
Thank you for the reminder that you saved me by your grace
when I believed. That I cannot take credit for your grace because
it is your gift to me. Thank you for your gift of grace. I pray that
all your children remember that you saved them by grace when
they believed. That they cannot take credit for your gift of grace.
That they each embrace rather than resist the gift of your grace.
I ask this in your son Jesus' name. Amen!

—————————●—————————

DECEMBER 17

Cultivate Delight

ANCHOR SCRIPTURE: PSALM 37:4

Take delight in the Lord, and he will give you
the desires of your heart.

True education flowers at the point when delight
falls in love with responsibility.
- *Philip Pullman*

Delight is sometimes defined as a high degree of gratification or pleasure, extreme satisfaction or something that gives great pleasure.
Embracing and cultivating delight daily is necessary.

Sometimes you wonder how a person can be so joy-filled when so much plagues them. Maybe it is because they are filled with gratitude despite their circumstances. Gratitude that no matter what, God is with them and by their side through it all. As long as you delight in the Lord, there is hope that the desires of your heart would eventually be met. Second, do not desire what someone else has. Remain focused on your desires and relationship with God. Not that of others. Psalm 37:1(msg) says, "Don't bother your head with braggarts or wish you could succeed like the wicked." Lastly stay clear of judgement as the table could turn at any moment.

Heeding these suggested steps may help you stay clear of distractions that may keep you from delighting in God and allowing God to shape your heart. No matter who you are or what you have done, you can delight in Lord. Today's verse is a reminder to take delight in the Lord, and he will give you the desires of your heart. Cultivate delight! I encourage you to read Psalm 37 in its entirety.

——————————— **PRAYER FOR THE DAY:** ———————————

Dear Father,
Thank you for the reminder to take delight in you, and you will give me the desires of my heart. To commit my way to you and trust you. I pray that all your children take delight in you and remember by doing this you will give them the desires of their heart. That they commit their way to you and trust you. I ask this in your son Jesus' name. Amen!

Be Resilient

ANCHOR SCRIPTURE: JAMES 1:12

Blessed is the man who perseveres under trial because when he has stood the test, he will receive the crown of life that God has promised to those who love him.

"Courage doesn't always roar. Sometimes courage is the quiet voice at the end of the day saying, I will try again tomorrow."
- Mary Anne Radmacher

What is the worst trial you ever faced? If you are reading this today, you made it! Yes, you made it through your "Why Me" toughest of pains. You remained resilient and persevered. Glory be to God!

Resilient is defined in Merriam Webster as the capability of withstanding shock without permanent deformation or rupture or tending to recover from or adjust easily to misfortune or change. Perseverance is sometimes defined as to persist in a state, enterprise, or undertaking despite counter influences, opposition, or discouragement. Can you imagine being bombarded by trials, tests, and tribulations and making it? One thing after the other. Sometimes all is needed is a gentle reminder that you made it through the worst, and you will make it through this as well. Even if it is worse than the last time, you will make it.

Somehow you managed to dig deep, found the strength and courage to carry on. To trust God through it all. To wake up each morning and say, let's try this again. At the time you were in your test, trial, or tribulation, you had no name for how you manage to keep going every single day. To press forward despite the height of the wall you need to climb or the thickness of your situation. James 1:2-4 reminds us "to consider it pure joy, my brothers and sisters, whenever you face trials of many kinds because you know that the testing of your faith produces perseverance. Let perseverance finish its work so that you may be mature and complete, not lacking anything." Continue the course even in the face of difficulty, lack of understanding or faint hope.

Giving up when you are tired of the tests or searching for answers is easy to do. Today's verse is a reminder, "Blessed is the man who perseveres under trial because when he has stood the test, he will receive the crown of life that God has promised to those who love him." Are you willing to stand the test to receive the crown of life that God promises to those who love him? I encourage you to read James 1 in its entirety and to persevere. Be resilient, Trust God!

——————— **PRAYER FOR THE DAY:** ———————

Dear Father,
Thank you for the reminder that blessed is the man who perseveres under trial because when he has stood the test, he will receive the crown of life that you have promised to those who love you. I pray that all your children endure the test given. That they remember that blessed is the man who perseveres under trial because when he has stood the test, he will receive the crown of life that you have promised to those who love you. I ask this in your son Jesus' name. Amen.

Called To Be Free

ANCHOR SCRIPTURE: GALATIANS 5:13

"For you were called to freedom, brethren; only do not turn your freedom into an opportunity for the flesh, but through love serve one another."

The secret to happiness is freedom...
And the secret to freedom is courage.
- *Thucydides*

Merriam Webster defines freedom as the quality or state of being free, such as the absence of necessity, coercion, or constraint in choice or action; restrain from the power of another; release from something onerous; or boldness of conception or execution. As you reflect on these various definitions consider this, are you free? Do you allow tiredness, guilt, worry, judgement of others keep you in an unlocked cell?

A few years ago, a dear friend and sister gifted me a book entitled LIFE, Six Principles for Successful Living by Kenneth Brown. LIFE is the acronym for Living in Freedom Every day. The book shared 6 keys to successful living that eliminates limiting beliefs and creates a freedom and success driven mindset. The Understanding that pursuing your life passion/purpose helps to get you unstuck and disable procrastination.

Are you familiar with what living In freedom everyday looks and feels like? Today's verse is a reminder, "For you were called to freedom, brethren; only do not turn your freedom into an opportunity for the flesh, but through love serve one another." You are called to be free.

Dear Father,

Thank you for the reminder that I am called to be free. To not turn my freedom into an opportunity for the flesh, but through love serve one another. I pray that all your children remember they are called to be free. To not turn their freedom into an opportunity for the flesh, but through love serve one another. I ask this in your son Jesus' name. Amen!

DECEMBER 20

Walk in Favor

ANCHOR SCRIPTURE: PSALM 5:12

"Surely, LORD, you bless the righteous; you surround them with your favor as with a shield."

"Favor is not achieved, it is received."

Favor is sometimes defined as approval, support, or liking for someone or something or an act of kindness beyond what is due or usual. Can you imagine being surrounded by gifts you cannot see; therefore, you do not open? Limited vision, circumstances, and little faith can prevent you from seeing favor that is already yours. That you are singled out for blessings and miracles.

This lack of vision of your favor may also lead to a disobedient, selfishness, rebellious, prideful life that destroys your favor. Each of you can access and be surrounded by this favor. It is yours to receive but not to keep for yourself. It is to help change lives and glorify the giver of the favor. 2 Corinthians 6:2 tells "For he says, "In the time of my favor I heard you, and in the day of salvation I helped you." I tell you, now is the time of God's favor, now is the day of salvation."

Today's verse is a reminder, Surely, LORD, you bless the righteous; you surround them with your favor as with a shield. See it, open it, walk in your favor. You are surrounded by it!

—————— **PRAYER FOR THE DAY:** ——————

Dear Father,
Thank you for the reminder that in the day of salvation you helped me, you bless the righteous; you surround them with favor as with a shield. I pray that all your children remember that you bless the righteous, you surround them with your favor as with a shield. That in the time of favor you heard them, in the day of salvation you helped them. I ask this in your son Jesus' name. Amen!

A Time for Everything

ANCHOR SCRIPTURE: ECCLESIASTES 3:1

*"There is a time for everything and a season for
every activity under the heavens..."*

The two most important requirements for major success are:
first, being in the right place at the right time, and second,
doing something about it.
- Ray Kroc

It is said that there is a proper time for everything a balanced and cyclical nature of life. I recalled the first time I deeply paid attention to today's verse. It was read at my cousin's funeral. During a very perplexing season of suddenly losing a loved one, I heard these words, "There is a time for everything, and a season for every activity under the heavens: a time to be born and a time to die, a time to plant and a time to uproot... The words that read brought a peace that could not be explained.

Sometimes it is important to understand that what you may be facing is just part of the cyclical nature of life. As I watched a recent baseball game, I thought about this passage that talks about seasons. If it is your season to harvest what you sow, nothing or no one will stop it. Sometimes "underdogs" may shock the status quo and surprisingly pull off a victory. That it may just be their season to experience victory.

Neale Donald Walsch says that the cycles of life are endless -- and always serve you because life is a process that serves life itself. When things seem to be shifting away from you, moving in the other direction, closing doors, shutting down opportunities, remember that all things are cyclical -- including life itself.

Today's verse is a reminder, "There is a time for everything and a season for every activity under the heavens..." I encourage you to read Ecclesiastes 3 in its entirety. Never envy someone else's season, yours will eventually come.

PRAYER FOR THE DAY:

Dear Father,
Thank you for the reminder that there is a time for everything and a season for every activity under the heavens. I pray that all your children remember that there is a time for everything and a season for every activity under the heavens. That they find peace in this reminder. I ask this in your son Jesus' name. Amen!

Way to Freedom

ANCHOR SCRIPTURE: JAMES 1:22-25

"Do not merely listen to the word, and so deceive yourselves. Do what it says. Anyone who listens to the word but does not do what it says is like a man who looks at his face in a mirror and, after looking at himself, goes away and immediately forgets what he looks like. But the man who looks intently into the perfect law that gives freedom, and continues to do this, not forgetting what he has heard, but doing it – he will be blessed in what he does."

"Between stimulus and response, there is a space.
In that space is our power to choose our response.
In our response lies our growth and our freedom."
- *Vicktor Emil Frankl*

Can you imagine spending your entire life in a maze and missing the exit because you refuse to follow instructions and you insist to do things your own way instead of as the "guide" instructs? Sometimes ego, pride, being hard-headed and self-righteousness keeps you in a mental incarceration and prevents you from living in freedom every day.

Why as humans we insist on doing things our own way or alter the instructions to get credit or lean on our own strength and understanding baffles me. I guess each of us must learn the hard way. Someone recently ask, how do you remain free? I said let's look at the book of instructions to see what it says (I refer to the Bible as the book of instructions.) There was the answer directly from the instruction guide. The book of James lays out the perfect law that gives freedom and is today's reminder on the way to remain free regardless of your circumstances, "Do not merely listen to the word, and so deceive yourselves.

Do what it says. Anyone who listens to the word but does not do what it says is like a man who looks at his face in a mirror and, after looking at himself, goes away and immediately forgets what he looks like. But the man who looks intently into the perfect law that gives freedom, and continues to do this, not forgetting what he has heard, but doing it – he will be blessed in what he does." I encourage you to read James 1 in its entirety and be FREE.

PRAYER FOR THE DAY:

Dear Father,
Thank you for the reminder that you have provided clear in-structions that gives freedom. To "Do not merely listen to the word, and so deceive yourselves. Do what it says." You remain faithful. I pray that all your children obey the clear instructions you have provided for them to remain free. That they not merely listen to the word, and so deceive themselves, that they do what it says. That they do not forget what they have heard and that doing what they have heard will bless what they do. I ask this in your son Jesus' name. Amen!

Purpose vs. Problems

ANCHOR SCRIPTURE: PHILIPPIANS 1:21 (NIV)

"For to me, to live is Christ and to die is gain"

"The purpose of life is not to be happy. It is to be useful, to be honorable, to be compassionate, to have it make some difference that you have lived and lived well."
- Ralph Waldo Emerson

I recently listened to a sermon by Pastor Rick Warren. In this sermon Pastor Warren said that happiness comes from service and giving your life away. "Until you understand this, you're not going to be happy for much of your life. Happiness does not come from self-gratification. It comes from self-sacrifice." This statement brought light to much in leadership and in life.

I wonder if everyone could be taught from a very young age to search for purpose rather than the deception of riches, the perfect mate, and materialistic things. To truly understand that happiness has nothing to do with how much you have, who you are with or what you look like. That as Pastor Rick says it comes from "service and giving your life away." If you are solely serving yourself, ask yourself that hard question, are you truly happy or are you playing tricks on your own mind? Are you focused on solving your problems or serving your God given purpose?

Some may say, "I don't know my purpose." Seek, ask and it will be shown to you. God is faithful. You exist for a purpose. Don't fall prey to the thoughts that you cannot make an impact in this world. Today's verse is a reminder, "For to me, to live is Christ and to die is gain." Remain focused on your purpose, God will solve your problems. I encourage you to read Philippians 1 in its entirety.

Dear Father,
Thank you for reminder to focus on my purpose and not my problems. That "For to me, to live is Christ and to die is gain." I pray that all your children seek you to find their purpose, true happiness and focus less on their problems. That they remember that you are working everything out for their good. That to live is Christ and to die is gain. I ask this in your son Jesus' name. Amen!

DECEMBER 24

Fearless

ANCHOR SCRIPTURE: 1 JOHN 4:18 (NIV)

"There is no fear in love. But perfect love drives out fear because fear has to do with punishment. The one who fears is not made perfect in love."

"Fear you have lost your hold on me"

Merriam Webster defines fearless as free from fear; brave or bold. I recently had an epiphany during a conversation with a young child. That no matter how fearful a situation may seem; love casts away all fear. That approaching most situations with love and no judgement, you can free yourself and others from fear.

The simple act of sharing genuine love and concern for others can be transformational. It can instantly transform fear to bravery, darkness to light. If we could only remember that God gave us a spirit not of fear but power and love and self-control. No matter what situation you face, be confident that God is with you, there is no need to fear.

Today's scripture is a reminder, "There is no fear in love. But perfect love drives out fear because fear has to do with punishment. The one who fears is not made perfect in love." Today I encourage you to read 1 John 4 in its entirety. Declare "Fear you have lost your hold on me." Be fearless and choose love!

────────────── **PRAYER FOR THE DAY:** ──────────────

Dear Father,
Thank you for the reminder that there is no fear in love. That perfect love drives out fear. I pray that all your children awaken to their power to be fearless. That they remember that there is no fear in love, and you did not give them a spirit of fear. That today they free themselves from fear and choose love. I ask this in your son Jesus' name, Amen.

Merry Christmas and Best Wishes for the Coming Year!

ANCHOR SCRIPTURE: PHILIPPIANS 3:13

"Brothers, I do not consider that I have made it my own. But one thing I do: forgetting what lies behind and straining forward to what lies ahead…"

"Seeking excellence means choosing to forge your own sword to cut through the limitations of your life."
-*James A. Murphy*

Forge Forward or Forge Ahead is sometimes defined as to suddenly make a lot of progress with something. Sometimes, we go through life in starts and stops. Sometimes those stops may be caused by focusing too much on what lies behind rather than what's ahead. This is a natural reaction, to hold on and replay what was as it is the familiar. Not realizing that one may be seesawing through life rather than forging forward. Life is meant to be lived forward, to keep growing. Imagine being a seed, and as you grow, have branches and fruits, you then decide you rather return to a being a seed. Not happening. The best is always ahead, never behind.

I share this reflection written by Lloyd Alexander. "Life's a forge! Yes, and hammer and anvil, too! You'll be roasted, smelted, and pounded, and you'll scarce know what's happening to you. But stand boldly to it! Metal's worthless till it's shaped and tempered! More labor than luck. Face the pounding, don't fear the proving; and you'll stand well against any hammer and anvil."

Today's verse is a reminder, "Brothers, I do not consider that I have made it my own. But one thing I do: forgetting what lies behind and straining forward to what lies ahead..." Seize seesawing through life and forge forward.

Dear Father,
Thank you for the reminder to seize seesawing through life. To forget what lies behind and strain forward to what lies ahead. I pray that all your children seize seesawing through life. That they focus on what lies ahead that behind. That they believe in you and your word. May your truth shine their path and will to forge forward. I ask this in your son Jesus' name. Amen!

Reflections

_____

_____

_____

_____

_____

_____

_____

_____

_____

_____

Forge Forward

ANCHOR SCRIPTURE: 2 CORINTHIANS 9:15 (NIV)

"Thanks be to God for his indescribable gift!"

"Christmas is not a time nor a season, but a state of mind.
To cherish peace and goodwill, to be plenteous in mercy,
is to have the real spirit of Christmas."
- Calvin Coolidge

Thanks to each of you for doing life with me this year. You made it amazing and made me a better person. My heartfelt gratitude to each of you!

May hope, peace, and love reign in your hearts and your homes throughout this holiday season and the coming year.

From my family to yours, Merry Christmas, Happy Holidays, and May 2019 be your best year ever!

Peace and Showers of Blessings!

Learn it. Live it. Lead it.

- Ilka V. Chavez
Author of the book: What Leaders Say and Do:
How to Inspire your tribe.

It is Not Over!

ANCHOR SCRIPTURE: EXODUS 12:1-2

"The Lord said to Moses and Aaron in Egypt, "This month is to be for you the first month, the first month of your year."

"It ain't over till it's over."
- Yogi Berra

I know many people are thinking, the year is already over. Where did time go? What did I accomplish this year? I only met two of my fifteen things I put on my vision board. Oh well, I guess I will do better next year. I say, the year is not yet over. You have 31 more days to meet a few more goals you set out to achieve. You have time to mend a few broken things you set out to mend this year. Don't give up. Finish the year strong, so you can start next year stronger.

Sometimes we stop just before we see God's best. We arrive at the finish line and give up before stepping over. Have faith, trust that God can help you accomplish a bit more this year. He will help you cross the finish line. We serve a faithful God. In Exodus, God delivered the Israelites from bondage at an unusual time. If he did it then, he can do it now. It only requires your faith.

Today's verse is a reminder that the Lord said to Moses and Aaron in Egypt, this month is to be for you the first month, the first month of your year. I encourage you to look at this last month as your first month of the year. As an opportunity for new beginnings to gather the faith to finish the year strong. It's not over! I encourage you to read Exodus 12.

Dear God,
Thank you for the reminder of the words you spoke to Moses and
Aaron. For the reminder that it is not over until you say it is so.
For the encouragement that this last month can be treated as my
first. I pray that all your children do not give up on what they set
out to accomplish this year. That they have enough faith to finish
the year strong and realize the year is not yet over. I ask this in
your son Jesus' name. Amen

DECEMBER 28

Changed Perspective

ANCHOR SCRIPTURE: ISAIAH 55:8 (NLT)

"My thoughts are nothing like your thoughts," says the LORD.
"And my ways are far beyond anything you could imagine."

"The real voyage of discovery consists not in seeking new lands
but in seeing with new eyes."
– *Marcel Proust*

Merriam Webster defines perspective as the capacity to view things
in their true relations or relative importance or the interrelation in
which a subject or its parts are mentally viewed. Can you imagine
someone walking up to you and saying, "Your perspective is upside
down or inside out?" That for the two, three, four, five and even eight
decades you have been around on this earth, you may have interpreted
life and how to live it completely wrong.

What if you were told that life gets better when you change the way you look at things. I had a conversation with a young man, who was experiencing a bit of frustration and guilt over his current situation. I shared that It is okay to question what you always held as truth and it was okay to change his mind if he encountered a different perspective.

Life is a mystery... One way to enjoy life may be to always remain curious. To remain open to having the impossible become the possible for you. Wayne Dyer is quoted as saying, "If you believe it will work out, you will see opportunities. If you believe it won't, you will see obstacles." Have you been approaching life with lens that only see obstacles and not opportunities? What if you flip the script, and only approach life as one that attracts opportunities and infinite possibilities to you?

Today's verse is a reminder "My thoughts are nothing like your thoughts," says the LORD. And my ways are far beyond anything you could imagine." Maybe it is time to change lens. To adopt a different perspective. Changing your mind is hard and it is not impossible. Look beyond what is in front of you!

───────────────── **PRAYER FOR THE DAY:** ─────────────────

Dear Father,
Thank you for the reminder regarding my perspective versus yours. That my thoughts are nothing like yours and your ways are far beyond anything I could imagine. That adopting your perspective allows me to see what is possible and not what is impossible. I pray that all your children continue to grow curious and understand that your thoughts are nothing like their thoughts. And your ways are far beyond anything they could imagine. That they remove the lens of looking at life filled with obstacles and change to one filled with infinite possibilities. That what today may seem impossible, is possible beyond their own imagination. I ask this in your son Jesus' name. Amen!

Comparison Steals Your Joy

ANCHOR SCRIPTURE: 2 CORINTHIANS 10:12 (NKJV)

*"For we dare not class ourselves or compare ourselves
with those who commend themselves. But they, measuring
themselves by themselves, and comparing themselves among
themselves, are not wise."*

"Comparison is the thief of joy"
- *Theodore Roosevelt*

Comparison is sometimes defined as an examination of two or more items to establish similarities and dissimilarities. Comparison is a chronic problem that cheats you of the riches you already have. It may cause you to devalue your power and your strength. It will blind you to hate rather than to love. To fear rather to have faith.

In times of trouble, it may cause you to even cry out, "it is not fair or just." Imagine if Jesus decided to be disobedient, pouted and complained about dying on the cross for us? Dr. Steven Maraboli is quoted as saying, "The only thing that makes life unfair is the delusion that is should be fair."

In pursuit of an antidote for comparison, I found this text in Philippians 4:11-12, "Not that I speak in regard to need, for I have learned in whatever state I am, to be content: I know how to be abased, and I know how to abound. Everywhere and in all things, I have learned both to be full and to be hungry, both to abound and to suffer need." Still in search of an antidote and for now, rest in finding peace in whatever or wherever you find yourself. God is with you and remains on the throne.

Do not surrender to the thief known as comparison. Today's verse is a reminder. "For we dare not class ourselves or compare ourselves with those who commend themselves. But they, measuring themselves by themselves, and comparing themselves among themselves, are not wise." May you find freedom and peace from comparison. I encourage you to read 2 Corinthians 10 in its entirety.

—————————— **PRAYER FOR THE DAY:** ——————————

Dear Father,
Thank you for the reminder that comparison is the thief of joy. To dare not class myself or compare myself with those who commend themselves. That comparing myself with others is not wise. I pray that all your children remember that comparison is the thief of joy. That they do not fall prisoners to comparison. That they remember your teaching that comparing themselves among themselves, is not wise. I ask this in your son Jesus' name. Amen!

Tell and Live Your Truth

ANCHOR SCRIPTURE: JOHN 8:32 (ESV)

And you will know the truth, and the truth will set you free

If you do not tell the truth about yourself,
you cannot tell it about other people.
-Virginia Woolf

Are you able to vow to always tell the truth about yourself and others? Imagine teaching this to our children at an early age. To always tell the truth about themselves and others. This could be the missing link in knowing who and whose you are.

Fear or embarrassment of others "finding out" may lead one to live a double life. To live a fake or fantasy life rather the truth. If you knew that those from who you hide, already know your secret, that you are not alone or the first, would it encourage you to live and tell your truth? Families have carried secrets across generations. Could living with secrets and lies be the cause of our bondage, brokenness, and division?

I wonder if this serves us and our legacy any good, to not live our full and authentic truth. God our Father loves each of us just the way we are. No need to keep secrets. You are his worthy possession. He forgives all his children, just say to Him, "Forgive my trespasses."

Today's verse is a reminder, "And you will know the truth, and the truth will set you free." There is power in owning and living your truth. Reevaluate your truth. Embrace your power to be free! I encourage you to read John 8 in its entirety.

Dear Father,
Thank you for the reminder of my worth to you. That no matter
what I may have done, you will forgive me. I just need to ask.
That knowing and living my truth will set me free. I pray that
all your children remember the truth that each are your prized
possession. No matter what they have done, you will forgive
them if they repent and ask for your forgiveness. That they know
the truth, and this truth will set them free. I ask this in your son
Jesus' name. Amen!

DECEMBER 31

Faith or Feelings First

ANCHOR SCRIPTURE: JEREMIAH 17:9

The heart is deceitful above all things, and desperately sick;
who can understand it?

"Feelings should follow not lead what you do"

Have you ever noticed whether your feelings or your faith dominate your decision making? Unbeknownst to many, their feeling is guiding them through life. Feelings sometimes direct our every steps. I can almost assure you countless times your feelings deceived you or lead you down a path with no return.

There is a verse in the book of Proverbs that is a reminder that "Whoever trusts in his own mind is a fool, but he who walks in wisdom will be delivered." You read the truth and you continue to trust your feelings. Why would you allow your feelings to continue to lead you? Is it because it "feels" good? Is it because you enjoy being the king and queen of drama? Or is it because it makes you "feel" you are in control?

Have you ever said, "I don't feel like doing something? Leaning on faith pushes you to do things you don't feel like doing." I wonder if you let your faith be your compass rather than your feeling or doubt, my how far could you go? Today's verse is a reminder "The heart is deceitful above all things, and desperately sick; who can understand it?" This verse blew my mind. Can you imagine your heart deceives you and is desperately sick yet plays a part in your feelings? I wonder if the root cause of our feelings issues is the condition of our heart. Let your feelings follow, not lead!

——————— **PRAYER FOR THE DAY:** ———————

Dear Father,
Thank you for the reminder that my feeling is a traitor. That the heart is deceitful and desperately sick. To consider relying on my faith rather than my feeling. I pray that all your children let their feeling follow, not lead what they do. That they remember that the heart is deceitful and desperately sick. To rely on faith and your word, your truth, to push through their feeling. I ask this in your son Jesus' name. Amen!